THE
FOOD
OF
GREECE

THE
FOOD
OF
GREECE

Vilma Liacouras Chantiles

ATHENEUM   NEW YORK

1975

DRAWINGS BY VILMA LIACOURAS CHANTILES

The author is grateful to the American School of Classical Studies at Athens for permission to use the translation of the Krates poem, which appeared in their book entitled *Pots and Pans of Classical Athens*, and also to the Loeb Classical Library and Harvard University Press for permission to quote from *Athenaeus: The Deipnosophists*, translated by Charles Burton Gulick, Vols. I, II, III, IV, and VII, 1927, 1928, 1929, 1930, 1931.

Dedicated to my parents,
and in memory of my maternal grandparents,
who brought the spirit of Greece to America

Acknowledgments

This book was conceived to fill the need for a cookbook that reflects the Greek culture, the present uses of food in relation to the past, and the radiating influence of Greece throughout the Western world through its emigrants. In respect to the last of these qualities, I acknowledge the life-long inspiration of my parents, my brother, and sisters—my nuclear family. Through our grandparents, many aunts, uncles, and cousins, and later with my husband's sisters, I developed a bond with our extended family. For their recipes, which I have enjoyed for most of my life, I am almost as grateful as for the warmth and expertise with which they shared them. And how much I appreciate my country, the United States of America, where my parents were able to continue their Greek customs and beliefs, facilitating my own freely valuing both Greece and America.

I thank these New York University School of Education faculty members for helping to provide useful insights in the study of foods: my gratitude to Dr. Henrietta Fleck, now Professor Emeritus, Home Economics, for suggesting that I write a Greek cookbook following my independent study of the cultural and historical implications of foods of Greece; also to Dr. David W. Ecker during my independent study of foods as an aesthetic experience; and to Miss Helen Shull, who had taught Cultural Understanding Through Foods. I appreciate the encouragement and suggestions of my editor Miss Dorothy Parker as well as the advice of numerous friends.

To the many cooks, chefs, food experts, agriculturists, retailers, farmers, priests, monks, nuns, and many families in Greece and Cyprus who have contributed generously of their time and experience in answering my questions, I am deeply obliged. I also thank officials of the Greek National Statistical Service, Agricultural Extension Service, Home Demonstration Agency, Hellenic Promotion Council, and the National

Tourist Organization. And I shall always be grateful to the outstanding Greek food importers and government officials in New York City and Washington, D.C., and the Office of the Greek Commercial Attaché, New York, as well as many men and women born in Greece and Cyprus who have answered my questions about Greek foods. Because the list is very long and extends throughout all the regions of Greece and Cyprus, I regret that it is impossible to name each individually.

I am grateful to the many Greek people who spoke the proverbs related to foods and Greek life through the centuries, which I now speak, and the fine Greek poets whose poetry I have quoted, and to the following publishers for their kind permission to use excerpts from various publications: The American School of Classical Studies at Athens; The Loeb Classical Library and Harvard University Press; and Random House, Inc.

I needed especially, and am particularly grateful for, the responsiveness of my family: I am indebted to my husband Nicholas who took me to Greece and who answered many of my questions about the Greek language, both modern and classical; and to our sons Dean and James, tireless photographers, and our daughter Maria Nicole, helpful researcher, on our various family trips to Greece.

V.L.C.

PROLOGUE

THE INCOMPARABLE BEAUTY OF GREECE stimulates all the senses and enriches the spirit. From the stunning azure of the Ionian and Aegean seas to the herb- and beehive-dotted mountains, honey-sweet fruit aromas fill the air, while the twisted trunks of old olive trees and the curling vines of the ubiquitous grapes delight the eye. Colors vibrate. Air seems fresher, the atmosphere lighter, than in other lands. You imagine you see Hermes flying gracefully across the cloudless sky on his winged sandals, or misty-eyed Nereids and Naiads dancing on the blue-green water. It is impossible to resist the attractiveness of the warm, volatile Greek people or to keep from falling in love with their country.

In Greece there is an intimate interaction of people with nature, and hence with food. This interplay is never more obvious than in the Greek markets, where fresh fruits and vegetables are piled high in baskets and young lambs and piglets hang along the sidewalks—a refreshing contrast to the packaged fruits, dehydrated herbs, and frozen, unrecognizable fish seen in markets in the United States. Invariably, instances of Greek *philoxenia* (hospitality) surprise tourists and at times befuddle them. Anecdotes such as that of the Americans who asked directions of a Greek woman in the Taygetos Mountains are common: "She did not understand English, but loaded the back seat of our car with oranges!" Unusual perhaps, yet visitors sense more than a warm gesture. They feel the fundamental tie that food expresses. Classical antecedents appear both in Homer's *Iliad*, when Achilles offers food to Priam following Hector's death, and again in the *Odyssey,* with the hospitality to Penelope's ardent suitors.

I have felt this elemental quality throughout a lifelong familiarity with both Greek people and Greek food. From an early age I realized that food provided more than nourishment. Memories of food keep recurring, associated with gaiety and music, with dancing and games. Food is such a strong part of Greek tradition, its seasonal and holiday prepararations, it pervades every aspect of our culture. Particularly, food is a way to befriend and link people. Serving Mother's quince, *vyssino*, or orange, rind spoon sweets was probably my earliest and most eloquent lesson in human relations.

Yet it was not until I was an adult, a mother with two infants, that I visited Greece for the first time. Furthermore, my parents, who as children had emigrated to the United States from Greece with their families, had become happy American citizens and had not returned to Greece in the interim. How did it happen, then, that our food preferences and habits were so similar to those of the Greek people whom I met during the first and subsequent trips?

Sociologist Oscar Handlin, in *The Uprooted*, focuses on cultural ties of immigrant groups that mitigate their feelings of alienation. Separation from familiar villages, loneliness, new concepts of life style and goals—these were some of the harsh realities that provoked reversion to the past. "These reactions reflected the urge to strengthen old values and to reaffirm old ideas. . . . All would seek to set their ideas within a fortification of religious and cultural institutions that would keep them sound against the strange New World." * Through their transplanted culture my own grandparents, then my parents, transmitted their traditional values to the next generation and maintained a continuity with their past. Like all Greeks, they have felt a kinship with their motherland throughout the years of separation.

Anthropologist Dorothy Demetracopoulou Lee, in *Cultural Patterns and Technical Change*, describes the resistance among Greeks to planned change that might have improved their economy through industrialization and technology: "Traditionally, food is not nutrition. Food is good. . . ." † As an example of Greek attitudes, Mrs. Lee cites the father who derides the raisin bread that is introduced to the child. Raisins are for snacks, to "pass the time," not to bake into bread, traditionally a sacred food. Research during my graduate studies and talks with many people in Greece have confirmed these observations.

Food attitudes and preferences, a recurring theme of Greek poetry and folk songs, were developed early in myth and legend and repeated in poetry, drama, philosophy, and the visual arts. Poets have elucidated the Greek bond with nature, the feeling for the seasons, the sacred asso-

* Handlin, Oscar, *The Uprooted* (New York: Grosset & Dunlap, 1951), pp. 115–116.

† Mead, Margaret, ed., *Cultural Patterns and Technical Change* (New York: The New American Library, Mentor Book, 1955), p. 87.

ciations with prized foods. Olives, honey, goat's milk and cheese, wine, seasonings, vegetables, grapes, figs, and pomegranates—these foods, so cherished by modern Hellenes, were favored by their ancestors of the Early Bronze Age. During the classical period, when the Greek cuisine reached its zenith, publishing of cookery books began. *Gastronomia* by Archestratus (fifth century B.C.) was among the earliest.

Visiting Greece, we are able to pass on our excitement to our children. They capture the spirit. We smell the wild oregano as we climb the pine-cushioned hills of Kavouri, overlooking the spectacular peninsula. We find dill growing from a rock on Delphi. Taste buds usually coated with peanut butter awaken to *kalamarakia tiganita* sprinkled with juice from lemons of Arta—to *oktapodi, melitzanosalata,* and *taramosalata.* Olive oil from Kalamata flavors artichokes from Dalamanara. Thessalian wheat turns crusty and rich in the *fourno* of the village baker. *Loukoumia* of Syros sweeten our lips on Corfu; Macedonian peaches delight us in Megalopolis; our appetites are sated with the melons of Argos and the early grapes arriving from Corinthian vineyards.

Chefs in taverns and seaside resorts, mothers in remote villages and in bustling cities, monks in Varlaam, Meteora, and nuns in Pantanassa, Mystras—all speak to me of their foods. Their answers to my queries reveal an intimacy with foodstuffs. Persons in Greece whom I questioned for recipes rarely needed to produce them in written form. They remember proportions rather than measurements, give principles rather than procedures—the clearest evidence of cookery enculturation from generation to generation. While they are explaining, however, they urge care and caution, and my mind buzzes back over the centuries, recalling the advice of a Greek chef mentioned by the comic poet Damoxenus, of the third century B.C.: "When you see them making a pickled sauce out of fish of contradictory qualities and grating a dash of sesame into it, take them in turn and tweak their noses."

Inevitably the argument arises as to the source of the Greek cuisine —as moot a question as that of the identity of the Greek people, which has never been settled. Some experts agree with Jacob P. Fallmerayer, who wrote in 1827 in *Geschichte des Kaisertums Trapezunt* that Greek country folk of the nineteenth century contained not one drop of blood of the ancient Greeks. Others maintain the belief of Greek folk historian Nicholas Polites, who advanced a theory of continuity supporting the direct descendancy of today's Greeks from the ancient Greeks. No matter which pole one leans toward, however, one must agree with C. M. Bowra, who wrote in *The Greek Experience* that even "the Greeks of historical times were physically a mixed people, and the advocates of 'purity' of breed will find in them no support for their views." *

As for the question of the politicogeographical identity of Greece, the answer is also enigmatical. Greece lies among the Mediterranean countries, yet many political scientists consider Greece a Balkan country. The United States State Department conducts official business with Greece through the Near East Division. Greece was part of the Byzantine Empire between A.D. 330 and 1453, then buckled under to Ottoman domination until 1832.

The impact of various races and cultures on the Greek people has remained a profound and lasting one. The Byzantine influence is so strong that Greek people refer to Istanbul (formerly Constantinople) as Polis (the city), and the Greeks who returned from Turkey during the exchange of populations early in this century brought with them foods and dishes that are still referred to as "Constantinopoleos" or "a la Polita." Many chefs we spoke to in Greece said they had been born in Polis.

Not the least powerful influence on food is the Orthodox Church, which developed from Byzantine roots. (The Orthodox Patriarchate continues to function from Istanbul.) The Three Hierarchs, regarded as the "three stars" of Orthodoxy, are commemorated reverently on their special feast days every year: Saint Basil, born in Caesarea; Saint Gregory the Theologian, born in western Cappadocia; and Saint John Chrysostom—a Syrian who was a great orator and author of the most frequently used Orthodox Divine Liturgy, which bears his name—born in Antioch. The *vasilopita* (Saint Basil's bread) is used traditionally in both churches and homes.

Though of humble origins, two empresses contributed conspicuously to the eclectic Byzantine cuisine. One was Lupicina of the Danube Valley, herself a cook; the other, Theodora, mistress and later wife of Justinian, who hired chefs for her court from Persia, India, Syria, and the Greek mainland. Just as the cultures of these various lands blended, so too did the cooking methods and ingredients.

In old letters and chronicles one can read of the daily life in the Byzantine period and see how much survives in today's Greek practices: festivals of the liturgical year; Lenten fasting and the Easter lamb; pilgrimages to Jerusalem and shorter excursions to shrines of local saints or monasteries; emphasis on baptism and the last rites of the deceased; the

* Bowra, C. M., *The Greek Experience* (Cleveland and New York: The World Publishing Co., 1957), p. 6.

practice of carrying food and drink to church for blessing. And we cannot overlook the Judaic influence, transmitted through the early Christians, on the meal patterns of the Greek family. It seems to me apparent, from studies of the Old and New Testaments, that the first Christians held communal meals called *agape* (love), at which food was shared. This custom was in sharp contrast to that of the ancient Greeks for men and women to dine separately; women present at men's meals were usually performers or companions, not wives. Other characteristics of the Byzantine period emphasized by historians are as follows: food prices were strictly controlled; monasteries were founded to help feed the needy, and the foods usually donated were wine and bread, dried or fresh vegetables and legumes, meat and fish; the diet of monks in monasteries was limited to fish and vegetables; there were guilds for fishmongers, butchers, bakers, and grocers; shops in the squares and streets were permitted to sell meat, salt fish, cheese, honey, olive oil, vegetables, and grains—the local products of the agrarian empire.

A noted Greek food authority, the late Nicholas Tselementes, demonstrates the Greek influence on western European foods via Rome; he traces the ancestry of such dishes as *keftedes, dolmades, moussaka*, and *yuvarelakia,* ancient preparations that subsequently became masked behind Turkish and European names. Among other dishes surviving since ancient times, Mr. Tselementes includes the famous *bouillabaisse,* French offspring of the Greek *kakavia.*

Polemics regarding the Greek cuisine will persist—assertion of the "Greekness" of things remains part of the Hellenic spirit, the *kefi.* Nevertheless, ingredients that migrated into the Greek kitchen long after the classical and Hellenistic periods have modified flavors, colors, and textures considerably: materials that now thrive in Greek soil and recipes traveled to Greece from India, Burma, China, Africa, Persia, and certainly from the New World, and French, Italian, German, and Turkish names for Greek dishes appear on menus. Greek food experts, tracing the origin of the white sauce, reckon it among the splendid inventions of ancient Greek chefs; nevertheless, they still refer to this essential component of many Greek dishes as "béchamel sauce." Reminiscent of the two-headed emblem of the Byzantine Empire, Greek cuisine faces both East and West. It is versatile and adaptable.

The fact remains that the Greek cuisine flourishes because of its intrinsic values and qualities—the feelings aroused by the foods and dishes. Without this emotional association, a collection of available vegetables, grains, meats, cheeses, and spices, plus a legacy of principles and techniques, would provide little more than a means of survival. Without aesthetics, the preparing or eating of meals deteriorates into a tasteless chore, a headache—a bellyache. When Greek people respond to the meaning in their foods, something deeper vibrates. Eyes sparkle, nostrils quiver, and salivary glands pump away, arousing the appetite. Watch a Greek break off a piece of crusty bread, or nibble *orektika* (appetizers). Fervor and flavor combine to create an instant *glendi* (feast and amusement) that is immediately contagious. And strangers report delightful reactions as well. Describing new foods they sampled in Greece, friends always simultaneously depict the setting, the sounds, the people. An acquaintance asking for my *spanakopita* recipe insists that she will make her own *filo*, rather than use the commercial kind I suggested, even though she is a novice cook who knows that *filo* requires much effort and considerable skill. The spirit of the dish, apparently, is automatically transmitted along with its ingredients.

In Greece we experienced a similar urge. Walking by the beautiful harbor of Rhodes, near the area where the great Colossus once stood, we saw a man pounding something on a flat rock. Mystified, we watched him, totally engrossed in the rhythmic motion of his hands—rolling, pounding, rubbing—and then saw that what he worked on was an octopus. When he noticed us, he paused to answer our questions. As I listened to him explain the tenderizing method and how he would cook the octopus, I particularly valued my knowledge of the Greek language. He smiled, his eyes shone, he gestured as he spoke; and we felt his cultural link with a tradition for tenderizing and cooking that dated back more than two thousand years. We immediately wanted to find our own octopus so that we could do likewise. And now, in the United States, we buy octopus from a specialty fish market not too far from our home, and in our garden we have a special "octopus rock" for tenderizing.

In such ways do Greek food specialties thrive and spread, thus providing for those who have emigrated to the United States, Brazil, Australia, and elsewhere a continuity with the spirit of the original Greeks. A cookery book must convey this culture and spirit as well as recipes and techniques. Culling from family experience, trips to Greece, and much research, I have not only selected favorite Greek dishes but have also tried to provide glimpses of the exciting Hellenic culture through its foods.

I find that Greek foods integrate qualities of the land, people, history and culture. Particularly when tasting fresh, delicious meals outdoors, I have felt Greek culture and nature pervading my spirit. Whether sampling foods rich and Thessalian, or frugal and Spartan, whether sitting by the quiet sea near the jagged, awesome coast by day, or reveling in a friendly, noisy tavern at evening, I have felt food become an elemental experience. I have sensed the meaning of the proverb *"Ola kala kai to meli glyko"* (All's well and the honey is sweet).

Crusty, sinewy, nappy, brittle, soft, flaky, smooth—textures of the foods reflect the landscape, the earth, sky, sea, marble, leaves, bark, stone. The prismatic colors of flowers, tomatoes, fruits, and herbs blend with the quiet tones of eggplant, grapevine, leaves, lamb, artichokes, and soups. Sparkling dashes of white feta cheese, bread, and yogurt contrast with the black of olives. Vivid sunlight seems to tint the lemons, olive oil, and wine. Dull brown sauces do not exist: the word for "brown" in the Greek language is *kastano* (chestnut)—a rich, warm color.

The flavors of food waken the taste sense—bitter, salty, sour or sweet. From the garlicky power of *skordalia* to the cinnamon-spiced *kapama*, from caprylic cheeses to resinous retsina, from *souvlakia riganato* to parsleyed-dilled *spanakopita*, from herbed *plaki* to pungent *tursi*—the message registers almost before reaching the taste buds. Clearly, dining in Greece is a thing of all the senses: taste, smell, sight, touch—and certainly not to be forgotten—sound.

Children growing up in a Greek environment absorb all these sensuous feelings for foods, as well as attitudes toward the family and character—all an inherent part of "Greekness." Children, constantly in the company of adults (who never heard of "baby-sitters"), develop a clear idea of their roles in life and of their self-images. They are constantly exposed to the *kouvenda* (banter) that characterizes the loquacious Hellenes. A wealth of games, myths, tales, songs, and other cultural expressions strengthens the family unit and the individuals in it. The result is that when a Greek grows up, he never dines or dances alone. And a snack more often than not grows into a *glendi*.

In Greece, laughter and the sound of clinking glasses are often heard as a counterpoint to words from the past, toasting the future in lusty voices: *"Eis hygeian*—to your health!"

CONTENTS

THE
FOOD
OF
GREECE

REGIONAL
FLAVOR

———————◆———————

IN THE APPROACH to Greece by air, the first glimpse is startling. After aerial views of Europe's lush valleys and fields, the rugged, brutally desolate Attic coastline shocks and disturbs. But while the earth is barren, the culture is such a rich one. Lessons from school textbooks and images from poetry and legend flash through the mind: the myth of Uranus falling in love with Gaea, a picture of God throwing rocks over his shoulder to form Greece, settlements of ancient civilizations, invasions, dispersions, a culture spreading and surviving. Can this rocky waste be the land that inspired Homer? With the same sense of mystery felt in reading the first line of his great epic, "Tell me, O Muse . . . ," the modern traveler's odyssey begins.

As the plane circles to land, you ask yourself the awesome question: "How can people live off those stones?" Disembarking into the dazzling sunlight, and looking down at the jagged boulders previously seen from the air, you hear tumultuous sounds from above. Jerking your head up defensively, you are amazed to see frantically waving Hellenes on an outdoor terrace, welcoming, cheering and beckoning. *"Kalos orises!"* *"Yeia sou!"* *"Ela'pano!"*

Spontaneously you wave, smile, and respond, regardless of whether the greetings are for you or for others debarking with you. The hearty, contagious Greek *philoxenia* has captured you. From that first emotional moment of arrival, until you depart laden with gifts of dried fruits, sweets and ouzo, there will be no looking down again. Greece will lift you up, over, and beyond.

On arrival you are immediately startled by contrast and contradictions, in architecture, communications, transportation, in personality and life styles—paleo and neo. Even before landing, your jet plane had

3

zoomed over the fashionable suburbs on the Attic shore, where you looked down and saw the rambling *manavi* on the road below, selling fruits and vegetables from his donkey-drawn cart or new truck—a prelude to the superimposition of the new ways on the old that you will notice throughout Greece. Within minutes of Athens Air Terminal, operating since the summer of 1969, you will see the Parthenon, a masterpiece of twenty-four centuries ago and still standing. The glorious temple to the goddess Athena high on the Acropolis and the sparkling new terminal are made from the same marble, cut from Mount Pentelikon overlooking Athens.

Around you in the airport now are Hellenes hugging relatives from overseas. These Greeks may never have been in an airplane, or even an automobile; they may be seeing Athens for the first time. But more important to them is greeting a returning brother who emigrated many years ago. The majority of Greeks, all but one quarter, were born in villages and have lived in the hills and fields. And despite the millions of dollars sent back by emigrants to their families, remote village life imposes primitive hardship and struggle. Tseria, near Gytheion, Lakonia, the village where my maternal grandmother and mother were born, had no electricity until the latter months of 1971!

Yet the emigrant returning to his homeland longs to reach the house where he grew up, to cry in his relatives' arms, to touch the olive and fruit trees, to smell the basil and thyme, to eat a fig, walk through the *ambeli* (vineyard) and drink the wine of its harvest.

"Ah, sweet *patrida*, when shall I see you again?" the Greek folk song cries. And Georgios Drossinis voices the same theme in his poem

> Let me take an amulet with me
> To keep me from all sorrow, from every evil,
> An amulet against sickness, an amulet against death,
> Just a little earth, Greek earth!

An emotional bond ties the expatriate to Greece, no matter how far he wanders. Greek ethos outwears hardship: it survives amid the ferment of new concepts and bustling modern economies. Greece maintains a strong hold on the child who has grown up in the motherland, even if his adult years are lived far to the west.

But you, the *xenos*, the visitor-stranger, you are suddenly aware that you are in the city where the very idea of liberty was born, the land protected by Pallas Athena since she produced the first olive tree. Breathe deeply the glorious air of the city where King Theseus established the

4

first commonwealth, where Socrates, Plato, and Aristotle made sacred the word "philosophy," where Solon created a body of law, and Pericles led the city into the Golden Age.

An unusual light glows about you, and the stimulating atmosphere banishes your aching weariness after the long trip. Driving through Leoforos Syngrou or the wider Kalirois into the city's center, you are drawn into the heart of Attica, of Greece.

GREEK LIFE STYLES: URBAN AND RURAL

Athens is a kaleidoscope of colorful contrasts, most significantly in the people—those transplanted from parts of the mainland, the islands, Asia Minor, Europe, Russia, as well as the retired emigrants, returned to Greece for their golden years. (The latter, dubbed Broukli, "from Brooklyn," by Greeks, are considered the lucky ones, the ones who made it.) Clothing is many-hued; racial and facial types are splendidly varied. Black-robed widows, bearded priests, white-aproned waiters carrying long-handled trays, modestly dressed tradesmen and office workers, a sprinkling of flashy international types—all represent Athens. Some are obviously poor, yes; but except for the gypsies, I have never seen tattered and torn beggars in Athens—or anywhere else in Greece.

From the center of Athens, major arteries radiate into the ten public squares and into the Acropolis. Flowing northeastward toward Kifissia are the elite suburbs of the wealthy class, dotted with luxurious villas. The Alpha Beta and Markopoulos supermarkets herald changes in food merchandising. Frozen foods, packaged goods, and convenience items gradually appear on the shelves there, and then quickly disappear into the arms of the affluent residents who enjoy the novelty of refrigerator-freezers and who live their lives at an increasingly fast tempo. The many foreign residents living near Athens have been influential in the increase of luxury goods.

But take a leisurely drive from Athens, past Mount Hymettus, where bees have been grazing on wild thyme for centuries, toward the eastern Attic coast, and another scene unfolds. Through quiet Koropi into the town of Markopoulon, a wine center, the traditional lifestream flows without visible change. Streets and townspeople focus around the *plateia* (square). Individual shops offer, separately, produce or cheese and dairy products or meats or bread, near the inevitable *pantopoleion* (general store) and *kafeneion* (coffee house). Shop owners close for the day's most important meal, *yevma* (dinner) about 1:30 or 2:00 P.M.

Except for those who cannot be home, Hellenes in the outlying districts of Athens and in the provinces cling tenaciously to established patterns of family life and food habits. The major meal of the day is a family affair, with everyone sitting together at the same table (in classical times women and children were relegated to separate quarters). The menu is usually legumes, vegetables, pasta, cheese, olives, yogurt, bread, wine, water, and fresh fruit. Sunday and holiday meals feature special meat dishes—perhaps *arni psito* or another roasted seasonal meat.

If you drive through a village during this mid- to late-afternoon period, you may wonder what happened to all the Greek activity that you have heard so much about and that you observed at the airport. The *plateia* is vacant, except for an occasional breeze rustling through the shrubs, or perhaps an infrequent bus, motorcycle, or automobile. Store doors are closed, curtains are drawn, large cloths protect the vegetables and fruits from the merciless Greek midday sun. Even the donkeys and chickens of nearby farms rest silently.

If you should happen to arrive in a town by bus and you have to wait for a connecting bus, as we frequently did, there will be a chair in the shade on which you can rest. Or if you are thirsty, you can always find a *kafeneion* to serve you a *portokalada* (orange drink) or a *koka* (Coca-Cola), the recent arrival sweeping through Greece. For in villages and towns it is compulsory for some shops to remain open to accommodate visitors. (When I queried a shop owner about this rule, which forced him to miss the big meal at home, he replied good-naturedly, "I am in business with my brother and we take turns keeping open.")

In Markopoulon, a town through which many buses pass en route from Athens to Sounion or to eastern Attic resorts and towns, the buses stop directly at the *plateia*. What a difference we observed between arriving during this strangely deserted period, and arriving after 5:00 P.M., when a general reawakening stirs through the village, the shops, the *plateia*. The scene was so lively, so utterly changed, when we passed through in the evening, en route to visit friends in Porto Rafti. The bus could barely turn the corner into the *plateia*; the entire town must have been out for the evening stroll.

This ebb and flow of Greek life seems to create two days in one. While it is very difficult for us to adjust to this traditional pattern, it is an accepted way of life for the Greek people. Schools and government support the rest period. For example, the *dimosia* (public schools), which open at 8:00 A.M., close for the day at 1:00 P.M., so that youngsters may go home for the main meal and rest period. Construction work must stop: Greek people feel imposed upon if their nap is interrupted by disturbing sounds. Hospitable in many ways, they usually consider it necessary to complain, especially at resorts, if the rest period is broken.

After the family meal, children as well as adults must "rest." They must be quiet even if they do not sleep. "Why do we have to rest?" our youngsters ask. It is through this pattern, we try to explain to them, that the Greek family stays closely knit; it is the reason that Greek people can stay up longer and need less sleep at night, and possibly can wait longer between meals—all so very different from American habits and life.

THE ATHINAS STREET MARKET

In central Athens, running north-south, almost halfway between the Acropolis and Plateia Omonias, is the great market on Athinas Street. This dominant agora, just a short walk west of Plateia Syntagmatos, the city's primary square, has vibrated to the same rhythms for decades.

Walking through the Athens market, which on a larger scale is the model for markets throughout the towns and villages of Greece, one is reminded of the passage in Aristophanes' poem "The Gourd":

> There you shall at mid-winter see
> Cucumbers, gourds, grapes and apples,
> And wreaths of fragrant violets
> Covered with dust, as if in summer.
> And the same man will sell you thrushes,
> And pears and honey-comb and olives,
> Beestings and tripe and summer olives,
> And grasshoppers and bullocks' paunches.
> There you may see full baskets packed
> With figs and myrtle, crown'd with snow.
> There you may see fine pumpkins join'd
> To that discovered bond, and mighty turnip,
> So that a stranger may well fear
> To name the season of the year.

All the foods mentioned, except for grasshoppers (which were a popular delicacy in the third century B.C.) are still highly favored. Beestings, the first milk of a cow after she has calved, may not be available in bottles; but milk fresh from the cow, goat, or sheep, boiled at home, is still a treat in the provinces, as is buffalo milk in Thrace.

It was on my initial visit to the Athens market in 1956 that I first saw the famed *barbouni* (red mullet) among the many varieties of fish —and observed its infamous price! The fish market, apparently a major attraction in all eras, is featured in much Athenian literature. The comic poet Antiphanes compared fishmongers to the gorgons of Greek mythology, who caused the petrifaction of any mortal who looked directly at them:

> Therefore I must necessarily talk to them with my face turned away, for if I see a small-sized fish it is for which they charge such a high price, I am then and there frozen solid.

Antiphanes is a gold mine of information on the food habits and attitudes of his period (fourth century B.C.).

The fish market opens early and soon fills with clamoring, boisterous Athenians. The floor is strewn with sawdust to absorb the melting ice, and the air is redolent with the smells of the sea and its products. Busy shoppers, open stalls piled high with fish, and the *psaropolides* (fishmongers) darting about enthusiastically calling out their wares combine to make a live portrait of another era.

Nearby in the meat market, whole lambs, piglets, calves, poultry, and game, varying with the season, hang on hooks, row on row. Hawking and bartering fills the air, the pitch rising and falling as the *kreopolis* (meat vendor) gestures and calls to passing marketers, extolling the virtues of his Greek imported meats.

Sweet, salty, caprylic, fragrant odors assail you as you weave your way into the cheese shop, where the tall *tyropolis* (cheese merchant) stands by his huge piles of cheeses, cutting off chunks to weigh for his customers: feta, 35.90 drachmas per kilo; mizithra, 30 per kilo; kasseri, 51 per kilo. *"Poso*—(how much)?" he asks. *"Eh, toso,"* replies the shopper, holding up two spread fingers.

Fruits and vegetables attract you with their enticing colors. Baskets piled high with deep purple eggplant, ruby tomatoes, emerald peppers, and the popular *horta* (greens). And the perennial staple roots complement the tubers and aromatic vegetables and bulbs.

The Greek shopper feels the meaning of foods, and is selective, discriminating, and very demanding. Impeccably ripe produce and perfectly tender meats are a must, not a fad, in Greece. I remember watching a woman bending over a bin of *bamyes* (okra), seriously involved

8

in selecting her vegetables for the day. "What do you think of frozen vegetables?" I asked her. Her spontaneous reply was a wince and a shudder.

There is in Greece, nevertheless, a new frozen fruit and vegetable industry, exporting from Athens to Europe and the United States. The canning and freezing industries are far flung, ranging from Elis, Sparta, Nafplion and Argolis in Peloponnesos to Arta, Thebes, Naoussa, and Thessaloniki in areas north and west of Athens, and including a tomato-canning plant in Kos in the Dodecanese. Yet the availability of frozen foods seems not to have cut into the business of the Athens central market on Athinas Street, where all the many stalls and shops seem to flourish.

Swept by the crowd into the tiny shop carrying all kinds of dried legumes, you feel a mounting excitement: nuts and fruits, coconut (the latest rage), and the favorite snacks *passa tempo* and *stragalia* (salted seeds and chick-peas). You walk through the labyrinth of fascinating shops and find yourself accumulating handfuls of small paper bags. You dart in and out of the tiny side streets, juggling your purchases as you jump to avoid the intruding automobiles. You stop at a kiosk (where they sell everything!) for a net shopping bag, into which you pop your dozens of small purchases. And now you will try to find the *bahariko* (spice shop) buried among a dozen other food shops in one of the smaller lanes, or you will look for the shops where you can buy cooking utensils.

As in other village shopping areas throughout Greece, cookery hardware is also sold in the Athinas market, each item in its own special shop. There is, for instance, the store where you can buy knives—in dizzying variety—and see them being made. (On Crete, knives are engraved with jingles and mottoes.) In another store you can buy anything *pilino* (earthenware), or a *yuvetsi* (traditional casserole) of any size. And then there is the tin shop—anything from a *röi* (oil funnel or cruet) to a *fanari* (oil lamp), each in various sizes, usually made by the retailer himself. There are also thousands of *tapsia* (baking pans) and *katsaroles* (pots). And the wood shops carry *goudi* and *goudoheri* (mortar and pestle), some made on Mount Athos; and *koutales* (spoons) for stirring, made by Greek or other European craftsmen, often German.

Obviously the more than two million people living in Athens and its environs cannot all market on Athinas Street (though on a crowded market day, as the hubbub increases and you can barely cross the street, you may think they all do!). Throughout the city are thousands of small food retailers at every conceivable corner, basement, or walk-in, some so tiny that they stock barely ten or twelve crates of fresh and dried fruits. Indeed, except for the increasing intrusion of the supermarket in Athens, small shops predominate, in the capital as in the islands and small villages.

INDIVIDUAL FOOD RETAILERS

What a range of shops—from tiny, cozy, basket-lined, leisurely, and informal ones to newer, modern shops equipped with streamlined refrigerator cases. In any of these, it is not unusual to see the owner chatting with a friend, who sits by the counter on a small chair. When you enter, they both look up as if to ask, "I wonder what she could want?" The merchandise is incidental—not as important as the chat, as life.

Each shop is named for its food specialty, with the suffix *-poleion* from the verb *polo* (sell) added to the name. Neat signs (usually including the owner's name) identify them:

Artopoleion, popularly referred to as *fourno* (oven) : Bakery shop

Ichthyopoleion, popularly called *psaropoleion*: Fish store

Kreopoleion: Meat store (butcher)

Allantopoleion: Sausage shop

Lahanopoleion: Vegetable shop

Oporopoleion, also called *froutaria*: Fruit shop

Tyropoleion: Cheese shop

Oinopoleion: Wine shop

Galaktopoleion: Milk and dairy shop (always has tables and chairs)

Zacharopoleion or *zacharoplasteion*: Sweet and pastry shop (always has tables and chairs)

Galaktozacharopoleion or *galaktozacharoplasteion*: Milk and dairy, sweet and pastry shop (usually in northern Greece and in some islands, including Crete)

We observed quite a few variations, especially in the northern regions. Some bread shops are called *artopoieion* (making of bread). Quite a few eating places combine the word *zytho* (beer) with coffee house or restaurant. And we were astonished to see *kafegalaktozacharoplasteion*, which reads (in Greek) two letters longer than the entire Greek alphabet.

I should also include the many street vendors selling chestnuts, corn, seeds, and more recently, frozen custard. These little stands are interspersed among the other shops—in case you should have a sudden appetite for snacks. And it is always so refreshing to stop at these stands, since the *bakali* (grocer) or *politis* (seller) is so pleasant, even when he is selling tiny portions that may add up to only a few drachmas.

The bakery and pastry shops are Greek landmarks as important as the *kafeneion*. The *allantopoleion* is less prevalent. Should you seek any of these specialty shops in villages and towns without success, be sure to ask for the *pantopoleion*. This Greek version of the general store (forerunner of the supermarket) has character; it is colorful and warm, carrying everything from canned milk to nuts.

Curiosity prompted me to query the National Statistics Service about the number of food retailers. I was told that in 1971 there were 7,344 *pantopoleia* in the Athens area; 2,655 *kreatopoleia*; and 2,111 *oporopoleia*. These shops employed 22,267 people. And in the summer of 1972 the total number of food retailers of all types, throughout Greece, was 45,556.

Supermarkets apparently spring up so quickly that statistics were not available. Between my trips to Greece in the fall of 1971 and the summer of 1973, I observed the heavy influx not only in food supermarkets in the wealthier suburbs, but also the hardware, toiletries, and other kinds of supermarkets in downtown Athens. This swift acceleration, I am sure, is partly in compensation for the economic lag that followed World War II.

In the face of this fierce competition, how can so many small retailers survive? Though their profits are meager and their working hours very long, food dealers in the small shops seem at peace; their warm, friendly, and fulfilled personalities are often a welcome change for those of us accustomed to the impersonality of supermarkets in the United States. Stopping by one of these tiny fruit stalls in Athens to buy delicious grapes (about 11 drachmas per kilo), one greets the gentle, pleasant proprietor, asking about his health and his business. He shrugs and good-naturedly replies, "*Etsi ketsi* (the Greek equivalent of the French *comme ci, comme ça*)," shaking his hand, palm down, in a typical gesture indicating "so-so."

ATHENS THE CORNUCOPIA

During the fifth century B.C., Thucydides wrote, "Attica, because of the poverty of its soil, from a remote period enjoyed freedom from faction and invasion." (Unfortunately, Attica subsequently failed to resist invasion; it was under constant siege by either the Franks or the Turks from 1204 to 1832.) Whatever advantages it may have enjoyed because of its barrenness, the fact remains that Attica ranks low as a productive area. Those stones that seemed so foreboding from the air, the poor soil, low rainfall, and dry summers—all contribute to the difficult growing conditions. Central Greece, of which Athens is a part, is one of the driest areas of the country. The valleys of Thebes and Lake Copais are also arid, but there the land is more fertile and the milder climate more suitable for crops. Despite adverse conditions, however, Attica has managed to improve some of her productive capacities. In 1968 Attica, of the eight crop areas of central Greece, achieved the highest production in grapes, raisins, okra, cucumbers, squash, eggplant, endive, peas, and leeks.

Athens, the population center of Greece, naturally assumes a major role in the distribution of the products of the more fertile regions, notably Thessaly, Macedonia, and Peloponnesos. The products of all regions appear in the Athens markets, on the carts of street vendors selling tidbits for munching and refreshment, and on the menus of the many taverns and restaurants.

At first glance, Athens menus may be confusing in their impressive variety. Athens is a cornucopia, frequently criticized by its ancient rival Thebes, which is traditionally more frugal in its nutritional tastes. Thirteen to sixteen food categories usually appear on an Athens bill of fare, with four to ten selections under each heading. Taverns in Plaka, the curved, cobble-stoned section of old Athens at the foot of the Acropolis, usually list ten or more *orektika* (appetizers), five to eight dishes under *diafora* (diversities) or *entrades* (entrees), four or five *tis oras* (made-to-order), and a variety of *salates* (salads), *psaria* (fish), *psita* (roasts), *zymarika* (pasta), *tyria* (cheeses), *frouta* (fruits), *krasia* (wines), *nera metallika* (mineral waters), and *glyka* (sweets). This menu format, incidentally, is typical of taverns of other regions, except that only few *glyka* are included, since they are the specialties of the sweets shops.

Menus are frequently printed in both Greek and French, or have some words transliterated from Greek to French, and increasingly to English. Most meals are listed at two prices, with and without service charge. Reading the menu adds another dimension to the total aesthetic effects; it is a riotous experience, even for those who can read the three languages!

The opulence of Athens dinners was objectionable to people of some city-states during the classical and Hellenistic periods. According to Athenaeus:

> . . . the cook sets before you a large tray on which are five small plates. One of these holds garlic, another a pair of sea-urchins, another a sweet wine sop, another ten cockles, the last a piece of sturgeon. While I am eating this, another is eating that; and while he is catching that, I have made away with this. What I want, good sir, is both the one and the other, but my wish is impossible. For I have neither five mouths nor five right hands.

Perhaps the difficulty of making a choice, rather than the profusion of foods, was the sticking point!

A Greek tavern is often a place not only for eating, but for singing and dancing as well. Dining under bright starlight, with the accompaniment of spirited Greek music, is truly a delight to all the senses.

Athenian liveliness also achieved notoriety early among the city-states, as we can learn from literature. Athenaeus, for example, quotes an author who asserts that Athenians "have but to take a sip of wine at the symposia to make them dance . . . they all begin to dance the moment they glimpse the smell of wine . . ." The spontaneous singing, dancing, and chatter is still typically Athenian, though perhaps not at symposia. The acute sense of smell also still exists, and fragrances are still considered tangible. *"Eides aroma?"*—see the aroma? a Greek asks, holding the food closer to you. A sniff sends waves of pleasure vibrating through the Greek body.

After the theater or concert, or for a late supper, Athenians can nibble, sip, and laugh into the wee hours of the next morning. Visitors can, too. Sampling *orektika* in a merry atmosphere puts them into the right frame of mind, and they find that the fun and revelry is contagious.

This is particularly true in the nightclubs, increasingly popular with rising affluence and the freedom that comes from more automobiles. Especially romantic in the outdoor, hillside settings in the Athenian suburbs, the nightclubs feature orchestras playing either Greek *bouzouki* or rock music, both with a powerful enough beat to inspire the dancers. And of course, as everywhere, the discotheques attract many fans. Nightclubs we visited were absolutely bouncing with activity—a condition one must quickly adjust to when in or near Athens. Our host managed to make the evening a family affair, inviting our daughters along with us. And, as we sat at one of the sea of tables under the trees and the stars, we found it a wholesome, delightful experience.

FESTIVALS AND FEASTS: THE TIES WITH NATURE

Family life, religion, national holidays, festivals, and carnivals strengthen the Greek culture and contribute to the food and eating customs that pervade Greece. Important religious holidays are also national holidays: schools are closed on these days, and offices observe the occasions by early closing.

Namedays are family events, celebrated with special meals and visits to acquaintances, and religious festivals are closely integrated with family life as well. During the period preceding Lenten fasting, which is carnival time (Apokreos), traditional gaiety mounts, with parades and plays enjoyed by the whole family. The series of Lenten services, fasting, Holy Communion, and Holy Unction that follow are solemn experiences for the family, highlighted on Good Friday by the grave street procession of parishioners bearing the *Epitaphio* (tomb of Christ). And the candlelight procession by a snakelike stream of Orthodox mourners down Mount Likavittos is an unforgettable annual experience in Athens.

The ancient wine festival is revived annually (to the joy of tourists, who sample free wine) at the charming Byzantine Daphne monastery and church not too far from central Athens. After viewing, in the church nave, the mosaics of the Christ Pantocrator, Baptism, and Nativity (among the most magnificent relics of the Byzantine era remaining on the mainland), you can attend the wine festival on adjacent grounds. Should your visit coincide with wine-pressing season in September and October, you can dance on grapes while sipping wine!

Culturally, Athens features both indoor and outdoor theater. I recall witty skits on popular and political themes in the early 1960s, and more recently a magnificent drama, *Aspasia*, which, in portraying the *hetaira* (companion-mistress) of Pericles, described the political turmoil and Black Plague of his era. The primary attendants are adults, but during summer music festivals, youngsters frequently accompany their parents. Last summer, listening for more than an hour to uninterrupted Mahler in the open air, my daughter and I blissfully forgot that the seats in the Herod Atticus Theater at the base of the Acropolis have no back rests.

Festivals, parades, and outdoor theater reinforce the ties with nature. Each religious ceremony and every outdoor activity relates somehow to food. Fruit and nut trees are never out of sight: Plateia Syntagmatos is studded with orange trees growing amid masses of tables and chairs, and we walk under olive trees when taking a shortcut through the Stadium to Pangrati and back. The Athens Hilton has transplanted a venerable olive tree to grow in its lobby; another aged olive tree, said to have been planted by Socrates, is a landmark. Apollo's laurel grows in the Athens Agora, and herbs and Dionysos' vines clamber over the quaint dwellings of Plaka.

Like most Greeks, Athenians spend much of their time outdoors in all seasons, a custom deeply rooted in history. The market as a meeting place has roots going back to Homer's time; witness the *Odyssey*'s second chapter, "The Council Meeting in the Market Place of Ithaca." When you visit the ruins of the ancient Athenian Agora, you can easily imagine the meeting there of the philosophers whose names have become milestones in the history of ideas. In the Athens market today the older men meet and chat while the women scurry home to prepare the important meal and finish their chores.

The exquisite climate and the long stretches of time between meals encourage outdoor activities. Walking to a *plateia* for the daily marketing; meeting friends for *meze* or *kafedaki* (little coffee) in one of the numerous *kafeneia*, where people can and do sit for hours without pressure from the waiters; strolling to the luxuriant Royal Gardens, recently renamed Ethnikos (National Gardens) or to the Zappeion (Exhibition Hall)—all of these habits involve communion with nature. So universal is this way of life that a song has been written about it: "In the Zappeion where I was walking one day," we sang in the United States, long before seeing lovely Greece. And when I first visited Athens and a relative took our youngster for a walk to the Zappeion, the words of the song came pouring back from my childhood memories—an exciting moment.

FAMILY ENTERTAINING

Experience leads me to believe that, with few exceptions, the finest food in Athens is prepared and served in private homes. A consistently high standard of food emanates from dwellings of very different life style, class, and income level. My family and I have had memorable meals in the prestigious Kolonaki area around Mount Likavittos in the mushrooming smart section near the Athens Hilton, in the established middle-class Pangrati southeast of the Stadium, in the vacation and resort sections of Porto Rafti, Vouliagmeni, and Kavouri, and in northern suburban homes. Unless the family formerly lived abroad, or is extremely upper class, its food patterns are typically Athenian—characterized by the pride of preparing and serving good food, a token of esteem to the guest.

When receiving visitors, Athenians customarily serve something made, grown, or gathered in their villages of origin—often noodles, wine, olives, fruit, oil, spoon sweets, or herbs. Sprinkling their tasty dishes with oregano, thyme, basil, or rosemary from their native villages reinforces their ties with the old home and with nature. I first tasted Cretan *tsikoudia* in Athens, a drink brought from "home" by the Cretan hostess. Many of our acquaintances in Athens were born in Asia Minor, Alexandria, and Russia—or their parents were—and through them we learned of exotic foods or new concoctions from their birthplaces. Favorite dishes from the islands—Spetsai, Samos, Crete, and Corfu—also appear regularly on Athenian tables, just as the specialties of Athens appear abroad. An example of the latter is *Kopenhai* (Copenhagen), a Greek dessert that was created especially for the coronation of King George, of Denmark, as king of Greece.

When our children travel with my husband and me, they are included in invitations to Athenian homes. The host family's youngsters greet us with their parents, for they have learned the art of *philoxenia* at an early age. The daughters help serve and clear the table between courses, the maids (where they exist) usually remaining unobtrusively behind the scenes. The hostess herself supervises the making of important dishes unless the family employs a highly skilled cook, and in most of the homes we have visited, the culinary arts have passed from mother to daughters. The oldest son joins the father in the traditional role of serving food and wine and coaxing conversation and laughter. And no matter how large the group, all adults and children are seated around one table. (Luckily, in our experience, the group has never exceeded fifteen!) Conversation and food games create an atmosphere of cordiality and relaxation.

After the meal, in the living room, the girls take turns playing the piano, and everyone joins in singing popular songs. My childhood had prepared me very well for these evenings: our family meals in America had climaxed with the joy of music, as well as with dancing on Sundays and holidays. Convivial feelings, therefore, highlighted our visits to Athenian homes as much as the unfailingly excellent food and drink.

The aesthetically pleasing evening usually continues with *kafe* on a balcony under the Milky Way, amid breezes perfumed with basil, rosemary, jasmine, and laurel. Before guests depart, another nice ancient custom is still observed: *epideipnis* (after-dinner) sweets—usually *loukoumia*, chocolate, or candied fruits—are passed, for a *glyko* (sweet) finale.

Over the years we have spent many memorable evenings with Athenians. Among these was a supper in a villa on the eastern Attic coast with a typical professional family—both parents high in educational echelons and three offspring in, or graduates of, universities. (In Athens their home is a spacious apartment, privately owned, very much like American condominiums.)

We were greeted by the entire family, and after a brief glimpse of the stars and deep breathing of sea air from their balcony (the time was after 9:00 P.M.), we were seated in the dining room around the spacious round table to await supper, which is usually a light meal. Following the delicate *soupa avgolemono,* served as a first course, several platters were brought to the father by the daughters. I clearly remember the variety and flavor: *psari tiganito* with *skordalia* (fried fish with garlic sauce), *kalamarakia me saltsa domata* (squid in tomato sauce), *angourodomatosalata* (cucumber-tomato salad), *avga yemista* (stuffed eggs), feta, olives, and anchovies. There was homemade bread on the table, of course, and water; and wine was served by the father, who rose and walked around in continental fashion instead of having glasses passed to him in the more usual Greek style. No milk was served to our youngsters (typical American types who missed fresh milk throughout Greece); but our older son, then sixteen, was offered wine mixed with water, a Greek way of drinking wine since Homer's time. He was too surprised to accept. The supper was climaxed with the fruit course— fresh *peponi* (melon) and *karpouzi* (watermelon), especially succulent in late summer.

17

After dinner we moved to the living room, which was equipped with a piano for the daughters' summer practice, and we sang popular songs and folk songs. Later, again on the balcony, we enjoyed liqueur under the stars amid fragrant breezes. Throughout the meal there was amiable conversation and a sense of repose, though all the food had been cooked and served by the hostess and her two daughters. How could we ever forget such an evening?

CONTRASTS: PALEO AND NEO

Though tradition is strong in Greece, innovation occasionally nudges custom. During a recent visit to Athens, a friend suggested that we stop by at 3:30 P.M., since our available time was limited. I gasped in surprise: the thought of visiting during the traditional rest time! But she insisted it would not be inconvenient for her since her husband (among the growing number of Athenians who work through the day) does not come home for a large dinner at midday. As we enjoyed refreshments on her terrace, carefully quiet so as not to disturb the naps of others, she whispered about changes in women's lives—more conveniences, more social and sexual freedom. "This little world isn't the same as it used to be," she said, sighing, and then went on to comment on the aspects of liberation that pleased her.

Leaving Athens, on my last trip, I thought of the exquisite poem "Athens" by Kostas Karyotakis (1896–1928), and how he captures the beauty of the great city:

Sweet hour. Lovely Athens lies down
Yielding to April like an hetaera;
There is pleasure from perfume in the air,
And the soul awaits nothing more.

Evening bends over the homes
And her silver eyelids grow heavy;
Like a queen the Acropolis yonder
Has robed herself in purple sunset.

A kiss of light and the evening star bursts;
Over on Ilisso the breeze falls in love
With shivering laurels, like rosy brides.

Sweet hour of joy and love, when
Birds chase one another
Flapping air around a pillar at the Temple of Olympian Zeus.*

And looking back over your shoulder at this fascinating land of paleo-neo contrasts, you will remember that, traveling in almost any direction, you will very likely soon see a black-clad woman on a donkey, hauling twigs to build her fire and cook her home-grown food.

A QUICK COOK'S TOUR OF THE PROVINCES

From Athens, drive past the ancient shrine of Demeter at Eleusis, along the fluid highway beside the brilliant Saronic Gulf—this is the magnet that draws you into Peloponnesos. After crossing the four-mile isthmus cut by the Corinth Canal, linking two great gulfs, you will be beguiled by the contrasts of the southern Greek region. In fact, in any direction from Athens the country is full of surprises. You see not only geographic diversity but visual stimuli so pure that the past never seems too remote.

There are constant reminders of the myths, of the drama and poetry of Greece. Mycenae, the oldest known mainland settlement, which reached its zenith under Agamemnon, grandson of Pelops (for whom the peninsula was named); the lovely Arcadian plain where Pan found pasture to romp in and Hermes played the shepherd-pipe; Olympia, site of the stadium and the museum where Praxiteles' statute of Hermes stands in marble perfection; and the magnificent theater of Epidavros, setting of the superb drama festivals. The Hellenes—who were, are, and always will be health enthusiasts—adore their mineral water spas and consider good health the greatest gift of life.

Patras is a spankingly new city, swinging with the vigor of youth, where the standard of living is higher than in other towns of this southern region. Yet the food habits are similar to those of the tiniest villages. People cling to their leguminous soups, cheeses, local wines, fruits, and vegetables. And much remains unchanged: Messenian land owners working with traditional methods dry their currants and figs outdoors in late summer; the village baker is still an early riser, at his *fourno* long before the cock crows; men otherwise unemployed spend each wakeful

* "Athina," *Neoelliniki Poeitiki Anthologia Papyrou* [New Greek poetry anthology papyrus] (Athens, Greece: Papyros Press Ltd., 1971), p. 237.

19

moment at the *kafeneion* catching up on the day's activity; and it is very exciting to stand at the quai and watch the fishermen bartering with villagers.

For in many beautiful ways (except for the obvious sad exodus of many, many Hellenes to Athens and other countries) the villages and towns of Peloponnesos reflect the life style of all Greek areas. Marketing is a daily affair, and family life continues to be closely knit. Women's lives center around their families, and though their routines may seem monotonous on the surface, their contentment is ensured by their knowledge of the essential role they play.

Every day is a day to walk in the *plateia* (even in large Thessaloniki there are endless walks along the lovely Thermaic Gulf, and, in Epirus, around the famous lake of Ioannina), which is usually also the most exciting historical or natural landmark.

Central Greece, known to the Hellenes as the mainland, lies beyond the northern shores of the Corinthian Gulf, extending from the Ionian to to the Aegean seas, and including the enormous island of Evia (Euboea). Also in central Greece are the *nomoi* (provinces) of Eurytania, Phthiotis, Aetolia-Acarnania, Phocis, Boeotia, and of course, Attica.

Culturally, Attica dominated the region in ancient times, especially during the Age of Pericles, the Golden Age of ancient Greece, when the arts flourished to an unsurpassed degree. In modern times its influence persists, with Attic Athens the nerve center and capital of all Greece; as well as Messologion, which for the Greek people is synonymous with the heroic siege during the War for Independence (1825–1826). Messologion is also famous as the place where Lord Byron died of fever while fighting with the Greek forces. His memory is revered throughout Greece, and his statue is a landmark where buses pause for passengers at the National Gardens in Athens.

During the seventh to fourth centuries B.C., however, the Delphic Oracle on Mount Parnassus, in Phocis, maintained an emotional grip that reached to the four corners of Greece and extended into the neighboring countries. Today Mount Parnassus provides one of the most spectacular experiences to be enjoyed in all of Greece. Among the other sights, from the awesome slope where the Delphic ruins lie, thousands of olive trees can be seen shining below in the Crisaean plain. Amphissa, capital of Phocis, produces an olive that is probably the most "Greek" of all (large, black, wrinkled and salty-bitter, as compared to the famous Kalamata type, which is smooth-skinned and sourish).

To say the word "Epirus" is to invoke an atmosphere of wildness and austerity. In the approach from Corfu, its island neighbor to the west, Epirus looks very much like its name, a "continent" of formidable majestic mountains rising from the blue Ionian Sea. Towering heights and wild gorges apparently inhibited thick settlement in Epirus, whose natives claim descendancy from Achilles. In legend Epirus is linked with misery and frustration, Greek people still sing the tragic folk songs: "The Bridge of Arta" tells of the sad ending of Kyra Phrossini, sweetheart of the son of Ali Pasha (who ruled during the Turkish period); another celebrates the women and children of Suli, who leaped from the cliffs of Zalongo to avoid surrendering to Turks. In Epirus, man first settled in the sacred oak forest, ate acorns, and drank from the Achelous, said to be the oldest river in Greece. These early people were named Hellenes, and according to legend, their cult grew into a nation. Austerity in Epirus, and other Greek regions as well, inspired rather than discouraged the people. They bake and broil delectable carp, trout, and eel dishes from the bountiful rivers, especially of Ioannina; local venison, hare, wild boar, woodcocks, and partridges are plentiful in the dense Pindus forests; olives thrive on coastal Parga; Zitsa wine delights everyone; and the incomparable citrus fruit brings particular fame to Arta. When not sampling Epirote culinary creations, you will be marveling at the contrasts in the terrain. The road from port Igoumenitsa (the ferry link to Corfu) to Ioannina pierces some of the most desolate, barren mountains I have ever seen. But arriving at Metsovon, nestled in the Pindus Mountains, is like coming upon an idyllic highland retreat.

Farther east, facing the magnificent plains of Thessaly, one is seized with a deep reverence for the land. Its great expanses of wheat fields have earned for Thessaly the sobriquet "the granary of Greece." The land is rich, secure, bountiful. How understandable the ancient devotion to Demeter, and how easy to imagine Persephone dancing in the fields of grain and wild flowers. But how amazing to see flat land in Greece!

It is not surprising that invaders from all directions tramped through Thessaly and that tourists invading Thessaly today experience great joy in its beauty. On the one hand, the sun's rays beat down on the fertile, expansive plains, and on the other, the cool tones of the mountains provide an astounding change. Mount Pelion, for example, is lushly covered with evergreens, olives, *firikia* apples and *aphroditi* peaches, growing side by side on the brilliant slope all the way down to the beach by the sea. *"Orgiazi i fisis!*—an orgy of nature!,," a Hellene exclaims at such a sight.

Thessalians, referred to in much ancient literature as having extravagant prandial tastes, contribute many ideas to Greek cuisine. They frequently crumble their *filo* sheets when layering them for their rich *pites* (pies); *spetsofagi* (page 160) is unique. Yet in the monasteries high in the gigantic Meteora above the village of Kalambaka, the monks and nuns lead lives of utter simplicity. The monks (of Varlaam) and nuns (of Agios Stephanos) adhere to the strictest rules of self-deprivation of their Orthodox faith. Watching them raising and gathering their food and water is a modern-day lesson in survival!

Aristotle and Alexander the Great were Macedonians. As if this were not sufficient claim to fame, Macedonia can boast of being the largest region, of having lush meadows and magnificent lakes, of yielding the greatest volume of crops, and of producing an industrial output triple that of any other region. Its people are among the handsomest, and their contributions to Greece—their foods, their woven goods and furs, and their educational center—are enormously important. The mere mention of the famous *yarmades* peaches of Macedonia makes the mouth water instantly!

Verdant and fruitful, this region attracted settlers from just about everywhere. Many of these, unfortunately, were conquerors—from north, west, and east—who coveted Macedonia (just as Macedonia subsequently was to covet the entire Western world). The capital, Thessaloniki, is calm and reserved (compared to the frenetic pace of Athens or bustle of Patras) and excels as a lively banking, administrative and university center, and a center of agricultural training as well. All the industriousness and productivity seems to fan out from Thessaloniki. It is also a rich architectural museum of the Byzantine period; many of the old churches are steeped in the miraculous lore of that fascinating age. The slick University City includes an agriculture and forestry department, and the most unusual American Farm School, operating both farm and school a short distance from the city center, teaches young Macedonian men and women agricultural and handicraft skills and operates a small supermarket that sells students' dairy products, including delicious ice cream in Dixie cups.

Most Hellenes (and visitors) associate Macedonia with its renowned fruits. Verria, Florina, Edessa, and Naoussa fruit trees are laden with bounty, and easy to see as you travel westward. On the Halkidiki Peninsula on the eastern side a similar richness awaits the eye and taste buds, but it is organized in an altogether different mosaic. Here the startling beauty of the fishing villages and each tiny cove surprise you at every turn; and there are thousands of olive trees (rarely seen in western Macedonia) along the coast, wheat fields, and the inevitable cows, goats, and sheep living in an orderly setting.

Leaving Macedonia, one thinks of its richness, its dynamism—all reminiscent of the periods of Aristotle and Alexander the Great—and one begins to know why its present glory is often referred to as the Macedonia Renaissance.

Thrace is small, heterogeneous, fertile, and fascinating. From earliest times its culture has been highly developed, music and poetry being its specialties. Two Greek mythological figures originated here: Orpheus, whose music entranced listeners into naming a constellation for him; and Dionysos, the god of wine. But it was as a deity of vegetation that the latter was worshiped in Thrace before traveling southward to Attica, where he rose to fame with his vineyards.

Like Macedonia, Thrace has a refreshingly opulent appearance. From Kavalla, in eastern Macedonia, also the primary port and communication center of Thrace, the road to Xanthi sustains this image. Many diverse elements distinguish themselves as you drive through the fertile valley from the Nestos River all the way to Alexandroupolis. In the villages, clothing patterns among women are sharply defined: Turkish ladies in long, heavy black robes, white or black scarves draped tightly around their heads, and black bloomer-trousers; Greek ladies in short Western dress; teen-agers in miniskirts and jeans. Thracian *pites* and specialties were fun to discover; you will feel a similar response trying the unusual recipes.

AND AT LAST THE ISLANDS

Charm, beauty, tradition, history, magic!—instant associations when we hear the phrase "the Greek Islands." To characterize them as a group, however, is impossible, for each is distinctive. But think of a collection of the world's finest stones, each different yet all gems, or of a basket of luscious fruit—peaches, pears, apples, grapes, cherries, oranges, plums, tangerines—every known variety . . . and then sail to the Greek Islands.

The islands that cling to Greece on the west are in the Ionian Sea; the others, which almost touch Asia Minor or the northern coast of Africa, east and south of mainland Greece, are sprinkled across the vast expanse of the Aegean. Both these seas were named for mythological characters. Io, sweetheart of Zeus, was changed into a heifer to fool jealous Hera, then, stung by a bee, plunged into the sea but swam to safety; the Ionian Sea was later named for her. When King Aegeus saw the black flag on his son's ship returning from Crete, he believed Theseus had died (Theseus had forgotten to switch flags to indicate his victory over the Minotaur); the father drowned himself, and since then the sea has been called the Aegean.

Though these lovely islands have an agriculture limited in quantity, most gained fame through the quality of their wines, fruits, and foods. Ionian wines are delightful, outstanding being the red wines of Lefkas and the dry white and red Mavroudi wines of Kefallinia. Samos wines have been celebrated in literature: Byron repeats throughout *Don Juan,* "Fill high the bowl with Samian wine!" The bountiful vineyards of Lindos, on Rhodes, yield both red and dry white wines; Tilos, Santorini, Nisiros, and Leros are among the many areas noted for their vineyards.

Among the islands famous for their dishes, Corfu leads with a distinctive blend of the Venetian, French, and British influence; Spetsai produced the renowned Psari Spetsiotiko (page 115); Syros makes Greece's finest *loukoumia,* jellied candies scented with rose and mastic. (Most distinctive of all Greek aromatics, mastic, produced in the villages of Chios, is used for flavoring and preserving, also to make the liquor *mastiha.*) The chestnuts of Ayassos and olive oil of Kalloni are among the culinary contributions of the island of Lesvos, which is also famous for desserts. The spoon sweets and preserves of Kalymnos are superb, as are the apricots of Karpathos. The latter also produces fine almonds, as do Tilos and Nisiros.

Food and life-style traditions continue to reflect the ageless rapport between man and sea, with a vigorous nudge to more aggressive selling on many islands, particularly Mykonos. Common sights: fishing boats, slim fishermen bending over their nets, fish being unloaded very early in the morning; a sudden flurry when a cruise ship arrives, Hellenes running home to watch the "sights" from safety behind a window.

Largest of all Greek islands, Crete flourished even during the early Bronze Age, and continues to dominate the island culture and foods. In its small arable area, Crete blooms with grapes, oranges, bananas, melons, grains, legumes, and many vegetables, including artichokes and eggplants. Cheeses, too, bring honor to Crete: anthotyro, manouri, mizithra; as do varied red and white wines and *tsikoudia,* a strong liquor. Cretan *pites* and desserts are inventive and distinctive.

Though not a "Greek isle" or one belonging to any other govern-ment since it became an independent republic in 1960, Cyprus must be included in a Greek cookbook. Its culture, religion, mores, and foods are strongly Greek, as anyone with Cypriot friends knows! Its burgeon-ing fields produce Commandaria, Othello, Ansinoe, and other delicious wines (including sherry, which is not produced on the mainland); excellent fruits, carob, wheat, barley, and the fabulous anari and haloumi cheeses. Like the Cretans, the Cypriots have used Greek ideas to produce highly distinctive dishes.

Leaving all these islands, you remember Homer's account of Calypso's cave in the *Odyssey* and his words about the fragrant scent over the island and the "luxuriant grapevine, with clusters of ripe fruit . . ."

AESTHETICS AND COOKERY

———◆———

The Cook at Work

The cook and the poet are just alike. The art of each lies in his brain. EUPHRON (3rd century B.C.)

GREEK COOKERY ASSUMES A fundamental feeling for food. The cook feels secure in working with familiar ingredients, always aware of their meaning as part of the culture. And the cook thoroughly enjoys serving others who will share in the joy of eating the favored foods.

The feeling for the food begins even before the preparation of a meal. Most Greek people, whether in villages or cities or towns, manage to keep a hand in the cultivation of herbs, fruit, olives, grapes, and vegetables, so that the physical contact with food starts early. Many people keep chickens for eggs, and a goat, sheep, or cow for milk and cheese; or they get these products from a neighbor in their community. As growing things ripen, the cook tests their color, texture, aroma. Particular care is lavished on the preservation of cheeses, wines, and other foods stored for the year's use. Fruits may be preserved in syrup or dried, vegetables pickled, olives marinated, herbs and legumes dried, fish salted, pork smoked, eggs and milk transformed into *trahana* and *hilopites* (noodles). By the time an ingredient is slated for a particular day's menu, the cook probably has seen, touched, and heard it, and has enjoyed its scent many times.

In addition, the Greek cook has a considerable bond with his environment, acquired through the traditional culture. All Greek parents, directly or indirectly, teach their children how food enriches life in myriad ways. Extremely exciting for children are the festivals involving group food production, in which the energies of the extended family are united in the preparation of a common meal, in preserving of foods, in celebration of the holiday. Kneading and rolling pastries and breads, drying figs and raisins, packing olives, pitting cherries, shelling nuts, roasting lamb on the *souvla* outdoors—all of these are done jointly. While learning these skills and attitudes toward food, the young also emulate the family "expert," a highly distinguished individual in Greek families. Recipes, spoken or written, usually convey the feeling of family and cultural unity (as I tried to demonstrate in the *hortopita* recipe on page 220): "We wash the spinach," and "After cooling the mixture, we stir in the wine." The use of the "we" enhances the feeling of food as a heritage.

The Greek cook, in speaking about his or her work, often seems like a poet seeking the word with exactly the right nuance to complete his verse. Or like the painter for whom elements like line, color, texture, form, and space are interrelated. If you ask about quantities of ingredients or about cooking time, the Greek cook will say, "It depends . . ." —on how salty the particular fish is, how ripe and juicy the tomatoes, how sweet the syrup, how large the eggplant, how young the chicken, and so on. How much vinegar do you add? "*Analogos*—in proportion," the cook answers. To reach a perfect balance, the cook has to use all five senses—touch, taste, smell, sight, and hearing—and he has to weigh each situation carefully before making a judgment.

Greek cooks also know and use scientific principles, though they may not use scientific terms. They utilize the principles of fermentation in making yogurt and wine, the process of protein coagulation in making *avgolemono*, of emulsions in making *taramosalata*, of hydration of proteins in preparing their marvelous breads, of osmosis in developing the flavor of *stifado, tzatziki, briami,* and the numerous stuffings and mixtures from *keftedes* to *dolmades.* They know the value of slow casserole baking and the need to cook greens with the lid partially off, as well as many tricks for tenderizing meats and fish.

In every Greek home and in good Greek restaurants, it is a pleasure to see the cook eagerly watching over his pots and kettles. Such a sight recalls Athenaeus' description of an ancient cook teaching his apprentices (all cooks should read Athenaeus for real inspiration):

> I sit nearby and . . . explain principles and result. . . . "Play
> fortissimo with the fire. Make the tempo even. The first dish
> is not simmering in tune with the others next it" . . . You see,
> I serve no course without study, I mingle all in a harmonious
> scale. . . . Some things are related to each other by fourths,
> by fifths, or by octaves. These I join by their own proper in-
> tervals and weave them in a series of appropriate courses. . . .
> "What are you joining that to?" "What are you going to mix
> with that?" "Look out, you are pulling a discordant string."

Any cook using the recipes in this book is encouraged to use his
or her own senses and judgment in interpreting them. Learn to measure
with the hand and eyes, allowing the Greek idea to work. For measuring,
Greeks use their fingers or fingertips, one hand or two, a water glass, a
teacup, a Turkish coffee cup or its saucer, or special measurers (in grams)
of their most frequently used liquids, olive oil and wine (the latter
serves to measure water also). In small *tavernes*, if you order wine, you
will probably be served wine in this special bright orange measurer
(your pitcher) and an empty wine glass (which you can keep filling).
These are handy measurers when the Hellenes cook, for 100 grams,
200 grams, and so on up to a *kilo* (1,000 grams). Solid volumes are
estimated by referring to a familiar product—the size of a lemon, an
orange, an almond, or a walnut. Sight and touch are the primary methods
of measuring—difficult but exciting. Mixing with the fingers, a cook
will look at the dough, batter, or *kima* and say, *Theli ki' allo*—"It
wants more." When a Greek cook challenges you with instructions like
"as much as it wants," or "as much as it will take," meaning oil or flour
usually, you have to use your own senses and judgment to create a delicious product. And also, at this point in time, facing a possible change
toward the metric system (as the Greek people did from Turkish
measurements a few decades ago) we might adapt more quickly.

Allow your eye to judge the ripeness of a fig, the tenderness of a
stuffed turkey, or the doneness of a cake or bread in the oven. Watch
for colors also, as Greek cooks do. When preparing gravies and jellies,
listen for the sizzling and unmistakable changes as they thicken, and for
the musical effects of butter being whipped, and wine or vinegar bubbling when poured into a hot savory sauce. Before adding herbs and
spices, sniff them to estimate how much of their volatile substances
they still retain, a great variable determining the amount needed, and

smell the vapors rising from the pot before adding salt. But while aroma is the first clue to flavor, you must taste, as you cook, for the harmony of flavor. Thus will you develop a fundamental feeling for food.

Having felt since childhood the warm feelings involved in family cookery projects and the joy of joining in the preparations, I find the task of sharing these recipes a pleasurable one. I have attempted to convey the simplicity of Greek cooking by making the recipes brief, but I also have made an effort to describe some of the well-known interpretations and variations.

TERMS, TIPS, AND METHODS OF COOKERY

"The kitchen ware
Will come when bidden. Table, stand by me.
Casserole, make ready. Flour-bag, knead the bread.
Pour, ladle. Where's the cup? Come clean.
Rise, barley cake. Now, cooking pot, disgorge the beet.
Here, fish." "But my other side's not cooked."
"Well, over you go, and salt and oil yourself."
                    KRATES (4th century B.C.), *Wild Animals*

The cook must know both the food she is working with and the varied avenues it may travel if she is to reach her goal—the special dish. An illustration of Greek awareness of food properties is the saying: "Oil from the top, wine from the middle, and honey from the bottom— always—when marketing." Both the physical and chemical properties are major factors in selection, preparation, and cooking of foods. This sensibility is mirrored in the variety of food uses, as I have tried to depict in the recipes.

Greek cookery terms show an acute knowledge of the properties of foods. Most frequently used cookery terms are basic verbs that apply to a variety of similar physical functions in relation to foods. For instance, the very same *kopto* (I cut) is used for "dice," "chop," "slice," "cube," "mince," and "trim"; it may also mean to divide dough or pastry (with a pastry wheel), and sometimes even to peel. But "peel" has a special verb, *xefloudizo* (literally, "I unskin"), which is also used for shelling nuts and seeds or removing husk or bark—and it may be used to describe a human after a good sunburn. To cite other examples, "drain," "strain," and "sift" may all be described by *strangizo* (I strain),

29

whether it be through *tsantila* (cheesecloth) or colander or strainer or *strangihtiri* (sieve). When boiling, poaching, or parboiling, the Greek says *vrazo* (I boil)—which also can mean "I'm furious!" "Scald" and "blanch" are from the verb *zematizo*, the same verb used when the cook burns her finger. *Ktypo* (I beat) may imply pounding, tenderizing with a mallet, whisking, beating by hand or with electric mixer or a spoon; and recently it has come to mean blending (with electric blender): However, the ageless pounding with mortar and pestle has a special verb, *kopanizo*. The word *tiganizo* (I fry) has a range of possibilities— deep-fat frying, pan frying, and sautéing.

During my visits to Greece, and while I was testing and writing recipes, I accumulated an enormous list of ideas that are usually classi- fied as "tips" in cookery. Rather than include the list here, I prefer to allow you to discover them in the recipes, where they have been noted. But here are a few personal ones (not mentioned in recipes): sheep and goat's cream for softening facial skin; lemons rubbed on hands after squeezing out the juice; spices on clothing in drawers; bay leaves in rinse water for clothing; thyme and marjoram for fragrance; and chew- ing on whole cloves after a large, delicious portion of Skordalia (page 49)!

You may find and read the Greek ideas easily. But to develop a strong feeling for the foods you use, you must become actively involved in the preparation—learn the techniques and methods. You have to pound eggplants, and nuts, and garlic; slap and beat the doughs and octopus; rinse and wash and dry the fruits; knead the breads and *kima* mixtures; you have to crack walnuts, rub the almond skins and peel the vegetables and chestnuts; stuff the grapevine leaves and vegetables and poultry; you have to roll *filo* and noodles and mold the little cakes by hand. You have to use your body, your senses. Whether you imagine each dish as an adventure: an exploit of Aphrodite or a conquest of Zeus; or as a challenge for Athena or Theseus or Herakles—you must travel the road yourself. There is no other way to the Greek imagination.

Aroma and the Senses

Anyone familiar with modern Greece quickly feels the bond between the people, their senses, and nature as expressed through food. Throughout the centuries scientists, philosophers, historians, and artists have helped to strengthen this bond. That it remains today in individual Hellenes is apparent from the way the poorest, humblest cooks spice their dishes.

Theophrastus (371–288 B.C.) was among the Greeks who became absorbed by plants and spices and wrote about them in scientific treatises. His *Enquiry into Plants,* one of the finest works of the third century B.C., is still exciting to read in the twentieth century. Theophrastus, who studied and classified odors, found that those with the longest-lasting properties were iris, marjoram, and myrrh (popular during his time). He also found that heat and sun could destroy odors (we know that spices and herbs should not be stored near the stove or in the sun), and that certain odors could not be combined satisfactorily; in fact, he stressed that the unpleasant could destroy the odor of the pleasant. In developing and compounding spices for perfumes (an experiment easy to try at home), he mixed whole spices, slightly bruised, in a container, sealed it, and allowed it to rest for several days. When the container was opened, the spice retaining the strongest smell was used on clothes for fragrance. Theophrastus also knew that the senses of smell and taste were inseparable, and that tastes and smells of foods vary considerably over a period of time.

Theophrastus was probably the earliest researcher of taste and odor in the Western world, but the field remained virtually untouched until the eighteenth century, when Jean Anthelme Brillat-Savarin wrote his *Physiology of Taste.* This gastronomer frequently referred to the ancient Greeks. In his chapter on the "Philosophical History of Cooking" he includes this passage: "Cooking and its amenities were held in high esteem by the Athenians, as was natural in a race so elegant and eager for the new; kings, rich citizens, poets, and scholars led the way, and philosophers themselves did not feel called upon to refuse pleasures wrung from the breast of nature."

The awareness of the senses of taste and smell early in their history heightened Greek consciousness of herbs and seasonings. The result is that Greeks adore their seasonings. Many of them, however, were and are eclectic in their tastes. Some cooks dribble oregano, mint, or basil into all their dishes; they savor a particular spice and find joy, not monotony, in its constant use.

The taste sense is by no means subtle. Greeks can be noisy eaters, without being a bit embarrassed. Table etiquette is not used in the in-hibiting sense; rather, it implies warmth, joviality, enjoyment. Hellenes relish and savor their foods, enjoying the basic flavors undisguised. They refer to *yefsis* of foods, implying both flavor and texture, which are considered equally exciting. They delight in breaking off crusty bread with the fingers and biting it with their teeth. They enjoy the relaxation of peeling fruit: they will try to cut off the orange peel in one continuous curl. They seem to delight in the crisp noises of cracking nuts and munching them slowly, and sip cool liquids between their lips, smacking them afterwards with satisfaction. I can remember watch-ing a family of five, sitting at the water's edge on a Thracian beach, cleaning mussels. For more than an hour they chatted among themselves, rubbing a large shell against the mussels to clean off the "beards." Occasionally the parents would turn to the children, but not to give them directions. The youngsters were already sensitized to the sight, touch, and sounds of cleaning mussels by the azure shore.

Women experience the touch sense in their daily cooking: rubbing, kneading, mixing doughs and stuffings, and measuring by hand. Most Greek pastries and cookies require long and vigorous handling. *Koulourakia, kourambiedes, melomakarona,* staples through the ages, are formed individually by hand.

Hellenes refer to the sense of hearing in metaphoric expressions, such as "Listen to the kneading of the trough and the swelling of the yeast." If a Greek is overcome with joy and eager to convey it to a listener, he might erupt with "Even my ears are laughing."

Sight is vital in cookery because eyes are an important center of the Greek being. Greeks speak with their eyes. A mother endearingly calls her child *"Matia mou—*my eyes." How frequently chefs who were giving me instructions cautioned me to watch the food carefully as it cooks, just as a mother warns her child who is leaving for a new adventure: "*Ta matia dekatessera*—keep your eyes open as if you had fourteen of them."

The olfactory sense is very important, and constantly responding to foods. A mere smell from the cooking pot will arouse a sharp sigh, and the Hellene will bend over and take another long whiff. But they loathe *bromio* (bad odor), and will use the term to express all forms of disgust. "The bad smell of a fish begins at the head," they will say, to indicate that corruption or mismanagement begins at the top. Of someone totally lacking in merit or virtue, a Hellene quips, "Sour wine, smelly fish!"—the most terrible qualities imaginable for wine and fish, favorite foods.

Through colors Greeks express strong preferences and prejudices. They use *mavro* (black) for the undesirable, as in "black fate," and "black luck." Jokingly a wife will say, "Black luck, my husband; everyone drowned, but you came back." For the two-faced person, Greeks use the expression "Black man, white words." Racial types, however, are not described as "black" and "white."

Skouro is the word for "dark," and *melani* (ink) conveys a particularly mysterious, sultry image. In referring to people, *melanchrino* means "dark-skinned"; it is also used as a nickname for *karydopita*, which is baked with cinnamon to a deep-colored tone.

At the other end of the value scale, since ancient times the light colors have been idealized. The word *xanthos* implies a handsome, fair-skinned, blond Apollo-type man. *Aspro* (white) is the best. *Ehi aspri gnosi* (literally, "He has white knowledge") means that one has sense. *Aspros helios mavri mera* (White sun, black day) is used to compare two extremes. Many other expressions reflect fondness for light, especially in foods; *anoikto* (bright) also means "open"; and *lefko* (white or blank) is frequently used for white wines.

Among the foods light colors—of bread, yogurt, cereals, pasta, *trahana*, cheeses, wines, confectioneries with powdered sugar, and whipped dishes—outnumber others. *Xantho* is used in referring to foods, as well as to people, of a pleasant color. *Chryso* (golden) and *chrysoxantho* (light golden) are popular cookery terms for baked crusts, or for onions sautéed in butter or oil. *Xanthokastano* (light chestnut) and *chrysokastano* (golden chestnut) imply radiant tones—in flaky pastries as they emerge from the oven, on *pastitsio* or *moussaka* or *pites*.

Reds, of course, are the adored bright colors, the terms of various shades being *kokkino* (red), *rodo* (rose), and *rodakino* (rosy peach). A rosé wine is *kokkinelli*. Meats and poultry seared in oil or butter are described as *kokkinisto,* not "browned" as in English. And breaded, fried, or sautéed foods achieve the rosy red of *rodokokkino.*

Very emotional, Greeks express their feelings and many situations in cookery terms, such as *vrazo* ("I'm furious" or "I'm boiling"). A vivacious woman is described as *petakti,* a man as *petaktos,* the same cookery term used for sautéing or frying quickly in a small amount of fat. Another example, roasts in Greek are described as *psita.* When a youth and girl fall in love and decide to marry, a Greek will quip *Ta psisane* ("They have roasted it").

They also express their feelings through temperatures. Coolness is a desirable quality, associated with water gushing from a spring, the herbs and wild greens they collect for their dishes, and despite their volatile tempers, in people. (Foods at room temperature are the rule in Greece rather than the exception—much to the dismay of tourists.) All the senses are vital to a Greek; they are not reserved for special occasions, but are part of the daily aesthetic experience, their *aisthisis.*

AROMA AND FAVORED INGREDIENTS

Hellenes invented *aroma* (pronounced in Greek with accent on the first syllable) and continually enjoy the essences of their beloved seasonings. These, I believe, through my study of Greek foods and feelings inspired among the people, are the staples—providing the continuity in new dishes and new combinations of foods. In Greece, security in the familiar manifests itself in popularity of choice flavorings. Although there is variation from region to region, from cook to cook, the frequent use of the same seasonings is common. The following are arranged in alphabetical order, not order of preference:

Acid seasonings: citric acid, lemon, lemon and orange rind, must, orange, pomegranate juice and seeds, tomato, vinegar, wine, yogurt.

Fat flavors: olive oil, olive-oil margarine, pork fat, sweet butter, *tahini* (sesame seed emulsion), vegetable oils (corn, peanut, sesame).

Herbs and aromatic bulbs and vegetables: basil, bay, carrot, celery, celery root, chervil, chives, dill, fennel, garlic, green pepper, juniper berries, leeks, marjoram, onion, oregano, parsley, rosemary, sage, savory, scallions, shallots, thyme.

Pungent seasonings: black pepper, capers, cayenne pepper, liquors, mustard, mustard seeds, paprika, *tursi* (pickle).

Salt seasonings: anchovies, caviar, cheese, olives, sardines, table salt, *taramas* (paste of salted fish roe).

Spices and seeds: allspice, aniseed, caraway, cardamom, cinnamon, cloves, coriander, cumin, *mahlepi*, nutmeg, sesame, vanilla.

Dessert flavorings: almond, apricot, brandy or cognac, bitter orange, cherry, honey, lemon, mastic, milk, orange, orange flower water, ouzo, rose geranium, rose water, spices, vanilla. Coconut and chocolate are newer flavorings.

Dried fruits and nuts (used in some dishes and beverages as well as desserts): almonds, candied fruits (fruit glacées), currants, dates, figs, filberts, pine nuts, pistachios, raisins, walnuts.

Spices and herbs should be replenished frequently, and are best purchased in small quantities. In Greece, herbs are frequently dried before used in cooking (admittedly home-grown varieties). When substituting dried for fresh herbs, use the rule of thumb-and-forefinger: pinch off ⅓ as much as the recipe requests since dried herbs are three times stronger than fresh. Add herbs as close to the end of cooking as possible.

Among many characteristic seasonings, the following two, salt and olive, rank very high.

SALT

The saltless man and his saltless wife
Had two children; they, too, have a saltless life.

Earliest records of Greek food history include the use of salt in cookery and as a preservative; salt was also a symbol of hospitality. The ancient chef Machon, using an analogy between cookery and music, speaks of salt as an essential for reaching a "harmony of flavor." He compares its use to the careful tuning of a lyre.

The ancient product salted fish paste, *garon*, is not used in modern Greece, although anchovies, fish roe, and salted cod are frequent ingredients in sauces and mixtures. *Garon* (which was probably the forerunner of *garum*, used in Apicius' recipes), was made of red mullet, anchovy, and sprats—salted and dried.

Modern Greek cooks are particularly cautious about the use of salt in dishes made of cheese, olives, fish, and meats because the amount of salt is a variable that depends on the saltiness of the ingredients themselves. Judicious seasoning with salt supports the cook: salt brings out the flavor of food and can help mitigate excessive sweetness. But salt can also overwhelm and demolish the spirit of a dish.

That Greeks are aware of the function and significance of salt is apparent in their language and their proverbs. The word *analatos* (unsalty), when applied to a human being, is the worst possible insult. (See the couplet above describing the *analatos* who married an *analati*, with devastating consequences to the children.) When hearing bland or listless talk, a Hellene may comment, "His conversation lacks salt." On the other hand *lissa* (very, very salty) is used to describe anything overly salty or excessive.

In the recipes that follow, except in those for doughs and batters, the amount of salt has been left to the cook's discretion. For soups and stocks, begin with ½ teaspoon per quart; for sauces, ¼ teaspoon per 2 cups. Tasting toward the end of cooking, after the various flavors have been absorbed and the liquid reduced substantially, will tell you if you need more salt.

There should be balance and harmony! Remember the Greek saying, "The entire ocean is *almyro*, but here and there *lissa!*"

THE OLIVE

Do you, master, love the ladies who are over-ripe or the virginal ones with bodies firm as olives steeped in brine?
ARISTOPHANES (446–385 B.C.)

Olives and olive oil are among the most important cash crops and food staples in Greece. Both are identified with Athena and her first olive tree, and with Aristaios, son of Apollo, who taught men to crush olives. Their cultivation, as well as their importance as an economic factor in Greek life, dates back to 3500 B.C., when Minoans traded oil for dyes and textiles with the Phoenicians. Despite the decline of olive tree culture during the Ottoman domination, Greece today ranks third in the world's output of olive products, exceeded only by Spain and Italy.

Olive trees thrive in dry, calcareous soil; once established, they bear olives for centuries. In recent years a million new seedlings have been planted annually, augmenting the hundred million olive trees already established in Greece. The finest Greek olives are produced in Peloponnesos (Kalamata) and in central Greece (Amphissa). Crete, Corfu,

Lesvos, and Volos rank slightly lower in quantity. Among other olive-producing areas are Sparta, Halkidiki, five areas of central Greece, Macedonia, Epirus, and Thrace.

Olives vary considerably in size, enough, in fact, to be classified in twelve standard sizes. They are packed in natural solutions of brine, or brine and vinegar. Greece produces about 47,000 tons of table olives annually, which are available in the United States in jars or in bulk in Greek, Jewish, Middle Eastern and Italian specialty stores. When purchased in bulk, store in glass jars and marinate with equal parts olive oil and red wine vinegar (or less vinegar if you do not like a sour taste). Also, use a Greek olive to test the amount of salt needed in brine to store feta cheese. The olive should float!

World production of olive oil is about 1,250,000 tons annually, and 75 to 80 percent of this total is consumed in the Mediterranean areas where it is produced. Of the 170,000 tons of olive oil produced annually in Greece, 150,000 to 155,000 tons are consumed by Hellenes. Greek per capita consumption of olive oil is even higher than that of Spain and Italy (17.0 kilos per year for Greeks, as compared to 9.5 kilos for Spaniards and 9.0 kilos for Italians). Luckily, Greece produces enough to meet the needs of her people, with some remaining to spread joy as exports.

Mechanical extraction of oil from the olive provides a flavorful, "pure" product, as Greek advertisements constantly stress. In addition, excellent olive-oil margarines are steadily increasing in use. No part of the olive is wasted, not even the pits, which are crushed to make *sporelaion* (seed oil); other by-products include soap and fertilizer. And the trees' branches and trunks are used for buildings, furniture, and fuel. (A Greek villager told me that an olive tree branch had sprouted long after his home had been built. Such stories add to the lore about the miraculous powers of the olive.)

The incomparable beauty of the olive tree, with its twisted, gnarled, grayish bark and its silvery-green leaves, may have been a factor that contributed to its traditional cultural value. Family trees, owned for generations, supply the family's olives and olive oil. The work of picking olives is difficult and tiring, yet indispensable. (My cousin in Tseria, Laconia, wrote me in December that the entire family had been picking olives for a month; all were exhausted but they had not yet finished.) Some of the remote villages have the basic equipment for making oil, but often it is done in a larger town nearby, the local "oil center." Relatives in Athens and other cities obtain oil from their families in the rural areas and villages, and those visiting from abroad receive oil—the supreme gift to carry back across the seas.

In the Greek home, the *ladi* (which is the word simply for "oil," but which means "olive oil") is undoubtedly the most important possession. It is stored in containers of various sizes—cruet, bottle, or *roï* (funnel-cruet)—according to its quality and intended use. Some qualities of oil are used for fuel; the finest is saved for cookery and salads. In Greek cookery oil dribbles into just about everything except syrups and spoon sweéts. In the villages the older generation often uses oil for pastries and cakes, whereas butter is used in the city.

In Greece high consumption of olive oil has a direct relationship to good health and well-being. Studies show that where olive oil consumption is high, particularly on Corfu and Crete, there is a low incidence of circulatory diseases, including heart disease, among all age groups. Olive oil is recommended for its unsaturated fatty acids and for its laxative properties. It is also prescribed for duodenal ulcers and liver ailments. The practice of prescribing olive oil for elimination of gallstones has declined, but the olive tree's bark and leaves are used in the treatment of high blood pressure. In fact, throughout Greek history, olive oil has been used for wounds, burns, earaches—it seems to be a cure for everything but a broken heart!

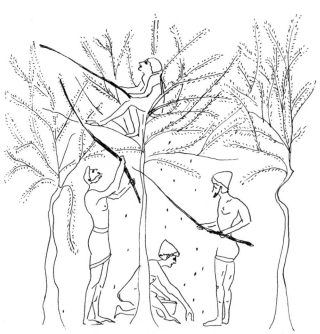

A Word About Basics

Not a single person has ever escaped scot-free after he wronged a cook. Our profession is somehow sacrosanct.

MENANDER

These are words from a play of Menander, poet of the New Comedy (343–291 B.C.), one of the many writers who reflected an admiration for the skills, achievements, and "inquiring minds" of Greek chefs. Earlier, Cadmus, the legendary Phoenician prince who founded Thebes and Boeotia, and introduced alphabetic signs to Greece, was also a cook! Athens, Rhodes, Sicily, Andros, and Chios produced the greatest chefs of antiquity. Reading about them in the *Deipnosophists* is an illuminating experience. I especially enjoyed learning an ingenious trick attributed to an unknown cook described by Alexis. It seems the cook scorched the pork he was stewing. Rather than admit defeat and toss it out, he placed the warm cooking pot (obviously earthenware) in a shallow pan full of cold vinegar. The heat from the upper pan absorbed moisture through the pan's pores, so that the meat did not dry up, but was "nice and savory." And he served the meat cold!

With such originality, it is not surprising that the ancient Greek word for cook—*mageiros*—has remained in the language. In addition, just about every related contemporary Greek word stems from the *mageira*: *mageireion* (kitchen), *mageiriki* or *mageirevma* (cooking or cuisine), *mageirikos* (culinary), *mageiriko* (lunch room). Is it mere coincidence that a similar-sounding word—*magia*—means sorcery, magic, witchcraft, spell, charm, and fascination?

Modern Greek cooks show their inventiveness in many ways, particularly thrift and versatility in their use of available ingredients whether in their natural form or as by-products of cooking, such as stocks and sauces. The charm of the cuisine, therefore, is in finding the basic preparations among the staple dishes, and then, using Greek resourcefulness and imagination, adapting them to other dishes. For example, chicken broth prepared as Kota kai Zomos (page 168) can be used to make soup or frozen as a stock for sauces, rice dishes, or savory pies. In a similar way, for a nice fish fumet, try the Greek method of making fish soup or poached fish dishes without using potatoes which will add starch to the stock.

Should you need an excellent marinade, you will find quite a few among the recipes, including one for vegetables in Selino Marinato (page 73), for meat and poultry in Kotopoulo Tiganito Marinato (page 174), for fish in Psari Marinato (page 118).

As for butters, their use is quite diverse, and therefore more difficult to isolate, which might explain why identification of the Greek cuisine with oil alone is common. But this is far from the truth. Butter is made by the shepherds, who care for the sheep and also make the cheeses. In addition, the Hellenes have developed a magnificent olive-oil margarine that tastes like *fresko voutiro* (fresh butter). In Greek recipes, for a taste more comparable to the delicious country butters, use sweet butter. For an ambrosial breakfast treat, mix sweet butter with honey to spread on homemade bread, as it is served in the *galaktopoleion* in Greece; for a tasty *makaronada* with little preparation, heat sweet butter very slowly in a heavy pan to light chestnut color and pour over hot, drained macaroni, spaghetti, or noodles, and top with freshly-grated mizithra cheese. Clarify butter in advance, particularly when using it for *filo* pastries and confectionery; over low heat or hot water, in a heavy saucepan, melt butter until a foam rises to the surface; skim off and discard or set aside this foam, then pour off the clear butter into a storage container and store in the refrigerator until ready to use. (The residue may be used for soups, etc.)

DOUGHS

Doughs are so important in Greece I would need an entire chapter to include all the variations I have tasted. Making doughs at home for *pites* (pies) is more the rule than exception. Although I was more timid about attempting them than any other culinary challenge, I found that with a new *plasti* (38-inch dowel with 1-inch diameter) added to our kitchen equipment, plus inspiration, it was not difficult to make a good *filo*. You must try one, for these skills will never die away if youngsters see the adults practicing them. For savory pies, try Zymi yia Filo (included below) and Filo Spitiko and Grigoro Filo Sfoliatas which follow. After these attempts for your delicious *pites*, you will be substituting different liquids and fats, just like the Hellenes!

At first, you might be happier beginning with commercial *filo*; you will certainly enjoy the many creations possible with this type—which requires more courage than expertise. The *filo* seems fragile, but is, in fact, delightfully versatile and strong *if* you keep it from drying. Suggestions for ready-made *filo* follow the homemade recipes.

Raw *kadaifi*, finely-cut dough which resembles endless strands of coconut, is not used as widely. Raw *kadaifi* pastry is named after the dessert for which it was named (page 334) and is used only for dessert. It is easier to work with than *filo* because it will not dry as quickly. You can buy the raw *kadaifi* pastry in Greek and Middle Eastern specialty stores which also stock commercial *filo*.

ZYMI YIA FILO
[*Homemade filo dough*]

Dependable and easy recipe, the dough should be mixed at least several hours before being rolled. Actual rolling takes 20 to 30 minutes, but is worth the time and effort.

TO MAKE 2 SHEETS FOR A 12 X 15-INCH PAN IF ROLLED AND STRETCHED AS THIN AS A DIME
TO MAKE 2 SHEETS FOR A 9 X 12-INCH PAN IF ROLLED TO THE THICKNESS OF 2 DIMES
TO MAKE 25 TO 30 4-INCH SQUARES OR CIRCLES FOR "PITAKIA"

> *3 cups all-purpose flour*
> *1 teaspoon salt*
> *1 teaspoon baking powder*
> *3 tablespoons softened butter or margarine*
> *5 tablespoons olive or other vegetable oil*
> *3/4 cup warm water, approximately*
> *2 tablespoons melted butter*

In a mixing bowl, sift the flour with the salt and baking powder. Using your fingers, a fork, or a pastry blender, work the butter and oil into the flour mixture until homogeneous. Gradually add only enough of the warm water to form a ball. Wrap in plastic or waxed paper and refrigerate for several hours. When ready to roll out, remove the dough from the refrigerator and divide into 11 equal balls, 6 for the bottom of the pan and 5 for the top if planning to make a large *pita*. (If using for individual pies or *pitakia*, divide into 10 balls and roll 5 at a time.)

Dust a marble or wood surface with flour. With the palms of your hands, press out the first group of balls you are going to roll into flattened circles, spread with melted butter and stack them. Using a broom handle or rolling pin begin rolling into one sheet, using the rolling technique as described on page 326, stretching as well as rolling. Repeat with remaining balls. Use immediately.

Note: When rolling smaller shapes, dust between each with cornstarch to prevent sticking and keep covered until stuffed.

FILO SPITIKO
[*Homemade filo dough with vinegar*]

Greek cooks imaginatively use soda water, beer, lemon juice, or vinegar among the liquids for homemade *filo*. Yet I have also seen successful paper-thin *filo* made of flour and water rolled on marble that has been spread generously with olive oil. Professional dough makers flip and slap the dough. Try it! Or use the following ingredients for a fine dough:

TO MAKE TOP AND BOTTOM PASTRY FOR A 10-INCH PIE

> *4 cups all-purpose flour*
> *1 teaspoon salt*
> *1 tablespoon vinegar*
> *1 cup water*
> *¼ cup olive oil*
> *Cornstarch (optional)*

In a large bowl, sift the flour with the salt. Make a well in the center, pour in the vinegar and water, and work until smooth. Add the oil, a tablespoon at a time. Knead until shiny and elastic. Cover and refrigerate. Roll out, using cornstarch or flour on the board. (See page 326.)

GRIGORO FILO SFOLIATAS
[*Quick filo pastry*]

A fine, professional cook referred to this as *sfoliatas* when she shared it with me. The name is from the Italian *sfogliata* (leaflike) or puff pastry but the similarity ends there. In adapting this, I used a fine olive oil, but a mixture of olive and another vegetable oil would work as well. She suggested working in the butter bits for increased flakiness as puff pastry is made, but it is excellent without butter. Use for savory pie or small *pitakia*; it is richer crust than plain *filo*.

TO MAKE TOP AND BOTTOM PASTRY FOR A 10-INCH PIE

> *½ cup cold milk*
> *½ cup light olive oil*
> *2¼ to 2½ cups all-purpose flour*
> *1½ teaspoons baking powder*
> *¼ teaspoon salt*
> *1 tablespoon cold butter cut into bits (optional)*

In a large bowl, combine the milk and oil. Mix the dry ingredients and add gradually to the milk and oil, mixing and kneading until the dough is soft. Cover and refrigerate at least 1 hour, then divide into 2 sections. Roll out the dough as fine as possible, working in the butter bits as you roll, if desired. The dough will be resilient. Use immediately as directed in your recipe.

FILO
[Commercial filo sheets]

Filo means "leaf," which describes the texture and fineness of fresh commercial *filo*. In Greece this type is usually referred to as *filo baklava* to differentiate it from homemade *filo*—*spitiko filo*—because *everyone* buys *filo* for *baklava*. In any country, *filo* pastry products, when well prepared of fresh *filo*, can be superlative. Each sheet of leaflike pastry, when lightly brushed with melted butter or oil, bakes to a flaky perfection. When unwrapped, fresh *filo* has a delicious fresh smell. If it has a sour odor, it is not fresh and should be returned. To ensure excellent results, first buy good, fresh *filo*, and second, work confidently when assembling. The storage, freezing, and baking, even the reheating, are relatively simple.

Most *filo* is available commercially by the pound package, rolled and frozen, and packed in airtight plastic bags. Before purchasing, open the carton and look at the edges. A good *filo* will have smooth edges, like a fabric. If crumbly, do not buy.

Most commercial *filo* packages contain 20 to 25 rectangular sheets about 11¼ x 15¼ inches. Makers of commercial *filo* may vary the sizes. After first using *filo*, the cook quickly learns how to measure and use it economically. It may be cut quickly with a sharp knife, and small pieces used for small *pites* or tucked between larger sheets. There need be none wasted. Only dry *filo* must be discarded.

Keep in the freezer, then move to the refrigerator for one day, or overnight, before using. Unroll on a board 15 to 20 minutes before using and cover with plastic wrap or waxed paper and a dampened towel. Keep covered, except to remove one sheet at a time. (This is not as difficult as it sounds, and well worth the effort to prevent drying.)

Lift a corner of the towel and count the sheets, checking the number against the amount needed in the recipe, and also measure the pan you are planning to use. If making small *pites* or Trigona (pages 65, 333), Bourekia (page 67), and so on, *filo* may be cut into thirds (across the width) and the *filo* stacked and covered. To make tiny *pites*, cut the *filo* in quarters (across the width). If using a small pan, cut the *filo* to fit the pan size, making sure the bottom and top sheets (according to the recipe) are large enough to allow for covering the sides of the pan and tucking together. When making Baklava (page 337), all Thracian *pites*, and others that need many layers, roll up, wrap and refrigerate top sheets to save them for the end. Now you will not run out of *filo* for the upper crust!

Have fillings ready, butter melted (and warm!), and all equipment at hand, including a good pastry brush and a very sharp knife. Work quickly. Keep the *filo* covered, and cover finished pastries when making small ones, until all have been formed. *Always* brush each sheet with butter or oil (or a mixture if you prefer), using a pastry brush lightly, or—as some Greek pastry makers do—dribble it evenly. Either way, the buttering or oiling is the necessary ingredient for flaky pastry. A very good trick when making any kind of *pita* or sheet-type pie, whether sweet or savory—but especially *baklava*—is to turn the pan around during the process for even distribution of both fat and filling ingredients.

Before baking all sheet pastry, *pites*, pies, and *baklava* they *must* be either cut or scored into the desired sizes and shape, a step not to be forgotten. Check the recipe.

Baklava must be cut from the top layers all the way down to the bottom into the desired size and diamond shapes. First decide on size desired, for instance, 7 lengthwise slashes will give you daintier-size *baklava* than 6 lengthwise slashes. After deciding the size, hold the pan

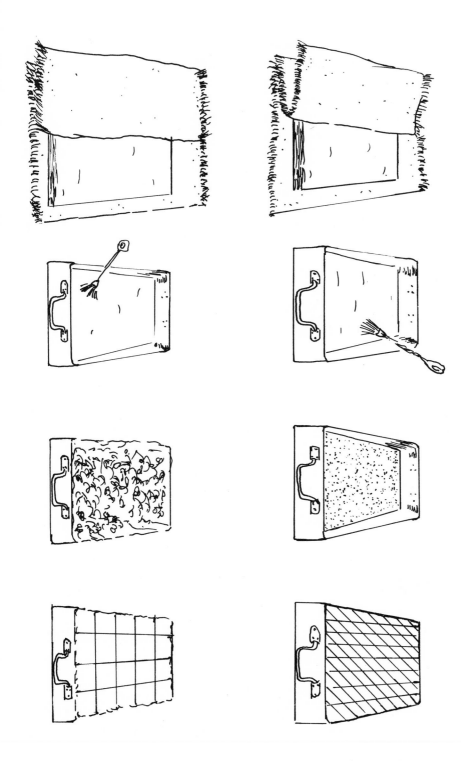

lengthwise and using a very sharp, long knife, begin cutting on the left side of the end farthest from you. Cut straight down until the tip touches the bottom of the pan and, keeping the knife straight, continue cutting in a straight line until the knife reaches the end of pan nearest you. (Left-handers will probably want to cut right to left.) Cut each consecutive slash the same size all the way down using the free hand to gently hold the *filo* behind the knife. When all the lengthwise cuts have been completed, begin at the upper left and cut diagonally across the lengthwise cuts. This is easy to do if you use the pan's corner as a visual guide. Again, you must be careful with the size of the first diagonal slash to determine size. Continue until you reach the opposite end.

Other pastries and *pites* which require scoring on the recipe are *not* cut all the way down to the bottom of the pan. Just use a sharp knife and cut the top few *filo* sheets, planning in advance the size and shape (diamond, square or rectangle) you wish. You will enjoy the flexibility of planning the sizes according to your needs for that particular day. Bake according to recipe, using the extra butter or oil to brush the top sheet.

SAUCES

If food were sacred in Greece (and it is), then sauces would be divine (and they are). From the moment the food begins to secrete its precious fluid while cooking, the *saltsa* is watched avidly. Is it thick, is it too thin, does it need more wine, more tomato, a touch of parsley, thyme, a speck of pepper? When the roast is tender and succulent, every drop of the remaining liquid is scraped from the pan, and the pan rinsed with water. This sauce is strained and used to serve with either the meat or an accompanying dish. When vegetables are simmered in oil and herbs, the consistency of the sauce tells the cook when the vegetables are ready. And when the dish is set before the Hellene, the sparkle in his eyes is the cook's reward for his painstaking care.

Several food writers of the Hellenistic period held the meat and fish sauces in higher esteem than the meat and fish. Among those described were sauces for roasted vegetable bulbs; honey-cheese sauce; pickled fish sauces; white sauce on fecund miscarried matrix (womb of an animal that had miscarried her calf); sauces of vinegar, cumin, and silphium; sauces of oxymel (honey-vinegar); sauces of vinegar-oil, beaten as a mayonnaise. Numerous marinades and dressings were dribbled on their dishes; white must and vinegar and vinegar-oil have been staples for centuries, with raisins, herbs, onions, garlic, spices, cheese, fish paste, eggs, and flour important ingredients. Honey blended with sauces of all kinds. Saffron and silphium were favored spices that have since disappeared from the cuisine. Tomatoes and yogurt are "new" acid ingredients; cornstarch is now popular as a thickener, much preferred to flour or arrowroot.

The naming of their sauces shows the influence of the French haute cuisine: "Béchamel sauce" is known throughout Greece as *saltsa Besamel*, and compound sauces and butters, dressings, and creams appear in Greek periodicals transliterated from French to Greek. But should observers doubt the authenticity of Greek sauces and dressings because of their names, I urge them to examine the methods and skills developed from the fifth to third centuries B.C. There they will find precursors of today's Western sauces and dressings. Consider the sauce in the "rose-dish" casserole described by Athenaeus, in which egg yolk is used as the thickener, olive oil as the fat, wine is the important acid, and aromatics are rose leaves, fish paste (for salt), and pepper. Are there any compound sauces in any cuisine more subtle and yet more imaginative?

> I crushed the most fragrant roses in a mortar, then laid on carefully boiled brains of fowls and pigs, from which the stringy fibres had been removed, also the yolks of eggs; then olive oil, garum-sauce (fish paste), pepper and wine. All this I stirred thoroughly and placed in a new casserole, giving it a fire that was gentle and steady.

When the cook uncovered the casserole the fragrance pleasantly overwhelmed the guests. One remarked that if uncovered in Zeus' mansion, the fragrance would have carried down to earth! And if any of us could find fragrant, unsprayed roses (which we could also use to make luscious rose-petal jam, Greek style), we could follow the ancient recipe and make another divine rose sauce.

By mastering some of these basic preparations, including sauces, the philhellene will be well on the way to becoming an accomplished Greek cook, utilizing classic methods and ingredients in an inventive way, with delicious results. "Let it rain oil and snow pepper," as the Greeks say—you will know what to do with them.

AVGOLEMONO
[*Egg-lemon sauce*]

Avgolemono is the most famous Greek sauce, named for its indispensable ingredients, *avgo* (egg) and *lemoni* (lemon). Light in color and of the prized lemony flavor, it is prepared with or without a roux base. But egg, lemon juice, and hot stock or broth from the dish for which it is being prepared are necessities. The sauce is then always added to the soup or dish, not served separately.

In Greek homes women usually make *avgolemono* with the egg whites included, while professional chefs more frequently omit the whites and thicken with cornstarch. Wonder and awe always recur as I prepare it; one of my earliest memories of cookery was adding hot broth in droplets while Mother warned, "Slowly, or the *avgolemono* will spoil." Subsequent food chemistry studies explained to me the process of egg coagulation and curdling, but never decreased the mystery of *avgolemono*.

Some Greek villagers, when adding the *avgolemono* to soup or dish, make a kissing sound, a magical trick to keep the egg from curdling. Nevertheless, Greeks in general don't trust too much to fate, and are very careful to keep the temperature below 160 degrees. Observing this rule, you will master *avgolemono*, a delicious addition to many soups and other specialties.

TO MAKE I TO 2 CUPS

2 eggs or egg yolks
Juice of 1 to 2 lemons, strained
1 to 2 cups hot stock or liquid from the dish for which the avgolemono *is being prepared*

Beat the eggs for 2 minutes. Continuing to beat, gradually add the lemon juice. Then add the hot liquid by droplets, beating steadily, until all has been added. Using a wooden spoon, stir the *avgolemono* into the dish for which it has been prepared while it is hot (not boiling). Keep the dish warm over hot water or minimum heat, stirring until the sauce thickens enough to coat a spoon.

Note: You can try another version usually made at home: Separate the eggs and beat the whites until stiff. Add yolks to the beaten whites and continue as directed above.

48

Or professional chefs' version: Prepare a roux by melting 3 table-spoons butter in a medium-sized saucepan. Stir in 2 tablespoons all-purpose flour, and after cooking over low heat for 1 minute, gradually add 2 cups hot stock. Stir until the sauce comes to a boil. Meanwhile, in a small bowl, beat 2 egg yolks and continue as directed above, adding the lemon juice and then the thickened sauce rather than the broth.

SKORDALIA

Skordalia is a sauce that provokes excitement at the mere sound of its name—from its most important ingredient, *skordo* (garlic). The sensation aroused in the mouth by *skordalia* is an indescribable mellow bite that travels from the tongue into the olfactory passages, a message that sharpens in proportion to the amount of garlic used.

Pounding garlic in a *goudi* (mortar) and smelling the pungent scents of garlic and vinegar awakens the appetite. The sauce may also be made in a blender or with an electric mixer, but the Greek way is more fun. The important skill in making *skordalia* is knowing how much oil and vinegar the garlic can absorb as it is being pounded and beaten. Though it's easy to prepare, all the senses must work together to make a sensational *skordalia*. And when everyone settles around the table to enjoy it, the *skordalia* runs through the party like an electric current. It is excellent with fish, rabbit, beets, zucchini, and eggplant.

TO MAKE 3 CUPS

> *6 cloves to 1 head garlic, peeled*
> *2 cups mashed potatoes (approximately 4 medium potatoes)*
> *4 or more large slices French- or Italian-type bread, crusts removed,*
>   *soaked in water, and squeezed dry*
> *1/2 to 3/4 cup olive oil*
> *1/3 to 1/2 cup white vinegar*
> *Pinch of salt*

Pound the garlic cloves in a large wooden mortar with a pestle until thoroughly mashed. Continue pounding while adding the potatoes and bread very gradually, beating until the mixture resembles a paste. Slowly add the oil, alternately with the vinegar, beating thoroughly after each addition until well absorbed. (The beating may now be transferred to a blender or electric mixer, or continued by hand. Use low speed when adding the small amounts of oil and vinegar, and increase to high speed after they have been added.) Add salt, taste for seasoning, and beat until the sauce is very thick and smooth, adding more vinegar or soaked, squeezed bread if necessary. Push the *skordalia* through a sieve if lumps have formed, then scoop into a glass or porcelain serving bowl. Cover and refrigerate until ready to serve; *skordalia* must be used within a week.

Note: Skordalia may also be made using all potatoes, all soaked bread, or cooked, drained chick-peas as the important starchy ingredient. Or the sauce may be varied by adding and mashing ½ cup chopped almonds, walnuts, or pine nuts after mashing the garlic.

SALTSA ASPRI
[*White sauce*]

Saltsa aspri, or white sauce, is important in Greek cooking, particularly as a climaxing layer for the casseroles *pastitsio* and *moussaka*. Thickness varies with cooks and dishes. Although the proportion of liquid increases to make a thinner sauce, the proportion of flour to fat remains the same, and so does the method of preparing. Use this table as a guide, to make one cup.

Sauce	Butter or margarine	Flour	Milk (warm)
Thin	1 tablespoon	1 tablespoon	1 cup
Medium	2 tablespoons	2 tablespoons	1 cup
Thick	3 tablespoons	3 tablespoons	1 cup

To make the sauce, in a heavy saucepan melt the fat and heat *without* browning. Using a wire whisk, stir in the flour. Cook for 1 to 2 minutes over low heat, then remove from the burner and gradually stir in the warm milk. Move the pan back to the heat and bring to a boil, stirring steadily for a smooth sauce. Add a pinch of salt and white pepper, and grate a little nutmeg over the sauce for a nice flavor.

As a general rule, thin white sauce is used for soups and sauces, medium for *pastitsio* and *moussaka* and other au gratin dishes, and a thick sauce for croquettes and soufflés.

Note: Using the above plan, by substituting broth or stock for the milk, you can make chicken, fish, and vegetable sauces. You will probably want to use a little fresh herb, chives, or diced scallions instead of the nutmeg.

SALTSA DOMATA ME LADI
[Tomato sauce with oil]

TO MAKE 3 CUPS OF SAUCE

2 tablespoons olive oil
1 small onion, chopped
1 to 2 cloves garlic, minced
2 pounds fresh tomatoes, peeled
   and chopped or 1 two-and-one-
   half-pound can plum tomatoes,
   chopped
1 teaspoon granulated sugar

¼ cup red wine
Salt and freshly ground pepper
1 small stick cinnamon
   (optional)
1 to 2 sprigs fresh parsley,
   chopped
1 sprig fresh basil, chopped or
   ½ teaspoon dried basil

Heat the oil in a heavy saucepan, stir in the onions, and cook gently until transparent. Add the garlic, tomatoes, sugar, wine, salt and pepper, and cinnamon, if desired. Taste for seasoning, then allow the sauce to simmer gently for 30 minutes. Add the parsley and basil and simmer for another 10 minutes. Remove the cinnamon stick before serving and serve hot.

    Note: For a thicker sauce, add ¼ cup tomato paste diluted with ¼ cup water when adding the tomatoes. For a smoother consistency, the sauce may be strained and seeds discarded just before the parsley and basil are added.

SALTSA DOMATA ME VOUTYRO
[Tomato sauce with butter]

To make 3 cups, use 3 to 4 tablespoons butter instead of the oil in Saltsa Domata me Ladi (above), and add 1 tablespoon each of chopped carrot, celery, and parsley along with the onion. With the seasonings, instead of the cinnamon stick add 1 bay leaf, ½ teaspoon dried thyme, and 2 beef bouillon cubes or 2 to 3 tablespoons meat drippings (without fat). If necessary, after simmering, dissolve 2 teaspoons cornstarch in 2 tablespoons cold water and add to the sauce. Simmer until thick.

SALTSA DOMATA KRASATI
[*Tomato sauce with wine*]

To make 3 cups, make Saltsa Domata me Ladi using oil or butter, and add 1 cup dry white or red wine when adding the tomatoes. During the last 15 minutes of cooking, if desired, add 2 sprigs fresh marjoram or savory instead of the basil.

SALTSA KIMA
[*Ground meat and tomato sauce*]

Saltsa kima is served over pasta or grains and used as a meat layer for baked casseroles such as Moussaka (page 233) and Pastitsio (page 98) and as a filling for many vegetables, poultry, and meats.

Flavor improves the second day, and will thicken considerably, a great help in composite dishes such as those just mentioned which need several processes before combining. Also—all the fat which collects on top after refrigerating overnight may be easily discarded.

TO MAKE 4 CUPS (ENOUGH TO SERVE 4)

1 onion, chopped fine
2 to 3 tablespoons butter, margarine or olive oil
1 pound lean lamb, beef, or veal, ground
1 clove garlic, chopped
½ cup dry red wine
1 one-pound can peeled tomatoes, chopped and drained

2 tablespoons tomato paste
½ teaspoon granulated sugar
1 stick cinnamon
1 bay leaf
Salt and freshly ground pepper
3 to 4 tablespoons chopped fresh parsley
1 sprig fresh basil or ½ teaspoon dried basil

In heavy saucepan cook the onion in a little water over medium heat until softened, then add the fat and cook the onion until translucent. Combine the ground meat with the onion, mashing with a fork and stirring until the raw color disappears. Add garlic and wine, then cover and simmer for 5 minutes. Stir in the tomatoes, the tomato paste, sugar, cinnamon stick, bay leaf, salt and pepper to taste, then simmer, covered, for 30 minutes longer. Add the parsley and basil during the last 10 to 15 minutes. Cook uncovered for the last few minutes, to allow excess liquid to evaporate; the sauce should be thick. Remove the cinnamon stick before serving.

SALTSA YAOURTI
[*Yogurt sauce*]

Saltsa yaourti may be poured hot over sautéed or fried chicken and small birds, or may be prepared as a sauce in which to simmer chicken parts or birds.

TO COOK A 2½-POUND CHICKEN

> ¼ *cup* (*4 tablespoons*) *butter or margarine*
> *1 small onion, minced*
> ¼ *cup all-purpose flour*
> *2 cups milk, warmed*
> *Salt and white pepper*
> ½ *teaspoon grated nutmeg*
> *1½ cups plain yogurt*

In a heavy saucepan, heat the butter, toss in the minced onion, and sauté over medium heat until soft. Add the flour and cook without browning, for a few minutes, then remove from the heat and add the milk gradually, while stirring with a whisk. Return to the heat and cook until the sauce has boiled for 1 minute, stirring constantly. Strain the sauce and pour back into the saucepan. Season with salt and pepper and the nutmeg, then stir in the yogurt and simmer for a few minutes.

DRESSINGS

LADOXIDO
[*Vinegar-oil dressing*]

Without oil, without vinegar, how can we take a trip?
GREEK PROVERB

The ancient recipes made over and over again, I have learned, are the most difficult to write out. *Ladoxido* is a classic example. To describe the typical Greek method: first, the olive oil cruet is held over the dish to be seasoned, tilted, and in a gentle, rotary motion allowed to pour in a slow stream over the food. The hand's movement begins on the outer perimeter and steadily turns and turns to stop in the center. This same circular movement is repeated with the vinegar cruet (red wine vinegar), but the movement is quicker than with the oil. Who can guess the amounts used?

If less than brave, combine 2 parts oil to 1 part vinegar in a bowl, mix with a fork and pour over the salad. Season lightly with salt. If the results are too sour, add a pinch of sugar to mitigate the vinegar and decrease the proportion of vinegar the next time! A Hellene will crumble a little oregano into the salad before tossing, and will certainly taste it before serving.

LADOLEMONO
[Lemon-oil dressing]

For poached, grilled or fried fish and shellfish, raw and cooked vegetables and salads.

Choosing finest quality olive oil, measure 2 parts oil to each part lemon juice. (For example, you will need 4 tablespoons oil to 2 tablespoons lemon juice.) Whisk together in bowl with a pinch of salt and a few grindings of black pepper. Add a small amount of chopped parsley, basil, oregano, thyme, or fennel and pour over the dish (the herb is not a must, but very flavorful on fish particularly). Serve immediately.

Note: Make enough *ladolemono* for one meal at a time. Lemon juice may be increased, a personal decision.

MAYONEZA
[Mayonnaise]

This dressing traveled from France to Greece where, as it was made at home by the ladies, it received a feminized name—*mayoneza*. It is ideal for lobsters, salads, and so forth. Fine flavor depends on perfect proportions of light olive oil and lemon juice.

TO MAKE 1½ CUPS

> *2 egg yolks, at room temperature*
> *¼ cup plus 1 teaspoon strained lemon juice*
> *¾ cup olive oil*

54

Put the egg yolks into mixing bowl and whisk by hand or electric mixer until thick enough to coat the beater. Gradually add the 1 teaspoon lemon juice beating constantly for 1 minute. Then begin to add the olive oil in droplets, increasing by teaspoonfuls as the sauce thickens. Gradually add remaining lemon juice and oil alternating and beating steadily. Taste for flavor.

Kali orexi!   *Eis hygeian!*
(Good appetite!)   (To your health!)

APPETIZERS

I like to see you eat, but not overeat.   GREEK PROVERB

THE WORD *orektika,* FROM *orexis,* means to desire, to long, to yearn for something—which aptly describes the Greek feeling for these varied, delicious samplings. Glancing through a Greek menu under *orektika* quickly confirms the Greek preference for miniature servings of their favorite foods! And this "sampling" may take the place of a more conventional meal, and go on for hours. The ancient habit of eating before and during the drinking of wine is a well-established one.

The author Alexis depicts one appetizer shaped like the "hemisphere of Heaven's vault. For all the beauties of the constellations were on it—fish, kids, the scorpion, the slices of egg represented the stars." In *The Republic,* Plato describes a meal of radishes, olives, cheese, cooked bulbs, green vegetables, figs, chick-peas, beans, myrtle berries, and acorns toasted before the fire—all while sipping wine, in moderation. In the 20th century that fare might be served at a typical Greek gathering (minus the myrtle berries and acorns). Adults today often dilute their wine or ouzo and children over twelve may be offered water-diluted wine with their foods.

Olives, cheeses, a fresh salad of tomatoes, cucumbers, and scallions, a whipped salad of eggplant or fish roe, and crusty bread with wine begin an exciting taste adventure—whether called *orektika* or by the Turkish word for tidbit, *meza* or *mezedaki.*

Bourekakia and *pitakia* of all kinds are delicious, and more likely to be served in homes than in restaurants because they need to be made fresh and served piping hot. Usually they are stuffed with cheese, meat, poultry, or fish mixtures, and wrapped in homemade or commercial *filo* in all imaginable shapes. (See sketches.) On the mainland or the islands,

56

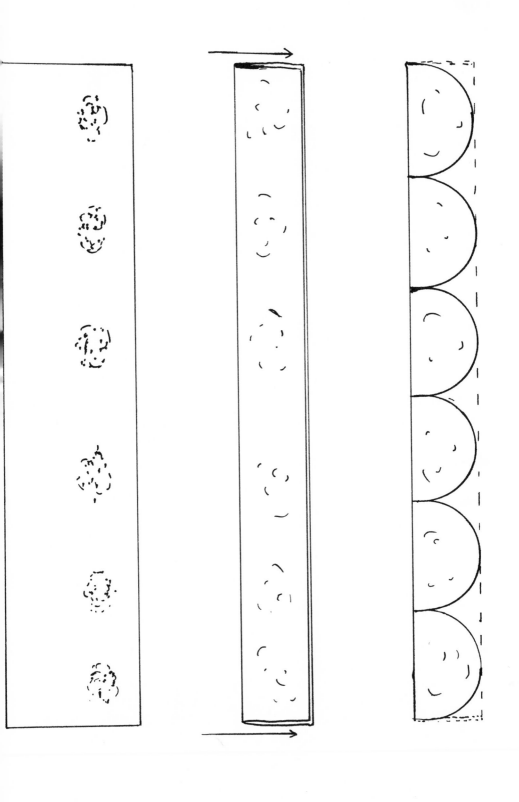

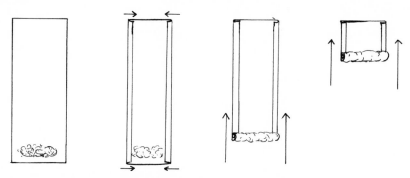

they are usually baked, sometimes fried, and always served hot. The creative cook may use these treasures to advantage.

Pickled, smoked, marinated, steamed, and fried fish and shellfish are very popular on both islands and the mainland, their seasonings varying regionally. Lamb is the traditional favorite, and may, during the lamb season, be served in the form of special dishes like broiled and fried lamb entrails. Veal, however, is not an unpopular meat, and among the specialties prized from the *mosharaki* (young calf) are the *ameletita* (testicles). Brains and *sikotaria* (liver) of veal or lamb are probably the universally favorite specialties.

Dolmadakia (small versions of the stuffed grapevine leaves), *keftedakia* (tiny spiced meat balls), as well as *kokoretsi* (barbecued lamb entrails) and *loukanika* (homemade sausages), reflect much effort in preparation. Eggs always represent high esteem because of their costliness and limited supply; they are usually stuffed, especially for the visitor.

Cheeses make their appearance undisguised, as well as fried or broiled, in salads or in *tyropites* (savory cheese pies). *Tzatziki* (page 74) is a popular appetizer. *Pikti* (jellied pork) (page 162), is served frequently in some regions as an appetizer, as is salami (invented on the island of Salamis), ham, and the "international" canapés, puffs, and croquettes gaining status with increased tourism.

In the recipes that follow I have included *orektika* sampled in various regions. For example, after the theater in a Plaka *taverna* we had *taramosalata*, pickled octopus, sardines, olives, *melitzanosalata, dolmades,* feta cheese, cucumber salad, fresh bread, and wine. On Corfu the *poikilia* (variety) included *kossiki salata, taramosalata*, sardines, salami, *dolmadakia,* and other essentials. On Crete, along with these familiar universals, *pikti* and *avga a la Rous* (eggs à la Russe) were included.

Appetizers become satisfactions to the appetite, or as the Greeks say, "*Trogontas erhete i orexi*—with eating comes the appetite!"

TARAMOSALATA
[*Fish roe salad*]

Greeks love to pass the time nibbling *orektika* and sipping ouzo or wine; they also enjoy all edible parts of fish and meat. These two seemingly disparate elements of the Greek life style blend incomparably in *taramosalata,* a fluffy, creamy, fish-roe dip Hellenes usually enjoy with crusty bread. For the American palate, *taramosalata* whets appetites with raw celery strips, or unsalted crackers and bread sticks. *Taramosalata* is a delicate creamy-orange color and has a subtle fish flavor.

TO SERVE 8 TO 10

3 slices Italian or French bread, crusts removed, soaked in water and squeezed dry; or 2 medium potatoes, boiled and peeled

5 ounces tarama *(fish roe), soaked in warm water a few minutes, then rinsed and drained*

1 cup olive oil of fine flavor
Juice of 1½ lemons
2 tablespoons vinegar
1 to 2 tablespoons water, if necessary
½ onion, grated (optional)

Using an electric blender or electric mixer (or old-fashioned mortar and pestle), thoroughly blend the bread or potatoes and the *tarama.* Add the olive oil as slowly as possible, blending at a medium speed; add the lemon juice and vinegar, blending at a higher speed, plus a little water if the mixture forms peaks. Add the grated onion, if desired, then whip at high speed for a few minutes.

Note: The flavor may be mitigated to suit taste by adding more bread or potato; a too-salty taste may be adjusted by dropping in a few tablespoons of sour cream while blending. Leftover *taramosalata* can be stored in a covered jar in the refrigerator for 7 to 10 days.

HAVIAROSALATA
[*Whipped caviar salad*]

TO SERVE 4 TO 6

3 tablespoons black caviar
2 slices white bread, crusts removed, soaked in water, and squeezed dry
1/2 cup olive oil
Juice of 1 1/2 to 2 lemons, more if desired
2 to 3 tablespoons water

Beat the caviar in a blender or an electric mixer (or use a mortar with a wood pestle). Beat in the bread gradually. Continuing to beat steadily, add the olive oil in a slow stream, then the lemon juice. Taste for seasoning, and add more lemon juice if desired. Slowly pour in droplets of water to adjust the consistency, which should be thick. Chill. Serve with unsalted crackers or toast as canapés.

ASTAKOS LADOLEMONO
[*Lobster with lemon-oil dressing*]

TO SERVE 1 TO 2

1 lobster, boiled or steamed
1/3 cup olive oil
Juice of 1 to 1 1/2 lemons
2 scallions, white parts only, minced
1 teaspoon prepared mustard or 1/4 teaspoon dry mustard

Salt and freshly ground pepper
A few tablespoons water, if necessary
Lettuce leaves

Cut the lobster meat, including the tail and claws, into rings. Remove the meat from the lobster shell, saving all liquid from the lobster in a small bowl and set aside. To the lobster liquid in the bowl, add the oil and lemon juice and beat until thick. Beat in the minced scallions and the mustard, then season with salt and pepper to taste. If necessary beat in a few tablespoons of water. Arrange the lobster on the lettuce leaves and pour the sauce over. Serve cold.

MIDIA KRASATA
[Mussels in wine sauce]

Diocles of Carystus in *Hygiene* (4th century B.C.) considered shell-fish—mussels, oysters, scallops, and cockles—very digestible, and the best food for the kidneys. Writers also tended to use shellfish a good deal in their description of imagery. Aristophanes wrote, "Every one of them began to open his mouth wide, like conches baking on coals."

TO SERVE 6

2 pounds mussels in shells
1½ cups dry white wine
4 to 5 scallions, chopped
1 to 2 sprigs fresh parsley and thyme
Salt and freshly ground pepper
Fresh parsley or watercress for garnish

Place the mussels in cold water and scrub, using a brush. Drain and rinse several times. Place the mussels in an enameled pan, cover with the wine, scallions, parsley, and thyme, and season with salt and pepper to taste. Cover and simmer over low heat until all the shells open (approximately 10 to 15 minutes), discarding any unopened mussels. Using a slotted spoon, remove the mussels to a serving dish and keep warm. Strain the sauce into a small pan and boil down until thick. Pour over the mussels, garnish with parsley or watercress, and serve immediately.

OKTAPODI ME LADOXIDO
[Octopus in vinegar-oil dressing]

Octopus in Greece can taste like lobster, and even the most squeamish of visitors have admitted this after sampling some. So many versions exist, and I wish I could include them all. This is a traditional method. Another is *oktapodi tursi* (pickled octopus). To enjoy the latter, marinate with additional wine vinegar in covered jars in the refrigerator for one week after preparing the following recipe.

TO SERVE 4 TO 6

> *1 small octopus (1 to 1½ pounds)*
> *⅓ cup olive oil*
> *¼ cup wine vinegar*
> *Freshly ground black pepper*
> *A few sprigs fresh parsley, chopped very fine*
> *Salt, if necessary*
> *1 sprig fresh dill, chopped (optional)*

Beat, pound, and rub the octopus from 20 to 30 minutes on a rough stone surface. The octopus will feel softer and will secrete a grayish liquid after pounding. Wash thoroughly, then drain and cook in a covered pan without adding water until the octopus turns bright pink-red and feels tender. Cool and cut into round, bite-sized pieces about the width of a heavy finger.

Meanwhile, prepare a dressing by mixing the olive oil, wine vinegar, a few grindings of black pepper, parsley, pinch of salt, and dill, if desired. Pour the dressing over the octopus, stir well, and store in covered jars in the refrigerator for several days before serving. Flavor will develop after marinating. Taste and season with salt, if necessary. Serve cold with a small amount of dressing.

KALAMARAKIA KRASATA KYPRIOTIKA
[*Spicy squid braised in wine, Cyprus style*]

TO SERVE 6 TO 8

1 pound small squid
¼ cup olive or corn oil
3 onions, peeled and sliced into rings
¼ cup vinegar

½ cup dry red wine
2 sticks cinnamon
4 whole cloves
1 bay leaf
Salt and freshly ground pepper

Clean the squid according to directions on page 128. Heat the oil in a pan, add the squid, including the tentacles, and onions, and cook slowly until the onions are translucent. Pour the vinegar and wine over the squid and onions, then add the remaining ingredients and enough water to almost cover the squid, if necessary. Cook, uncovered, over low heat until the squid are tender and all the wine has been absorbed, approximately 1 to 1¼ hours. Remove the spices and bay leaf. Cut the squid into bite-sized pieces and serve warm or cold.

KALAMARAKIA TURSI
[Pickled squid]

A most delectable way to serve squid. This is excellent as canapés on crisp toast squares, with a few drops of the marinade sprinkled on top before serving.

TO SERVE 5 TO 6

12 to 15 medium squid
2 to 3 tablespoons olive oil
Salt
Freshly ground pepper
¼ cup chopped fresh parsley
Few sprigs fresh rosemary or
½ teaspoon dried rosemary

2 cups white vinegar, approximately
Pickling spices and herbs (8 black peppercorns, 2 cloves garlic, 1 bay leaf, 1 sprig fresh rosemary or pinch dried rosemary)

Prepare the squid as directed on page 128. Cut the sacs into ½-inch-wide rounds. Heat the oil in a frying pan and slip in the squid rounds, heads and tentacles. Cover and simmer until bright pink and tender (approximately 30 minutes), adding salt and pepper to taste, parsley and the rosemary during the last 15 minutes. Half fill a clean quart-sized jar with the squid and all the juices remaining in the pan. Add white vinegar almost to the top, then the pickling spices and herbs. Seal the jar tightly and shake. Marinate at least one day before serving. Keep in the refrigerator.

To serve, remove from the marinade and serve cold, within 10 days.

MARIDES MARINATES
[Marinated smelts]

The lowly smelt becomes sublime for those who try this Greek recipe. I use frozen smelts when fresh are unavailable, thoroughly defrosted before beginning to cook.

TO MAKE APPROXIMATELY 30

2 *pounds smelts, cleaned and
drained*
Juice of 1 lemon
Flour for dredging
*Vegetable oil for frying,
preferably olive oil*
½ cup dry white wine
¼ cup wine vinegar
*2 tablespoons chopped fresh
parsley*

*1 tablespoon chopped fresh
thyme or 1 teaspoon dried
oregano*
*½ teaspoon dry mustard mixed
with 1 tablespoon cold water*
2 tablespoons olive oil
Salt and freshly ground pepper

Sprinkle each smelt with lemon juice, roll in flour, and fry in hot oil about a half-inch deep. Drain on absorbent paper.

Meanwhile, in a small saucepan combine the wine, vinegar, parsley, thyme or oregano, diluted mustard, oil, salt, and pepper. Simmer 8 minutes, then add the smelts. Bring to a boil and remove from the heat. Cool, then chill before serving. Serve cold.

Note: The smelts will keep several days in the refrigerator. Sliced garlic, shallot, or onion may also be added to the marinade.

SAGANAKI
[*Fried cheese*]

This delicious appetizer takes its name from the *saganaki*, a two-handled shallow pan in which the cheese is fried and served.

TO SERVE 4 TO 6

⅓ pound kefalotyri or kasseri cheese
2 tablespoons butter
Juice of 1 lemon

Cut the cheese into bite-sized cubes. Melt the butter in a *saganaki* (or another frying pan), and fry the cheese on all sides until crusty and chestnut colored. Squeeze lemon juice over the cheese and serve with bread, other appetizers, and wine or ouzo.

TYROPITES

[Savory cheese triangles]

Combinations of cheese for fabulous *tyropites* vary both with available cheeses and Greek moods. Feta, mizithra, or manouri are most frequently used, and when the mixture is combined, kasseri or kefalotyri may be grated in to supplement the amount or the taste. The cook must taste the cheese to be able to control the amount of salt in it and the butter or margarine. Soft ricotta or cottage cheese, as well as cream cheese, are excellent choices to mitigate the sharpness of the accompanying Greek cheeses. Rolled and frozen in advance, *tyropites* are invaluable for unexpected guests—and they will evoke praise for their crispness and flavor.

TO MAKE ABOUT 60 TRIANGLES (2½ INCHES)

½ pound cream cheese
½ pound feta cheese, crumbled
2 eggs, lightly beaten
1 tablespoon all-purpose flour
Pinch of salt (optional)
½ to 1 teaspoon grated nutmeg

1 cup (½ pound) plus 3 table-spoons melted butter or margarine
1 pound commercial filo *pastry sheets, cut in thirds (3 x 11 inches)*

In a bowl combine the cheeses, eggs, flour, salt (unless the feta is very salty), nutmeg, and 3 tablespoons butter. Cover the bowl and chill several hours or overnight, removing from the refrigerator an hour before using.

Pile up the *filo,* covering it with waxed paper and a damp towel. Take out one sheet at a time and keep the rest covered. Butter the *filo,* one sheet at a time, using the pastry brush and the ½ pound melted

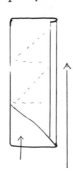

butter or margarine, warmed. Place 1 teaspoon of the filling 1 inch from the end nearest you. Fold the *filo* back over the filling so the bottom edge meets the left edge, forming a right angle. Continue folding back at right angles to make the triangular shape (see sketch). Place on baking sheets and keep covered until all are ready to bake. Bake in a moderate oven (350 degrees) for 20 to 25 minutes or until golden and crisp, turning once. Serve hot.

Note: Tyropites may be stacked upright in cardboard boxes and frozen. When ready to bake, separate while still frozen, spread on baking sheets, and bake as directed above, allowing an additional 10 minutes baking time.

TYROPITA TRIFTI THRAKIS
[*Crispy grated cheese squares, Thracian style*]

Delicious! And simple to make in a large batch for appetizers. As made in Thrace, the soft dough may be spread into a sheet and cut in squares before baking, or each shaped individually into dainty *bastounakia* (little canes or sticks). The word *trifti* identifies the texture—crisp and crumbly in the mouth. (They are also called *kourou* [cut small].) If making the individual "little canes," they should be half a (dainty) finger wide and a finger in length. The secret of the crispness is in adding only enough flour to make a soft dough.

TO MAKE 100 ONE-INCH SQUARES

> *½ cup (¼ pound) butter*
> *½ cup light olive oil*
> *⅓ cup plus 2 tablespoons milk*
> *1½ teaspoons baking powder*
> *½ teaspoon salt, less if the cheese is salty*
> *1 cup grated Greek cheeses of your choice*
> *2 to 2¼ cups all-purpose flour*

The mixing of the dough may be begun with an electric mixer, but should be finished by hand. Beat the butter until fluffy, then lower the speed and add the olive oil. Continue beating, and when fluffy beat in the milk, baking powder, salt, if necessary, and cheese. Begin adding flour, but after 1 cup stop beating with the mixer and beat in the remaining flour by hand, adding only enough to make a dough soft enough to roll into strips. Knead a few minutes. Spread or roll on buttered sheet (jelly roll tray, cookie sheet, or any flat pan) to a thickness of half-finger's width and cut into squares of desired size (the smaller the better, since they are rich). Bake in a moderate oven (350 degrees) for 20 to 25 minutes, moving to the top shelf for the last minutes to achieve a golden chestnut color. (If making the "little canes," the baking time will be 10 to 12 minutes.) Remove when done and cook on a rack.

Note: Stored in covered tins, these will keep for several weeks.

BOUREKIA APO KIMA (KREATOPITAKIA)
[Baked savory pastries stuffed with seasoned meat]

Bourekia apo kima and *kreatopitakia* are examples of the diverse family of small savory pastries. These are stuffed with meat and rolled in various ways, rolls and triangles usually being the most popular and attractive for appetizers. Seasonings vary, but these pastries are always well seasoned and delectable. And if you are very expert, roll your own *filo* (see page 41).

TO MAKE ABOUT 60

3 tablespoons butter or margarine
2 shallots or onions, minced
1 pound lean meat (ground lamb or beef)
½ cup dry white wine
3 sprigs fresh parsley, chopped
1 tablespoon chopped fresh mint or dill
½ cup tomato sauce, canned or homemade

Salt and freshly ground pepper
½ cup grated kefalotyri or Parmesan cheese
1 egg, lightly beaten
1 tablespoon bread crumbs, if necessary
1 pound commercial filo *sheets, unrolled flat*
1 cup (½ pound) butter or margarine, melted

Heat the butter and cook the shallots until soft, then add the meat and mash with a fork over medium heat until the color changes. Add the wine and simmer a few minutes. Stir in the herbs and tomato sauce; season with salt and pepper to taste and simmer for 20 minutes. Cool. Add the cheese and egg, and if the mixture is very liquid, stir in the bread crumbs immediately before stuffing. Roll like the Tyropites (page 65) or another favorite shape.

KEFTEDAKIA MARINATA
[Marinated spiced beef balls]

TO SERVE 4 TO 5

1¼ pounds lean ground beef

2 thick slices white bread, crusts
removed, soaked in cold water,
and squeezed dry

4 to 5 sprigs fresh parsley,
chopped fine

2 tablespoons chopped fresh dill
or mint leaves

1 teaspoon ground coriander or
cinnamon

1 small onion, crushed

2 large cloves garlic, crushed

Salt and freshly ground pepper

Flour and pligouri or substitute
burghul or wheat germ,
pounded for dredging

Vegetable oil for frying

2 cups hot Saltsa Domata Krasati
(page 52)

In a large bowl combine the meat, bread, herbs, coriander or cinnamon, onion, garlic, salt, and pepper. Knead thoroughly for 3 to 4 minutes, until thoroughly blended and aromatic. Cover and refrigerate for at least 3 hours or overnight. When ready to fry, break off pieces slightly smaller than a walnut in size and shape into balls by rolling between the palms of the hands. Roll the balls in the flour-wheat mixture and prepare to fry.

Heat oil to a depth of ½ inch to the smoking point in a deep, heavy frying pan. Add the balls to the pan one layer at a time, turning to color all sides evenly. Removed with a slotted spoon to drain on absorbent paper. Continue until all the keftedakia are fried; then place them in the hot saltsa and allow to cool in marinade. Serve, hot or cold, in the marinade.

Note: Ground lamb or pork may be substituted for beef. Use sage or rosemary with pork instead of dill. Incidentally, pounding the pligouri or substitute is not essential but will produce a finer coating.

DOLMADES YIALANDZI
[Stuffed grapevine leaves]

This is by far the appetizer most favored by hostesses and chefs throughout Greece. If fresh grapevine leaves are available to you use the young, tender ones and you will enjoy the results.

TO MAKE 60 TO 70

3/4 cup olive oil
1/2 small onion, chopped
8 scallions, chopped fine
2 large cloves garlic, chopped
1 cup raw long-grain rice
1 bunch fresh dill, chopped

1/2 bunch fresh parsley, chopped
Juice of 1 1/2 to 2 lemons
Salt and freshly ground pepper
*   to taste*
1 cup hot water
1 one-pound jar grapevine leaves

Heat 1/2 cup of the oil in a skillet. Add the onion and scallions and sauté for about 5 minutes, until soft and transparent. Add the garlic and cook for a few minutes, then add the rice, dill, parsley, lemon juice, salt, pepper, and remaining 1/4 cup olive oil. Stir well, then add the hot water. Cover and simmer about 5 minutes. Remove from the heat and cool.

Meanwhile, carefully remove the grapevine leaves from the jar, leaving the brine in the jar. Wash grapevine leaves thoroughly and drain, then with a sharp knife cut the heavy stems from the leaves. (If using fresh grapevine leaves use the same procedure, parboiling leaves for 5 minutes when not tender, then drain.) Line an enameled pan with a few heavy grapevine leaves and set aside. To stuff a grapevine leaf, put it on your working surface rough side up and stem end near you, and place a teaspoonful of the rice mixture near the stem end. Using both hands, fold the part of the leaf near you up and over the filling.

Then fold the right side of the leaf over the filling, then the left side, and roll tightly and back away from you and toward the pointed end of leaf. Place the *dolma*, seam side down, in the prepared pan. Continue stuffing grapevine leaves until the mixture has been used. (If any grapevine leaves remain, replace in the reserved brine for future use.) Place an inverted plate on the *dolmades*, then add enough water to cover the *dolmades* (about 1 to 1½ cups). Bring to a boil, then cover the pan, lower the heat, and simmer as slowly as possible for 1¼ hours, then taste one to see if the rice is tender, and continue cooking slowly if necessary. Cool, then chill. Serve cold, as an appetizer or as an entrée.

Note: An important variation, particularly in Macedonia and Thrace: add a few tablespoons of raisins and pine nuts to the filling when adding the rice. Also, you may vary the size of *dolmades* as you wish by adding 1½ teaspoons of the filling. However, be consistent to allow them to cook at the same rate. They may be stored in the refrigerator for a week or so.

MANITARIA TURSI
[*Pickled mushrooms*]

TO SERVE 4 TO 6

> *1 pound small mushrooms*
> *Salt*
> *Juice of ½ lemon*
> *¼ cup olive oil*
> *1 cup white vinegar*
> *¼ teaspoon peppercorns, bruised*
> *½ teaspoon dried oregano or thyme*

Wash the mushrooms, trimming off and saving the stems for another purpose. Leave the caps unpeeled. In a small pan, bring enough salted water to cover the mushroom caps to a boil, then add the lemon juice and mushroom caps and simmer 5 minutes. Drain, then dry the mushroom caps by wrapping them in a clean towel. Put into a large jar or divide into smaller jars, filling each jar only two-thirds full.

Meanwhile, prepare a marinade by bringing the oil, vinegar, peppercorns, and oregano or thyme to a boil in a saucepan. Pour immediately over the mushrooms, then seal the jars and cool. Store in the refrigerator for one week before using.

ANGINARES SALATA
[*Artichoke salad*]

Delightful as an appetizer or salad.

TO SERVE 4 TO 5

> 8 *small artichokes*
> *1 lemon, halved*
> *Salt*
> *1 tablespoon olive oil*
> *Juice of 1 lemon or 3 citric acid crystals (see note below)*
> *¼ cup Ladolemono (page 54)*

Pull off the tough outer artichoke leaves and snip off the tips of the remaining leaves, using shears. Cut off the stems, then cut the artichokes
in half lengthwise, immediately rubbing all the cut parts with a lemon
half. Scoop out and discard the choke.

In an enamel pan, combine enough water to cover the artichokes
with salt to taste, the olive oil, and lemon juice or citric acid (which has
to be dissolved in a little hot water). Bring to a boil, then drop in the
artichokes, cover partially, and simmer for 25 minutes, or until tender.
Drain, arrange in a salad bowl, and pour the *ladolemono* over. Cool,
then chill. Serve cold.

Note: Citric acid crystals are available wherever spices are sold, an
excellent substitute for lemons in acidulated water.

MELITZANOSALATA
[*Whipped eggplant salad*]

Cold, thick, and aromatic, when well seasoned, *melitzanosalata*
leaves a lasting impression on the taste buds. Invariably included on
taverna menus, *melitzanosalata* is usually among the first appetizers
Hellenes order following the theater or concert, with wine and olives.

TO SERVE 4 TO 6

2 eggplants (1 to 1½ pounds each)

3 to 4 cloves garlic

2 to 3 fresh tomatoes, peeled and chopped or 3 canned, peeled tomatoes, drained and chopped

Salt and freshly ground pepper

2 tablespoons chopped fresh parsley

1 teaspoon crumbled dried oregano

⅓ to ½ cup olive oil, more if necessary

6 tablespoons red wine vinegar, more if necessary

Bake the eggplants for 45 minutes in a 375-degree oven or in hot ashes. Peel off and discard the skin, then chop the eggplant flesh while still hot. Rub a wood or earthenware bowl with one of the garlic cloves, cut. Add the eggplant and beat with a wooden spoon—or if available use a wood mortar (*goudi*) to pound eggplants. Continue pounding or beating, meanwhile adding the tomatoes, a little salt and pepper, 2 to 3 cloves garlic, crushed, and the herbs. Continuing to beat, gradually add the olive oil alternately with the red wine vinegar. Taste, adding oil and vinegar, if necessary; *melitzanosalata* should be thick and smooth. Serve cold with fish, meat, or fresh, crisp bread.

Note: You will have excellent results by whipping *melitzanosalata* in a blender. Another, milder whipped eggplant dish (excellent with meats) is *melitzanes poure*, whipped with butter, salt, pepper, and a little milk after baking the eggplants.

HUMUS ME TAHINI
[Chick-pea salad with tahini]

Tahini achieves particular status during fasting periods, when it is used in many dishes. This hearty appetizer, which—scooped on lettuce or tomato rings and sprinkled with chopped parsley—is excellent as a salad, makes a superb accompaniment for fish dishes. It may be whipped in the blender.

TO MAKE 2 CUPS

1 cup dried chick-peas
¼ teaspoon baking soda
2 to 3 teaspoons tahini
⅓ cup water
Juice of 1 lemon
¼ cup olive oil
2 cloves garlic

½ teaspoon ground coriander
(optional)
½ teaspoon ground cumin
(optional)
Salt and freshly ground pepper
Chopped fresh parsley

Wash the chick-peas, then soak overnight with the baking soda in cold water to cover. The following day, drain and wash the chick-peas, then cover with fresh water. Bring to a boil, then lower the heat and simmer until tender, 1½ to 2 hours. Drain and push through a sieve or food mill, discarding the coarse fibers remaining in the sieve.

Meanwhile, put the *tahini* in a small bowl and beat it with the ⅓ cup water until dissolved, using a whisk or fork. Beating briskly with the whisk, add the *tahini* mixture, a teaspoonful at a time, to the chick-peas, alternating with the lemon juice and olive oil. When all has been added, crush the garlic over the mixture and sprinkle with optional spices, salt, pepper, and 1 tablespoon chopped parsley. Beat for another minute, then taste for seasonings and chill overnight—if possible. Serve cold, sprinkled with additional chopped parsley.

SELINO MARINATO
[*Marinated celery*]

Hellenes usually serve celery, with or without meat, as a main dish. This very tasty recipe will also make an excellent appetizer. It must be made in advance.

TO MAKE APPROXIMATELY 1 QUART

1 bunch Pascal celery
½ cup olive oil
Juice of 1½ lemons
2 tablespoons chopped fresh
fennel leaves
1 to 2 sprigs fresh thyme,
chopped

2 sprigs fresh parsley, chopped
1 small bay leaf
Salt and freshly ground pepper
Lemon slices and fennel leaves
for garnish

Scrub the celery stalks, scraping only the tough ones. Using a sharp knife, cut the stalks diagonally into 1½-inch pieces, cutting large pieces in half lengthwise.

Meanwhile, in an enameled pan large enough to accommodate all the celery, combine the oil, lemon juice, herbs, seasonings, and ½ cup water. Bring to a boil, then drop in the celery and enough water to half cover the celery. Invert a dish over the celery and simmer for 15 minutes, or until tender but still crisp. Remove from the heat and cool in the marinade. Store, marinade and all, in a glass jar in the refrigerator. (If the marinade is very watery, boil it down in a small saucepan and pour over the celery.) Serve garnished with lemon slices and fennel leaves.

Note: This marinade may also be used for artichokes, beans, fennel, leeks, mushrooms, or canned wax or green beans. (For the canned beans, drain and bring to a boil in the marinade. Cool.) After cooking, use within a week.

TZATZIKI (TALLATORI)
[Herbed yogurt and cucumber]

Such a delicious salad or appetizer, this is another traveler from the Middle East made ravishingly popular in Greece—so much so that it is now available in disposable cartons in Athens. When making it at home with homemade yogurt, thicken the yogurt by any of the methods mentioned on page 245 and make *tzatziki* a day in advance.

TO SERVE 3 TO 4

2 cups plain yogurt
1 medium cucumber, peeled,
    seeds removed, and diced
1 clove garlic, minced
2 to 3 teaspoons fine olive oil
1 tablespoon white vinegar

1 tablespoon finely chopped fresh
    dill
1 teaspoon finely chopped fresh
    mint
Pinch of salt

Combine all the ingredients in a glass or earthenware bowl and chill, to allow flavors to penetrate the cucumber. Serve as a "dip," or on lettuce leaves as a salad, or with fried zucchini, eggplant, or fish.

ELIES
[*Olives*]

A recipe section of Greek appetizers without olives would be as incomplete as a Greek table of *orektika* or *mezedakia* without them. Serve any preferred type: Kalamata (smooth-skinned purple), or Amphyssis (black and wrinkled) or the small black island varieties. Marinate to the desired flavor, then serve each type separately in small bowls.

If a good friend has an olive harvest and offers some, this is the way to prepare olives, Greek style:

Collect the olive as ripe as possible (late November in Greece). Slash or stamp each olive with the side of knife or board to make an opening, then soak in cold water in earthenware or glass containers for 10 days, changing the water daily. Soak in a brine solution for 24 hours, then wash off the brine and soak for 24 hours in vinegar. Drain. Store in jars in olive oil. This method will preserve olives indefinitely. (If sourer olives are preferred, add a little vinegar to the oil.)

ELIES ME KOLIANDRON
[*Green-olive relish with coriander, Cyprus style*]

A most delicious combination.

TO MAKE ABOUT 2 CUPS

> *1 twelve-ounce jar green Spanish-type olives*
> *¼ cup olive oil*
> *¼ cup red wine vinegar*
> *2 large cloves garlic, crushed*
> *2 teaspoons coriander seeds, crushed or ground*

Drain the olives. Remove and discard the pits, then chop the flesh of the olives and combine in a small bowl with the oil, vinegar, garlic, and coriander. Cover and refrigerate overnight, stirring a few times. Serve on toast, as canapés.

SOUPS

My garlic, my onions, every bite with tears.   GREEK PROVERB

SOUP HAS A TRADITIONAL PLACE in Greek culture, in the villages especially. Who knows how many families have survived the centuries on soup?

The favorite Greek soups are meals in themselves. They have names without needing the "soup" identification. Kakavia (page 77), Mageritsa (page 84), Faki (page 89), Faba (page 90), Fassoulada (page 90)—each has its personality, aroma, time, situation, and blessings. Picked over, soaked, and sprinkled with whatever aromatics are on hand, the legumes absorb the cook's affection, hunger, and yearning. Soup as the main course is thick and substantial, accompanied by bread, cheese, and fresh onions, perhaps topped off with fresh fruit. A more elaborate meal develops when Greek cooks use fish, poultry, and meats for soup. The broth extracted becomes the base for the soup, and the fish, meat, or poultry follow the soup course, served on a separate platter garnished with vegetables cooked in the broth—a traditional and very practical use of foods, which I have tried to reflect not only in this section, but throughout the entire book. Greek cooks have used court bouillons, stocks, and fumets for generations—they are the soups made in the family *kakavia, chytra, tsoukali, katsarola*, or whatever you want to call the pot—and enjoyed to the last drop.

In large cities, among the "continental" restaurants, the character of the soup can be deceivingly untypical—more of an appendage than the backbone of the meal. "Potage crème de legumes" and "Potage aux champignons" appear in miniature servings.

Mageritsa (Easter soup made with herbs and lamb innnards, page

76

84) enacts an important cultural role—the breaking of the long fast of Great Lent. And *tyrozoumi* (broth with herbs and cheese) is served on the evening of Cheese Sunday preceding Lent. *Zomos* (broth, see Kota kai Zomos page 168), in the diminutive *zoumaki* is spoken in an endearing tone, with the quality of a mother's hand gently spooning the broth into her child's mouth. Kakavia (below) the most ancient Greek fish soup for all its variations (large fish or small, various combinations, various seasonings, some methods using a little sea water, etc.) has one basic characteristic: fish is served *in* the broth. And this soup really belongs in the hands of the Greek fishermen who invented it—and invent it anew every time they make a *kakavia* full!

With the growing affluence in Greece and a parallel rise in the use of convenience foods, soups may diminish in their overall importance. But there is a stabilizing reminder of their significance in old proverbs like "Some lentils got mixed in with the cooked food," and "If we had bread and onions, our neighbor would lend us a pot."

KAKAVIA

Put the kakavia *on the fire . . .*   ARISTOPHANES

It is no secret that *kakavia* is the most ancient of Greek fish soups. The recipe traveled with colonists in 600 B.C. to Marseilles (ancient Massalia), where it developed into the famous *bouillabaisse*. The latter is a fabulous soup seasoned with saffron and served with a peppery *rouille*. *Kakavia* also traveled in Greece in an easterly direction, and is still made in the Aegean islands—and in fact, anywhere in Greek-speaking regions where fishermen still fish. The Greek and French soups have three distinct similarities that have survived the centuries: (1) they are both named for the pot—*kakavia* (the *kakavi*) and *bouillabaisse* (the *bouillet*); (2) they are both made with a flexible variety of fish, depending on availability; and (3) the soups remain individual expressions of simple fishing villages, not the "big city." Although not as excellent as in a sea setting, the soups can be made at home, if the most important principle is maintained—a strictly fresh and good variety of fishes. In Greece the "catch" determines the ingredients.

TO SERVE 8 TO 10

1 cup sliced onions, scallions, or leeks

½ cup olive oil

4 tomatoes, peeled, seeded, and chopped

½ stalk fennel or celery, sliced

3 sprigs fresh parsley

1 bay leaf

2 sprigs fresh thyme

1 cup dry white wine plus 5 or 6 cups water, more if necessary

Salt and freshly ground pepper

4 pounds of 3 to 4 kinds of fish for poaching (bass, cod, hake, haddock, halibut, trout, pollack, snapper, rockfish, whiting, etc.), cleaned and sliced

1 lobster (optional), cut up and claws cracked

1 pound shrimp, peeled and deveined

1 pound scallops or mussels in shells (optional), scrubbed

8 to 10 thick slices bread, toasted

Croutons

In a soup pot with a wide bottom, sauté the onions in the oil, without browning, until soft. Add the tomatoes, fennel, herbs, wine, and water and bring to a boil. Season with salt and pepper to taste and simmer for 45 minutes. Pour the stock into a large bowl through a sieve, squeezing all the pulp from the vegetables before discarding the fibers remaining in the sieve. Return the soup stock to the pot and bring to a boil.

Meanwhile, lightly salt the fish and let stand for 10 minutes, then rinse with water and lower into the soup, adding water only if needed to cover the fish. Lower the heat and simmer for 5 minutes, then add the lobster. Cover and simmer 5 minutes longer, then add the shrimp and scallops or mussels and simmer an additional 10 minutes. Taste and adjust the seasonings.

Arrange the toast slices in large soup plates. Serve the varied fishes and broth in each bowl, hot, with croutons in a separate plate.

Note: Kakavia is frequently made in the following variation: Cook 2 to 3 fish with the vegetables and strain with the vegetables to make a thicker stock. Continue to cook the remaining seafood as described above.

PSAROSOUPA ME HORTA KRITIKI
[Fish soup with vegetables, Cretan style]

A thick and rich red fish soup originating in Agios Nikolaos, Crete, so delicious we decided to make a meal of it. Use large fish slices or smaller ones: carp, cod, hake, mackerel, salmon, skate, trout, turbot, perch, haddock, swordfish.

TO SERVE 6

¼ cup olive oil
1 onion or 3 scallions, chopped
2 carrots, chopped
1 large stalk celery, chopped
2 tomatoes, peeled and chopped
1 small zucchini, peel left on, diced

¼ cup chopped fresh parsley
2 tablespoons all-purpose flour
1 pound fish of your choice
Juice of ½ lemon
Salt and freshly ground pepper
Parsley for garnish (optional)

In a large frying pan, heat the oil, then add the onion and cook until transparent, then add the carrots, celery, tomatoes, zucchini, and parsley. Cover, and simmer until tender but not mushy, adding only enough water to keep the vegetables from sticking to the pan. Remove the lid, stir in the flour, and cook for a few minutes until it is light chestnut in color.

Meanwhile, wash the fish and poach in 4 cups salted water until tender (approximately 25 minutes). Remove the fish and set aside. Strain the stock and add to the vegetables, stirring until the mixture boils and thickens, then strain through a colander into another saucepan. Using a spoon, remove those vegetables which retain their shape and add them to the soup. Push the remaining vegetables into the soup through the colander, using a pestle or spoon and discard the fibers remaining in the colander. The soup will be thick. Skin and bone the poached fish, cut into small cubes and add to the soup. Add the lemon juice and salt and pepper to taste, then heat to the boiling point. Serve piping hot, garnished with parsley, if desired.

79

PSAROSOUPA PATMOU
[*Fish soup, fish and vegetables, Patmos style*]

Patmos, smallest island of the Dodecanese, immediately impresses you with its quiet, reserved air which seems to originate in the monastery and grotto where St. John wrote the Apocalypse. Sparkling white homes are trimmed in blue or green around the window frames and graceful eucalyptus trees line the narrow lanes. In its comparable simplicity, this recipe, similar to many of the mainland, outlines a fundamental method of cooking fish from the serene sea.

TO SERVE 4 TO 6

2 pounds fish suitable for soup, washed and cleaned	2 bay leaves
	1/4 cup olive oil
Salt	3–4 potatoes, peeled and quartered
2 onions	
2 stalks celery	Salt and freshly ground pepper
4 tomatoes	1/2 cup fide or 1/3 cup rice

Place the fish in a shallow bowl, salt lightly and allow to rest for 15 minutes. Meanwhile slice the onions, celery stalks and tomatoes and place them with bay leaves in a soup pot. Add the oil and enough water to cover. Bring to the boil and simmer until vegetables are almost tender, about 25 minutes. Add the potatoes and continue cooking for 10 minutes. Rinse the fish, drain and lower into the soup. Simmer until the fish is tender. Season with salt and pepper. Carefully lift the fish to a warm platter, then lift the vegetables and arrange them around the fish. Strain the broth and place back into the soup pot. Bring to the boil and add the *fide* or rice, allowing 1/2 cup crumbled *fide* or 1/3 cup rice for 8 cups of broth.

Soup is the first course, followed by fish and vegetables. Fish is frequently served with *ladolemono* dressing and oregano crumbled over the top and the soup served Avgolemono style (page 48).

SOUPA FIDES
[Vermicelli soup]

A popular soup in Greece for convalescents, the next food for the patient after broth. For a family meal, it would most likely be made with *avgolemono*. *Fide*, incidentally, is also called *mallia angelou* (angel's hair).

TO MAKE 2 QUARTS

> 2 quarts broth or stock of your choice
> 2 rolls fine fide noodles
> Chopped fresh herb of your choice (see note below, optional)   2

In a large pot, bring the broth or stock to a boil. Crush the *fide* noodles between your fingers into the stock. Stir, then lower the heat and simmer until tender (approximately 20 minutes). Serve hot, with or without chopped fresh herb sprinkled on top.

Note: Mint is delicious with lamb broth, thyme or marjoram with beef, and parsley or dill with chicken and any favorite with fish stock (especially rosemary).

TAHINOSOUPA
[Tahini soup]

Tahini in Greece is most identified with fasting days, when the sesame seed emulsion is beaten into soups, cakes, and breads, and spread on bread.

TO SERVE 4 TO 5

> 7 cups salted water
> 1/3 cup rice
> 1/2 cup tahini
> 1/2 cup cold water
> Juice of 1 to 1 1/2 lemons, strained
> 1 teaspoon tomato purée or paste (optional)
> Freshly ground black pepper

In a soup pot, bring the salted water to a boil. Slowly add the rice and cook until tender (approximately 20 minutes). Meanwhile, in a small bowl, beat the *tahini* with the ½ cup cold water, using a fork. Gradually add the lemon juice, then take 1 cup of the water in which the rice is cooking and add it by spoonfuls to the *tahini* mixture. Stir the *tahini* into the same soup pot, then add the tomato purée and remove from the heat. Serve warm, with a few grindings of fresh black pepper.

SOUPA AVGOLEMONO
[*Chicken rice soup avgolemono*]

Traditionally, *soupa avgolemono* is made using chicken broth or stock and rice with *avgolemono*, unless otherwise specified. Sometimes very fine noodles, *fide* or *kritharaki*, called vermicelli and orzo by the Italians, are substituted for rice, and less frequently beef stock is used in lieu of chicken. A fabulous soup, *psarosoupa avgolemono* is made using fish fumet or court bouillon and *fide*.

TO SERVE 5 TO 6

> 2 quarts chicken broth, strained
> ½ cup raw long-grain white rice
> 2 whole eggs or egg yolks
> Juice of 1½ to 2 lemons
> Salt
> 2 tablespoons butter (optional)

Bring the broth to a full boil in a soup kettle. Gradually add the rice, stirring constantly until the broth boils again. Reduce the heat, cover, and simmer until the rice is just tender, not mushy, 12 to 14 minutes. Remove from the heat and keep warm while preparing *avgolemono* according to the directions on page 48, using the eggs or yolks and lemon juice. After slowly adding hot broth to the egg-lemon mixture, stir it into the soup and cook over minimum heat, without boiling, until the soup thickens enough to coat a spoon. Swirl in the butter, if desired, taste for salt, and keep warm over hot water until ready to serve. Pass the pepper mill at the table for additional zest.

YUVARELAKIA SOUPA AVGOLEMONO
[Meat-rice "barrel" soup, Epirus style]

We sampled this in the charming Metsovon in the Pindus Mountains, a traditional dish throughout Greece. If made with less liquid, this is simply called *yuvarelakia*, an excellent one-pot family dish!

TO SERVE 6

1 pound ground beef, veal, or lamb	1 teaspoon dried oregano or thyme
1 onion, grated	Salt and freshly ground pepper
2 cloves garlic, crushed (optional)	3 eggs
6 tablespoons raw long-grain white rice	5 cups water or stock
Chopped fresh parsley	1 onion, chopped (optional)
2 tablespoons chopped fresh mint, basil, or dill	1 stalk celery, chopped (optional)
	½ carrot, chopped (optional)
	Juice of 1 to 1½ lemons

In a large bowl, combine the meat, grated onion, garlic, rice, 3 tablespoons chopped parsley, the mint, oregano, salt and pepper, and 1 egg, slightly beaten. Knead for a few minutes, then shape into walnut-sized barrels and set aside.

In a soup pot, bring the water or stock to boil with the chopped onion, celery and carrot, and salt and pepper to taste. Lower the heat and add the meat-rice barrels. Simmer, covered, for 30 minutes, then remove from the heat. Prepare *avgolemono* according to the directions on page 48, using the remaining 2 eggs and the lemon juice. Add to the soup and heat, being careful not to let it boil. Serve hot, garnished with parsley.

Note: This soup is frequently made without the additional vegetables added to the liquid. Also, you may enjoy this soup without *avgolemono*, in which case add ½ cup canned tomato sauce to the liquid and reduce the water to 4½ cups.

MAGERITSA
[Easter lamb soup]

Traditional *mageritsa* is unusual in flavor and cultural significance. Its dark color, herby aromas, and heavy lamb-organ tastes evoke thoughts of sorcerers' brews and love philters. Whether it was originally created for a sweetheart or not remains a moot question. However, the soup as made in the provinces is a practical one, using all remaining parts of the paschal lamb that are not barbecued. The soup's name sounds like a derivative of the Greek words for "cook" and "cuisine," (see page 39), and justly so. For with the favored leguminous soups, *kakavia* and *soupa avgolemono*, *mageritsa* is distinctively Greek.

Mageritsa breaks the long fast following midnight services on Easter eve. Everyone enjoys it with red eggs and Easter bread. The making of *mageritsa* is fascinating to observe and to be involved in—the braiding of the intestines, the washing and cutting up of organ meats and fragrant herbs. Since the fast continues during its preparation, the cook may use all senses but taste. It is a substantial meal, meant as it is to provide nourishment. This from the provinces is traditional; a very fine, quick adaptation can be found in Athens.

TO SERVE 6 TO 8

Intestines, heart, lungs, liver of 1 lamb
Lamb's feet and tripe of 1 lamb (optional); (see note below)
1 lamb's head (optional); (see note below)
Salt
Juice of 1½ to 2 lemons
Small bunch of scallions, chopped

⅔ cup chopped fresh parsley
½ cup chopped fresh dill
¼ cup chopped celery leaves
6 tablespoons raw long-grain white rice
½ teaspoon aniseed (optional)
Freshly ground pepper
2 to 3 whole eggs

Clean the intestines thoroughly by turning them inside out, using a long skewer or stick (this turning will be quicker if the intestines are first cut into 2-foot lengths), then wash under cold running water until clean. Rub the intestines with salt and the juice of ½ lemon, rinse again in cold water and drain. Braid the intestines or tie the ends together with clean string. Put in a large soup pot with the lamb's head, if using, and cover with cold water. Bring to a boil, then lower the heat, skim, and simmer for 30 minutes. Remove the intestines, drain them, and cut into ¼-inch pieces with the scissors and set aside. If using the head, remove the brain, cut into small pieces, and set aside to add to the soup later. (Use the remaining portion of the head for another dish.)

Bring the soup stock to a boil and add the scallions, parsley, dill, and celery leaves. Cut the heart, lungs, and liver into small bite-sized cubes, and add them to the soup, and simmer for 15 minutes. Add the rice, cut-up intestines, aniseed, salt and pepper to taste and continue simmering until the rice is tender, approximately 15 minutes, adding more water as needed and the brains during the last few minutes of cooking.

Half an hour before serving, bring the soup to a boil, remove from the heat, and add *avgolemono* (prepared as directed on page 48) using the eggs and remaining lemon juice. Serve warm, but avoid boiling the soup after adding the *avgolemono*.

Note: If using the lamb's head, wash it, then soak it in cold water for 3 hours. Drain. Cut the head in half, using a sharp knife, and tie with a clean string.

If using the lamb's feet and tripe, prepare as described on page 86. Discard the water used to blanch the feet and tripe. Cube the tripe, remove the meat of the feet from the bones, and add to the *mageritsa* at the same time as the cut-up intestines, adjusting the liquid by adding more water.

A richer *mageritsa* can be made by sautéing the scallions in 3 tablespoons butter or oil before adding to the soup.

PATSAS SOUPA
[*Tripe and lamb's feet soup*]

Patsas is a controversial dish, but the average Greek will never admit to it. *Patsas* (lamb's feet) and *skembe* (lamb's tripe) are usually used preparing this dish. Yet if you ask 5 Hellenes what *patsas* is made from, they will answer, "Stomach of a lamb." So for cooks who enjoy a tasty controversy, this version is worth trying. Save the knuckle bones to play the age-old Greek game *veziris*.

TO SERVE 6 TO 8

1 lamb honeycomb tripe
1 to 2 lamb's feet, cleaned and plucked
2 onions, sliced
1 stalk celery, sliced, or ½ celery root, sliced
1 carrot, chopped (optional)

2 to 3 garlic cloves, sliced (optional)
Salt
2 egg yolks
Juice of 1 to 1½ lemons
Freshly ground pepper

If the tripe is not partially cooked, cut open with a sharp knife and clean the inside thoroughly under running water. Put in a pan with cold salted water to cover and soak for 30 minutes, then drain and wash with cold water. Cut into small pieces and put in a large soup pot with the lamb's feet. Cover with cold water, add the vegetables and simmer until tender, adding salt to taste during the last minutes of cooking. Strain the stock into another pot, then pick out the tripe from the colander and add to the stock. Remove the bones from the lamb feet, cut up the meat, and add it to soup. Prepare *avgolemono* according to the directions on page 48, with the 2 yolks and lemon juice, using the hot stock. Serve warm, with a few grindings of pepper.

HORTOSOUPA HIMONIATIKI
[*Winter vegetable soup*]

Greek ingenuity prevails in their vegetable soups. A mosaic of colors and flavors develops naturally when vegetables currently in season are used along with other available ingredients. In the spirit of this flexibility, two soups are suggested for the creative cook—this one for winter and the following one for summer, each made using a different method.

TO MAKE 2 QUARTS

2 quarts broth or stock
2 cloves garlic, sliced
½ cup chopped onion or shallots
1 leek, chopped
1 large stalk fennel or celery,
  chopped
2 medium carrots, chopped
1 turnip or parsnip, chopped
¼ small head cabbage, shredded
1 medium potato, diced

2 tablespoons legumes (dried
  peas, lentils, beans, soaked;
  see note below)
or, 2 tablespoons cracked wheat
  or barley
Herbs of your choice (bay leaf,
  parsley, dill, fennel, basil or
  mint, to taste)
½ cup tomato juice or tomato
  sauce
Salt and freshly ground pepper

In a soup pot, bring the broth or stock to a boil, then add the vegetables and legumes or cracked wheat. Simmer until tender, about 1 hour, adding the desired herbs, tomato juice, salt and pepper after the first 30 minutes. Check for amount of liquid in the soup; it should be thick but may be thinned by adding more broth, stock or water. Taste for seasoning and serve hot, sprinkled with additional herbs.

Note: Soak the dried peas, lentils, or beans, if using, in advance according to the package directions (usually beans need to be soaked overnight).

HORTOSOUPA KALOKERINI
[*Summer vegetable soup*]

TO MAKE 2 QUARTS

3 tablespoons oil, butter or
  margarine
1 small onion or shallot or 3
  scallions, chopped
1 carrot, chopped
1 stalk celery, chopped
½ cup of any 3 vegetables (green
  beans, green peas, okra,
  peppers, eggplant, zucchini,
  lettuce, cucumber)

3 fresh tomatoes, peeled and
  chopped
Parsley, mint, or basil to taste
Celery or fennel leaves to taste
2 quarts broth, stock or water,
  more if necessary
Salt and freshly ground pepper

In a soup pot, heat the oil or butter and cook the onions until soft. Add the carrots and celery, cover, and cook for 5 minutes. Uncover and add the vegetables of your choice, which have been peeled and cut into uniform cubes. (Okra should be soaked at least 15 minutes in vinegar, rinsed, and drained before adding.) Cover and cook slowly for 15 minutes, then add the tomatoes, herbs, celery or fennel leaves, and broth. Stir, cover, and simmer until tender but not mushy (approximately 40 minutes). Season with salt and pepper to taste, adding additional broth or water if necessary. Serve hot.

REVITHIA SOUPA THESSALIAS
[Chick-pea soup, Thessaly style]

Chick-pea soup is undoubtedly one of the Greek basics. In fact, it was one of the dishes the monks selected when I asked for recipes at the magnificent Varlaam Monastery in the Meteora, Thessaly. I was advised to be sure and use onions, which help thicken the soup; to add olive oil at the beginning of cooking and salt at the very end; and to begin with only enough water to cover chick-peas and continue adding as necessary.

Incidentally, climbing the spectacular peaks to the monastery is one of the most awesome, breathtaking experiences in all of Greece. The old ropes and baskets remain as relics of the days before roads were built, when the monks were hoisted up by the cables.

TO SERVE 6 TO 8

> *1 pound dried chick-peas*
> *2 teaspoons baking soda*
> *2 onions; chopped*
> *1/3 to 1/2 cup olive oil*
> *Salt*
> *Fresh lemon juice or wine vinegar*

Wash the chick-peas, drain and cover with cold water. Soak overnight. The next day, drain again, discarding the water. Pour the chick-peas into a bowl, mix in the soda, and allow to stand for 1 hour. Rub the chick-peas with your fingers, or wrap in a towel and rub, to loosen the skins. Rinse several times in clear water, discarding the skins. Drain.

In a soup pot, bring 2 quarts of water to a boil and add the chick-peas. Remove the scum, then add the onions, and simmer until tender (approximately 2 hours), adding the olive oil at the beginning of the simmering. Season with salt when the chick-peas are tender. Serve hot with fresh lemon juice or vinegar on the side.

FAKI

[Lentil soup]

For bulb-and-lentil soup is like ambrosia in the chilly cold.
CHRYSIPPUS (3RD CENTURY B.C.)

Faki is "soul food" for many Hellenes, one of the most ancient of dishes, whose ancient name has survived along with its popularity. Also a cultural food, when made without oil, it is fare on the strictest fasting day, Good Friday. The secret for either the Greek or non-Greek palate is to make it thick, redden it with good-quality tomatoes, and flavor it with a fine oil, herbs, and a little vinegar.

TO SERVE 10

1 pound lentils	*1 large bay leaf*
1 large onion, chopped	*4 sprigs parsley*
2 to 3 cloves garlic, chopped	*Mint, basil, or oregano to taste*
2 small or 1 large stalk celery, chopped fine	*⅓ cup fine olive oil*
	Salt and freshly ground pepper
5–6 canned Italian-type plum tomatoes and their juices	*Red wine vinegar*

Wash the lentils and place in a soup pot with warm water to cover (about 2 quarts). Let stand for 1 hour, then bring to a boil. Add the onion, garlic, celery, and tomatoes. Cover, and simmer for 1 hour. Stir in the herbs and oil and season with salt and pepper to taste. Continue to simmer, covered, for another 1½ hours, until very thick and tender, stirring occasionally and adding 2 tablespoons vinegar toward the end. Serve hot, with additional vinegar on the side.

Note: You may like to freeze half of the soup for another meal since the flavor improves after cooking *faki*.

FAVA
[Split pea soup]

Fava *without onions, wedding without games.*
GREEK PROVERB

Prepare *fava* as directed in the previous recipe, substituting dried split peas for the lentils and using more onions (the indispensable ingredient) and more oil but *no* vinegar. Strain the peas when tender (*fava* is thick) and serve warm with lemon juice. Equally delicious cold.

FASSOULADA
[Bean soup]

Serve *fassoulada* with verve, remembering that beans have sustained many Hellenes since the Bronze Age. Modern Greeks can make a feast of *fassoulada*, olives, feta or kasseri, bread, a heady local wine and fresh fruit. Beans are such a part of life that in the proverbs they are used to describe such attitudes as patience: *Fassouli to fassouli yemizi to sakkouli* (Bean by bean the sack is filled), which might be a good thought to pursue while waiting for the first spoonful of *fassoulada* to cool.

TO SERVE 6 TO 8

1 pound dried navy beans, washed and soaked overnight in cold water	1 cup chopped, drained fresh or canned tomatoes
2 onions, chopped	1 bay leaf
2 stalks celery with leaves, chopped	2 to 3 sprigs fresh mint or thyme
2 to 3 carrots, scraped and diced	Salt and freshly ground pepper
4 to 5 sprigs chopped fresh parsley	1/3 cup olive oil or 1 ham bone

In a soup kettle, bring the beans to a boil in the soaking water. Skim off the foam, then add the remaining ingredients, cover, and simmer gently until the beans are tender, about 3 hours. Remove the bone, if used. Serve hot.

Note: Less frequently, the soup is puréed through a sieve. Also, you may add the herbs during the last hour or so of cooking, if you wish.

GRAINS AND PASTA

As when along the hallowed threshing floor the wind scatters chaff, among men winnowing, and fair-haired Demeter in the leaning wind discriminates the chaff and the true grain . . . HOMER, *The Iliad*

WHEAT IS THE GRAIN most deeply associated with Greece throughout its history, since its cultivation spread westward from the Fertile Crescent. Demeter became the goddess of grain and harvests; her image was sacred and blessed, her bounty rich and generous. Consequently, the reverence for her transferred strongly to her products, which explains the sacred aspects of wheat, bread especially, in everyday use. In villages it is customary to make the sign of the cross on the bread before cutting it and the last wheat stalks are taken to church for blessing, then hung over the house beams as a talisman. By ancient tradition the grain from this sheath, symbolizing fertility, is mixed with that sown for the new crops. Grains in general and wheat are both called *sitari*.

Along with wheat, barley and millet have been cultivated in Greece since the Neolithic era. Archeologists found that bread was made of barley as well as wheat, coarse and unleavened. And wasn't barley among the foods to appear on the earliest Greek coins (along with the vine, wild parsley, and silphium)? An early testimonial to the feeling for wheat is the graceful Harvester Vase in the Heraklion Museum, Crete.

In modern Greece, wheat production is geared to the national demand, and for the last fifteen years has been enough to feed the Hellenes with little surplus. Greece harvests nine soft and four hard wheat varieties, and of the latter group, Electra and Methoni are considered superior.

Rice cultivation since the early part of the twentieth century has expanded throughout Greece, and rice has become a very popular grain. Served in an enormous variety of ways, rice, which spread westward from India and Indonesia, reflects the Middle Eastern influence on the Greek cuisine, and more recently, with the rising use of converted rice, an influence from the United States.

Rice is served with meat, fish, poultry, game, and vegetables and in combinations with legumes and potatoes less frequently. Rice may be spooned into a round or tube pan after cooking and flipped onto a warm platter; this may be topped with meat or poultry, the style is called *atzem pilafi*—for a nice version try Kota Atzem Pilafi Ipiriotiko (page 173).

Rice with herbs and seasonings makes a delightful stuffing served frequently throughout Greece. Ground meat is often mixed with the rice, providing a nutritional variety including grain, meat, and vegetables. After a little experimentation, the cook stirs up a savory stuffing, soon learning to include the pulp and centers of vegetables being stuffed whenever possible. Most frequently stuffed vegetables include artichokes, eggplants, zucchini and zucchini blossoms, grapevine leaves, cabbage, lettuce, green peppers, and tomatoes. You will find a selection of these stuffed vegetables in a later chapter.

Corn is a relative newcomer to Greece, used more extensively in the form of cornstarch thickening or as corn oil. Corn still has a low status, due to the tasteless corn breads of World War II; it has become associated with poverty and animal fodder. But it is oats that remain at the very bottom of the grain hierarchy, food for animals, a status clearly described in their name, *bromi*.

In cooking, grains are subject to regional preference. *Pligouri*, cracked wheat, is more prized on the islands and in the villages, while in large cities rice has risen in popularity. Semolina has survived for ages in Greece.

The tradition of commercially made pasta expanded with post—World War II industrialization, twenty-two modern factories producing some 58,000 tons annually. Exports have risen correspondingly. During the last six years, for instance, commercial pasta exports increased from 54 to 1,121 tons, primarily to North America, Great Britain, Scandinavia, and Africa. While increasingly available in the United States, most of the commercially made Greek favorites may be substituted for by American and Italian pasta. As you might expect, pasta products are among the Greek "filler" foods, among which *kritharaki* is my family's favorite. *Kritharaki* is harder and better textured than the substitute, orzo. Since it is excellent commercially, *kritharaki* is made less at home.

Noodles, *hilopites*, however, are among the home specialties. When we saw noodles made in Tseria, the village in the Taygetos Mountains where my mother was born, we saw a collaborative effort in food preparation. It seemed like the many joint cooking ventures we observed as youngsters, watching Mother and several aunts prepare jellies, *trahana*, baked sweets, and holiday foods together. But we finally saw it in its original setting, where mutual assistance is for survival, not for fun.

For these occasions, it is not unusual for helpers to bring their own equipment, special knives for cutting, for example. One neighbor carried her *soffras*, a low, round table that had been used for many decades (obviously a carry-over from the Middle-Eastern custom of dining around a low table). Sitting on her low stool, using the *plasti* (a clean broom handle), with nimble fingers she rolled and unrolled the dough, repeating until the dough covered the table's three-foot diameter. An architect couldn't have designed a better piece of equipment.

Probably rolling requires the most skill, but what the mixing, cutting, and drying of noodles needs is the right touch. The simplest aspect, of course, is eating them. Cooked on the same day they are made with fresh eggs and goat's milk, noodles have a flavor as glorious as can be. During the drying period, when thousands of noodles are spread on white linen-covered surfaces, their name—*hilopites* (a thousand *pites*)—seems very appropriate.

How the women talk, joke, and laugh the entire day, bustling back and forth, between rolling and cutting, to their homes just down the hilly, rocky slope. Undoubtedly, this was the most interesting discovery for me—an awareness of the rapport among these women, who for so long have endured experiences and hardships together: living without electricity in their villages until December, 1971; seeing brothers, sisters, and children leave for the big cities. Nevertheless, noodle making never suffered.

Trahana, another home product made of wheat flour combined with eggs and sour or sweet milk, is probably the most distinctive Greek grain product. Provincial Greeks probably invented *trahana* as a means of preserving milk and eggs long before the advent of refrigeration. Nutritionists would agree it is an excellent food, providing animal proteins from the eggs and milk as well as vegetable proteins from the wheat.

93

Grain thickeners have a hierarchy of their own, each imbued with special qualities for particular dishes. Cornstarch (known in Greece as "corn flour") leads in usage for most dishes and sauces. Nevertheless, arrowroot and flours of wheat, rice, and potato are not strangers to the Greek cook. Still another thickener, toast and bread crumbs of wheat bread (*galetta*), is of tremendous importance in cookery, an aid in preparing the extensive casseroles and baked, layered dishes. Crumbs form a surface crust and may be sprinkled throughout to absorb excess moisture as well.

Macaroni and spaghetti products are enjoyed by the Hellenes very much like their Italian neighbors, except for the cooking which is much softer than *al dente*. On the other hand, cooking pasta products with meats and poultry in the same dish, baked together, is a Middle-Eastern influence. I believe the Greek people combined these two notable influences and devised the sensational *pastitsio*, baked macaroni and meat topped with thick white sauce, included among these recipes.

KOLYVA
[*Memorial wheat and seasonings*]

Kolyva is a most fascinating food of the Greek people. When asking for a "recipe" for this special memorial dish, one usually gets a vague answer. Yet when the tray appears in church for the special service for the deceased, the sight of the beautifully decorated confection is one of sheer perfection!

Kolyva represents one of the many traditions continued for hundreds of years among the Greek Orthodox. Earliest records indicate that it originated around A.D. 362, associated with the sprinkling of blood from sacrificial animals in the marketplace. Christians reacted to the pagan rite and refused to eat meat. Instead, they brought wheat from Christian farms and cooked grains during fasting days. At the same time the All Souls' Day memorial services, celebrated on the first Saturday of Lent preceding Easter, became a tradition. *Kolyva* is brought to church on All Souls' Day, and also for the forty-day, one-, five-, and ten-year anniversaries of Orthodox deceased. Sweet and munchy, *kolyva* is distributed in tissue or white paper bags among the parishioners following the service.

TO MAKE 1 LARGE TRAY, SERVING 45 TO 50

2 pounds whole wheat kernels
Salt
½ pound sesame seeds, toasted
  in a moderate oven (350
  degrees) for 10 minutes
3 cups finely chopped walnuts
1 pound light raisins or sultanas
1 cup minced fresh parsley
½ cup minced fresh basil leaves

2 teaspoons ground cinnamon
¼ cup pomegranate seeds
  (optional)
1½ to 2 pounds confectioners'
  sugar
White or silver candy balls,
  raisins, or blanched almonds
  for garnish

Cook the wheat until tender in a large quantity of lightly salted water, about 1½ hours, stirring frequently to prevent sticking and burning. Drain, then roll in dry towels to absorb excess moisture. In a large mixing bowl, combine the wheat with the sesame seeds, walnuts, raisins, parsley, basil, cinnamon, and pomegranate seeds, and at least 1½ cups of the sugar. (The wheat should have a sweet taste.)

Spread white doilies over a large rectangular tray, cover with waxed paper or plastic wrap, and mound the *kolyva* slightly in the center to form a smooth, wide circle that slopes down at the perimeter of the tray. Carefully sift the remaining sugar over the entire top, pressing down gently with waxed paper until a thick layer covers the surface like a frosting. Clip away any excess waxed paper or plastic wrap around the edges. Using cardboard, cut out a small Greek cross (all sides equal) and the initials of the deceased. Press the cross pattern in the center and the initials on each side. Outline the edges of the cross and initials with candy balls, raisins, or almonds, and also around the circumference of the *kolyva*, stressing simplicity in your design.

Note: After preparing *kolyva*, store in the refrigerator.

PLIGOURI
[*Cracked wheat*]

Pligouri (also known as *pourgouri* and *hondro* on some islands) is cracked wheat and undoubtedly a modern version of the ancient grain. It is usually available in various degrees of coarseness, and the medium coarse type will serve you well for these dishes. Try them all. The cooking of *pligouri* and rice is similar, both in methods used and in the yield

(1 cup dry *pligouri* yields about 3 cups when cooked). The taste, however, is very different. Plan to substitute *pligouri* for pasta or rice, well worth the effort for its cost is low and nutrient value much higher than that of white rice. *Burghul* (burghur) may be used as a substitute, or the more familiar wheat germ.

TO MAKE 3 CUPS

> 2 cups stock or broth
> Salt
> 1 cup pligouri

Bring the stock or broth to a boil, add salt to taste, and gradually stir in the *pligouri*. Cover, lower the heat, and simmer for 15 minutes or until the liquid has been absorbed. (Cooking time increases with the coarseness of the wheat.) Remove from the heat, uncover, drape with a dry towel and let stand for 10 minutes. Flip over to unmold on a warm platter. Serve warm, with meat, poultry, or vegetable dishes; this is particularly good with yogurt or sour cream.

Note: You can also heat 2 tablespoons butter in a saucepan and add 1 small minced onion or scallion (white part only). Cook until soft, then add the broth and proceed as above.

Or you can serve this topped with any of the sauces suggested for rice, or use in *yuvetsi* dishes (see pages 102–103) instead of pasta. Proportions should be slightly more than 2 parts liquid to 1 of the *pligouri* when added to meat or poultry dishes. Garnish with greens.

HILOPITES
[Homemade egg noodles]

Begin early—just after the cock crows—for that old-fashioned flavor! And be sure the weather is dry, preferably sunny.

TO MAKE ABOUT 8 CUPS DRIED NOODLES (ENOUGH FOR 4 TO 5 MEALS)

> 8 cups all-purpose flour
> 4 teaspoons salt
> 2 eggs, plus 1 egg yolk, at room temperature
> 1 cup light cream, warmed
> 1½ cups milk, warmed

Combine the flour and salt in a large mixing bowl and make a well in the center. Break the eggs into a smaller bowl, add the yolk and mix slightly with your fingers or a whisk. Pour into the well along with 1½ cups of the combined milk and the cream, and mix with the flour as if mixing bread; knead on a board until soft and smooth, adding the remaining milk and cream, if necessary, to make an elastic, shiny dough. Cover and let rest for 1 hour, then uncover and divide into 3 balls. Roll out one of the balls on a floured table or board, using a *plasti* if you have one, as described for rolling Diples (page 325).

When the dough is paper-thin and transparent, wrap it around the *plasti* and carry it to an airy, cool surface covered with clean linen or cotton (Greek women use a bamboo lattice covered with linen sheeting to allow air circulation from below as well as above the surface). Unroll the dough and allow it to rest for 1 to 3 hours, until dry enough to be cut. Repeat with the remaining balls of dough.

When the dough is dry enough to be cut into noodles, fold as the Greek villagers do: fold one sheet at a time in half, and bend over the curved ends toward fold, and fold again like a tablecloth. Lift, drape over the arm, and carry to a clean surface for cutting. Lay the sheet on the cutting surface folded, as you had lifted it. Using a sharp knife, cut the dough into 3 or 4 sections across the length, producing workable, easy-to-cut sections 4 thicknesses deep and about 5 inches square. Using a clean ruler for a guide (when cutting, Greek women use the side of a hand as a guide for the knife, dangerous for the inexperienced) and with a sharp knife, cut each section straight across into ¼-inch strips (see note below). Holding in place, cut again at right angles the same width to make square-shaped noodles. (If you can turn the board or table, it will be quicker than turning the noodles.) Run your fingers through the noodles, then allow them to rest while cutting the remaining noodles in that group. Transfer to a dry tray and spread on your airy, cool linen or cotton surface for about 4 days, turning at least once daily for air circulation. When thoroughly dry, store in dry, airtight containers. Use in any dish that requires noodles.

Note: If you wish long noodles, only cut the first step, and they will be macaroni lengths. Also, you do not have to dry all the noodles; cooked the same day, noodles are delicious and cook more quickly than dry ones, in 15 minutes.

MAKARONIA ME KIMA
[Macaroni with meat sauce]

TO SERVE 6

Probably the most popular pasta dish in many regions, almost as enjoyed in the homes as *makaronada*—pasta with butter melted to a chestnut color with the local grated cheese.

> 1½ pounds macaroni or spaghetti
> ¼ cup (½ stick) butter or margarine
> Saltsa Kima (page 52)
> Grated cheese (kefalotyri, mizithra, or Parmesan)

Cook the macaroni or spaghetti according to package directions, then drain and arrange on a warm platter. Melt the butter, pour it over the pasta, top with hot *saltsa kima*. Serve with grated cheese.

Note: Frequently, the sauce is mixed with the pasta and served on a warm platter.

PASTITSIO ME KIMA
[Baked casserole of layered meat, macaroni, and white sauce]

Steaming hot and spicy, *pastitsio me kima* is a treat for the palate and eye, probably the most famous of Greek baked macaroni dishes. Equally versatile as a first course or cut into smaller squares for a buffet, *pastitsio* stands firmly when cut, a cross-sectional study of layered macaroni and ground meat topped with thick white sauce. Each mixture is prepared separately, then the casserole is layered in a large *tapsi*, or baking pan, baked, cut, and served warm. Variations of *pastitsio* prepared with feta cheese and with tomato sauce are not as well known, even among the Hellenes. By using cut macaroni and small ovenproof earthenware servers, you can readily adapt the large recipe to make individual servings, a practice I first noticed in Macedonia. When made for an individual serving, *pastitsio* is aptly dubbed *atomiko*.

The procedure may be simplified (and flavor improved) by making the meat mixture a day in advance. This is a good-sized recipe designed to serve a large group. For a family meal, use half the recipe and a baking pan about 8 x 10 x 3 inches.

98

TO MAKE 20 TO 24 SQUARES

1½ to 2 pounds ziti thick, uncut
  macaroni
Salt
2 cups grated mizithra and
  kefalotyri or hard ricotta and
  Romano cheese
6 tablespoons melted butter or
  margarine

7 to 8 eggs
6 cups Saltsa Kima (page 52)
6 cups medium Saltsa Aspri
  (page 50)
1 teaspoon ground cinnamon
½ teaspoon grated nutmeg
1 cup bread crumbs

In a large pot, boil the ziti in salted water until almost tender. Drain thoroughly. In a large bowl, combine the macaroni, 1½ cups of the grated cheeses, the butter, and 4 to 5 of the eggs, lightly beaten.

Butter an 11 x 15 x 3-inch baking pan, and in it layer half the macaroni mixture. Separate 2 of the eggs and combine the 2 egg whites plus 1 more whole egg with the *saltsa kima*. Spread it evenly over the macaroni in the pan and cover with the remaining macaroni. Meanwhile, combine the *saltsa aspri* with the 2 egg yolks and the spices. Pour over the macaroni, spreading it into the corners with a spatula. Sprinkle the top lightly with the remaining cheese and the bread crumbs. Bake in a moderate oven (350 degrees) for 45 minutes or until a golden crust develops and the sauce bubbles. Remove from the oven and allow to stand for 15 minutes before cutting into squares. Serve on a warm platter.

Note: Try this once using 1½ pounds of ziti for an elegant *pastitsio*. A very rich recipe; you can safely reduce the meat sauce and *saltsa aspri* by one cup, if desired.

PASTITSIO MAKARONIA ME FETA
[Pastitsio with feta cheese]

A medley of whites and with a nutmeg fragrance, this version of *pastitsio* is made with *filo*, like a pie. You may try it without the pastry sheets, for fewer calories.

TO SERVE 9 TO 12

1 pound macaroni, boiled in salted water and drained
7 to 9 tablespoons warm melted butter or margarine
3 eggs, lightly beaten
½ cup grated cheese

1½ cups feta cheese, cubed
Salt and white pepper
1 teaspoon grated nutmeg
12 sheets commercial filo pastry, cut to fit the pan and kept covered to avoid drying

In a large bowl, combine the macaroni, 3 tablespoons of the melted butter, the eggs, grated cheese, and feta. Season with salt, white pepper, and nutmeg and mix with a wooden spoon. In a buttered 9 x 12 x 3-inch baking pan, spread 6 sheets of *filo*, brushing butter between each with a pastry brush. Spread the macaroni-cheese mixture over the *filo* and cover with the 6 remaining sheets of *filo*, brushing butter between each and on the surface. Using the tip of a sharp knife, score the top 3 to 4 sheets to indicate 9 or 12 servings, as preferred. Bake in moderate oven (350 degrees) for 30 minutes, or until the surface is crisp. Remove to a rack for 10 minutes, then cut and serve on a warm platter.

HOMEMADE TRAHANA
[Sour-milk pasta]

The pleasant sight and scent of *trahana* drying on clean linens is one I remember vividly from childhood. We always use sour milk at home, allowing it to sour naturally. It's delicious to nibble on the *trahana* as it dries for days. In many regions of Greece, we tasted *trahana* of sweet milk, but it somehow lacks the zest of the sour-milk variety. Try making *trahana* on a glorious late summer day and store it for winter. Use in soups as you would noodles or rice, delicious with a dash of tomato and sweet butter.

TO MAKE 22 CUPS UNCOOKED "TRAHANA"

5 packages active dry yeast
1 teaspoon granulated sugar
1½ cups warm water
2 quarts soured milk, at room temperature
¼ cup salt

¾ cup vegetable oil
8 eggs, lightly beaten
26 to 26½ cups sifted all-purpose flour (approximately 6½ pounds), more if necessary

In a small pan or mixing bowl, combine 3 packages of the active dry yeast, the sugar, and warm water. Cover and allow to double in size. Meanwhile, in a large mixing bowl, stir the soured milk, salt, vegetable oil, and eggs; set aside.

In a very large mixing pan, combine the flour and remaining 2 packages active dry yeast. Make a well in the center of the flour and pour in the swollen yeast mixture and the soured milk mixture. Work into the flour by squeezing your hands through the liquids, gradually combining and removing all lumps, until you have a soft but not sticky dough. (If necessary, add sifted flour by half cupfuls at the bottom of the pan and gradually work into the dough.) Knead for 15 to 20 minutes, on a board as you would knead bread, until smooth and elastic. Cover and set in a warm area to rise overnight.

The following morning, spread clean linen or cotton on a surface where the *trahana* may dry undisturbed. Break off the dough in cup-sized pieces and allow to dry for 8 hours, turning once. Break into smaller pieces until dry enough to push through a wide-holed colander (¼-inch holes). Continue turning and drying for several days, until thoroughly dry and hard as pebbles. Store in sealed containers.

Note: The drying process is hastened by dry weather and impeded by moist, humid weather. In Greece, *trahana* is placed in the hot sun during the day and brought into the house at night.

TRAHANAS TIGANITOS
[Fried trahana]

Probably the most traditional way of making this zesty peasant dish.

TO SERVE 5 TO 6

    3 tablespoons butter
    3 tablespoons olive oil
    1¾ cups dried Trahana (page 100)
    2 quarts water
    ½ cup cubed kefalotyri cheese or hard cheese of your choice

In a heavy frying pan, melt the butter, then add the oil and heat together for 1 minute. Add the *trahana*, stirring with a wooden spoon, and stir over medium heat until the *trahana* turns a light chestnut color; do not let it brown. Pour in the water, stir, and simmer for 25 to 30 minutes, until all the liquid has been absorbed and the *trahana* is tender. Stir a few times and add the cheese cubes during the last 5 minutes. Serve with meat, poultry, or vegetables, or just enjoy it as a luncheon dish with fresh salad.

YUVETSI KRITHARAKI ME KIMA KYPRIOTIKO
[Spicy ground meat and pasta casserole, Cyprus style]

The dish *yuvetsi*, or *giouvetsi*, means different combinations in different Greek regions, but it originated by taking its name from the pot in which it is baked. The *yuvetsi* is made in Greece of various sizes of ovenproof earthenware, clay-colored interior, roughish cream-colored exterior with two curved handles. The fact is that the dish *yuvetsi* could be cooked in any suitable ovenware and the mouth would water just as much.

Yuvetsi may be pasta (macaroni, *kritharaki*, spaghetti, noodles) baked with or without meat. It is a quick, easy, and nutritious dish either way, because cheese accompanies the pasta when meat is not used, providing the animal proteins. The *yuvetsi* recipe below is based on meat, while the one on page 103 is baked without meat.

TO SERVE 4 TO 6

2 tablespoons vegetable oil or margarine
1 pound lean meat, ground
1 onion, minced or grated (optional)
Salt and freshly ground pepper
3 whole cloves

1 stick cinnamon
2 tablespoons tomato paste mixed with 1 cup hot water
1 quart stock, preferably same flavor as meat
1 1/4 cups kritharaki or orzo
Parsley or watercress for garnish

Heat the oil and mash the meat into it with a fork, then cook over moderate heat, stirring constantly until the raw color disappears. Add the onion, salt, and pepper to taste, spices, and tomato paste diluted with hot water. Cover and simmer for 20 minutes, then remove the spices. Add the hot stock and *kritharaki* and transfer to a buttered *yuvetsi* or baking casserole. Taste and adjust seasonings.

Bake in a moderately hot oven for 40 minutes, or until the pasta is tender and all liquid has been absorbed, stirring once. Remove from the oven. Drape with a dry kitchen towel to absorb moisture. Serve hot, garnished with parsley or watercress.

YUVETSI
[Baked kritharaki]

In Greece, this dish is usually planned for Sundays, when food is taken to the community *fourno* (oven) to be baked. The baker first roasts the meat, then adds the pasta (either spaghetti or *kritharaki*) and returns it to the oven to finish. Watching him pull casserole after casserole of cooked food out of his oven and hand each one to the right customer is a marvel.

TO SERVE 5

    6 cups tomato juice or 1 cup tomato sauce diluted with 5 cups water
    3 to 4 tablespoons meat drippings from a lamb or beef roast, fat skimmed off
    Salt and freshly ground pepper
    1½ cups kritharaki *or orzo*
    Kefalotyri, Parmesan, or mizithra cheese, at least ½ cup, freshly grated

Combine the tomato juice and meat drippings in a saucepan and bring to a boil. Season with salt and pepper, then add the *kritharaki,* stirring constantly. Transfer to a buttered *yuvetsi* or casserole and bake in a moderately hot oven (350 to 400 degrees) for 40 to 45 minutes, until tender and all the liquid has been absorbed, stirring once and allowing a fine skin to form on the surface. Remove from the oven and drape with a dry towel for 5 minutes. Serve hot, with the grated cheese either sprinkled over the top or served separately.

    Note: This is a perfect accompaniment to a carved roast and vegetables.

RIZI PILAFI
[Rice pilaf]

Rice cooked in any of three different methods is usually called *rizi pilafi*, and is tender but with each grain glistening and separated. Mushy, overcooked rice is not popular in Greece, unlike pasta cookery, which is usually much softer. When estimating the amounts of rice to cook, a good rule is that rice triples in volume; that is, 1 cup of uncooked rice will yield 3 cups of cooked rice. The amount per person varies with appetites. Greek cooks prefer long-grain hard white rice and wash and strain the rice several times before serving.

TO YIELD 3 CUPS COOKED RICE

> *Salt*
> *3 to 4 quarts water*
> *2 tablespoons lemon juice*
> *1 cup raw long-grain white rice, washed and drained*
> *2 tablespoons melted butter*
> *White pepper*
> *Fresh parsley for garnish*

In a large pan, bring lightly salted water to a boil, then add the lemon juice and stir in the rice while maintaining a rapid boil. Cook, briskly, uncovered over high heat until the rice is tender (approximately 18 minutes). Drain. Turn the rice into a warm serving dish and toss lightly with a fork while adding the butter. Drape with a dry towel for 10 minutes, then sprinkle lightly with pepper and garnish with parsley. Serve hot.

Note: Each serving may be set into a cup then turned out on individual dishes or a platter around the meat, fish, or poultry dish.

PILAFI STO FOURNO
[*Baked rice*]

This method of first frying the rice, followed by baking, may also be used to cook over the burner, with excellent results either way.

TO SERVE 4

> *3 to 4 tablespoons butter*
> *1½ cups raw long-grain white rice*
> *Salt and white pepper*
> *3½ cups hot chicken stock*

In a frying pan, heat the butter, then add the rice and sauté without browning until transparent, stirring constantly. Transfer to a buttered baking dish or casserole and add salt and pepper to taste and the hot stock. Stir, then cover and bake in a moderate oven (350 degrees) for 40 minutes, or until the rice is tender and all liquid has been absorbed.

Remove from the oven, uncover, and drape with a dry towel for 10 minutes. Serve warm.

LAHANODOLMADES ME RIZI AVGOLEMONO
[Stuffed cabbage with rice and pine nuts avgolemono, Macedonia style]

One of the more unusual versions of the substantial cabbage roll.

TO SERVE 6

2 medium heads cabbage, washed, parboiled, and drained
3 tablespoons clarified butter (see page 40)
1 medium onion, chopped, or 3 to 4 scallions, chopped fine
1 cup water
1 cup raw long-grain white rice
1/4 cup raisins or currants

1/2 cup pine nuts
1/4 cup chopped fresh parsley
1/4 cup chopped fresh dill
Salt and freshly ground pepper
3 eggs
Juice of 1 lemon
2 tablespoons butter, cut into bits

Prepare cabbage leaves as in Lahanodolmades Makedonika Avgolemono (page 153). Set aside while you prepare the filling. In a heavy skillet heat the clarified butter, add the chopped onions and cook until soft and transparent. Add the water and bring to a boil, then add the rice and stir. Lower the heat and simmer gently until the rice has absorbed the liquid, approximately 15 minutes. Remove from the heat and add the raisins or currants, pine nuts, parsley, dill and season with salt and pepper. Cool. Separate 2 of the eggs and mix the egg whites into the filling. Reserve the yolks for the *avgolemono*.

Stuff and roll the cabbage leaves, using one heaping tablespoon filling, roll up snugly, then place, seam side down, in a casserole. Dot with butter and add water to cover, then cover the cabbage rolls with an inverted plate and cover the casserole. Simmer for approximately 1 hour, then transfer to a warm serving dish and keep warm. Strain the remaining liquid for the *avgolemono*.

Prepare *avgolemono* as directed on page 48, using the remaining egg, the reserved yolks, and 1½ cups of the cooking liquid. Cook over hot water, not boiling, stirring constantly until the sauce thickens enough to coat a spoon. Pour over the cabbage rolls and serve hot.

KALAMARAKIA PILAFI
[*Squid baked with rice*]

A delicate blend of flavors, and simpler to prepare than the stuffed squid. Pick out the smallest sizes in Italian and Spanish specialty markets.

TO SERVE 4

1 pound medium squid
Salt
¼ cup olive oil
3 cloves garlic, sliced
¼ cup dry white wine
2 tomatoes, peeled, seeded, and
    sliced

3 tablespoons butter
1 cup raw long-grain white rice
Chopped parsley
1 tablespoon chopped fresh
    rosemary or 1 teaspoon dried
    rosemary
Freshly ground pepper

Clean the squid as described on page 128, then rub wth salt, rinse and slice into uniform rings, between ½ and 1 inch wide. Heat the oil in a frying pan and add the squid and garlic and sauté for 5 minutes. Stir in the wine and tomatoes, cover, and simmer until the squid is almost tender (approximately 30 minutes). Transfer to a baking dish.

Meanwhile, heat the butter and sauté the rice, without browning, until transparent, stirring constantly. Add the rice to the squid and sprinkle with ¼ cup chopped parsley, the rosemary, and salt and pepper to taste. Add enough hot water to cook the rice, slightly more than 2 cups including the tomato sauce. Cover and bake in a moderate oven (350 degrees) for 30 to 40 minutes, or until the rice is tender. Sprinkle with additional chopped parsley and serve hot.

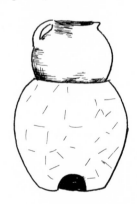

SPANAKORIZO
[Spinach and rice]

One of the classic modern-day Greek dishes, a great one-pot meal, or accompaniment to other dishes.

TO SERVE 6 TO 8

2 tablespoons clarified butter (see page 40) or olive oil
1 small onion, chopped
½ cup raw long-grain white rice
½ cup canned tomato sauce or tomatoes, drained
¼ to ½ cup water
2 pounds fresh spinach, washed, drained, and stems trimmed

¼ cup parsley, chopped
2 sprigs fresh mint, chopped
Salt and freshly ground pepper
Grated nutmeg
3 slices bacon, crumbled (optional)
4 hard-cooked eggs, sliced (optional) and lemon wedges for garnish

Heat the butter or oil in an enameled pan, then add the onions and cook until soft and transparent. Add the rice and sauté for a few minutes, stirring constantly, then add the tomato sauce or tomatoes and water, cover the pan and simmer until the rice is almost tender (aproximately 10 minutes). Uncover and stir in the spinach, parsley, mint; season with salt and pepper. Partially cover the pan and continue cooking, stirring with a wooden spoon until the spinach has wilted. Grate a little nutmeg over the top and continue cooking until all the liquid has been absorbed and the *spanakorizo* is tender, not mushy. Remove from the heat and drape with a dry towel until ready to use. Transfer to a warm serving dish, sprinkle with the bacon bits, if you like, and garnish with the sliced eggs and lemon wedges. Serve warm.

Note: To make *prassorizo*, substitute 1½ pounds sliced leeks for the spinach and add with the liquid. Leeks need longer cooking time.

BOURANI
[Tomatoes and herbs baked with rice]

An excellent brunch dish with ham or sausages and hot rolls. In Greece the ripe tomatoes made this a splendid sight and gave it a splendid flavor.

TO SERVE 3 TO 5

1/4 cup vegetable oil
1 1/2 pounds fresh or canned
tomatoes, peeled, seeded, and
sliced
1 cup tomato juice
Salt, freshly ground pepper, and
granulated sugar to taste
2 cloves garlic, crushed

1/3 cup chopped fresh parsley
2 to 3 sprigs fresh basil, or mint
leaves, chopped
1 small stick cinnamon
1 1/2 cups raw long-grain white
rice
Fresh parsley or watercress for
garnish

In a casserole, heat the oil, then add sliced tomatoes and juice and sauté for 5 minutes. Season with salt, pepper, and a little sugar, the garlic, parsley, basil, and cinnamon stick, then cover and simmer for 10 minutes. Remove the lid and measure the liquid, adding enough hot water to make 3 cups, then pour back over the tomatoes and bring to a boil. Taste and adjust seasonings, then stir in the rice. Cover and transfer to a moderate oven (350 degrees) for 35 to 40 minutes, or until the rice is tender. When done, remove the cinnamon stick and drape casserole with a dry towel for 5 to 10 minutes. Garnish with parsley or watercress and serve hot or cold. Excellent with smoked meat or fish, green vegetables, and chilled dry Greek wine.

FISH AND SEAFOOD

No creature's so unlucky as a fish!
When caught, to die at once it well might wish
And in the stomach snugly buried lie;
But now on salesman's slab left high and dry
More stale it gets, until some greedy ass
Who has no eyes to see shall chance to pass.
To him the festering corpses to remove
The right is given (for something more than love).
He brings them home, but straightway from him throws
His parcel when its odour meets his nose.

ANTIPHANES *

FIE ON THE FISHMONGER IN GREECE who tries to sell fish not strictly fresh—a concern that preoccupied Antiphanes in his comic poetry. Fishing villagers protect themselves by waiting for the caïque returning with the morning catch, bargaining on the spot, and never allowing the fish to leave their sight before carrying it home to cook.

While waiting for a fishing boat to dock, we once heard the woes heaped on those sly fishmongers who dripped blood on the eyes and gills of fish to make them appear fresher: they straightaway landed in jail! Against such deception, Greek people market with sharp eyes, looking for fresh fish characteristics: pink eyes, pink gills, firm scales and back, and a fresh sea smell. After cooking, a fresh fish emerges tender and succulent, with white, flaky meat and white bones. And the glorious moment of relishing a flavorful dish of fresh fish has preoccupied Hellenes for centuries.

* Paley, F. A., trans., and Moses Hadas, ed., *The Greek Poets* (New York: Random House, Inc.) p. 278.

109

Variety in diet had increased considerably by the fifth century B.C. in Greece as compared with Homer's era, although Homer described the Hellespont and waters around Ithaca as teeming with fish. In addition to the plentiful fish of the Saronic Gulf, the red mullet was brought from the Gulf of Corinth and the glaukus and *marides* (very small smelts) from the Peloponnesian coast. Lobsters, oysters, prawns, mussels, and sea urchins were seasoned with parsley and mint, cooked in honey and wine. In addition, a special cookery method for each fish was proclaimed by the great chefs.

Archestratus, probably the greatest chef of all, treated fish like children born with the proverbial gold spoon in their mouth. For tunny (tuna), he ordered that you get a piece of she-tunny, slice and roast it, sprinkling it with just a little salt and rubbing it with oil, and eat the slices hot, dipping them in piquant sauce. As for the roe, wrap it, in autumn, in fig leaves with a very little marjoram—no cheese, no nonsense—then push it under the ashes to bake. For sea bass, when cleaned and scaled, bake them whole gently and serve them with pickle. Harpfish (a fish with firm white flesh) should be boiled in clear brine with herbs thrown in. "But if reddish and not large, grill after being nicked with a sharp knife. Rub it with oils and lots of cheese, for it's a fish that loves to have much made of it, and very demanding. . . ." The fish developed personalities and characters under the spell of these chefs of ancient times.

Most of the prolific writers wrote about fish, including Aristotle in his *History of Animals.* Hippocrates also classified fish, including shellfish, in his *Regimen.* He selected pickled fish for a drying effect on the metabolism, and considered oily fish very laxative.

Seafaring and fishing are two of the traditional trades of the Greek man. Yet until World War II Greek fishermen stayed close to shore. Only recently has deep-sea fishing begun, with the limited number of 48 deep-sea fishing boats out of the total of 18,400 in the fleet. Nevertheless, of the some 130,000 tons of fish hauled from Greek waters yearly, about 30 percent are caught in the deep sea. And though the increased demand for fresh fish since World War II has been met, large quantities of salt cod, smoked herring, and canned fish must be imported. It's safe to say that the Greek people eat lots of fish.

An important factor in fish eating is the periods of meat fasting, when fish assumes the major billing. With herbs, oil, tomatoes, and seasonings, fish can be cooked by many methods and in many styles. Simply grilled with lemon juice, a flavorful fish becomes sublime. Large fish in thick slices, fried and served with Skordalia (page 49), ensure a feast. Poached or broiled and served with cooked greens and fried potatoes, preceded by *psarosoupa avgolemono* (page 82), a fish can make a meal unforgettable.

The fish, of course, is strongly identified with the early Christians, and *ichthys* written using Greek letters is an acronym for Jesus Christ Son of God Savior. In monasteries where meat is not allowed, fish becomes the Sunday dinner. And for all Hellenes during Great Lent preceding Easter, the fast may be flexed to include a fish dinner on Palm Sunday.

That aspect of the fishing industry that deals with freezing fish has begun to affect both the fisherman and the cook. Fishes netted in the small caïque, if not sold to the waiting villagers and islanders, are sold to the local merchant, who quickly freezes them and sends them off to retailers, usually in Athens. Nine firms in Athens and Piraeus specialize in frozen fish exporting. (Incidentally, the largest exporters of fresh fish, in addition to those in Athens, are in Thessaloniki, Patras, and Kavalla. Those specializing in salted fish are located in Lesvos [Mytilini], Volos, Kavalla, Thessaloniki, Piraeus, and Athens.)

As for the home cook, even in the most isolated areas she has learned to cope with frozen fish, not the favorite by any means, but a necessity since fishing is strictly controlled during spawning seasons. Cooks using frozen fish thaw the fish thoroughly and then treat it like fresh fish.

After I had finished writing this chapter on fish, I was especially rewarded to find the following excerpt, again from Antiphanes:

> Let's have a sliced mullet, a stewed electric ray, a split perch,
> a stuffed squid, a baked smooth-tooth, the first cut of a greyfish,
> the head of a conger eel, the belly of a fishing frog, the flanks
> of a tunny, the back of a ray, the loin of a spot fish, a mite of
> sole, a sprat, a shrimp, a red mullet, and a wrasse. Let none
> of these dishes be absent.

Let none of these dishes be untasted!

BAKALIARO TIGANITO ME SKORDALIA
[Fried cod with skordalia]

A prized combination, extremely popular in many Greek regions. Dried salt codfish is most frequently used, although fresh cod may be substituted. Cod has nourished many Hellenes since the days of Aristotle, who wrote of it, "The cod . . . has a widely gaping mouth, and is not gregarious. This is the only fish in which the heart is contained in the belly, and in its brain it has stones resembling millstones . . ."

TO SERVE 6

> 1½ pounds dried cod (see note below)
> 1¼ cups all-purpose flour
> ⅔ cup cold water
> Pinch of salt
> ¼ teaspoon baking powder
> Vegetable oil for frying to depth of ½ inch
> Skordalia (page 49)

Cut the cod into 4-inch sections. Place in a glass or earthenware bowl, cover with cold water, and soak overnight. The next day, drain and discard the water. Put the cod in a pot and cover with cold water. Bring to a boil, then remove from the heat and lift out the cod with a slotted spoon. Remove the bones and the black skin.

In a medium bowl, combine the flour, water, salt, and baking powder to make a thin batter. Dip the cod in batter and fry in hot oil on both sides, then lower heat and cook until tender, turning once again. Serve hot, with the *skordalia,* which is cold or room temperature.

Note: If the cod is excessively salty, change water 2 or 3 times during the soaking period.

HELI PSITO
[Roast eel]

Eels belong to the genera of teleostean fish lacking ventral fins. The distinctions between eels and other fishes were first described in Greek literature by Homer. And the comments of subsequent writers express sheer rapture for eel dishes. When an eel was served to Epicurus, the Greek philosopher cried, "Here comes the Helen of all feasts; I, therefore, shall be Paris." The six- to ten-foot conger eel was considered "glorious" enough to make a "dead man sniff." Eels remain popular in Greece, although more for home cookery than in restaurants and *tavernes*. Eels are usually roasted (as below), fried, broiled, or served in tomato sauce.

TO SERVE 4

> *1 eel*
> *Salt and freshly ground pepper*
> *2 to 3 cloves garlic, sliced*
> *½ cup vinegar*
> *2 bay leaves, crushed*

Skin, wash, and dry the eel, or have it skinned by the fishmonger. Cut across into 1½-inch rounds, then arrange in a bowl. Season lightly with salt and pepper, then add the garlic and vinegar, and sprinkle the crushed bay leaves over the top. Allow to marinate for 2 hours, turning occasionally, then transfer to a baking dish and roast in a moderate oven (350 degrees) about 20 to 25 minutes. Plan a very light meal around the eel including fresh salad, a dry white wine and fresh fruit.

HELI SKARAS
[*Broiled eel*]

TO SERVE 4

> *1 eel*
> *Juice of 1 lemon*
> *Vegetable oil*
> *Salt and freshly ground pepper*
> *Ladolemono (page 54)*

Skin, wash, and dry the eel or have it skinned by the fishmonger. Cut into pieces, then squeeze a lemon over the eel and allow to stand for 15 minutes. Brush the eel with oil, season lightly with salt and pepper and grill or broil on all sides until fork tender. Serve with the Saltsa Ladolemono.

Note: The eel may be lightly floured and fried in a little oil, if preferred.

XIFIAS SOUVLAKIA
[Swordfish on skewers]

So enjoyable to see and taste, this dish is found most often in the villages and towns of eastern Macedonia, although it is made throughout Greece.

TO SERVE 6

2 pounds swordfish, boned, skinned, and cubed
Salt and freshly ground pepper
Juice of 1½ lemons, strained
¼ cup olive oil
Chopped fresh thyme to taste

3 firm ripe tomatoes, quartered, or 8 cherry tomatoes
8 bay leaves
2 green peppers, seeded and cubed

Season the cubed swordfish lightly with salt and pepper and set aside. In a medium bowl, whisk together the lemon juice, oil, and thyme. Dip the swordfish in the marinade for a few minutes, then thread on cane or metal skewers, alternating with the tomatoes, bay leaves, and peppers. Broil 4 to 5 inches from the heat or grill over coals, for approximately 15 minutes, turning frequently and brushing occasionally with the remaining marinade. Serve hot.

Note: Delicious over steaming rice and served with a green salad.

PSARI FOURNOU ME AMBELOFILA
[Fish baked in grapevine leaves]

The fragrant aroma of this dish brings the Greek provinces into the kitchen.

TO SERVE 5

5 medium whole fish, cleaned but with heads left on
2 to 3 tablespoons olive oil
Juice of 1 lemon
1 tablespoon chopped fresh parsley
1 tablespoon each chopped fresh thyme and fennel

Salt and freshly ground pepper
3 to 4 anchovy fillets, rinsed and minced or mashed
2 tablespoons butter
12 to 15 large grapevine leaves
Lemon slices and fennel leaves for garnish

Wash and dry the fish. In a glass or earthenware bowl, beat the oil, lemon juice, parsley, thyme, fennel, and a pinch each of salt and pepper. Dip each fish in the mixture, turning to coat and allow to marinate an hour or two in the refrigerator.

Remove the fish from marinade and drain. Meanwhile, beat the anchovies and butter together and spread on the fish with a knife. Wrap each fish in grapevine leaves and place, seam side down, in an attractive baking-serving dish. Bake in a moderate oven (350 degrees) for 30 minutes. Serve hot, garnished with lemon and fennel.

PSARI STO LADOHARTO
[Fish baked in paper]

You may prefer this variation, fish wrapped in heavy paper and tied like a parcel. Season the fish with lemon, garlic, bay leaf, capers, and parsley. Then wrap and tie and brush the outside of the package with oil before baking.

PSARI SPETSIOTIKO
[Fish, Spetsai style]

Pine-forested Spetsai, the Saronic Gulf island that guards the entrance to the Argolikos Gulf, claims this dish as a specialty. It is not only the most famous of the excellent fish island styles in Greece, it is also a feature of luxury cruise chefs in the Aegean.

TO SERVE 4 TO 5

2 pounds fish (snapper, porgy, mullets, or any favorite), cleaned and left whole or sliced into steaks
Juice of 1 lemon
Salt
1/3 cup olive oil
4 ripe fresh or canned tomatoes, peeled and chopped
1/4 cup white wine, more if necessary
4 cloves garlic, sliced
1/2 teaspoon granulated sugar
Salt and freshly ground pepper
1 cup chopped fresh parsley
Bread crumbs for good flavor
Tomato juice, if necessary

Wash and dry the fish (if using dried cod be sure it was soaked overnight), then sprinkle with salt and lemon juice, particularly inside the neck area if using fish with heads on. Arrange on a baking-serving dish and set aside while you prepare the sauce.

Heat the oil in a saucepan, add the tomatoes, wine, garlic, and sugar and simmer for 10 to 15 minutes. (The amount of garlic may be reduced, but it *is* the most important ingredient.) Season with salt and pepper.

Sprinkle the fish with a light coating of bread crumbs and then with the chopped parsley, then spoon the hot sauce over the fish. Repeat this procedure until all the sauce has been used, ending with a topping of bread crumbs. Bake in a moderate oven (350 degrees) for 30 to 40 minutes, depending on the size of the fish, basting twice with the sauce. (A golden crust will form on the fish, characteristic of this famous style.) During the baking period, add some wine or tomato juice if necessary; some sauce should remain around the fish. Serve hot.

Note: This makes an excellent first course with dry white Demesticha or Samos wine.

PSARI PLAKI
[*Fish, Plaki style*]

A popular style named for the aromatic ingredients used to cook other dishes such as Fassolia Plaki (page 193). The success of *psari plaki* depends on the delicate balance of herbs and seasonings. *Psari plaki* is usually poached in the sauce, or baked, as in the recipe below as we tasted it on the famous island Mykonos, in the Cyclades, also famous for its tasty fish dishes.

TO SERVE 4 TO 5

2 pounds fresh, seasonal fish, cleaned and washed
Salt and freshly ground pepper
Juice of 1 lemon
½ cup olive oil
1 onion, chopped
½ cup white wine
½ to 1 cup water
3 fresh or canned tomatoes, peeled and chopped

¼ cup each chopped fresh celery, carrots, and sorrel or spinach
4 tablespoons chopped fresh parsley
2 tablespoons chopped fresh dill
1 to 2 cloves garlic, crushed (optional)
1 fresh tomato, sliced

Cut the fish into slices, if large, or leave with heads on if using small varieties. Sprinkle with salt, pepper, and lemon juice and arrange in a baking dish. Set aside while you prepare the sauce.

In a medium saucepan, heat the oil and cook the onion until soft and translucent, then add the wine, ½ cup water, chopped vegetables and herbs using 2 tablespoons of the parsley, garlic, if desired, then season with salt and pepper to taste. Mix thoroughly and adjust the consistency by adding water if necessary to cover the fish, but do not add fish yet. Simmer the sauce for 15 minutes, then pour over the fish. Arrange the tomato slices on the fish, sprinkle with additional chopped parsley, and bake for 30 to 40 minutes, or until fork-tender.

Note: An optional method is to gently lower the fish into the sauce, poach at low heat until tender, then remove to a warm serving platter. Reduce the sauce, if necessary, and spoon over fish. Garnish and serve warm.

PSARI SAVORI
[*Fried fish with savory sauce*]

A tangy (and very popular) method of serving fried fish in Greece.

TO SERVE 4 TO 5

1½ pounds small fish or slices of large fish	1 tablespoon tomato purée or sauce
Salt	2 cloves garlic, sliced
Vegetable oil for frying	2 sprigs fresh rosemary or 2 teaspoons dried rosemary
¼ cup olive oil (optional)	
¼ cup all-purpose flour	1 bay leaf
½ cup vinegar	Salt, pepper, and granulated sugar to taste
1½ cups water	
½ cup dry white wine	Fresh parsley for garnish

Wash, dry, and salt the fish. Heat a small amount of oil in a frying pan and fry fish on both sides, without browning, until tender, adding more oil if necessary. Drain the fish on absorbent paper, place on a warm serving platter, and keep warm while you prepare the sauce.

Pour off all except ¼ cup oil from the pan, or wipe the pan and add ¼ cup olive oil. Heat the oil and add the flour, stirring with a whisk. Cook over low heat until the flour is a light chestnut color, then stir in the vinegar (it will sizzle), water, wine, tomato purée, garlic, half the rosemary, and bay leaf. Season with salt, pepper, and a little sugar. Cook until thickened, stirring constantly. Taste and adjust seasonings. Strain the sauce, add the remaining rosemary, and pour over the fish. Garnish with parsley and serve warm.

PSARI MARINATO
[Marinated fish]

TO SERVE 4 TO 5

Salt

2 pounds fresh fish (whole or large slices), cleaned and washed

Juice of 1 lemon

Flour

Freshly ground pepper (optional)

Vegetable oil for frying to depth of ½ inch

½ cup olive or vegetable oil

½ cup red wine vinegar

2 to 3 tablespoons white wine

½ cup tomato juice or diluted tomato purée

Herbs: 1 bay leaf, 2 sprigs fresh parsley, 1 sprig fresh rosemary, or 1 teaspoon dried rosemary

½ teaspoon granulated sugar

2 to 3 cloves garlic, sliced

1 whole lemon, quartered, and chopped fresh rosemary for garnish

Salt the fish, then sprinkle with lemon juice and roll in seasoned or unseasoned flour. Heat the vegetable oil in a heavy frying pan, and fry the fish, turning once. Drain on paper toweling, then arrange on a serving platter, allowing space between each fish. Set aside while you prepare the marinade.

Pour off the oil from the pan, but do not scrape clean. Put in the olive oil and heat gradually, then add 3 tablespoons of flour, stirring constantly with a wooden spoon until a very light chestnut color. Add the vinegar (it will sizzle), then continually stirring, add the wine, tomato juice, seasonings, herbs, sugar, and garlic. Simmer for 15 to 20 minutes, then strain immediately over the fish. Allow to cool uncovered. Garnish with lemon wedges and sprinkle with a little rosemary. Serve cool.

Note: If planning to serve several days after preparing, add a few tablespoons more vinegar.

PSARI VRASTO KRITIKO
[Poached fish, Cretan style]

Various regions vary the basic recipe below by adding other vegetables—carrots, celery, and shallots in lieu of onions, small squash and such favorite herbs as dill, in addition to potatoes. The vegetables are arranged around the fish and the fish stock transformed into a delicious soup, usually *psarosoupa avgolemono,* an unforgettable taste when made by a good cook in Greece.

TO SERVE 5 TO 6

2 pounds fish suitable for poaching (such as cod, mackerel, carp, trout, haddock, salmon)
Lemon juice
2 quarts water
1/4 cup olive oil

Herbs: 2 bay leaves, 8 peppercorns, 2 sprigs fresh thyme, 3 sprigs fresh parsley, tied in a cheesecloth
10 small onions, peeled but left whole
10 small potatoes, peeled but left whole
Salt and freshly ground pepper
Chopped fresh parsley for garnish

Slice large fish into inch-thick steaks and leave small fish whole, if desired. Sprinkle with lemon juice and set aside.

In a soup kettle or fish poacher, bring the water to a boil, then add the oil, herbs, and onions. Cover and simmer 15 minutes, then add the potatoes and continue simmering until the vegetables are tender. Remove with a slotted spoon and keep warm.

Carefully lower the fish into the court bouillon and poach over low heat, below the boiling point, for 15 minutes, or until tender (one-inch cod steaks require less than 15 minutes). Season with salt and pepper. Carefully lift the fish, without breaking, and arrange on a warm platter, then surround with the potatoes and onions. Garnish with chopped parsley.

Note: Greeks rarely need a dressing with their delicious fish, but prefer Ladolemono (page 54). The remaining fish bouillon is strained for *psarosoupa avgolemono* (page 82) which is served as the first course.

PSARI KRASATO
[Poached fish in wine with herbs]

Mackerel, tuna, eel, or whatever—suitable for stewing or poaching —may be your choice for this favored and quick style for fish.

TO SERVE 5 OR 6

2 pounds fish suitable for stewing
Salt and freshly ground pepper
Juice of 1 lemon
½ cup olive oil
2 large onions, chopped
1 cup dry white wine, approximately

1 cup tomato juice, approximately
1 clove garlic, sliced (optional)
1 small bunch fresh parsley,
  chopped
1 small bunch fresh dill,
  chopped

If using a large fish, cut it into ½-inch slices; cut smaller fish in half. Wash and dry, then sprinkle with salt and pepper and squeeze lemon juice over all sides. Set aside.

Heat the oil in a large pot and cook the onions until soft. Stir the wine into the onions, then add the tomato juice, garlic, and herbs, and simmer for 15 minutes. Slip the fish into the sauce, along with additional wine, or water, or tomato juice to cover. Cover and simmer (about 20 to 25 minutes) until the fish is fork-tender and the sauce is thickened. Using a spatula, carefully lift the fish to a warm platter. Spoon the sauce over the fish and serve warm or cold.

PSARI STIFADO
[Fish, stifado style]

Stifado means "stew" in Italian, but Greek people gave the word another meaning—all stifado dishes are cooked with small white onions, wine, and spicy seasonings. In Greece, plentiful cod is used most frequently, but other available thick slices of any stewing or braising fish may be substituted.

TO SERVE 6

1½ pounds salt or fresh cod
⅓ cup olive oil
1 cup tomato juice
½ cup dry red or white wine
2 tablespoons red wine vinegar
1 teaspoon granulated sugar
2 bay leaves
3 whole cloves

Salt and freshly ground pepper
2 cloves garlic, sliced
1½ pounds small white onions,
peel and root end slashed with
a knife tip
Fresh parsley or watercress for
garnish

If using salt cod, soak overnight or longer in cold water, changing the water at least once. Cut into serving pieces and combine in a baking-serving casserole with all the other ingredients except the garnish. Cover and cook in a slow oven (250 degrees) for 1½ hours. Serve hot or cold, garnish with parsley or watercress with olives, fresh salad, and Greek wine.

BOURTHETO
[Peppery fish stew, Corfu style]

This lovely island in the Ionian Sea enjoys quite a few hot dishes including this one which is especially good made with assorted fish.

TO SERVE 4 TO 5

¼ cup olive oil
1 cup water, more if necessary
2 large onions, sliced in rings
Salt and freshly ground pepper
Paprika

Dash of cayenne pepper
1½ to 2 pounds assorted fish for
stewing (carp, perch, trout,
cod, mackerel, etc.)
Fresh parsley for garnish

In a large pan, combine the oil, water, onions, salt and pepper, ¼ teaspoon paprika and cayenne and simmer until the onions are almost tender. Wash and slice the fish into large, uniform pieces, then set the pieces carefully in the pan with the onions, adding a little water if necessary to cover the fish. Partially cover the pan and simmer over low heat for 15 to 20 minutes, or until the fish is tender. Using a spatula, lift the fish out onto a warm serving platter. Surround with the onions and pour the remaining sauce in the pan over the fish. Sprinkle lightly with additional paprika, garnish with parsley, and serve warm. This is especially good with boiled greens served with *ladolemono* dressing, followed by thick, fresh yogurt.

ASTAKOS
[*Lobster*]

Greek seas produce the rock, or "spiny" lobster, which lacks heavy claws, having instead long, thin ones as well as long, thin antennae and spines on body and legs. Lobster is a luxury as it must have been for 2300 years. When returning from a coastal trip, the first thing Greek friends asked us was, "Did you eat lobster?" Archestratus stated it more bluntly in the third century B.C. when he said, "But letting a lot of trash go, buy yourself a lobster, the kind which has long claws, and heavy withal, with feet that are small. . . ." Despite years of adulation, however, lobster cookery is quite simple. The cookery methods used for rock lobster may also be used for northern lobsters.

TO SERVE 1 TO 2

1 quart cold water	*2 sprigs fresh thyme*
1 stalk celery, sliced	*1 bay leaf*
1 onion, sliced	*1 cup white wine*
1 carrot, sliced	*1 teaspoon salt*
3 sprigs fresh parsley	*1 large lobster*

In a pot large enough to accommodate the lobster, put the 1 quart cold water, then add the sliced vegetables, parsley, thyme, bay leaf, wine, and salt. Bring to boil, plunge in the lobster, and simmer for 20 to 30 minutes or until tender. Remove from the heat and allow the lobster to stand in the cooking water for 10 minutes, then remove from the pot with tongs and drain. Reserve the cooking liquid (see note below). Separate body from tail. Cut open the body shell and remove and discard the intestinal vein, liver, gills, and stomach but reserving the pink coral if a female lobster; see note below. Remove all the lobster meat, including the sweet meat between the "bones," and in the long claws. Cut the meat into bite-size slices.

Note: The female's pink coral should be saved for a garnish, to color the sauce, or to form the base for Coral Sauce.

Strain the liquid in which the lobster was cooked and use for stock in cooking soup, rice, or sauce.

CORAL SAUCE

Pink Coral (eggs) from a cooked female lobster
2 to 3 tablespoons olive oil
Juice of ½ lemon
½ teaspoon prepared Dijon-style mustard
Pinch of fresh marjoram or thyme (optional)

Remove the coral from the lobster and beat in a medium bowl using an electric mixer, or in a blender, or use a mortar and pestle. Continuing to beat, gradually add the olive oil, lemon juice, and prepared mustard. A pinch of herb may also be added, if desired. Spoon over the cold lobster meat.

Note: Prepare the sauce as close to serving time as possible to prevent separation.

ASTAKOS MAYONEZA
[*Lobster mayonnaise*]

One of the more popular methods of serving lobster in seaside *tavernes* of Corfu and a favorite on Mykonos and, in fact, wherever you can find lobsters.

TO SERVE 2

1 large lobster, prepared and meat
removed as directed on page
122, body shell reserved
1 cup mayonnaise (page 54)
Squeeze of fresh lemon juice
Dash of vinegar

1 tablespoon minced shallots
Pinch of cayenne pepper
Milk, if necessary
Finely chopped fresh parsley or
rosemary for garnish

Cut up the cooked lobster meat into finger-sized rounds. Wash and dry the reserved shells. Spice the mayonnaise with the lemon juice, vinegar, minced shallots, and cayenne pepper. Whip for a minute, and add a little milk if necessary to lighten the mayonnaise. Fill the lobster shells with the sliced lobster, spoon the mayonnaise over, and sprinkle with finely chopped parsley or rosemary.

OKTAPODI MARATHO KRASATO
[*Octopus and fennel in wine, Cretan style*]

Delicious and an excellent appetizer. If made with scallions or onions and a clove or two of garlic instead of the fennel, the dish would be like the mainland favorite *oktapodi krasato* (octopus in wine).

TO SERVE 4

> *1 medium octopus*
> *1 medium onion or 5 scallions, chopped*
> *⅓ cup olive oil*
> *1 cup dry red wine*
> *1 bunch fennel, chopped*
> *3 to 4 fresh or canned tomatoes, peeled, seeded, and chopped*
> *Salt and freshly ground pepper*

Beat and flay the octopus according to the directions on page 62. Using a sharp knife, cut into rounds the width of a small finger. Heat the oil in a *tsikali* or any pot, add the onion, and cook until translucent and soft. Add the round octopus slices to the onion, pour in the wine, and simmer for 15 minutes. Put the fennel and tomatoes on top of the octopus, season with salt and pepper to taste, and give the pot a good shake to mix. Cover and simmer until the octopus is fork-tender (approximately 45 to 50 minutes). Serve warm or cold.

GARIDES KOKKIYIA ME FETA
[*Baked shrimp and feta in shells*]

The squirming shrimp leaped forth like dolphins into the rope-twined pot. ATHENAEUS

A favorite at the taverns of Tourkolimano near Piraeus.

TO SERVE 6

2 pounds large shrimp, shelled
 and deveined
Juice of 1/2 lemon
1 onion or shallot, minced
3 tablespoons vegetable oil or
 butter
1/2 cup canned tomato sauce plus
 2 to 3 tomatoes, peeled,
 chopped and drained

1/4 cup chopped fresh parsley
2 tablespoons chopped fresh basil
 or dill
2 cloves garlic, crushed
Salt and freshly ground pepper
1/2 pound feta cheese
Fresh basil leaves (or parsley)
 for garnish

Wash and drain the raw shrimp, then sprinkle lightly with lemon juice. Heat the oil or butter in a frying pan and cook the onion until soft. Add the tomato sauce, herbs, garlic, and salt and pepper to taste. Simmer for 25 minutes, then remove from the heat and strain.

Butter large scallop or other shells, or individual ovenproof dishes, and spoon a little sauce into each. Fill with the shrimp and spoon the sauce over, then crumble the feta over the top. Set into a baking pan and bake for 15 to 20 minutes in a moderate oven (350 degrees), or until the shrimp is cooked and the cheese melted. Garnish with fresh basil or parsley and serve hot.

HOHLI BARBOURISTI
[Fried snails with vinegar, Cretan style]

The Greek gift for having a word for it applies richly to snails, usually called *salingaria* on the mainland, but *hohli* on Crete and *karaoli* on Cyprus. *Hohli* are a favorite Cretan food, and the delicious cooking methods explain why. Snails are scrupulously avoided except in summer, when they are considered safe to eat. Since snails absorb the odors and taste of foods on which they feed, Cretans catch them after a rainfall, put them in a covered container, and feed them for several days on wheat, flour, and perhaps some thyme. Then the real fun begins.

The amounts of the other ingredients in this recipe and the next are based on a pound of snails. One pound of snails serves 1 to 2.

First be sure all the snails are alive, then wash them thoroughly in cold water and place in their shells in a container large enough to hold them. Pour hot water over them to cover and bring to a boil. Add a teaspoon of salt for each quart of water and continue to boil for 20 minutes, skimming off the foam. Drain the snails, then wash in cold water and drain again.

In a deep, heavy pan, heat olive oil almost to the boiling point, using ½ cup olive oil per pound of snails. Add the snails and fry for 10 minutes, turning carefully with tongs to avoid spattering the oil. Pour in ¼ cup red wine vinegar for each pound of snails. Remove from heat and stir constantly for a few minutes. Remove the snails to individual plates and serve hot with a little of the remaining sauce, and some bread and wine, as an appetizer or first course.

HOHLI ME DOMATES
[Snails braised with tomatoes, Cretan style]

Cretans appear to eat snails with everything. Some other favorites are *hohli me hondro* (with wheat), *hohli me kolokithakia* (with zucchini) and *hohli me patates* (with potatoes).

Prepare the snails according to directions on page 125. Then, in a deep, heavy pan, heat ½ cup olive oil per pound of snails, add some salt for seasoning and then the snails. Cover, lower the heat, and cook for 10 minutes, turning once. Add a grated onion and ¼ cup chopped fresh parsley per pound of snails. Stir over medium heat for a few minutes, then add a pound of peeled, chopped tomatoes for each pound of snails. Cover and simmer for 30 minutes, or until the tomatoes are tender. Serve with fried potatoes and baby zucchini salad.

TARAMOKEFTEDES
[Seasoned fish roe keftedes]

Tarama, available in jars commercially, makes an excellent base for tiny croquettes for appetizers or larger ones for an entrée. Either size needs the right touch in seasoning.

TO MAKE 25 TO 30

1 cup tarama
2 medium potatoes, boiled, peeled, and mashed
4 slices white bread, crusts removed, soaked in cold water, and squeezed dry
1/4 cup fresh minced parsley
2 tablespoons fresh minced dill

2 to 3 mint leaves, minced
Freshly ground pepper
1 tablespoon lemon juice
3 tablespoons all-purpose flour
3 scallions, minced
Vegetable oil
Crushed zwieback, if necessary

Place the tarama in a bowl and cover with warm water for 30 minutes. Drain through a fine-mesh strainer or 4 thicknesses cheesecloth, then rinse with cold water and drain. Combine the mashed potatoes and the tarama in a large bowl, then add the soaked bread, parsley, dill, mint, a little pepper, the lemon juice, and flour. Knead thoroughly. Sauté the scallions in the 1 tablespoon oil and add to the tarama mixture, then cover and refrigerate overnight, if possible, or for several hours at least. Taramokeftedes may be dropped by teaspoonfuls into boiling oil, and deep-fried, or if preferred rolled into walnut-sized balls with enough crushed zwieback added to thicken the mixture. When they rise to the surface, taramokeftedes should be turned over with tongs to fry on the other side. Drain on paper towels and serve hot.

KALAMARAKIA YEMISTA
[Baked stuffed squid]

A delicacy that calls for cries of "bravo" when prepared by skilled fingers. Delicious the second day, cold—if any leftovers remain!

TO SERVE 5

1 pound squid (approximately 16 medium size)
Salt
6 tablespoons olive oil
1 onion, chopped
1/3 cup raw long-grain white rice
1/2 cup chopped fresh parsley
1/4 cup chopped fresh mint leaves

1/3 cup plus 2 tablespoons white wine
1/4 cup pine nuts
1/4 cup black raisins
Freshly ground pepper
4 to 5 fresh or canned peeled tomatoes, drained

Wash and clean the squid, separating the outer sacs from the heads and tentacles, removing and discarding the translucent cartilage, and small sand bag and ink. Rub salt on the outer sacs and rinse them inside and out with cold water. Heads and tentacles should be rinsed thoroughly and cooked along with the sacs after you stuff the latter. Drain and set aside.

Heat 1/4 cup of the oil in a heavy frying pan, then add the onion and cook, without browning, until transparent. Stir in the rice and sauté a few minutes, until golden. Blend in the parsley, mint, 2 tablespoons wine, pine nuts, and raisins, and season with salt and pepper to taste. Add enough water to half cover and cook for a few minutes, then stuff the squid sacs with the mixture using a very small spoon and allowing enough liquid in each for the rice to cook. Seal opening with skewers or toothpicks. Place the stuffed sacs with the heads and tentacles in a baking-serving dish. Sprinkle with salt and pepper and set aside.

Meanwhile, combine the tomatoes, 1/3 cup wine, and a little salt and pepper in a small saucepan and simmer for 5 minutes. Pour the sauce over the squid and dribble the remaining 2 tablespoons olive oil over the top. Bake in a medium-slow oven (300 degrees) for 1 1/2 hours or until the squid and rice are tender and the sauce has thickened. Serve warm or cold.

KALAMARAKIA KRASATA
[Squid in wine sauce]

Do not make the stuffing for the squid, but otherwise prepare the same as for the recipe above. To the drained tomatoes for the sauce, add 2 chopped cloves garlic, 1 bay leaf, and a large sprig of fresh rosemary with the wine and simmer for 10 minutes before adding the squid, then bake for 1 1/2 hours in a slow oven (250 degrees).

128

MEATS

CULTURAL HABIT GIVES TO MEAT (*kreata*) a special position among foods, reserving it for Sundays, holidays, celebrations—a blessing, considering the high cost. Provincial families reserve meat for the special Sunday dinner. And in the cities Hellenes happily survive with meat for dinner twice, or three times at most, weekly. Cheese, yogurt, fish, and seafood supply joy (and animal proteins), allowing meat to remain on its pedestal.

This does not indicate prejudice or religious taboo. Greek Orthodoxy has not imposed sanctions against any meats, as the Hindu, Moslem, or Judaic religions have. On the contrary, Greeks have eaten many meats throughout history since the Bronze Age, according to archeological evidence. Homer's testimonial for many meats remains a clear record. And except for small philosophical sects such as the Pythagorean one, no compulsory meat fasting was practiced. Periodical abstinence from meat and dairy products is imposed on the Greek people for spiritual reasons. The principle is to curtail physical indulgence in order to improve self-examination and the spiritual life.

Hippocrates in his *Regimen* classified many meats that were consumed, some of which have gradually disappeared from Greek eating habits, such as horse, ass, dog, fox, and hedgehog, although wild boar, deer, and hare are still specialties today. The great physician specifically suggests dog flesh for the treatment of diarrhea. But although dogs are no longer eaten in Greece, there persists a general animosity toward the dog, most forlorn of creatures—except possibly for the miserable cats that wander into outdoor *tavernes*.

Comparing the relative effects of flesh on the human metabolism, Hippocrates names birds "drier" than beasts, and includes among the favorites of his times doves, partridges, and pigeons.

Literary sources before the Christian period are rich with meat references—methods of cooking, tricks and skills used in preparation, and how they are served and enjoyed. The cookery was varied: smoking, salting, boiling, stewing, preserving in salt and vinegar, roasting on spits or in pots. Even the Spartans, considered frugal eaters, enjoyed the *aiklon*, consisting of loaves of bread and a piece of meat following meals.

A certain mystique of meats is reflected in tales and proverbs. Beast fables have been used for centuries in Greece to explain human motives. A particularly Greek favorite is, of course, the lamb. "A lamb that God looks after won't be eaten by a wolf," they say. The sheep, adored and protected throughout its pastoral history, has always been supreme in Greek folk culture. Hellenes will explain the behavior of a "wild" child with "The wolf cannot become a sheep!"

Lamb is also king of beasts when it comes to eating. Tradition repeats the annual outdoor spitting and roasting of lamb, Arni Souvlas (page 131), on Easter, a particularly festive day and the highlight of Greek religious and outdoor life. Lamb is cooked and eaten very young, under one year whenever possible. Young lamb cooks more quickly, is more tender, and has much better flavor than older lamb and mutton (unknown in Greece). Lamb is also most plentiful, with about three million heads of lamb slaughtered for food annually, twice as much as goat, and more than four times as much veal less than one year old. Calves slaughtered between one and two years are fewer in number.

Based on a seasonal market, meats rotate from lamb in spring to veal in summer and pork in winter with a great deal of overlapping, particularly with imported meats. We saw Bulgarian lamb in the large Athens market in midsummer, when Greek lamb was more expensive. (While Greek annual meat production increased to three hundred thousand tons in recent years, more than double its volume of a decade earlier, Greece must still import to meet the demand from Hellenes.) Other available animal-flesh foods include buffaloes, piglets, heifers, oxen, poultry, and rabbits.

One of the favorite ways of serving meat, in addition to outdoor barbecues, is as a roast, usually served in combination with pasta, grain, potatoes, or other vegetables (one at a time), and with sauce from the meat. All over Greece, including Athens, people continue to enjoy the privilege of having their Sunday meat baked in the community oven— the *fourno*. As they carry it home, their eyes relish the food, while their noses absorb the aroma in eager anticipation.

In homes and typical Greek *tavernes*, braised dishes outnumber others. With the increased circulation of popular Greek magazines, the old Turkish names are gradually being displaced by others. Greek? *mais non*, mostly French and English anonyms! *Yiahni* and *kokkinisto* (on menus in all regions) are being simmered as *braisé* and *ragoût* But the dishes taste like the marvelous *katsarolas* (pot) dishes, for, after all, the pinches of flavorful herbs and the fingers of the cooks are Greek. Does it matter if the Greeks keep finding a new word for them? From tradition emerge the fabulous rolled, sliced, stuffed, wrapped, jellied, cold, glazed, steaming, bright, and saucy specialties.

A note about the recipes that follow: To make the Greek principle work (because meats as well as other Greek foods are chosen on seasonal availability), many dishes can be made by the same method using available meat: pork, veal, and lamb usually, but also goat and some beef in Greece.

ARNI SOUVLAS
[*Barbecued whole lamb*]

The most climactic, traditional Greek method of preparing and serving lamb—outdoors. Easter preparation of lamb on the *souvla* (spit) is an unforgettable experience, a joint cooking venture of many ages in a very large family setting. Festivities mount during the cooking of the paschal lamb, which requires hours, expertise, lots of willing hands, and patience, to turn and baste the lamb and regulate the heat. Whole lambs are plentiful in spring in Greece, but not in American supermarkets. They are, however, available in specialty meat markets if ordered in advance. Buy the entire lamb, have it cleaned, and save all the parts to cook in any number of tasty ways.

After the head, trotters and innards are removed, wash and dry the lamb. Sprinkle with salt and pepper inside and out and fasten securely to a strong spit that is at least a foot longer than the lamb on each end (the Greeks use strong tree limbs). Strong twine should be used at both ends and also at the center of the backbone to control turning of the lamb on the spit.

Meanwhile, both the fire and the marinade should be ready. The coals must be banked so that the maximum heat is aimed toward the thighs and shoulders and the least toward the breast. The marinade may be whisked in a bowl. (The usual Greek marinade is 1 cup of oil, juice of 2 to 3 lemons, 1 tablespoon crumbled oregano, and salt and pepper,

which will have to be replenished several times during the cooking.)
Rub the marinade into the lamb's entire surface and use it to baste
periodically.

The length of cooking will vary considerably according to the size
of the lamb, the air temperature, and the heat in the coals. The smaller
lambs in Greece, approximately 22 to 25 pounds, may be roasted in 3
hours. Larger lambs may need 5 to 7 hours of slow cooking to avoid
burning the exterior, plus frequent turning and marinating. Crush
oregano over the lamb when roasted and serve warm.

Note: The other outdoor Greek meat festival is on August 15,
Assumption Day, when suckling pig takes star billing for the day. *Hirino
souvlas* is delicious with its crisp skin and tender meat. The marinade is
the same, with lots of lemon juice.

ARNI FRIKASEE
[Lamb braised with vegetables and herbs]

Greek cooks prepare this dish by stewing or by braising as in this
recipe.

TO SERVE 4 TO 5

1/4 cup olive oil or shortening	1/4 cup chopped fresh parsley
2 1/2 pounds lean lamb, cut into serving pieces	3 sprigs fresh thyme or 1 teaspoon dried thyme
2 medium onions, chopped	1 bay leaf
2 cloves garlic, sliced	Salt and freshly ground pepper
2 carrots, sliced	3 tablespoons margarine
2 stalks celery, sliced	3 tablespoons all-purpose flour

In a heavy braising pot, heat the oil, then add the lamb and onions and
sauté for 5 minutes, turning the lamb on all sides. Add the garlic, carrots, celery, parsley, thyme, bay leaf, and salt and pepper to taste and
cook for a few minutes, stirring constantly. Add hot water to cover the
meat and vegetables. Bring to a boil, cover, then lower the heat and
simmer until the meat is tender, about 50 minutes, removing the carrots
and celery when cooked and reserving in a bowl. Remove the meat,
arrange on a serving platter with the cooked vegetables, and keep warm.

Put the remaining broth through a sieve, pushing through as much
of the vegetables and herbs as possible, then discard the rough fibers

remaining in the sieve. Skim the fat from the broth and discard, then boil the broth down to 1½ cups. Prepare sauce as suggested for Saltsa Aspri (page 50) using the margarine, flour and remaining broth instead of milk. Pour over the meat and vegetables and serve warm.

Note: Peeled, quartered potatoes may be added during the last 20 minutes of cooking time and served arranged on the platter with the lamb and other vegetables.

ARNI ME ANGINARES KAI ANITHON
[Lamb with artichokes and dill]

A sensational combination made in this style, with tomatoes, or minus the tomatoes with the familiar *avgolemono*.

TO SERVE 4

2 to 3 tablespoons olive oil
1 pound lean, stewing lamb or
  rib chops, cut into serving
  pieces
2 onions, chopped
3 fresh or canned tomatoes,
  peeled and sliced
2 teaspoons tomato paste

6 globe artichokes, cleaned and
  quartered lengthwise
Juice of 1 lemon
Salt and freshly ground pepper
Small bunch of fresh dill,
  chopped
4–5 sprigs fresh parsley, chopped

In a heavy pan, heat the oil, then add the lamb and onions and sauté for a few minutes, stirring constantly. Reduce the heat, add the tomatoes, tomato paste, and enough water to almost cover the meat, stir, cover the pan, and simmer for 30 minutes.

Meanwhile, sprinkle the artichokes with lemon juice to prevent discoloration, then slip them into the pan with the lamb, adding water if necessary, cover, and continue cooking until artichokes are tender and meat is falling off the bones. Season with salt and pepper and add the dill and parsley during the last 20 minutes of cooking. The sauce should be thick. Serve warm with feta cheese, a crisp salad, and a full-bodied Greek wine.

ARNI EXOHIKO
["Surprise" lamb, country style]

An exciting way to surprise family or guests, this dish originated in the provinces.

TO SERVE 8

2 tablespoons olive oil or clarified butter (see page 40)
8 loin lamb chops, or 8 ¾-inch slices leg of lamb
16 to 18 sheets commercial filo pastry
6 tablespoons hot and melted butter or margarine
2 cups fresh or canned garden peas, cooked and drained

16 potato balls, parboiled and drained
16 cherry tomatoes, peeled
½ pound kasseri cheese, cut into 8 pieces
Salt and freshly ground pepper
¾ cup chopped fresh parsley
Pinch of dried oregano

In a heavy skillet, heat the oil or butter and fry the lamb over high heat, turning frequently. Lower the heat and simmer for 15 minutes, then remove from the heat. Meanwhile, unroll the *filo* sheets and cover with a damp towel. In a small pan over low heat, have the butter hot without letting it brown. Remove two sheets of *filo*, brush hot butter over the first, then cover with the second sheet and brush it with butter. In the center of the buttered *filo* place 1 lamb chop, 2 tablespoons peas, 2 potato balls, 2 cherry tomatoes, and a slice of kasseri. Sprinkle with salt and pepper, a heaping tablespoon of parsley, and a pinch of oregano. Fold the *filo* around the lamb and vegetables like a sealed parcel. Place, seam side down, on a buttered baking pan (approximately 11 x 15 x 3 inches) and set aside while you repeat the procedure with the remaining ingredients to make 8 "parcels." Brush hot butter on the tops, then bake in a moderate oven (350 degrees) for 45 to 50 minutes or until golden in color. Remove from the oven and arrange on a warm platter or on individual dishes. Serve warm, with a fresh-cooked or raw vegetable salad.

Note: The vegetables and herbs may be varied. Substitute green beans or lima beans for peas, use thyme or basil instead of oregano. *Arni exohiko* is frequently prepared using buttered waxed paper or aluminum foil rather than with *filo*.

ARNI PSITO ME KASTANA
[Rosemary-flavored lamb roasted with chestnuts]

Lamb is traditionally the favorite Greek meal, and it is no secret that *arni psito* is a festive method of cooking the leg and shoulder particularly. A certain amount of moist heat accompanies the roasting process, for Greeks invariably add a little water during the cooking, or perhaps tomatoes, or wine, or some of each. The precious *saltsa*, or liquid from the lamb during roasting, is never wasted (see page 103), but becomes the base in which to cook potatoes, tomatoes, pasta, and vegetables planned to accompany the lamb during the meal. Greek cooks are not prone to thicken the drippings, but will pour the hot sauce over the meat if any remains.

Greek lamb is always eaten very young, consequently it is less fatty and cooks more quickly than American varieties. Lamb roasting methods may be applied to other meats—particularly leg of veal or fresh ham.

TO SERVE 6 TO 8

> *1 leg of lamb*
> *Salt and freshly ground pepper*
> *Juice of 1 lemon*
> *Fresh rosemary*
> *1½ to 2 pounds chestnuts, parboiled and peeled*

Wipe the lamb with a damp cloth, then rub with salt and pepper and sprinkle generously with lemon juice. Using the tip of a sharp knife, make small slashes in the flesh of the lamb and insert sprigs of rosemary using about 6 small sprigs. Roast in a moderate oven (350 degrees) allowing 25 to 30 minutes per pound, until an internal temperature of 180 degrees, basting with meat drippings frequently and turning the meat so it roasts evenly on all sides. Put the chestnuts around the meat after the first hour of cooking. Remove from the oven and transfer the chestnuts to a warm serving platter, but allow the lamb to rest in the pan for 15 minutes before carving. Place on the platter with the chestnuts and serve warm, garnished with additional rosemary.

Note: Strain meat drippings, refrigerate until fat is chilled, remove and discard. Use the remaining liquid as a base.

MOSHARI ME KASTANA
[*Veal with chestnuts*]

For another superb combination, substitute 2 pounds lean veal in
1-inch cubes, but sauté the meat in butter first, then simmer in ½ cup
dry white wine before adding the chestnuts as described above. Add 1
bay leaf and 3 tablespoons raisins during the last 15 minutes.

ARNI ME YAOURTI
[*Roast lamb with spicy yogurt sauce, Cretan style*]

TO SERVE 8

1 leg of lamb
Salt and freshly ground pepper
2 cloves garlic, cut into slivers
1 cup canned tomatoes or tomato
  sauce (optional)

1½ cups plain yogurt
1 egg (optional)
½ teaspoon ground cinnamon
½ teaspoon all-purpose flour

Wipe the lamb with damp towels, then rub with salt and pepper. With
a sharp knife, slash the meat and insert the garlic slivers. Put in a baking
pan and roast in a moderate oven (350 degrees) until cooked but not
dry, adding the tomatoes during the last hour, if desired. Remove the
tomatoes and drippings from pan and save for future use, leaving the
lamb in the pan. Meanwhile, combine the yogurt, egg, cinnamon, and
flour in a bowl and whisk hard for 2 minutes. Pour over the meat and
continue baking for 10 to 15 minutes, or until the sauce is firm. Serve
warm, with grain or potato dish and salad.

ARNI STO LADOHARTO
[*Lamb baked with seasonings in paper*]

Traditional, delicious, and dependable. Wrapped meats are frequently called *klephtika* (thieves). The story goes that the Greeks
had to steal meat from the Turks and that they cooked it in skins so the
Turks could not smell the aromas. Best served steaming when first unwrapped after roasting, this is easier to carve if boned.

Veal, beef, or pork may be substituted for lamb in this recipe.

TO SERVE 6 TO 8

1 leg of lamb, boned
2 cloves garlic, slivered
Salt and freshly ground pepper
2 bay leaves, crushed
½ cup chopped fresh parsley
¼ cup chopped fresh thyme or
*   2 teaspoons dried thyme*

Grated rind of 1 lemon (about
*   1 tablespoon)*
Juice of 1 lemon
Greaseproof baking paper and
*   string*
Olive oil

Wipe off the lamb with a damp cloth and cut off the excess fat. With the tip of a sharp knife, make incisions here and there in the flesh of the lamb and insert the garlic slivers. Rub the lamb with salt and pepper, then sprinkle the crushed bay leaves, parsley, thyme, and lemon rind over both sides of the lamb and roll tightly lengthwise. Set the lamb roll on a piece of greaseproof paper and pour the lemon juice over it, then brush lightly with olive oil. Roll the paper tightly around the lamb and close sides as you would a parcel. Tie with string. Brush the outside of the paper with olive oil and set the wrapped lamb in a baking pan. Bake in a moderate oven (350 degrees) for 30 minutes, then reduce the heat to 325 degrees for an additional 1½ hours. Serve warm, with potatoes or grain dish, yogurt, and fresh vegetables, and of course, a Greek wine.

KOTOLETTES ARNIOU LADORIGANI SKARAS
[Barbecued lamb chops marinated with lemon and oregano]

If you prefer, instead of barbecuing, the chops may be fried in a small amount of vegetable fat, breaded or plain. Veal or pork chops may be substituted in either method.

TO SERVE 6

Landolemono (page 54) using ¼ cup olive oil, juice of 1 lemon
*   and ½ teaspoon oregano*
6 to 8 loin or rib lamb chops
Salt and freshly ground pepper
½ teaspoon dried oregano leaves
1 lemon, cut into 8 wedges

Whisk the oil, lemon juice, and oregano in a glass or earthenware bowl large enough to hold the chops. Add the chops to the marinade and allow to marinate for 2 hours at room temperature or 4 hours in the refrigerator, turning twice. Barbecue over hot charcoal, turning once, sprinkling with salt and pepper and using the remaining marinade to baste the chops. Place the chops on a warm platter and crumble oregano over. Garnish the platter with the lemon wedges. Serve hot. Delicious with Horiatiki Salata (page 212).

SOUVLAKIA APO ARNI
[Marinated lamb on skewers]

Equally delicious with veal using marjoram or thyme as seasoning.

TO SERVE 8

1 leg of lamb, boned and cut into walnut-sized cubes

5 baby lamb sweetbreads, cubed the size of the lamb (optional)

4 baby lamb kidneys, cubed the size of the lamb (optional)

1/4 cup olive oil

Juice of 1 lemon

1/4 cup wine

1/4 teaspoon each thyme or oregano and rosemary

1 bay leaf, crushed

2 garlic cloves, crushed

Freshly ground black pepper

8 bay leaves, cut

Firm tomatoes, quartered (optional)

Firm green peppers, cubed (optional)

Salt

Oregano and lemon quarters for garnish

Place the lamb, sweetbreads, and kidney cubes in a large glass or earthenware bowl. Make a marinade of the oil, lemon juice, wine, herbs, garlic, and pepper and pour over the meat. Marinate in the refrigerator, preferably overnight, or for at least 3 hours. Thread the meat on long skewers alternating the bay leaves with the tomatoes and peppers, if desired. Grill over hot coals or broil 6 inches from the heat, brushing with the remaining marinade and turning frequently. Season with salt and pepper, then remove the meat from the skewers to warm platter and crush oregano over the top. Garnish with lemon quarters and serve hot.

SKORDOSTOUMBI
[Braised garlic-flavored steaks, Zante style]

Lamb or veal steaks are usually used for this dish, which is identified with the Ionian island of Zante. But thin beef flank or round steaks may be substituted. Similar dishes are prepared in other regions wherever strong garlic preference lingers. When one Athenian was reminiscing about *skordostoumbi* as made by his mother, all he could remember in vivid detail was the garlic!

TO SERVE 4 PER POUND

Have the steaks cut ½-inch thick, and allow at least one per person. Using a mallet-type meat tenderizer or the side of a cutting board, pound the steaks until flat. Cut into convenient serving pieces and season each side of each piece with salt, pepper, and ½ teaspoon vinegar. Flour lightly and sauté on each side in a thin layer of hot oil. Drain, then arrange in a cooking-serving pan, and surround with as much minced garlic as desired (1 clove garlic per person would be a reasonable amount, though conservative by Greek standards), and 2 peeled, sliced tomatoes per pound of meat, salt, pepper, and a little sugar, chopped parsley, and 1 teaspoon basil. Pour ½ cup white wine over each pound of steaks, and give the pan a shake to mix, cover tightly, and simmer for 50 minutes, or until tender. (Or *skordostoumbi* may be baked in a moderate oven.) Serve with cooked grain, pasta, or potatoes, and a fresh salad.

ARNI/MOSHARI KOKKINISTO
["Reddened" lamb or veal]

Lamb seared and braised with tomatoes, aromatic vegetables, and herbs is "reddened" during the searing process and named *kokkinisto*. This standard method of preparing lamb, as well as veal, is also known as *katsarolas* (pot), *yiahni* (the Turkish word for braised dishes), *entrada* (entrée), and more recently *ragoût* (the French word for braised dishes). Combinations of lamb (or veal) with one vegetable or pasta are usually the rule, whether cooked together from the start, combined for part of the time, or cooked separately and served together. Variations are

139

infinite, possibly adding to the dish's great popularity with Greek cooks, who may create a combination according to whim or mood.

TO SERVE 6

2½ pounds lean lamb or veal,
preferably leg or shoulder
Salt and freshly ground pepper
All-purpose flour for dredging
5 tablespoons vegetable oil, and
butter or margarine, combined
1 medium onion, chopped, or
3 to 4 scallions, chopped

1½ to 2 cups canned tomatoes,
strained or canned tomato sauce
or juice
Aromatic seasonings (chopped
celery, parsley, mint, dill,
basil, bay leaf, garlic, carrot,
thyme, savory, etc.)
½ cup dry white wine (optional)
½ teaspoon granulated sugar

Cut the meat into uniform serving portions or walnut-sized cubes, then dredge with salt, pepper, and flour. (The latter will insure a thicker sauce.) Heat the fat in a heavy braising pot and sear the meat on all sides, then lower the heat and add the onions. Cook, stirring constantly, until the onions soften. Meanwhile, in a small pan heat the tomatoes with seasonings of your choice, preferably a little chopped celery, very little carrot, parsley and another herb, and salt and pepper. (Plan to add the herbs toward the end of the cooking, whenever possible.) Stir the tomatoes into the meat, then add the wine and enough water to cover. As the liquid begins to boil, lower the heat to keep at a simmer. Cover and cook slowly for 40 to 60 minutes, until the meat is tender. Plan in advance to include any one fresh vegetable, a grain, or perhaps a pasta (see note below). Serve warm, with feta cheese or yogurt and olives, bread and wine.

Note: Each variation of *arni kokkinisto* or *moshari kokkinisto* is made with a different vegetable or pasta, and each creates a unique aroma. The most popular are *araka* (green peas); *bamyes* (okra); *fassolia* (dried beans, presoaked and simmered separately and then added to the meat); *kolokithakia* (small zucchini or squash); *melitzanes* (eggplant); *patates* (potatoes); *stifado* (with onions); and *yuvetsi* (with pasta, usually *kritharaki*). Care must be taken to add additional water or tomato juice for cooking pasta or vegetable and to see that the quick-cooking vegetables are added during the last 10 minutes, not before. Be sure to add the herb or spice suitable to each vegetable. Bake in a slow oven or over a low burner, and serve warm.

KREAS ME ANGINARES AVGOLEMONO
[Artichokes and meat braised with aniseed, Cretan style]

This dish is frequently cooked with one pound of peeled, sliced tomatoes, without adding the *avgolemono*.

TO SERVE 4

2 *tablespoons olive oil or butter*
1 *small onion, minced*
1 *to 1½ pounds lamb, veal, or beef, cut into serving pieces*
Salt and freshly ground pepper
1 *to 1½ teaspoons aniseed*

8 *large quartered or 12 small whole artichokes, cleaned as described on page 203 and sprinkled with lemon juice*
2 *eggs*
Juice of 1 lemon

Heat the oil or butter and sauté the onion and meat until the meat is seared on all sides. Lower the heat, cover, and simmer for 10 to 15 minutes. Turn the meat over, season with salt, pepper, and 1 teaspoon aniseed, and enough water to cover. Cover the pan and simmer until the meat is tender, then remove the meat to a flameproof casserole and keep warm. Add the artichokes to the pan and simmer gently, uncovered, until tender (approximately 30 minutes). Using a slotted spoon, remove the artichokes and keep warm with the meat. Taste the cooking liquid and add more aniseed if desired; boil down until 1½ cups remain, then strain. Using the 2 eggs, the lemon juice, and the strained cooking liquid, prepare *avgolemono* as directed on page 48, then combine the sauce with the meat and artichokes, heat without boiling, and serve warm.

MOSHARI STIFADO
[Aromatic veal, stifado style]

"*Stifado* style" refers to the small white onions, usually used in equal weight to veal or rabbit, the two favorites, or less frequently with another vegetable such as eggplant. Beef may be substituted for the veal in this recipe, provided the chosen beef cut will cook within the same time required for the onions. As in many Greek dishes, *stifado* depends on the flavor of all ingredients permeating each other. Therefore, *stifado* flavor improves when cooked slowly the day before serving, stored in the refrigerator, then heated slowly. For an excellent party dish, double or triple the recipe and cook in an attractive cooking-serving casserole. Tender lamb, beef, or lean pork may be substituted for a very different flavor.

TO SERVE 5

2 tablespoons olive oil
1½ pounds lean veal, cut into walnut-sized cubes
2 cloves garlic, sliced
Salt and freshly ground pepper
¼ cup red wine vinegar
2 tablespoons dry red wine
3 canned or fresh tomatoes, peeled and chopped, or 1 cup tomato sauce
1 large bay leaf

1 tablespoon white or brown sugar
1½ pounds small white onions, peeled but left whole (see note below)
¼ cup chopped fresh parsley
2 tablespoons butter, cut into bits
1 stick cinnamon
3 whole cloves or ¼ teaspoon cumin

In a baking-serving casserole, heat the oil, then add the veal and sauté on all sides. Add the garlic and season with salt and pepper. Stir with a wooden spoon, then add the vinegar, wine, tomatoes, bay leaf, sugar, and enough water to cover the veal. Arrange the onions over the meat, sprinkle the parsley and butter bits over the top, and slip the spices in between the meat and the onions. Shake the casserole a few times, then cover with an inverted plate to keep in place and cover tightly with a lid (using a little flour-water paste around the inside of the lid to seal, if you wish). Bake in a slow oven (300 degrees) for 2 to 2½ hours or over minimum heat on a burner, until the veal and onions are tender. Remove from the heat and serve warm.

Note: After peeling the onions, pierce the root end of each onion with the tip of a small, sharp knife, then slash again at a right angle to make a cross. This will keep the onion whole and intact during the cooking process.

PASTITSADA KORFIATIKI
[Festive veal and macaroni, Corfu style]

Pastitsada is a favorite Sunday dinner on the Ionian island of Corfu.

TO SERVE 6

1½ pounds lean leg or shoulder of veal	1 bay leaf
⅓ cup olive oil	1 stick cinnamon
2 large onions, minced	1½ pounds ripe fresh or canned tomatoes, chopped
2 large cloves garlic, sliced	1 to 1½ pounds macaroni
Salt and freshly ground pepper	¼ cup (4 tablespoons) butter
½ cup dry white wine	½ cup grated kefalotyri or Parmesan cheese
1 tablespoon vinegar	
3 cloves	

Wipe the veal with a damp cloth and cut into cubes slightly larger than a walnut. Heat the oil in a large casserole, add the meat, and sear on all sides over high heat. Put the minced onions into the pan, then lower the heat, cover, and cook until soft (approximately 5 minutes). Add the garlic, season with salt and pepper, and pour the wine over the meat. Shake the pan to mix, then add the vinegar, cloves, bay leaf, cinnamon, and tomatoes. Cover and bake in a slow oven (300 degrees) for 2 to 2½ hours or until the veal is tender (or cook over the lowest heat on a burner). The sauce should be thick; if necessary, pour the liquid into a small pan and boil down. Remove the cloves and cinnamon stick.

Meanwhile, boil the macaroni in salted water, according to package directions. Drain. Select a large, deep serving dish, place the macaroni in the center. Heat the butter to bubbling in a small pan, then pour over the macaroni. Sprinkle the cheese over the macaroni and spoon the hot veal and sauce over the top. Serve immediately.

SOFRITO KORFIATIKO
[Pungent braised veal, Corfu style]

Sofrito originated in Spain and spread into many areas, changing costumes like a spy. It is a mystery how the Corfiotes developed this dish, for it bears no resemblance to *sofrito* in the Caribbean, Italy, or the Middle East (was it possibly brought by the Venetians?). It is popular on Corfu served with mashed potatoes.

TO SERVE 6

> 6 *loin veal chops or 6 half-inch slices veal shoulder*
> *Seasoned flour (with salt, pepper, and herbs) for dredging*
> *⅓ cup olive oil*
> *3 cloves garlic, minced*
> *2 tablespoons vinegar*
> *2 tablespoons chopped fresh parsley*

Wipe the veal with damp towel, then dredge with the seasoned flour. Heat the oil in a large casserole, add the chops, and sear on both sides over high heat. Lower the heat and add the garlic, vinegar (it will sputter), parsley, and enough hot water to cover the meat. Stir with a wooden spoon, cover, and cook over the lowest possible heat—or transfer to a slow oven (300 degrees)—for 1½ hours, or until the veal is fork-tender. Serve warm.

STAMNAKI

["Little jug" or veal baked in a jug, Thracian style]

A delightful and delicious dish made only in Thrace, this takes its name from the earthenware *stamnaki* (tiny version of the ancient water jug) in which it is baked. The jug's mouth is narrow enough to accommodate a fresh tomato, which serves as a lid!

TO SERVE 6

> *1¾ pounds veal shoulder or leg, cubed*
> *4 cloves garlic, chopped or sliced*
> *1 onion, sliced*
> *½ green pepper, sliced in rings*
> *1 bay leaf*
> *Pinch of dried oregano*
> *Chunk of kefalotyri or Romano cheese*
> *2 tablespoons olive oil*
> *Few grains black pepper*
> *Pinch of salt*
> *1 fresh, firm tomato*
> *½ cup all-purpose flour*

Combine the veal with all the seasonings and the cheese in a bowl. Using a long-handled spoon, put the veal into the *stamnaki* (or use a small earthenware bean pot). Place the tomato in the opening, stem side down, without pushing it through to the bottom. Set the jug aside. In a small bowl, mix the flour with enough cold water to make a dough. Roll it out flat and use it to seal the opening of the jug. (Or, if desired, use aluminum foil.) Bake in a moderate oven (350 degrees) for 1 hour, then remove and discard the dough or aluminum sealer. Transfer the seasoned veal and liquids to a warm platter, and serve accompanied by the tomato.

HIRINO SELINO AVGOLEMONO
[Pork braised with celery avgolemono]

Celery and pork are favorite Greek combinations, but during lamb and veal season, these meats are substituted successfully. Try it with pork first—you may never need a substitute.

TO SERVE 4 TO 5

3 pounds lean shoulder or leg of fresh pork, cut into 1½-inch cubes	3 cups hot water, approximately
	1 bunch celery
	2 tablespoons flour
4 tablespoons butter or margarine	2 egg yolks
1 onion, finely chopped	Juice of 1½ lemons
Salt and freshly ground pepper	Fresh parsley or celery leaves for garnish

Wipe the pork with damp paper towels. (The fat and skin may be left on during cooking and removed later.) Melt 2 tablespoons of the butter in a heavy pan or Dutch oven. Add the onion and cook until soft and transparent, then add the pork and cook, stirring, over medium heat until the raw meat color disappears. Season with salt and pepper, add hot water to cover, then cover and simmer gently (or bake in a 325-degree oven) for 30 to 35 minutes, or until almost tender. (The timing is important because the celery is to be added and cooked with the pork only until both are tender but not overcooked.)

Meanwhile, prepare the celery. Wash the stalks and scrape the heavy ones slightly. Cut each stalk once lengthwise (if large) and then across into 1½-inch slices. (Use the leaves as well, if desired, but a few might be saved for a garnish or an accompanying salad.) Add the celery to pork and continue simmering 25 minutes until both are tender. Using a slotted spoon, remove the pork and celery and place in a serving dish, first removing and discarding the fat from the meat. Keep warm. Skim the fat from the cooking liquid, then add water or boil down rapidly to make 1½ cups. Keep hot while you prepare the *avgolemono* as described on page 48, using the remaining 2 tablespoons butter and flour for the roux, and adding the egg yolks, lemon juice, and hot cooking liquid. Pour the hot sauce over the pork and celery, garnish with parsley or celery leaves and serve warm.

Note: Celeriac may be substituted for the celery. Use 2½ pounds of celeriac, and peel, quarter, and cut it into ½-inch slices before adding it to the pork. A little scraped, diced carrot may be added with the celery.

HIRINO ANDIDIA AVGOLEMONO
[Pork braised with curly endive avgolemono]

Hellenes who adore the pork and celery combination are usually just as delighted with this blend of flavors. You may substitute 2 large heads of curly-leaf endive, leaves separated and thoroughly washed, for the celery. Remove the pork from the liquid when partially cooked, add the endive and cook rapidly until the leaves release their liquid and collapse, then add the pork and continue cooking until both the vegetable and meat are tender. Make the *avgolemono* as described above.

HIRINO AFELIA
[Pork braised with wine and coriander, Cyprus style]

Afelia is a delightful style, used also for some vegetables—notably potatoes, artichokes, and mushrooms, each cooked separately—as an accompaniment to fish or meat dishes.

TO SERVE 4 TO 5

> *3 tablespoons corn oil*
> *1½ pounds lean pork, cut into 1-inch cubes*
> *Salt and freshly ground pepper*
> *½ cup dry red wine*
> *1 tablespoon coriander seeds, pounded*

Heat the oil in a heavy pan, add the pork, and sear the meat at a fairly high temperature on all sides, stirring constantly. Lower the heat and sprinkle with salt and pepper. In a small pan, heat the wine and pour it over the meat. Cover and cook over the lowest possible heat or transfer to a slow oven (300 degrees) for 1½ hours, or until the meat is tender and the wine has been absorbed. Check and stir several times, adding more hot wine or hot water if necessary. Stir in the coriander seeds during the last 20 minutes of cooking time. Serve warm with a grain dish and a crisp salad and white wine.

Note: Pork chops may be substituted for pork cubes and cooked until the meat is falling off the bones.

HIRINO RIGANATO
[Roast pork with oregano and wine, Cretan style]

Beaches in Greece are never difficult to spot anywhere along the vast coastlines. Along with sparkling surf, increasing numbers of Greek bathers, and frolicking games of paddle tennis, one finds the seaside restaurants and their sense-arousing food and music. All combined, these beach-eating places constitute a *plaz*, a very recent development in Greek summer family entertainment. The food is usually very good, and always better when the resort is geared for Hellenes, not tourists. Serving is informal, typical of other Greek restaurants. Ordering may be done from the kitchen, inspecting dishes *tis imeras* (day's specialty). Visiting a Cretan resort, we returned to compliment the chef-owner for our excellent meal. He promptly cut a slice off this version of roast pork and handed it to us on a fork to sample. Served cold, and sliced thin, this dish is excellent for a buffet dinner.

TO SERVE 6 TO 8

> *1 pork roast (5 pounds), preferably the shank half of fresh ham*
> *2 cloves garlic, slivered*
> *Salt*
> *2 teaspoons dried oregano*
> *½ cup dry red wine*
> *½ cup tomato juice or canned tomatoes, drained*
> *Juice of 1 lemon*

Wipe the pork with damp paper towels. With the tip of a sharp knife, pierce the meat on all sides and insert the garlic slivers. Rub the meat all over with salt and oregano, then place in a shallow roasting pan, uncovered, in a moderate or moderately slow oven (325 to 350 degrees) until thoroughly cooked (185 degrees on a meat thermometer). Pour the wine over the meat and the tomato juice around the meat after the first half hour of cooking, and baste occasionally with drippings. Remove from the oven and pour the lemon juice over the meat. Cool thoroughly, then carve into very thin slices and serve cold.

Note: Strain the remaining sauce, then chill. Skim and discard the fat. Use for gravy or to flavor *pilafi* or pasta.

HIRINO PSITO ME THYMARI KRITIKO
[*Roasted pork on thyme sprigs, Cretan style*]

Pork roasted in this way forms a delicious surface crust, suitable for large roasts in the oven or for chops and cutlets in pans over hot coals outdoors. Select a tender cut of roasting pork. The evening before roasting, wipe with damp towels, then, using a small skewer or knife, pierce the meat every few inches and squeeze lemon juice over it on all sides. Allow to marinate overnight in the refrigerator.

When ready to cook, rub salt into the meat, brush with olive oil and place on fresh thyme sprigs, using the branch as well as the leaves. Bake in a slow oven (300 degrees), allowing 25 minutes per pound for small roasts and 35 minutes per pound for large. (A 7½-pound shank end of fresh ham requires 5 hours.) Baste occasionally with lemon juice and fat from the pan, and sprinkle with thyme or marjoram during the last 20 minutes of roasting. Grind black pepper over the pork before slicing and serve warm or cold.

SOUVLAKIA APO HIRINO
[*Pork grilled on skewers and seasoned with lemon and oregano*]

Any tired summer traveler in Greece knows the delicious aroma of *souvlakia apo hirino*, eaten off the *kalamaki* (cane skewer). Usually skeptical about putting any non-homemade food except sesame *koulouria* (bread rings) into their mouths, Greek people make an exception for this treat.

To prepare, cut lean, tender cuts of pork into rectangles about 1 x ½ inch. Thread the pork lengthwise on 8-inch round or flat cane skewers. Grill over hot coals or a griddle until thoroughly cooked, then sprinkle with salt and pepper and dip quickly into lemon juice. Crush oregano over the meat. Pierce the tip of the skewer with a good slice of home-made or French-type bread and serve immediately.

The Greek way to eat it: hold the skewer with one hand harmonica-style and nibble, eating alternately with the bread.

Variety Meats and Ground Meat Dishes

Variety and specialty meats are very much of a delicacy in modern Greece. Through the prolific writings of Alexis, Aristophanes, and Anaxandrides, we can be sure that during their eras trotters, head, ears, tripe, jawbones, and paunches were supremely enjoyed. In one of his plays Alexis jibes that a contemporary of his would die for a boiled sow's paunch. Numerous recipes remain of specialties containing *vulva eiectitia* (matrix of miscarried sows). Hipparchus wrote, "Rather, let me be cheered by a casserole of the lovely countenance of a miscarried matrix, or a suckling pig whose smell comes deliciously from the oven."

Noted Dutch gynecologist Dr. Theodore Van de Velde in his discussion of aphrodisiacs in *Ideal Marriage*, wrote that the ancient Greek use of animal glands (testes and ovaries) and calves' brains were excellent choices for use in love philters. In fact, he believed that the philters of the Thessalian women "were the forerunners of modern organic therapy for sexual deficiency." * Considering the tenacity of Greek food habits, it is not surprising that variety meats include a popular appetizer *ameletita*—unmentionables (veal testicles).

In addition to glands and other specialties, the use of ground meat also flourished during the same period, as seasonings became diverse and imaginative ideas developed in chefs' minds. Artemidorus called these mixtures *myma*, which is similar to the modern Greek *migma* (mixture). A quote from Athenaeus:

* Van de Velde, T. H., *Ideal Marriage. Its Physiology and Technique* (New York: Random House, 1961), p. 260.

A myma of any kind of meat, including fowl, should be made by cutting up the tender parts of the meat into small pieces, mashing in the viscera, intestine, blood and spicing with vinegar, toasted cheese, silphium, cumin, fresh or fried thyme, savory, fresh or dried coriander, horn onion, peeled roasted onion, poppy head, raisins, or honey or the pips of an acid pomegranate. You may also have the same myma with fish.

With the replacement of certain ingredients, such as silphium, which has dropped from use, the recipe sounds very familiar—the family of *keftedes,* whether of a fish, meat, or vegetable base. *Keftedes* now may have a Turkish name tacked onto them (as many Greek foods have), but authorities consider them descended from the ancient *myma.* Certainly *keftedes*—all ground-meat mixtures, in fact—are highly seasoned. To arrive at their own individual *keftedes,* cooks use their senses of sight, smell, and feel, kneading with fingers and palms. Writing a recipe for *keftedes* becomes a risky affair because they are blended specially each time they are made, and personal taste at that moment may dictate a new recipe. One Hellene we know well uses garlic, mizithra cheese, ouzo (anise-flavored liqueur), oregano, salt, pepper, soaked bread, and a little onion to flavor her *keftedes.* In addition to the challenge of seasoning the meat, there is another one that must be met, that of teaming the seasoned meat with appropriate sauce, vegetables, poultry, and pasta in layered casseroles, in which two or three separate mixtures must be united in harmony with each other, as in Pastitsio (page 98) and Moussaka (pages 233–236).

Should the cook prefer fresh, available beef or pork, the same methods may be applied as given in the recipes for the more usual lamb and veal ground meats. Since ground-meat dishes are enjoyed as much cold as hot in Greece, for maximum flavor, only lean meat, such as leg and shoulder cuts, should be used in mixtures.

ROULO ME FILO
[*Veal roll in filo pastry*]

Though trickier to cook than the average meat loaf, this one, brought to the table in a crispy *filo* roll, will impress both family and guests. The steaming filling delights the eye and olfactory nerves. If possible, prepare the meat mixture a day in advance.

TO SERVE 4 TO 5

*2 tablespoons butter or
margarine
1 small shallot or onion
1½ pounds veal, ground
½ cup chopped tomatoes or
tomato juice
1 stick cinnamon or 1 teaspoon
ground cinnamon
Salt, if necessary, and freshly
ground pepper
1 or 2 teaspoons chopped fresh
basil
2 eggs, separated*

*1½ cups thick Saltsa Aspri
(page 50)
½ cup grated mizithra or
kefalotyri cheese
½ teaspoon grated nutmeg
Heavy greaseproof paper (about
20 x 20 inches)
10 to 12 sheets commercial filo
⅓ cup butter or margarine,
melted and warm
2 hard-cooked eggs, sliced
1 tablespoon chopped fresh
parsley*

Heat the butter in a large frying pan, then sauté the onion until soft. Add the meat, mashing it with a fork until the raw color disappears. Add the tomato and cinnamon, cover and simmer about 20 minutes, stirring once or twice. Remove the lid and season judiciously (if the cheese is salty, don't add salt until the very end). Stir in the basil, then remove the cinnamon stick and cool. Using a wooden spoon, mix the egg whites into the meat. Meanwhile, prepare the *saltsa aspri* (it must be thick) and combine with the egg yolks, cheese, and nutmeg. Taste to see if salt is needed.

To make the loaf, spread the baking paper flat on your work surface. Lay a sheet of *filo* (keeping the rest covered with a damp towel or waxed paper) in the center of the paper and brush with butter. Continue laying *filo*, one sheet on top of another, brushing each with butter, to make a large "base" on which to roll the meat loaf (about 15 x 15 inches). Spread half of the *saltsa aspri* in the center of the *filo*, allowing wide margins for turning later. Spread the meat mixture over the sauce to a length of about 9 inches. Lay the egg slices over the meat, cover with the remaining sauce, and sprinkle with parsley. Turn the edges of the *filo* up over the meat and roll into a loaf. Fold the paper over the loaf, secure it, and place, seam side down, in a baking pan. Bake for 1 hour in moderate oven (350 degrees), removing the paper after 35 minutes to allow the *filo* to get crisp. Brush the outer surface of the *filo* with butter or margarine for a higher golden chestnut color.

With wide spatulas, lift the loaf onto a warm platter. Serve immediately, with fresh green salad, black olives, and a heady wine.

SOUTZOUKAKIA SMYRNEIKA
[Ground meat sausages, Smyrna style]

Most famous of the Smyrna meat mixtures, made and known throughout Greece. The most distinctive spice is cumin, which I first tasted in Athens during my first visit there. I bought a special shallow, round, wide-bottomed *soutzouki* pot and lid, and have used it ever since.

If possible, prepare the meat mix early, or even the night before you cook the dish.

TO MAKE 20 SAUSAGES

4 tablespoons melted butter
1 pound fresh or canned
  tomatoes, peeled
1 teaspoon granulated sugar
Salt and freshly ground pepper
  to taste
3 cloves garlic, crushed
1/4 cup dry white wine
1 small bay leaf
1 pound lean beef, ground

2 slices bread, crusts removed,
  soaked in water and squeezed
  dry
1 teaspoon ground cumin
1 egg, lightly beaten
2 teaspoons finely chopped fresh
  parsley
1 to 1 1/2 teaspoons salt
Pinch of freshly ground black
  pepper
Vegetable oil or clarified butter
  (see page 40) for frying

Combine the melted butter, tomatoes, sugar, salt and pepper, 1 clove of garlic, wine, and bay leaf in a saucepan. Simmer for 30 minutes, then strain through a fine sieve or food mill.

Meanwhile, combine the remaining ingredients in a large bowl and knead thoroughly. (The mixture should not be stiff.) Pinch off pieces a little larger than a walnut and shape with the hands into elongated egg shapes about 1 x 3 inches. Either fry them lightly on all sides in hot oil or clarified butter and then drain on paper towels, or arrange them in a baking dish and bake in a 375-degree oven for 20 minutes, turning once. Drop the *soutzoukia* in sauce and simmer for 15 minutes. Serve with a steaming grain dish and fresh, cooked vegetables or salad.

LAHANODOLMADES MAKEDONIKA AVGOLEMONO
[*Stuffed cabbage with avgolemono, Macedonia style*]

Balkan influences filtered into the Greek cuisine through Macedonia as well as through Epirus. Some Macedonians use caraway in the stuffed cabbages.

TO SERVE 6 TO 8

3 *medium or 2 large heads cabbage*
Salt
2 *tablespoons vegetable oil or butter*
1 *medium onion, chopped, or 4 scallions, chopped fine*
1 *pound lean pork, veal, or beef, ground*
½ *cup raw long-grain white rice*

½ *cup finely chopped fresh parsley*
2 *tablespoons chopped fresh dill leaves*
Salt and freshly ground pepper
1 *egg, lightly beaten*
1 *pound sauerkraut, washed and drained (optional)*
2 *egg yolks*
Juice of 1 lemon

Plunge the cabbages into boiling salted water and cook for about 8 minutes, then drain thoroughly and set aside while you prepare the stuffing.

In a heavy skillet, heat the oil or butter, then add the onion and cook until soft and transparent. Add the ground meat and sauté for a few minutes, then remove from the heat and add the rice, parsley, dill, salt and pepper to taste, and egg. Knead. Spread the sauerkraut evenly in an enamel, earthenware, or stainless-steel pan. Roll the cabbages as described on page 105, then lay them, seam side down, over the sauerkraut. Add water to cover, spread a few large cabbage leaves on top and cover with an inverted plate. Simmer gently 1 to 1½ hours, then transfer to a warm serving dish and keep warm.

Reduce the cooking liquid by boiling rapidly or add enough water to make 1½ cups. Using the egg yolks and lemon juice, prepare *avgolemono* as directed on page 48, adding the hot cooking liquid drop by drop. Heat without boiling and pour over the stuffed cabbage. Serve warm.

DOLMADES ME KREAS AVGOLEMONO
[Meat-stuffed dolmades avgolemono]

One of the most famous Greek dishes may be made using Dolmades Yialantzi and meat (page 68) with *avgolemono*, suitable for a family meal and very nutritious while combining meat, grain and vegetable!

TO MAKE 60 TO 70

In the recipe for *dolmades yialantzi*, use only ½ cup rice and add 1 pound of ground meat to the onions before adding the rice. Save the lemon juice for the *avgolemono*. Simmer with the other seasonings and stuff the grapevine leaves. Cook the same as the other recipe, using 1 cup of the remaining liquid to make *avgolemono* (see page 48). Pour over the *dolmades* and heat without boiling. Serve warm.

KEFTEDES TIGANITES
[Fried keftedes]

Spicier *keftedes* are made by Greeks from Smyrna, using ground lamb seasoned with ½ teaspoon each of aniseed and cinnamon.

TO MAKE 3 DOZEN TINY OR 2 DOZEN MEDIUM "KEFTEDES"

1 *pound lean beef or veal, ground*
1 *medium onion, grated*
1 *clove garlic, crushed (optional)*
2 *slices bread, crusts removed, soaked in water and squeezed dry*
1 *egg, lightly beaten*
3 *tablespoons minced fresh parsley*

2 *sprigs fresh mint, chopped*
½ *teaspoon ground allspice, cinnamon or coriander*
1 *tablespoon dry red wine*
2 *to 3 tablespoons water, if necessary*
Salt and freshly ground pepper
All-purpose flour for dredging
Vegetable oil for frying to depth of ½ inch

In a large bowl, combine the ground meat with the onion, garlic, bread, egg, parsley, mint, spice, and wine and knead for 2 minutes. The mixture should be soft; add a few tablespoons of water if necessary. Season with salt and pepper to taste, then cover and refrigerate for at least 1 hour. Pinch off small pieces the size of walnuts or smaller and roll into balls between your palms, then dredge lightly in flour.

Heat the oil in a frying pan to the smoking point, slip in the *keftedes,* and fry until crisp, turning constantly with tongs. Remove with a slotted spoon and drain on absorbent paper.

Note: Keftedes Tiganites may also be simmered, after frying, in Saltsa Domata (page 51) and served over a favorite grain dish accompanied by green vegetables and a little wine.

KEFTEDES TOU FOURNOU KRASATA
[Baked keftedes in wine sauce]

TO MAKE 2 TO 3 DOZEN "KEFTEDES"

Prepare Keftedes Tiganites (see above), but instead of frying, arrange close together on a baking pan approximately 8 x 11 x 2 inches. Bake for 10 minutes in a hot oven (425 degrees), turning after 5 minutes.

Meanwhile, in a small pan combine 1 cup canned tomato sauce, 2 cups dry red wine, 1 large bay leaf, 2 whole cloves, ½ teaspoon dried oregano or marjoram, salt and freshly ground pepper. Boil for 5 minutes then pour over the *keftedes* in the oven. Reduce the oven heat to 300 degrees and bake for 40 minutes. Remove the bay leaf and cloves and serve warm.

GYRO
[Spitted spiced lamb]

Gyro, gyro oli is a favorite children's game, comparable to farmer in the dell, which describes the round-and-round motion of *gyro*. Since spreading to Greece from the Middle East, industrious Hellenes have brought it to the United States (New York is spinning with *gyro* restaurants), and one more snack has been added. On a vertical spit, which turns electrically, or is run manually by the *mikro* (apprentice), the meat is roasted to flavorful crispness. I adapted this recipe from a tasty snack in Crete. To make at home, grill outdoors (horizontally when lacking a vertical grill), and indoors, broil—delicious.

TO SERVE 6 OR 7

2 pounds lean lamb, ground

2 slices homemade bread, toasted and crushed

1 teaspoon allspice, pounded

1 teaspoon coriander, crushed

1 clove garlic, crushed

1 onion, grated

1 teaspoon chopped fresh savory

Salt, freshly ground pepper

3 slices bacon

6 to 8 flat Middle Eastern breads or any substitute bread or rolls

2 tomatoes, chopped or sliced thin and seasoned with vinegar and oil

1 cup chopped fresh parsley

1 cup plain yogurt

In a large bowl, combine the ground lamb with the bread, allspice, coriander, garlic, onion, savory, and salt and pepper, and knead thoroughly. The mixture should be spicy, though not too herby, and hold its shape. Break into 5 sections, each as large as a navel orange, then break each section into 6 balls. Knead and flatten slightly to a thickness of about ¾ inch. Cut the bacon slices into widths equal to these balls and place one on each ball. Continue shaping the balls, keeping the slices of bacon between them. Slip a cane skewer through the centers and roll gently with the palms to smooth the edges. (There will be 5 or 6 skewers, depending on their length.) Cover and refrigerate overnight.

When ready to cook, set on a broiler tray or grill and cook under moderate heat, turning every 5 minutes. (The bacon will baste the meat.) The surface will be crusty and the inside cooked within 25 minutes.

To serve: Put out the bread, meat, tomatoes, parsley and yogurt in separate dishes. Guests may open pocket bread or rolls and stuff them with meat and seasonings.

SOUVLAKIA APO ENTOSTHIA
[Entrails on skewers]

TO SERVE 6 TO 8

5 baby lamb's sweetbreads
3 to 4 baby lamb's livers
4 baby lamb's kidneys
2 to 3 baby lamb's spleens
1/4 cup olive oil
Juice of 1 lemon
1 teaspoon dried oregano

2 to 3 tablespoons chopped fresh
  parsley
Salt and freshly ground pepper
1 to 2 tablespoons chopped
  onion (optional)
Fresh parsley for garnish

Select young, fresh entrails. Wash, cut into chestnut-sized pieces, and place in a glass or earthenware bowl. Make a marinade of the olive oil, lemon juice, herbs, salt, pepper, and chopped onion and pour over the entrails. Mix thoroughly and allow to marinate 1 hour.

Thread the marinated entrails on wood or metal skewers and broil, brushing with marinade or oil, for 15 to 20 minutes. Remove the entrails from the skewers, arrange on a platter, and garnish with parsley. Serve hot.

SIKOTIA KAI MELITZANES KYPRIOTIKA
[Livers and eggplants, Cyprus style]

TO SERVE 4 TO 5

1 medium eggplant
Salt
3 tablespoons corn oil
2 1/2 cups tomato juice

Freshly ground pepper
2 large onions, sliced into rings
2 tablespoons red wine vinegar
1 pound liver, cubed

Wash and dry the eggplant, cut off the green end and slice into 1/3-inch rings. Salt on both sides and let stand for 30 minutes. Rinse with cold water and drain.

Pour the oil and tomato juice into a *yuvetsi* or other casserole. Season with salt and pepper, then layer the eggplant and onions, sprinkle with the vinegar, and tuck the liver in between the vegetables. Cover and bake in a moderate oven (350 degrees) for 1 1/4 to 1 1/2 hours, or until tender and the sauce has thickened. Remove from the oven. Serve hot, with Pligouri (page 95) or Pilafi (page 103) and fresh cucumber salad.

Note: If using chicken livers, add them during the last 20 minutes of baking time. This dish may also be cooked on a slow burner.

GLYKADIA KRASATA
[*Sweetbreads braised in wine*]

Though sweetbreads are frequently broiled in Greece, they are usually sautéed or braised, as in the recipe below.

TO SERVE 4 TO 6

1 pound sweetbreads	*2 sprigs fresh parsley*
Vinegar, lemon juice, or 4 citric acid granules	*2 sprigs fresh thyme, marjoram, or savory*
Salt	*1 small bay leaf*
¼ cup butter (4 tablespoons)	*1 cup hot stock or broth*
2 to 3 tablespoons chopped celery	*½ cup dry white wine*
2 to 3 tablespoons chopped carrot	*Freshly ground pepper*
2 to 3 tablespoons chopped shallot or scallions	*Cooked asparagus tips for garnish*

Soak the sweetbreads in cold water for several hours, then drain. Remove the covering membrane carefully and soak in acidulated water (1 quart water to 1 tablespoon vinegar or lemon juice, or citric acid granules dissolved in a small amount of hot water) for 50 to 60 minutes. Remove the sweetbreads and set aside. Bring the acidulated water to a boil, add 1 teaspoon salt and dissolve. Add the sweetbreads, lower the heat, and blanch the sweetbreads without boiling, for 15 minutes. Lift out and rinse under cold water.

In a large frying pan, melt 3 tablespoons of the butter and sauté the vegetables over low heat for 15 minutes, stirring occasionally. Add the sweetbreads and the herbs to the vegetables and continue simmering for 10 minutes. Pour over the hot stock or broth and the wine. Stir and transfer the contents of the pan to a heatproof casserole. Cover and bake in a moderate oven (350 degrees) for 25 minutes, or until tender. Pour off the stock, strain it, and boil down to 1 cup, meanwhile keeping the sweetbreads warm. Add 1 tablespoon butter to the stock, along with a pinch of salt and pepper. Slice the sweetbreads and arrange them on a platter. Pour the hot sauce over and garnish with asparagus tips.

Note: If you wish to broil or sauté sweetbreads, change the water twice during the soaking period. To sauté, dredge first in seasoned flour and then sauté in butter.

LOUKANIKA
[*Sausages*]

Homemade *loukanika* in the provinces is one of the finest specialties *tou spitiou* (of the home), and a visitor is honored when served some. Usually stored in pork fat in a large container, *loukanika* are particularly delicious with eggs or in regional dishes such as Spetsofagi (page 160), from Pelion, and Phroutalia (page 161), from Andros. There are many more, too numerous, in fact, to include. Neither does this recipe presume on the merit of the "real thing" in Greece. But it is fun to make, certainly better than the commercial kind—and the orange rind is especially Greek. With artful seasoning, your *loukanika* can be great, so be sure to add more fat (needed as a tenderizer which will melt during the cooking) and spices than for a normal meat mixture. Make it spicy!

TO MAKE 20 FOUR-INCH SAUSAGES

*1 pound lean pork shoulder,
    ground*
*½ pound fresh pork rind, boiled
    for 2 hours, drained, ground*
½ pound pork fatback, ground
1 teaspoon salt
Grated rind of 1 navel orange
*1 teaspoon crushed dried
    marjoram or thyme*

1 bay leaf, ground in a mortar
⅓ cup dry red wine
*1 teaspoon ground allspice or
    coriander or both*
Freshly ground black pepper
*2 cloves garlic, crushed
    (optional)*
*Sausage casing (available in
    German pork stores)*

Grind the pork, pork rind, and fatback through the fine blade of a meat chopper. Combine in a large bowl with all the seasonings. Knead thoroughly. Store in the refrigerator while you prepare the casing.

Usually salted, the casing (pork intestine) especially the interior, must be rinsed under cold running water several times. (To avoid losing the casing down the drain while doing this, be sure the casing is inside a very large pan!) Allow to drain on a linen towel.

Use a pastry bag to force the stuffing into the casing. Pinch at 3½-
to 4-inch intervals allowing space between to form the sausage links.
Normally the casing will not break, but if it does, that section must be
discarded and a knot tied in the new "end." To cook, poach in water for
1 hour, then drain, discarding the cooking water. Fry the sausages in a
frying pan over moderate heat, or use as suggested in any recipe. Drain
and serve hot.

Note: To store, freeze uncooked in meal-sized batches. The sausages
should be used within a day or two if not frozen.

SPETSOFAGI

[Homemade sausage stew, Pelion style]

Pelion in eastern Thessaly is rich with pines, olives, chestnuts, and
the abundant *firikia* apples and *aphroditi* peaches. A specialty of the
mountain villages is *spetsofagi* which owes its fame to the local *loukanika*, made with available meats and seasonings. I especially enjoyed
the texture and flavor of the other indispensable ingredient—green peppers—and the green pepper seeds, which the chefs admitted they will
include only when very tender.

TO SERVE 5

> 6 to 7 long green peppers
> 2 tablespoons olive oil
> ¾ pound Loukanika (page 159) or Italian sausage, sliced
>   in ¼-inch rounds
> 1 pound fresh or canned tomatoes, peeled and chopped
> Salt and freshly ground pepper

Wash the peppers. Using the tip of a sharp knife, cut around the stems
and discard the tough seeds and stems. Cut the peppers lengthwise into
½-inch slices and then in half.

Heat the oil in a flameproof casserole and sauté the peppers for a
few minutes before adding the sausages. Turn the sausages to crisp on
both sides, then stir in the tomatoes and season with salt and pepper to
taste. Cover and simmer for 30 minutes, or until the stew is tender, the
sauce thick. Serve warm.

PHROUTALIA
[Potato and sausage omelet, Andros style]

This northernmost Cycladic island is almost as famous for the omelet as it is for the nut and honey desserts. Try it for brunch!

TO SERVE 5

> *½ pound Loukanika (page 159) or Italian sausage*
> *4 large all-purpose potatoes*
> *8 eggs, lightly beaten*
> *Salt and freshly ground pepper*
> *2 tablespoons chopped fresh mint*
> *2 tablespoons butter (optional)*

Slice the sausages into rounds as thick as your little finger and fry in an omelet pan until crisp. Remove with a slotted spatula, drain on paper towels, and set aside. Pour off all but 3 tablespoons of the fat. Meanwhile, peel and slice the potatoes into thin circles. Add them to the hot fat, then reduce the heat, cover the pan tightly, and simmer 25 minutes until tender, turning once. Mix the sausages into the potatoes, pour the eggs over, sprinkle with the mint, and dust ever so lightly with salt and a grinding of black pepper. Cook over low heat until the egg has set on the bottom, then flip over to cook on the other side. (The simplest way to do this is to invert pan over a large platter, add butter to the pan, and slide the omelet back into the pan until the uncooked side is [hopefully] a golden chestnut color.) Serve hot.

MYALA
[Brains]

Veal brains are preferred for their fine flavor, but you may use lamb, pork, or beef brains for these recipes if necessary. Wash brains and soak for several hours in cold water, changing water once. Rinse the brains and carefully remove the membranes. Rinse under cold water. In an enamel pot pour enough water to cover the brains, add 2 tablespoons vinegar, lemon juice, or diluted citric acid granules, and 1 teaspoon salt and bring to a boil. Remove from heat and lower the brains into the hot liquid, cover and allow to blanch for 30 minutes. (Brains may be simmered to shorten cooking time but be sure not to boil. Young animal brains need 10 minutes and beef brains up to 20 minutes.) Remove from water, rinse under cold water and drain. Now the brains may be sliced or sautéed and served in any preferred style including one of the following:

With Ladolemono.   Mix ⅓ cup olive oil, juice of 1 lemon, salt and freshly ground pepper, chopped fresh parsley, dill or fennel leaves with ¼ cup water. Bring to a boil then add the brains as prepared above and simmer 5 minutes. Serve warm.

With Ladoxido.   Cover cool, drained brains with Ladoxido dressing (page 53). Allow to marinate a few hours. Serve cold.

MYALA ME MAVRO VOUTYRO
[Brains with black butter]

Brains served in this style reflect the growing French influence in Greek cities. The dish tastes much better than it sounds, and of course the butter must not burn in any country.

In a heavy frying pan slowly heat 2 tablespoons butter to a deep chestnut color without burning. Stirring constantly, stir in 2 sprigs fresh, minced parsley, 1 teaspoon vinegar, and a pinch of salt. Add the brains, prepared as above and sliced; spoon the butter over the brains and serve warm.

PIKTI
[Jellied pork mold]

Traditional throughout Greece, *pikti* uses pork head and feet in a delicious dish, one of the many pork loaves. Since pork head is increasingly difficult to obtain, this recipe is a newer adaptation in Greece, using lean pork from the body. Prepare a day in advance. Serve as an appetizer or first course.

TO SERVE 6 TO 8

4 pounds lean fresh ham
3 small pig's feet (optional)
1 stalk celery
2 bay leaves
6 peppercorns
3 sprigs fresh parsley
2 tablespoons plain gelatin
6 tablespoons cold water
½ cup bitter orange juice or plain
   orange juice

Juice of 3 to 3½ lemons
2 to 3 tablespoons white vinegar
1 clove garlic, crushed
Freshly ground black pepper
Salt
Cherry tomatoes, black olives,
   and fresh parsley for garnish

Wash and dry the ham and pig's feet. Place in a large pot and cover with boiling water. Add the celery, bay leaves, peppercorns, and parsley, lower the heat, and simmer until the meat falls off the bones. (Be sure to keep the water below a boil to avoid toughening the meat.) Strain the broth into another pot. Skim off all fat from the surface and boil down to 1½ cups.

Meanwhile, cut off all fat from the meat and dice into uniform pieces. Place the pork in an attractive mold of at least 6-cup capacity. Dissolve the gelatin in the 6 tablespoons cold water, add to the stock, and boil for 1 minute. Stir in the bitter orange juice, lemon juice (if using plain orange juice, use 3½ lemons), vinegar, and garlic. Add pepper according to taste and season with salt. Pour over the pork in the mold and refrigerate, covered with plastic wrap, overnight.

To unmold, run a sharp knife around the outer rim of the jelly, set for a moment in warm water, and invert over an attractive platter. Garnish with black olives, cherry tomatoes, and parsley and serve.

GLOSSA
[Tongue]

Then buy a large flounder, and the roughish ox-tongue; this last only in summer, when it is good at Chalcis.
ARCHESTRATUS, in ATHENAEUS, *The Deipnosophists*

Glossa in Greek means both "tongue" and "language." The English words *glossary, glossolalia* are among derivations from the Greek, while a considerable number of idioms and proverbs spice Greek everyday conversation. For example: "The tongue elevates, and the tongue humbles man," or "The tongue doesn't have bones but breaks bones," and "The tongue is a double-edged, terrible knife." A gossip is dubbed *glossou*, and gossiping frowned on as *glossofagoma*, or "tongue-eating."

In cookery, however, the tongue is not frowned upon. Since the classical period, when the tradition of enjoying all edible parts of the available meats began, Greeks have been smoking and spicing tongues of calf, beef, and lamb with cloves, cinnamon, bay and coriander. The following Greek method may be applied to all available smoked tongues, preferably 3 pounds or lighter. If nonsmoked types are used, add 1 teaspoon salt per quart of liquid.

TO SERVE 5 TO 6

1 onion studded with 5 whole cloves
1 celery stalk, sliced
1 carrot, sliced
Herbs: 3 parsley sprigs, 1 bay leaf, 2 thyme sprigs, 1 to 2 garlic cloves (optional), tip of stick cinnamon, 2 to 3 coriander seeds, cracked, tied in cheesecloth
1 to 2 anchovy fillets, rinsed and drained or 3 Greek olives, pitted

1 tablespoon pine nuts
1 clove garlic
1/2 teaspoon capers
1/2 slice bread, soaked in water and squeezed
1 hard-boiled egg yolk (optional)
1/2 cup olive oil
2 to 3 tablespoons red wine vinegar
Salt and freshly ground pepper
Cherry tomatoes and fresh parsley for garnish

Wash the tongue thoroughly in cold water. Soak overnight in cold water. Drain then put the tongue back into the pot and cover with fresh cold water. Bring to a boil, lower the heat, then add the onion, celery, carrot, herbs and spices which are tied in cheesecloth. Simmer from 1 to 3½ hours until the tongue is fork-tender. (Lamb tongue requires from 1 to 1½ hours; calf tongue from 1½ to 2 hours; beef tongue from 3 to 3½ hours.) Rinse the tongue under cold water, drain, then trim off the fat and gristle and peel off and discard the skin. Put the tongue back into the court bouillon until cool. Drain, then slice diagonally, arrange on a serving platter and set aside.

Prepare a sauce by pounding in a mortar or blending in an electric blender the anchovies or olives, pine nuts, garlic, capers, bread, and egg yolk. Gradually add the olive oil alternating with the vinegar to make a smooth sauce. Season with salt and pepper. Garnish the tongue with cherry tomatoes and parsley and pour the sauce over the tongue or serve separately.

ARNI KEFALAKI PSITO
[Roast baby lamb's head]

Food habits differ from country to country. Baby lamb's head is the best Greek example of this truth: a delicacy for a Greek, while the name of the dish alone makes the average American shudder. The recipe is included with full awareness of both attitudes.

Use only the head of a baby lamb for this dish. Older ones may be used for soups.

SERVES 1 TO 2

> 1 baby lamb's head
> 1/4 cup olive oil
> Lemon juice to taste
> 2 to 3 tablespoons tomato sauce
> Crumbled dried oregano to taste
> Salt and freshly ground pepper

Soak the lamb's head for one hour in cold water, then drain and dry. If the butcher has not split it, the head should be cut in half. In small bowl, whisk together a marinade made up of the olive oil, lemon juice, tomato sauce, and crumbled oregano. Sprinkle the head lightly with salt and pepper, set on a baking tray, brains up, and brush with the marinade. Roast in a moderate oven (350 degrees), basting frequently until the brains are tender. They may be removed and kept warm until the other portions are tender (approximately 1 hour, possibly shorter).

Note: In addition to the brains and tongue, there is another prize. But the reader must seek the answer, if he does not already know.

KOKORETSI
[Barbecued lamb organ meats]

The complicated preparation of *kokoretsi* is forgotten in the fun and excitement of Easter and a huge family gathering. While the paschal lamb is roasting on the spit, some family members grill the *kokoretsi*, timed for nibbling before the lamb is finished. Slow cooking is essential, since none of the innards have been parboiled, as in making Mageritsa (page 84). *Kokoretsi* may be grilled over an outdoor charcoal burner, but the heat must be controlled to a minimum for approximately 2½ hours.

TO SERVE 6 TO 8

> *Intestines, heart, liver, lungs, and sweetbreads from 1 lamb*
> *Salt and freshly ground pepper*
> *¾ cup olive oil*
> *Juice of 2 to 3 lemons*
> *2 teaspoons dried oregano*
> *1 to 2 cloves garlic, crushed (optional)*
> *Lamb membrane or casing, washed and drained*

Wash all the lamb innards in cold water. Turn the intestines inside out, using a long spit, then rub with salt and the juice of one or more lemons and wash in many waters. Cut the heart, liver, lungs, and sweetbreads into large pieces and slide, alternately, onto a skewer. Sprinkle with salt and pepper. Beat the oil, juice of 2 to 3 lemons, the oregano, and garlic in a small bowl and use it to brush the innards. Allow to marinate for 1 hour. Wrap the lamb membrane around the meat to form a large sausage and secure carefully by twisting the intestines around and around the casing. Secure with a skewer or tie knots. Brush with the marinade, place over a slow fire, and turn every 15 minutes. (Avoid placing the spit too close to the heat or the intestines will burn before the encased organs absorb the heat.) Continue cooking for 2½ hours, or until tender. Remove from the spit to a carving board. Cut into bite-sized pieces and serve hot, on forks or toothpicks, with bread.

Note: Lamb casings are available from specialty butchers who will also sell the entire lamb. Casings are usually stocked in pork specialty stores.

Poultry and Game

POULTRY, GAME, AND GAME BIRDS

Buy four or five partridges, three hares, sparrows to gobble greedily, some goldfinches and parrots, chaffinches, and kestrels and anything else you can find.

EUBULUS (3RD CENTURY B.C.)

Greek chicken dishes are exciting, easy, varied and have, in fact, provided for me a rich resource of recipes while raising our youngsters. I cannot imagine a cooking failure or remember leftovers.

If you have been to Greece and leaf through these recipes, a few of the many varieties, you may ponder my strong position. After all, one rarely finds a chicken specialty on Greek menus (although lamb and veal dishes are printed as staples on the bill-of-fare) and one rarely hears much about chickens, except in the proverbs. Yet the chickens and roosters living, pecking happily for centuries in Greek gardens and along roadsides (as they continue to do) were destined to create a unique symbiosis with village cooks. And they have. Chickens, hens, chicks, and roosters have special names, though classified with ducks, geese, turkey, and small birds as *ornitha* or *poulerika*. The latter sounds like our "poultry."

Turkey has interesting names: *galo* ("Frenchman" probably because the turkey was introduced into Europe through France); and a nickname *'diano* ("Indian" of the New World where turkeys originated). (Greeks also named the orange *portokali* for Portugal believing oranges had arrived from the west, but they were wrong that time.) Turkeys are used less than chickens in Greek homes. Southern Hellenes were amazed when I described to them some of the northerners' turkey dishes.

As for game and game birds—just the thought will produce instant rapture, a sigh. I have found this feeling and anticipation similar to the enjoyment of figs, very keen, very deeply rooted in history too.

Middle Comedy poets particularly raved about the delicious birds, a delicacy of that period. The practice in Greece has not died away. Crete, Peloponnesos, Macedonia, and central Greece produce vast numbers of pigeons (and Macedonia triples production of all poultry and game— hens, geese, ducks, turkeys, rabbits, and pigeons—as compared to other regions).

Among the delicacies usually braised in butter and simmered in wine are *becatses* (woodcocks), *perdikes* (partridges), *pitsounia* (pigeons) and *tsichles* (thrushes).

This enjoyment is contagious. We enjoyed *ortikia skaras* (charcoal-broiled quail) in a family-owned *taverna* in the *messoghion* (midland area east of Athens). They were difficult to resist, even though we saw them flying in cages as we arrived. Relishing the tiny birds, our host urged us to use fingers, remarking, *To pouli kai i gynaika theloun heri*— "Birds and women need handling!"

KOTA KAI ZOMOS
[*Chicken and broth*]

An old hen is worth forty chicks!   GREEK PROVERB

Traditional family recipe for broth and chicken, with wishbone saved to play the philopena game *viantes*. Ask a Greek friend the rules of this game for two, and enjoy the fun.

TO SERVE 4 TO 6

1 2½- to 3-pound stewing chicken	2 to 3 carrots
2 onions, chopped	Herbs: 3 sprigs parsley, 1 bay leaf, 2 to 3 sprigs thyme, mint, basil, or dill
1 leek, chopped	
2 stalks celery, scraped and chopped	Salt
	2 to 3 peppercorns

Wash the chicken and place in a soup pot with enough cold water to cover. Bring to boil, remove from heat and skim. Return to heat, add the onions, leek, celery, carrots, herbs, salt to taste and the peppercorns. Simmer until chicken is tender, approximately 2 hours. Remove from heat and lift the chicken from the pot using a slotted spoon. Strain the broth through a double cheesecloth draped over a sieve set into a bowl. Use chicken for salad, pie or fricassee. Broth will make a wonderful soup or can be used as stock for sauces.

Note: To clarify the broth, after straining, beat 2 egg whites until the soft peak stage and add to the stock with the 2 egg shells. Bring to a boil stirring steadily. Strain through the double cheesecloth and discard residue and shells in the cheesecloth.

KOTA KAPAMA

[Spicy chicken braised with cinnamon and cloves]

A superb dish for family or guests. I have seen Greek cooks slip a few hot red pepper seeds into the pot, but *kapama* is delectable without them. Another meat, especially lamb, may be used as a substitute for the poultry.

TO SERVE 5

*1 frying or roasting chicken
(2½ pounds), cut into serving
pieces
Juice of 1 lemon
4 to 5 tablespoons sweet butter
and vegetable oil, mixed
½ cup dry white wine (optional)
1½ pounds fresh or canned
tomatoes, peeled, chopped,
and drained*

*1 tablespoon tomato paste diluted
in ¼ cup water
1 large stick cinnamon
3 whole cloves
Salt and freshly ground pepper
Fresh parsley or watercress for
garnish*

Arrange the chicken parts in a glass or earthenware bowl and rub all over with lemon juice. Allow to stand while heating the butter and oil in a heavy braising pot. Slip the chicken into the fat and cook over medium heat, turning with tongs to avoid pricking the flesh; sauté until light chestnut in color. Heat the wine in a small pan, pour over the chicken, shake the pan, and continue cooking over low heat. Stir in the tomatoes and tomato paste, slip the cinnamon and cloves in among the pieces, and cover. Simmer over the lowest possible heat for 1½ hours, or until the chicken is tender and the sauce thick. Or, transfer to a medium slow oven (325 degrees) to complete the cooking. Season with salt and pepper. Serve warm over cooked grain or mashed potatoes with green raw or cooked vegetables and chilled wine. Garnish with parsley or watercress.

KOTOPOULO KOKKINISTO
["Reddened" chicken]

TO SERVE 5 TO 6

*1 frying or roasting chicken (3
pounds), cut into serving
pieces*
*3 tablespoons vegetable oil or
butter*
1 onion or 2 scallions, chopped
2 tablespoons butter
*2 tablespoons all-purpose flour
(optional)*

*1 cup dry white wine, more if
necessary*
*2 cups chopped, drained fresh
tomatoes*
*2 tablespoons chopped fresh
parsley*
*Pinch of dried marjoram or
thyme*
Salt and freshly ground pepper
Water, if necessary

Wash and dry the chicken. In a frying pan, heat the oil or butter and
sear the chicken over high heat, turning constantly to avoid burning the
chicken. Remove each piece when reddish in color. Lower the heat and
sauté the onion until soft, adding the butter while stirring. For a thicker
sauce, add the flour and cook 2 minutes, then add the wine and tomatoes.
Simmer until thickened, then strain the sauce into a baking-serving casserole. Bring to a boil, lower the heat, and slip the chicken into the
sauce. Sprinkle the herbs over the chicken, season lightly with salt and
pepper, and shake the casserole gently. Chicken should be almost covered with liquid; if not, add a little water. Cover tightly and simmer
over low heat or transfer to a medium oven (350 degrees) to bake for 1
hour, or until the chicken is tender and the sauce thick. Serve warm.

KOTOPOULO YEMISTO KYPRIOTIKO
[Stuffed chicken, Cyprus style]

The stuffing for this is crunchy and flavorful, and may be used with turkey by doubling the recipe.

TO SERVE 5 OR 6

1 roasting chicken (2½ to 3 pounds), liver reserved	*½ cup dry white wine*
	1¼ cups water
3 tablespoons vegetable oil or butter	*Salt*
	1 teaspoon ground cinnamon
½ cup almonds, blanched and quartered lengthwise	*Pinch of granulated sugar*
	½ cup currants
¾ cup raw long-grain white rice	*Melted butter or vegetable oil*

Wash and dry the chicken and set aside. In a medium saucepan, heat the oil or butter and sauté the almonds and liver, then remove with a slotted spoon. Chop the liver and set aside with the nuts. Add the rice to the fat in the pan and sauté over medium heat, stirring constantly, then pour in the wine, water, salt, cinnamon, and sugar. Cover and cook for 12 minutes, or until the rice is almost tender. Stir in the almonds, liver, and currants and remove the pan from the heat.

Spoon the stuffing into the large cavity of the chicken and close tightly with skewers. Truss the chicken and brush the surface lightly with melted butter or oil. Set in a baking pan, breast side up, and bake for 1¼ hours, or until tender, in moderate oven (350 degrees), turning with 2 wooden spoons every 20 minutes and basting frequently with drippings. Remove the stuffing from the cavity and transfer to the center of a warm platter. Carve the chicken and arrange around the stuffing. Serve warm.

Note: For a popular mainland version, substitute pine nuts, nutmeg, and a little chopped celery and parsley, and soaked bread for the almonds, cinnamon, and rice.

KOTOPOULO YEMISTO
[Roast chicken stuffed with pine nuts and herbs]

This stuffing has a subtle blend of textures and flavors, and is often used for stuffing small birds (*pitsounia*).

TO SERVE 5 TO 6

1 roasting chicken (3 to 3½ pounds), liver and heart reserved
Salt, pepper, and grated nutmeg to taste
2½ tablespoons butter
1 small onion, minced
2 tablespoons chopped celery
3 tablespoons chopped parsley

2 to 3 tablespoons chopped dill leaves
3 slices bread or toast crumbs (about ½ cup)
⅔ cup milk, more if necessary
2 tablespoons pine nuts
3 to 4 tablespoons melted butter
Fresh parsley for garnish

Wash the chicken inside and out, dry, then sprinkle inside and out with salt and pepper and grate some nutmeg into the cavity. Set aside while you prepare the stuffing.

Sauté the chicken liver and heart in ½ tablespoon of the butter, then chop and set aside. Heat the remaining butter in an enameled frying pan and cook the onion until soft and transparent. Add the celery and sauté for several minutes. Add the parsley and dill and stir in the toast crumbs. Remove from the heat, stir in the milk, using a wooden spoon, and season with salt, pepper, and nutmeg. Return to the heat until the mixture boils, then add the pine nuts and chopped liver, heat and stir. (There should be less than 2 cups.) Add a little milk if the stuffing is too thick and cool slightly. Stuff the body cavity and close it securely with 3 or 4 skewers. If any filling remains, stuff the neck cavity; fold the skin over and secure with a skewer. Truss the chicken, brush with melted butter, and place, breast side down, in a 9- or 10-inch baking dish. Bake on the center rack of a moderate oven (350 degrees) for 1¼ to 1½ hours, turning the chicken every 25 minutes, using 2 wooden spoons and brushing often with drippings. (The chicken will be reddish-chestnut and crisp.) Remove the skewers and strings. Carefully remove stuffing with a soup spoon and put into a warm serving bowl. Place the chicken on a warm platter, breast side up, and garnished with parsley. Serve warm.

KOTA ATZEM PILAFI IPIRIOTIKO
[Chicken sautéed with tomatoes and rice atzem-style (Epirus)]

In Epirus, a familiar method of cooking poultry (and meats as well) is called *atzem*: combined with rice and served from the baking dish. *Atzem*, both word and method, comes from Asia Minor, so dishes prepared in this way are most popular in areas with a strong Turkish influence, Epirus among them. This is particularly festive if the chicken is boned.

To make *arni atzem pilafi* (lamb with rice) substitute 2 pounds lean lamb chunks for the chicken.

TO SERVE 4 TO 5

*1 frying or roasting chicken (2½ pounds), washed, dried, and cut into
   serving pieces
4 to 5 tablespoons butter or vegetable oil
1 large onion, diced
Salt and freshly ground pepper
1 stick cinnamon (optional)
½ cup tomato sauce
1½ cups raw long-grain white rice*

In an attractive cooking-serving casserole, heat the butter, and sauté the chicken and the onion, turning the chicken pieces constantly. Sprinkle with salt and pepper, then add cinnamon stick, tomato sauce, and enough water to almost cover the meat. Cover and simmer on top of the stove or bake in a moderate oven (350 degrees) for 40 minutes. Pour out the liquid, measure, and if necessary add enough water to make 3 cups. Pour back into the casserole, add the rice and shake the pan a few times to mix the rice in. Continue cooking, uncovered, for 20 minutes longer, or until all the liquid has been absorbed by the rice. Remove from the heat and drape with a dry towel for 5 minutes. Serve hot.

Note: This is excellent with yogurt and green salad.

KOTOPOULO TIGANITO MARINATO
[*Marinated fried chicken*]

Hellenes like marinades. The one presented here can be used with poultry or meat.

TO SERVE 4 TO 5

1 frying chicken (2½ pounds), washed, dried, and cut into serving pieces
Marinade for Poultry or Meat (see below)
Salt and freshly ground pepper
¾ cup all-purpose flour
Olive, corn, or peanut oil for frying
Cherry tomatoes and watercress or parsley for garnish

Dip the chicken in the marinade, coating the pieces on all sides. Cover and refrigerate for at least 2 hours or overnight if desired. Drain, then season lightly with salt and pepper. Put the flour in a paper bag, add the chicken, and shake lightly until coated with flour. Put oil in a heavy frying pan to the depth of ½ inch and heat almost to the smoking point. Slip the chicken into the hot oil and fry to a light chestnut color, turning on all sides. Using tongs, remove the chicken to a baking pan, discarding the remaining oil in the frying pan. Bake in a moderate oven (350 degrees) for 50 minutes, or until tender, pouring off the oil as it collects in the pan. (The chicken will be crisp and a rich chestnut color.) Arrange on a platter, with tomatoes and watercress or parsley alternating around the chicken.

Note: If you do not wish to marinate the chicken, simply shake it in seasoned flour, sprinkle with paprika, and fry as above.

MARINADE FOR POULTRY OR MEAT

¼ cup olive oil
¼ cup white wine vinegar
¼ cup lemon juice
½ cup white wine
2 cloves garlic, cut
½ onion, sliced

1 bay leaf, crushed
1 teaspoon dried thyme, marjoram, or oregano
2 peppercorns, crushed
2 to 3 juniper berries
4 coriander seeds, cracked

Combine all the ingredients in a bowl and dip in poultry or meat to coat on all sides.

KOTOPOULO SALTSA KARYDIA
[Chicken braised in walnut sauce]

TO SERVE 4 TO 5

1 frying or roasting chicken
(2½ to 3 pounds), cut into
serving pieces
Salt and freshly ground pepper
1 large onion, sliced
4 to 5 tablespoons butter
1 bay leaf

1 sprig of fresh thyme
1 cup milk
2 egg yolks
1 teaspoon grated nutmeg
1 cup shelled walnuts, crushed
in a mortar or blender

Wash and dry the chicken parts and season lightly with salt and pepper. In a heavy frying pan, sauté the onion in the butter until soft, then add the chicken parts after a few minutes. Sauté on all sides, then add the bay leaf, thyme, and enough hot water to almost cover. Tightly cover the pan and simmer the chicken until tender (approximately 1 hour). Using a slotted spoon, remove the chicken to a warm platter and keep warm while you prepare the sauce.

Strain the remaining pan liquid into a small saucepan and bring to a boil. Meanwhile, whisk the milk with the egg yolks, then add, slowly, to the strained pan liquid and cook over very low heat until the sauce boils, stirring constantly. Sprinkle in the nutmeg, then stir in the crushed walnuts. Simmer another minute and pour over the chicken. Serve warm.

KOTOPOULO KRASATO
[Chicken braised in wine and Cognac]

TO SERVE 4 TO 5

1 broiler or roasting chicken
(2½ to 3 pounds), washed,
dried, and cut into serving
pieces
Salt and freshly ground pepper
All-purpose flour
2 tablespoons butter or
margarine
2 tablespoons olive oil

6 to 8 small white onions, peeled
and a cross cut in the stem ends
¼ cup chopped fresh parsley
1 small bay leaf
1 cup mushroom caps, canned
or fresh (optional)
Fresh thyme
¼ cup Cognac
1 cup dry red wine

175

Season the chicken pieces with salt and pepper and dust lightly with flour. Heat the butter and oil in a heavy braising pan and sauté the chicken on all sides, adding the onions during the process. Add the parsley, bay leaf, mushrooms, and a few thyme leaves. Pour the Cognac over the chicken so all the pieces are saturated and simmer for a few minutes, then pour in the wine, cover, and simmer for 1 to 1½ hours, or until the chicken is tender. (Or you may transfer the pan to a medium slow oven [325 degrees] and bake until tender.) When cooked, the chicken and sauce should be arranged on a warm platter along with a steaming rice or other grain dish. Serve warm, garnished with fresh thyme, with black olives, fresh salad, and chilled white wine.

KOTA FOURNOU LADORIGANI
[Roast chicken oregano, Peloponnesos style]

A very popular method in Peloponnesos.

TO SERVE 4 TO 5

> *1 roasting chicken (2½ to 3 pounds)*
> *Salt and freshly ground pepper*
> *¼ cup olive oil*
> *Juice of 1½ lemons*
> *1½ teaspoons oregano*
> *Sliced tomatoes and cucumbers for garnish*

Wash, dry, and truss the chicken, then season inside and out with salt and pepper. Whisk the olive oil, lemon juice, and 1 teaspoon of the oregano in a small bowl and brush over the chicken. Place the chicken in a shallow pan and roast in moderate oven (350 degrees) for 1¼ hours, turning every 20 minutes and basting with the remaining marinade. Sprinkle the remaining oregano on the chicken and serve warm, garnished with tomatoes and cucumbers.

Note: This dish is nice served with potatoes, if desired, which may be roasted with the chicken. Peel and quarter 4 to 5 medium all-purpose potatoes (or 10 small, round ones). Season them with salt, pepper, and the juice of 1 lemon and set around the chicken after the first 20 minutes of cooking. Add 1 cup of hot water and continue cooking until fork-tender. The potatoes will turn a rich color if the oven temperature is turned up to 400 degrees after the chicken is removed, during the last 10 minutes or so; turn them once. Garnish the chicken with the potatoes and serve the cucumbers and tomatoes as a salad.

KOTA ME SALTSA YAOURTI
[Chicken sautéed with nutmeg and yogurt]

TO SERVE 5

1 frying or roasting chicken (2½ pounds) cut into serving pieces
Salt and freshly ground pepper
2 tablespoons butter or margarine
Grated nutmeg
Saltsa Yaourti (page 53)

Wash, dry and season the chicken with salt and pepper. Heat the butter or margarine in a large pan and add the chicken pieces. Sauté until a rich gold color, then remove from the pan and sprinkle lightly with grated nutmeg.

Prepare the *saltsa yaourti* in a flameproof casserole, add the sautéed chicken, and simmer over minimum heat for 1½ hours, or until the chicken is tender. Delicious with Horiatiki Salata (page 212) and crusty bread.

GALOPOULO YEMISTO ME KASTANA
[Roast turkey with chestnut stuffing]

Chestnut stuffing is a favorite and may also be used to stuff chickens.

TO SERVE 6

1 turkey (7 pounds)
1 pound chestnuts
3 tablespoons butter or margarine
1 onion, minced
¾ cup milk
2 dried sage leaves
1 small bay leaf

Pinch of dried thyme
½ cup toast crumbs, approximately
Salt and freshly ground pepper
Juice of 1 lemon
Melted butter or oil
½ cup hot water

Wash and dry the turkey, inside and out. With a sharp knife cut a small cross in the flat side of the chestnuts, then place on a baking dish. Bake for 15 minutes in a moderate oven (350 degrees), or until the outer skin curls back. Remove, breaking off and discarding the outer skin. Place in a small pan with water to cover and boil until the inner skin loosens. Drain and peel. Cook in water to cover until soft but firm (approximately 10 more minutes). Drain.

Meanwhile, heat the butter in a frying pan and sauté the onions until soft, then add the milk. Crush the herbs and sprinkle over the milk, then bring to a boil. Add the chestnuts, enough toast crumbs to absorb the liquid, and season lightly with salt and pepper. Rub salt over the turkey and dust inside with salt. Stuff the large cavity with the chestnut mixture and close the opening with skewers, or sew with needle and thread. (Use any remaining filling to stuff the neck opening.) Brush the surface of the turkey with the lemon juice and melted fat, then truss the turkey and place on a rack in a shallow baking pan. Add the ½ cup hot water to the pan and bake in a moderately slow oven (325 degrees) for about 3 hours, or until golden and tender, turning and basting the turkey frequently. Remove the turkey from the oven and transfer the stuffing to a warm bowl. Serve both the turkey and the stuffing warm.

GALOPOULO ME LAHANO TURSI THRAKIOTIKO
[Turkey braised with sauerkraut, Thracian style]

One of the delights in writing this book has been the enthusiasm of people in many Greek regions to help. The Thracian ladies among them have become avid researchers, and they exposed me to this delicious dish which is served in Thrace on Christmas Day. When I tested the recipe with an under-7-pound frozen turkey, thoroughly thawed, I saved the neck, wings, and back to make turkey soup *avgolemono* (my own invention), but used the remaining pieces to prepare this Thracian specialty, sprinkled with paprika. Begin early to insure very slow baking.

TO SERVE 5 TO 6

> *1 turkey (6½ to 7 pounds), cleaned and washed*
> *3 to 4 tablespoons butter and olive oil, mixed*
> *Salt and freshly ground pepper*

¼ cup canned tomato sauce or tomato juice
½ cup water
1 to 1½ pounds prepared, uncooked sauerkraut
Paprika (optional)

Dry the turkey inside and out and cut into serving pieces. Heat the butter and oil in a heavy pan and sauté the turkey pieces without browning on all sides. Season lightly with salt and pepper, then cover and cook over low heat for 5 minutes. In a small saucepan, heat the tomato sauce with the ½ cup water and pour over the turkey. Continue simmering for 30 minutes.

Meanwhile, drain the sauerkraut, and using the fingers, squeeze thoroughly to remove all liquid. Tuck in among the turkey pieces and allow to heat through. Transfer to a *yuvetsi* or earthenware casserole, cover, and bake in a very slow oven (225 degrees) for 3 hours, or until tender, turning at least once every hour. (The sauce should be thick when the turkey is tender.) Sprinkle lightly with paprika and serve warm.

GALOPOULO YEMISTO ME KREAS KAI KOUKOUNARIA
[Roast turkey with meat and pine nut stuffing]

Pine nuts and raisins in stuffings are particularly popular in the northern regions. Use this stuffing also for chickens, Cornish hens and other game birds.

TO SERVE 6 TO 8

1 turkey (10 to 10½ pounds),
cleaned and washed, heart and
liver reserved and chopped
Salt and freshly ground pepper
Melted butter
3 scallions, minced
2 tablespoons butter
1 pound lean veal, ground
2 tablespoons chopped fresh
parsley

1 bay leaf, crushed
3 juniper berries
Pinch of thyme or sage
¾ cup raw long-grain white
rice
1 cup boiling water
⅔ cup pine nuts
⅔ cup raisins
Fresh parsley, pine nuts, and
cherry tomatoes for garnish

Dry the turkey inside and out. Season lightly with salt and pepper, and rub with melted butter. Set aside while you prepare the stuffing. Sauté the scallions in the 2 tablespoons butter until soft, then mash in the veal, using a fork, and cook over low heat until the raw color disappears. Cover and simmer a few minutes, until the meat secretes some liquid, then add the reserved, chopped turkey heart and liver and cook for 2 minutes. Stir in the herbs, rice, and 1 cup boiling water. Cook, uncovered, until the fat rises to the surface. Skim off the fat, season lightly, and simmer uncovered, until the rice absorbs the liquid (approximately 15 minutes). Stir in the pine nuts and raisins and allow to cool slightly. Stuff the turkey (you will have enough for both cavities), truss, and roast as described on page 178. Remove the stuffing and serve warm in a separate bowl, garnished with parsley and pine nuts. Carve the turkey and arrange on a platter, surrounded with cherry tomatoes.

Note: This is very tasty with cold marinated vegetables and Greek retsina wine.

PAPIA PSITI ME SALTSA PORTOKALI
[*Roast duck with orange sauce*]

In this recipe, stuffing ingredients are used to absorb the heavy duck odors, a popular method. Celery may be substituted for parsley, or prunes for the apple.

TO SERVE 4 TO 5

1 duck (5 pounds), cleaned and washed, neck and giblets reserved
Salt and freshly ground pepper
1 teaspoon dried sage
1 apple, peeled, cored, and cubed
4 to 5 sprigs parsley
1¼ cups orange juice
2½ cups meat stock
2 tablespoons butter

2 tablespoons all-purpose flour
3 tablespoons sugar boiled with ¼ cup water until thick
¼ cup Mavrodaphne (semi-sweet) wine (optional)
Rind (zest only) of 1 orange, cut into thin strips, boiled 5 minutes in water and drained
Lemon juice, if necessary
2 oranges, segmented

Season the duck cavity with salt, pepper, and the dried sage. Stuff with onion, apple, and parsley and truss securely. Prick the duck on the lower breast and thighs with the tines of fork and rub ¼ cup of the orange juice into the holes. Place, breast side up, on a rack in a shallow roasting pan. Roast in a hot oven for 15 minutes, then add ½ cup of the stock to the pan and continue roasting the duck for approximately

2 hours, or until the juices drain yellow when a leg is lifted. Remove and discard the stuffing. Transfer the duck to a warm platter, carve into serving pieces, and keep warm while you make the sauce.

Simmer the remaining 2 cups of stock with the reserved neck and giblets until reduced to 1 cup. Meanwhile, skim off all fat from the pan juices and discard, but save the other drippings (for quick separation use ice cubes). Strain the nonfat liquid into a saucepan, add the butter, and stir until the butter melts. Stir in the flour and cook for 2 minutes. Then add the 1 cup reduced stock, the sugar syrup, wine, and remaining orange juice. Simmer until thickened. Add the orange rind and taste. For more flavor add a few drops of lemon juice and season lightly with salt and pepper. Bring to a boil, then pour over the duck. Serve warm garnished with orange segments and bright leaves from a fruit tree, if available.

Note: This is delicious with rice and crisp vegetables.

PHASIANOS PSITOS
[*Roast pheasant*]

Pheasants traveled to Greece from the Phasis River in Asia and were available locally by the fourth century B.C. Pheasants and all the Greek favorites make their appearance in Aristophanes' satire *The Birds*. During game season, pheasants and quail are among the favored game, with pots simmering, particularly in the northern areas. Nevertheless, all provinces develop their favorite combinations, which on close scrutiny are simply the standard methods using locally favorite ingredients.

You should prepare pheasants (2½ to 3 pounds) by hanging them in a cool place for 4 to 5 days to develop flavor. They should then be cleaned, plucked, and washed like any other birds.

TO SERVE 2 TO 4

> *1 pheasant (2½ to 3 pounds), cleaned and plucked*
> *Salt and freshly ground pepper*
> *2 to 3 thin slices lard or salt pork*
> *4 to 5 tablespoons butter or margarine, melted*
> *Fresh radishes and scallions for garnish*

Season the pheasant inside and out with salt and pepper. Truss the bird securely, then tie the lard across the breast with string. Dip double-thickness cheesecloth into the melted butter and wrap around the pheasant. Place on a rack in a shallow baking pan and roast in a moderate oven (350 degrees) for 20 minutes per pound, basting and turning every 20 minutes. Remove from the oven, untie, and remove the cheesecloth and fat. Serve garnished with fresh radish roses and scallion curls.

Note: This is delicious with Kastana Poure (page 192) or puréed lentils.

PHASIANOS KRASATOS
[*Pheasant baked with wine*]

In a small saucepan combine 1 cup dry white or red wine with ½ cup tomato juice, 1 tablespoon each of chopped fresh parsley and celery, a small bay leaf, one clove garlic, a little salt and black pepper. Simmer for 20 minutes, strain, and keep warm. After removing the cheesecloth from *phasianos psitos*, cut the pheasant into serving pieces and arrange on a warm platter. Pour the warm wine sauce over the pheasant and serve.

PHASIANOS STIFADO
[*Pheasant stifado style*]

Substitute pheasant, cut into serving pieces, for the veal in Moshari Stifado (page 141) using pearl onions equal in weight to the pheasant.

LAGOS/KOUNELLI FOURNOU
[*Baked hare or rabbit*]

The finest Greek chefs of ancient times preferred rabbit or hare served without sauces. Archestratus, who was known as the "inventive genius of cookery," simply salted, spitted, and roasted rabbit and served it hot. Alcaeus liked hare sprinkled with coriander.

Greek chefs of today not only prefer cooking rabbit or hare in sauces, but also suggest marinating first to improve the flavor. Washing in both fresh water and vinegar first are also recommended.

TO SERVE 4 TO 6

1 *rabbit or hare, cleaned and skinned*
1 *to 2 stalks celery, leaves included, chopped*
2 *medium onions, chopped*
1 *carrot, sliced*
½ *cup chopped fresh parsley*
1 *bay leaf, crumbled*
1 *to 2 sprigs fresh rosemary*
6 *peppercorns, bruised*

2 *cups dry red wine*
½ *cup vinegar*
¼ *cup (4 tablespoons) butter or margarine*
Salt and freshly ground pepper to taste
3 *to 4 fresh tomatoes, chopped, or 1 can (8 ounces) tomato sauce*
A few allspice berries

After washing the rabbit or hare thoroughly and cutting into serving pieces, place in a large glass or earthenware bowl. Make a marinade by combining the celery, onions, carrots, herbs, peppercorns, wine, and vinegar and pouring over the meat. Cover and refrigerate for a day or two, turning the pieces over occasionally.

On serving day, drain, reserving the marinade, and wipe dry. Transfer the marinade to a casserole and simmer for 15 minutes. While the marinade is cooking, heat the butter in a large frying pan, and when very hot sear the meat over high heat until it is reddened in color without browning. Remove from the heat, and with a spatula lift the rabbit or hare pieces into the simmering marinade, then pour in the remaining butter. Taste for seasoning, then add the salt and pepper, tomatoes, and allspice. Weight the meat with a small plate to keep it under the sauce, then bake it in a very slow oven (225 degrees) for 2½ hours, or until the meat is tender and the sauce thickened. Serve warm with Melitzanes Poure (page 202) or other vegetables and a light wine.

LAGOS/KOUNELLI STIFADO
[Hare or rabbit stifado style, with onions and cloves]

Undoubtedly the favorite, a delicious method of braising hare, we sampled this dish on the island of Evia—unforgettable. On the island of Santorini we enjoyed rabbit braised in wine and tomato, with potatoes; in Macedonia the flavor was unique when the hare was marinated and then baked with wine, onions, and bacon bits.

183

TO SERVE 6

1 rabbit or hare, cut into serving
  pieces and marinated for 1 to
  2 days as directed on page 183
¼ cup butter or oil
1½ to 2 pounds small white
  onions (equal weight of rabbit
  or hare)
1 cup canned tomato sauce

3 whole cloves
2 cloves garlic
1 tablespoon raisins (optional)
1 bay leaf
1 teaspoon granulated sugar
½ cup dry white wine
2 tablespoons wine vinegar
Fresh rosemary

Remove the rabbit or hare from the marinade and wipe dry. In a large casserole, heat the butter or oil and sear the rabbit or hare over high heat until reddened in color, without browning the fat. Meanwhile, peel the onions and cut a cross in the root end with a sharp pointed knife to keep them from falling apart during cooking. Arrange around the rabbit or hare, then stir in the remaining ingredients, add enough water to cover, place an inverted plate over the meat and bring to a boil. Transfer to a very slow oven (225 degrees) and bake for 2 to 2½ hours, until the rabbit or hare and onions are tender. Remove from the oven and carefully pour off the sauce into a small saucepan. Boil down to 1½ cups. Remove plate from casserole, pour the sauce over, and garnish with additional rosemary. Serve warm.

  Note: The flavor improves the second day.

VEGETABLES
AND SALADS

Do not ask just to appear, but also to create.
GREEK PROVERB

A RAPT CONCENTRATION SHARPENS faces and wits in the lively Greek markets. Bending low over the baskets and stalls to see and touch the vegetables, women often seem to be murmuring, "What fine vegetables you are," and "Hmmm, you will make perfect *melitzanes yemistes* for dinner." And heaven help the vegetable that looks dry and wilted!

How many times we heard the *manavi* asked the same question, *"Einai fresko?"* as he stopped at door after door to sell his vegetables. In the luxury resort Porto Rafti on the eastern Attic shore, where hucksters are now elegantly motorized with thundering loudspeakers echoing off the hills, the women still ask the same questions every day, "Is it ripe?" "Are they tender?" "Are they fresh?" On Corfu, and Crete and Rhodes, where the *manavi* still has a donkey to pull his cart, demands for fresh vegetables make daily conversation. To us the produce looked outstanding. Yet many Hellenes growl and glower that the best is exported.

The Minoans picked mint, coriander, anise, and sesame to spice their dishes, which were by no means products of a "primitive" culture, according to the archeological study "Food in Early Greece" by Kenton Vickery.* Western herb and spice cookery certainly developed from

* Vickery, Kenton. "Food in Early Greece." Thesis: Illinois Studies of the Social Sciences, 1936.

185

these early experimenters. While, alas, no recipes remain, we know that among the Greek vegetable staples included in the recipes that follow, a significant number were the culinary fare of the Minoans on Crete during the early Bronze Age. Chicory, celery, cucumbers, leeks, garlic, onion, parsnip, squash, chick-peas, beans, peas, lentils, and of course olives were eaten twenty-five centuries B.C., archeologists say. A strong habit. When Greek people like particular foods, they like them for eons!

Furthermore, ancient utensils in the Heraklion Museum substantiate claims of archeological studies that these early chefs used both dry and moist cookery methods to cook their vegetables, as well as their meats. We marveled at their craftsmanship, and their varied, practical designs. Their tools would be delightful to use in 1975. By the time of Pericles, the Greek Golden Age, the herbs and spices in use included basil, rosemary, sage, savory, capers, oregano, marjoram, saffron, salt, pepper, caraway, mustard, parsley, bay leaves, garlic, onion, and leek, in addition to favorites of the Minoans. All remain significant in Greek cookery except saffron, which comes from the *krokos* (crocus) flower.

In the fourth century B.C., Antiphanes recorded the imaginative use of seasonings and vegetables, including radishes, asparagus, lupine, beets, carrots, turnips, mallow, sorrel, nettle, orach, iris, bulbs, artichokes, cactus, truffles, many varieties of squash and zucchini, and of course cabbage. About this time, naturalists and classifiers had a field day with Greek plant life. The great Hippocrates of Cos (479–399 B.C.) probably influenced Greek attitudes toward the respective status of vegetables and herbs more than anyone. He inaugurated the empirical system of diagnosis of physical and psychical symptoms, and he classified plants, attributing medicinal qualities to many herbs. Among the various plants in his fascinating *Regimen* Hippocrates listed wheat as more nourishing than barley; legumes as "heating"; mint, endive, parsley, and nettles as "cooling." Garlic, clover, fennel, and leek juice were distinguished as "diuretic"; nettles and mint as agents to stop vomiting. He suggested warm chamomile to treat wounds, and advised juices of chick-peas, lentils, barley, beet, and cabbage as purgatives. Smelling celery, he said, would stop sneezing.

Theophrastus, avidly following his predecessor's example, wrote the widely quoted reference *Enquiry into Plants*. He described vegetables in detail, including the truffles of Mytilini, Elis, and Cyrene (a Greek colony in northern Africa), those of the last having the odor of meat. It is no wonder that Greeks became aware of the physical qualities of vegetables. They cared about the effects on metabolism, the alimentary tract, and virility. Carrots, for example, were believed to have "semen-producing powers," while conversely, cucumbers were believed to inhibit coition. Lettuce was supposed to check sexual desire, and to make matters worse, was also soporific!

From Lydia to Sicily, cookery was refined to its zenith following the Persian Wars. Some of the dishes of that period have never been surpassed. Turnips, to give one example, were cooked in many ways: they were boiled, or roasted, or pickled. Prepared as appetizers, they were first cooked in vinegar, then spiced with mustard. Pickling, forerunner of the popular *tursi*, involved slicing, drying in the sun, dipping in boiling water, soaking in brine, or marinating in equal parts of white must and vinegar. Cooks sometimes seasoned the marinade with crushed raisins and mustard seeds.

And if that was not enough for the lowly turnip, it could also be disguised to fool the king. When King Nicomedes of Bithynia craved anchovy, his cook Soterides satisfied this longing without anchovy. The clever chef sliced a fresh turnip in the shape of anchovy, parboiled it, poured oil over, sprinkled it with salt, and spread on exactly forty seeds of black poppy. With such inventiveness, a cook has to make history.

Unfortunately, the lower classes could afford neither inventive chefs nor exotic foods. Historians remind us that they survived substantially on leguminous soups and porridges, no doubt seasoned with the yield of their sparse vegetation. But it is in how the poor use their foods that one can admire a country's cuisine. It is not surprising that beans became a Greek "soul food." The proverbs and idioms are rich with allusions to beans, and the treasured recipes pass from generation to generation.

Other vegetables gradually migrated to Greece and became esteemed there. Eggplant came from Arabia, okra from Ethiopia, and spinach from Persia, all very significant. Furthermore, tomatoes, green peppers, corn, peanuts, and potatoes traveled to Greece much later, after their discovery by Columbus and other Spanish explorers in the New World. Greek cookery—in fact, all Mediterranean cookery—seems unthinkable without tomatoes, peppers, and potatoes. America, therefore, has contributed color and zest to the cuisine of Greece.

Cooking in the pot and naming the dish for the pot began in early Greece. Casseroles, stews, and herb blends have been established for centuries. "First of all put some marjoram at the bottom of a large casserole, over that the liquor, diluted with vinegar in just measure, colouring it with must and silphium; then whip it vigorously," Alexis wrote in the *Love-Lorn Lass*. Except for silphium, which disappeared centuries ago, the recipe sounds like a sauce for the popular braised vegetable dishes of today. Herbs and spices enliven vegetable dishes because they arouse the senses of both cook and diner, as visitors are prone to observe in Greece.

When a Hellene impulsively pinches a sprig of basil growing in an herb pot, he inhales the aroma, sighs, and his face reflects unmistakable joy. And if we bend over to smell, the owner quickly snips off sprigs to give us for "food" on our trip, as he waves *sto kalo* (to the good). A smell is tangible and edible.

To a Greek, the cultural and aesthetic properties of vegetables often transcend the nutritional value, and some vegetables take on human characteristics. Human beings, on the other hand, don't mind being compared to vegetables or using them in banter to quip to a friend: "My sweetest leek, how can I forget you?"

As for the salads . . . when someone makes a mess of a situation, Greeks typically throw up their hands expressively and say, *"Ta'kame salata!"* meaning "He made a salad of it!"

In Greece, salads may be served as appetizers, as a first course, or a separate plate with the fish or meat course, as a garnish, or simply brought to the table in a huge bowl to be passed around, divided and enjoyed by the entire party. Salads are raw, cooked, whipped, or pounded. And except for the whipped and pounded styles, which require skill and taste to season judiciously, winter and summer salads are simple to prepare.

Salata for most Hellenes means one seasonal vegetable, served raw or cooked, hot or cold, seasoned with olive oil and lemon or vinegar. This is an ancient custom. Athenaeus referred to salads as *filla* (leaves) with vinegar dressing. One appetizer he described was seasoned with myrrh, sedge, pepper, and Egyptian perfume. Most of these aromatics have since moved from the kitchen to the dressing room; nevertheless, piquant seasonings are still adored by Greek people. Capers, bulbs (shallots, garlic, and onions), herbs (basil, rosemary, sage, parsley, and marjoram) have been recorded as important seasonings by Antiphanes and were used also by the Minoans, although no one knows exactly how.

Tavernes catering to a Greek clientele continually offer Horta Vrasta (page 207), the traditional cooked vegetable salads, sometimes simply called *horta*, because the Greek joy in eating them defies description. You will believe it to taste them, however. They are tender and mild. Villagers walk for miles to pick wild greens—*radikia, vrouva, vlyta, endidia,* and *scarollia*—as a special tribute to visitors, and also enjoy them cooked with pork or lamb, one at a time, of course, such as in Hirino Andidia Avgolemono (page 145).

Raw vegetables most frequently tossed together in summer are cucumbers, tomatoes, and scallions or onions. By the addition of green peppers, olives and feta cheese, the colorful salad becomes Horiatiki Salata ("village" salad; page 212) often referred to as *helleniki* (Greek) or *therini* (summer) in the provinces. *Marouli* (lettuce) is preferred cooked with meat, with or without *avgolemono*, but whenever available, the raw lettuce salad is delightful, and local varieties are very tasty. In winter, cabbages are plentiful, and enjoyed raw or cooked. Cauliflower and broccoli are cooked until very soft, as they are in other Mediterranean countries. Roots and tubers make staple cooked salads. Among the latter favorite combinations, Pantzaria Salata (beet salad) is delicious with Skordalia (page 49), both cold.

Salad dressings vary only slightly from region to region. Wine vinegars and fresh lemon juice with a good-flavored olive oil, fresh or dried herbs, salt, pepper, capers, pickles, hard-boiled eggs, and mustard are prized ingredients. Most frequently used salad dressings are the popular Ladoxido (vinegar oil; page 53), Ladolemono (lemon-oil; page 54), Mayoneza (mayonnaise; page 54), and individual variations on the familiar themes.

Vegetables

LADERA

[*Vegetables cooked in oil*]

A bevy of vegetables cooked in oil are a frequent selection on Greek menus. Tourists often reject these dishes as "too oily." Probably because bread is not buttered when eaten with dinner and supper, the additional oil in the sauce seems natural to Hellenes.

In cooking, the amount of oil becomes a variable. The method is excellent to master, because frozen vegetables may be cooked in place of unavailable fresh ones, and once cooked, the vegetables may be served at room temperature or cold. Try using one tablespoon of oil for each cupful of vegetables. The important rule: Add only enough liquid to cook the vegetable, and serve all the sauce with the dish.

Prepare vegetables as you would for any dish: wash, peel, scrape, and so on. Eggplant should be sliced, salted, and rinsed (although I frequently omit this step) and okra soaked first in vinegar and rinsed (I never omit this step). For each cupful of vegetable:

1 tablespoon olive oil or other vegetable oil
½ cup tomato sauce, tomato juice, or canned tomatoes (see note below)
Salt and freshly ground pepper
1 tablespoon chopped fresh parsley (optional)
1 sprig fresh or ¼ teaspoon dried herb of your choice
1 pinch of spice of your choice

Combine all the ingredients, add the vegetable of your choice (see below), and simmer until tender. Serve warm or cold, with broiled or roasted meats, poultry, fish, and egg dishes.

Note: You may prefer to use water instead of tomato with the cabbage, lettuce and potatoes.

Vegetable	*Suggested seasonings*
Cabbage	Dill or caraway, bay leaf
Eggplant	Garlic, oregano, or basil; allspice
Green beans	Mint, savory, or marjoram; nutmeg
Green peas	Basil or thyme; chives
Lettuce	Fennel or dill; celery, onions
Okra	Garlic; onion; leek
Onions, leeks, or shallots	Wine or vinegar, cloves, cinnamon, bay leaf, sugar
Potatoes	Rosemary, oregano, dill, or mint
Spinach	Mint or dill; nutmeg or mace
Tomatoes, fresh or canned	Cinnamon; basil, mint or marjoram
Zucchini	Onions, green pepper, oregano, basil, or thyme

Use chicken or other stock (instead of tomato) with the following group after preparing to cook. Incidentally, artichokes and celery are delicious with Avgolemono (page 48).

Vegetable	Suggested seasonings
Artichokes	Lemon; aniseed
Carrots	Onions and thyme; cloves
Cauliflower	Celery or dill leaves; lemon juice
Mushrooms	Garlic and oregano; savory; rosemary
Parsnips	Scallions or chives; allspice or coriander
Turnips	Chives; thyme; dill

Asparagus is an ancient Greek vegetable, highly esteemed for its healing powers. Anaxandrides described a dish of asparagus and squills seasoned with marjoram and coriander and served with smoked fish, which would taste delicious in the year 2000. The popular name for this vegetable is *sparangia*. Other modern asparagus dishes are made with Saltsa Aspri (page 50) and Greek grated cheese, and are baked until bubbly.

ASPARAGOS LADOLEMONO
[*Asparagus with lemon-oil dressing*]

TO SERVE 6 TO 8

> *2 pounds asparagus*
> *Salt*
> *1 sprig of fresh basil, marjoram, or rosemary*
> *½ cup Ladolemono (page 54)*
> *Capers for garnish*

Trim the asparagus spears with a small, sharp knife to remove the tough outer parts of the stalk. Cut off and discard the tough butt ends, wash thoroughly, and drain. In an enameled pan with a removable rack, fill to a level of 3 inches with water and lightly season with salt and the herb. Bring to a boil and add the asparagus, placed in the rack with tips up. Partially cover the pan and cook only until tender but firm, not limp and mushy (between 8 and 12 minutes depending on the diameter). Lift the rack and arrange the asparagus, without breaking, on a warm platter.

191

Pour the *ladolemono* dressing over and garnish with capers. Serve cold or warm, with grilled fish, meat, poultry, or egg dishes.

Note: If substituting frozen asparagus, cook in salted water (with the herb) according to the package directions. Save cooking water for a chilled drink with lemon juice, for a soup, or to add to tomato juice as an appetizer.

KASTANA POURE
[*Puréed chestnuts*]

Excellent with pork and game dishes, straight from the many Greek villages called Kastania!

TO SERVE 4 TO 6

1 pound chestnuts
1½ to 2 cups stock or water, more if necessary
Salt and freshly ground pepper
3 to 4 tablespoons butter

To peel the chestnuts, cut a cross on the flat side with the tip of sharp knife, then set on a baking sheet and bake in a 400-degree oven for 15 minutes, or until the outer skins curl. Peel.

Put the chestnuts in a saucepan with the stock or water, then cover and simmer until the liquid has been absorbed and the chestnuts are soft, adding more stock or water if necessary. Drain the chestnuts, peel off inner skins and push through a ricer or food mill into a bowl. Season with salt, pepper, and butter and beat with a wooden spoon. Serve warm.

Note: The Hellenes also make a delicious dessert made in a similar way using chestnuts, milk instead of stock or water, and seasoned slightly with sugar. After pushing through the food mill, arrange the chestnut purée in dessert plates shaped as a "nest" or a "mountain," and fill the nest with whipped cream, or top the mountain with whipped cream "snow."

FASSOLIA PLAKI
[Baked beans, plaki style]

Good health to you, old man, I'm sowing beans.
GREEK PROVERB

Aromatic vegetables and herbs used for *plaki* dishes with fish might have originated with beans. Steaming and herby, they make a meal in one dish.

TO SERVE 6 TO 8

1 pound dried navy beans, black-eyed peas or lima beans
2 medium onions, chopped
2 cloves garlic, sliced
1/3 cup to 1/2 cup olive oil
3 fresh or canned tomatoes, peeled and chopped, or 1/2 cup canned tomato sauce or juice
1/2 carrot, chopped

1 stalk celery with leaves included, chopped
1/3 cup chopped fresh parsley
1 large bay leaf
1 teaspoon dried oregano or 3 sprigs fresh thyme, chopped
3 teaspoons chopped fresh basil leaves or 1 teaspoon dried basil
Salt and freshly ground pepper
Crisp fresh scallions for garnish

Wash the beans and soak overnight in cold water to cover. The following day, bring to a boil, then discard the soaking water and cover the beans with fresh warm water. Simmer until half tender and water is absorbed (approximately 1 hour).

Meanwhile, sauté the onions and garlic in the oil until soft. Stir in tomatoes, carrot, celery, parsley; cover and simmer for 10 minutes. Combine the vegetables with the beans in a large bean pot or heatproof casserole, add the herbs and season with salt and pepper. Cover and bake in a slow oven (300 degrees) for 1½ to 2 hours, or until the beans are soft and all liquid absorbed. Serve warm, garnished with crisp scallions.

Note: The flavor improves the second day.

193

FASSOLAKIA ME PATATES MORAITIKA
[Green beans braised with mint and potatoes, Peloponnesos style]

A flavorful vegetable combination.

TO SERVE 4 TO 5

3 tablespoons olive oil and margarine, mixed
1 cup tomato juice or tomato sauce
1 pound fresh green beans, washed, trimmed, and cut
1 tablespoon chopped fresh parsley (optional)
1 large or 2 medium potatoes, peeled and cut in sixths lengthwise
Salt and freshly ground pepper
Chopped fresh mint

Heat the fat in an enameled pan and mix in the tomato juice. Add the green beans and parsley to the pan with enough water to almost cover. Tuck the potato slices in between, partially cover the pan, and simmer for 25 minutes, then stir and season with salt, pepper and 2 tablespoons chopped mint. Cook uncovered until the beans and potatoes are fork-tender, about 10 more minutes. If the sauce has not thickened, pour it into a small pan, and boil down to one cup, then combine with the beans and potatoes in a warm serving bowl. Sprinkle with a little additional fresh mint and serve warm. Excellent with grilled chops, fish, or egg dish, but equally good as a main course with cheese.

KOUKIA ME YAOURTI
[Lima beans with yogurt]

Beans are staples in Greece, always plentiful in markets. There are many varieties, with many special ways of identifying them, but in the proverbs and in jokes, they are all *koukia*. Very tender ones may be cooked in the shell, and the large ones require long cooking time. *Koukia* are usually cooked in oil, or served in a sauce, and occasionally cooked with tomatoes rather than meat. Invariably, however, they are tastily seasoned with herbs.

TO SERVE 5 TO 6

3 tablespoons vegetable oil or
   butter
1 small onion or shallot, chopped
3 cups shelled lima beans, fresh
   or frozen
3 tablespoons chopped fresh
   parsley

2 tablespoons chopped fresh dill
   or mint leaves
Salt and freshly ground pepper
½ teaspoon granulated sugar
1 cup plain yogurt

Heat the oil or butter in a flameproof casserole or pan and sauté the onion until soft. Stir in the lima beans and herbs and season with salt and pepper and the sugar. Add enough water to cover. Place cover on casserole, and simmer until tender (or bake in moderate oven [350 degrees]). Pour off the remaining liquid and save all but ½ cup for a soup. Cool the ½ cup liquid and mix with the yogurt in a small pan. Heat and pour over the beans. Serve warm.

BROKOLI
[Broccoli]

As a Mediterranean vegetable, broccoli is known to Hellenes and cooked like the other similar member of the cabbage family, cauliflower. However, for broccoli a steamer or a special cooker with a holder is preferable, to allow lower stalks to cook in water while the flowers steam.

Before cooking, cut off the tough ends of the stalk, wash, and drain. Cut several slashes lengthwise up the stalks. Set the stalks in boiling salted water, partially cover, and cook until tender but not mushy, about 15 minutes. Remove from water. To serve, pour Ladolemono (page 54) over the broccoli. Or, if preferred, heat butter to a chestnut color, pour on the cooked broccoli, and top with freshly grated mizithra cheese. Delicious warm with fish dishes.

KOUNOUPIDI ME MIZITHRA
[Cauliflower with cheese, Peloponnesos style]

TO SERVE 5

> *1 medium head cauliflower, washed*
> *1/3 cup butter or margarine*
> *1/2 heaping cut grated mizithra or hard ricotta cheese*

Prepare the cauliflower by steaming as described for Brokoli (page 195), remove from pan without breaking and set aside on a warm platter.

In a small saucepan, heat the butter or margarine slowly without browning, and just as the color begins to change to a pale chestnut, pour over the cauliflower. Scoop up the grated cheese and allow it to filter through your fingers over the cauliflower. Serve immediately. A fine accompaniment for roast meat, poultry, or grilled fish dishes.

PRASSA ME DOMATA
[Leeks stewed with tomatoes]

Leeks lack the status of onions and garlic in Greece, though they have been cultivated for centuries, and approved by Diocles of Carystus in his *Health* (fourth century B.C.). Leeks are used in seasonings and also stewed, baked in *prassopita*, and also combined with rice for *prassorizo*, which is similar to *spanakorizo*.

TO SERVE 4 TO 5

2 bunches leeks	*Few sprigs fresh parsley*
1 cup canned tomatoes or	*Pinch of thyme or oregano*
tomato juice	*3 tablespoons butter or vegetable*
1 cup stock or broth	*oil*
1 onion, chopped	*Salt and freshly ground pepper*
1 stalk celery, chopped	*2 tablespoons lemon juice*

Cut off the stem ends and green parts of the leeks, then wash thoroughly and cut into 1-inch slices. Soak in hot water for 5 to 10 minutes, then drain and discard the water. In an enameled pan, combine with the tomatoes or tomato juice, stock or broth, onion, celery, parsley, thyme or oregano, 3 tablespoons butter or oil, and salt and pepper. Simmer until tender (approximately 20 minutes), adding the lemon juice during the last 5 minutes. Serve warm or cold.

BAMYES YIAHNI
[Okra braised with tomato and parsley]

Okra is the pod of a plant originating in Africa, named from the West African name *nkruman*. I do not know where the word *bamyes* originated or the chemical composition of the gummy, gluey substance in the pods. But I would guess the latter chemical composition is basic because vinegar (an acid) dissolves it. This is why Greek cooks always soak okra in vinegar (½ cup per pound of okra) before cooking, and discard the gluey liquid, rinse, and drain the okra. Prepare okra an hour before cooking it, and try to pick young, tender pods. Along with *Kota me Bamyes* (Chicken and Okra), this is the most popular okra dish.

TO SERVE 6

1½ pounds okra	1 pound canned or fresh
¾ cup white vinegar	tomatoes, peeled and chopped
⅓ cup olive oil and butter mixed	½ cup chopped fresh parsley
3 scallions or 2 small onions,	2 cloves garlic (optional)
chopped	Salt and freshly ground pepper
	1 teaspoon sugar

Trim the stem ends of the okra with a small knife, then wash the pods thoroughly and drain. Place in a glass or earthenware bowl and pour the white vinegar over; mix thoroughly, cover, and allow to stand for at least 30 minutes, but no longer than an hour. Rinse in cold water (discarding the gluey liquid), then spread okra on a dry towel to drain.

In a frying pan, heat half the oil or butter and sauté half the scallions until soft. Add half the okra and sauté, turning on all sides, for 2 minutes. Using a slotted spoon, remove the okra and onions and reserve in a flameproof casserole. Repeat, using the remaining oil, scallions, and okra, then add to the casserole.

Put the tomatoes in the frying pan with the parsley, garlic, a little salt and pepper, and the sugar. Simmer a few minutes, then pour over the okra. Add enough warm water to almost cover the okra, invert a plate over the okra (to keep in place during the cooking period) and continue simmering until the okra is tender, but avoid stirring. (Or *bamyes yiahni* may be transferred to a moderately slow oven [325 degrees] to bake for 40 minutes.) Serve cold or warm (if cooked with oil) and warm (if cooked with butter) with poultry, fish, egg, or cheese dishes.

Note: If using frozen okra, defrost partially and saturate with vinegar, turning a few times during the soaking period.

PATATES YIAHNI
[Braised potatoes, Peloponnesos style]

A delicious and quick dish with an extremely rich flavor.

Feta cheese and a crisp green salad provide a fine balance of color and texture.

TO SERVE 5

> *5 medium potatoes*
> *4 tablespoons olive or vegetable oil*
> *1 medium onion, chopped*
> *2 cloves garlic, minced*
> *1½ cups Italian plum tomatoes, drained*
> *3 tablespoons chopped fresh parsley*
> *Salt and freshly ground pepper*

Peel, quarter, and soak the potatoes in cold water. Meanwhile, heat the oil in a medium frying pan and sauté the onions until soft. Add the garlic and stir in the drained potatoes, stirring over medium heat for a minute. Pour in the tomatoes and enough water to almost cover the potatoes, if necessary. Sprinkle in the parsley and season with salt and pepper. Cover and simmer over low heat for 30 minutes, then uncover and continue cooking over low heat until the potatoes are tender and the sauce thick, turning the potatoes occasionally. Transfer to a warm bowl and serve warm.

PATATES YEMISTES ME LOUKANIKA
[*Potatoes stuffed with sausages*]

A delectable dish when made with homemade country sausages in Greece. Finely seasoned sausages may be substituted.

TO SERVE 6

> *6 large baking potatoes, scrubbed*
> *1 cup thin Saltsa Aspri (page 50)*
> *¾ cup grated cheese*
> *½ teaspoon grated nutmeg*
> *2 to 3 sausages, fried and chopped*
> *Salt and freshly ground pepper*
> *Fresh parsley for garnish*

Bake the potatoes in their jackets in a hot oven (425 degrees) until tender to the touch (approximately 1 hour). Cut in half lengthwise and scoop the insides of the potatoes into a bowl. Arrange the shells in casserole and set aside. Mash the potatoes in the bowl with a fork or masher. Add the *saltsa aspri*, all but 6 tablespoons of the cheese, the nutmeg, and sausages and stir with a wooden spoon until smooth. Taste and add only enough salt to season and a few grindings of black pepper. Stuff the potato shells and dust the tops with the remaining cheese. Bake in a moderate oven (350 degrees) for 15 minutes, or until golden. Insert a fresh parsley sprig at the end of each potato and serve hot, with egg and green vegetable dishes.

Note: Fried, crumbled bacon, or leftover diced ham may be used instead of the sausages.

PATATOKEFTEDES
[*Potato and cheese croquettes*]

Though the potato is a relatively new vegetable for Greece, tried and true methods have made the potato dishes exciting. The ancient mixtures have been adapted to include the potato. This is a splendid accompaniment to meat and fish dishes and needs a creative cook to season artfully and knead to the right consistency before frying.

199

TO MAKE 20 CROQUETTES

5 all-purpose potatoes
Salt
2 tablespoons melted butter or
   margarine
1 small onion, minced
½ cup grated kefalotyri or
   Parmesan cheese

Freshly ground pepper
Grated nutmeg
2 eggs, lightly beaten
1 teaspoon all-purpose flour, if
   necessary
Vegetable oil for deep frying

Scrub the potatoes, place in lightly salted water to cover, and boil until tender, then drain and peel while still hot. Place in a pan and put over moderate heat until dry, shaking the pan to keep from burning. Put the potatoes through a food mill, then combine in a bowl with the butter, onion, cheese, and season only very lightly with salt if the cheese is salty. Grate in a little pepper and nutmeg and add the eggs, beating with a wooden spoon. Knead thoroughly with the fingers and add 1 teaspoon flour if necessary to thicken. Form into balls or flat circles.

Heat oil in a deep pan to 375 degrees and slip in 4 to 5 croquettes at a time. Turn to fry on both sides, then lift out with slotted spoon to drain on paper towels. Serve hot.

SPANAKI VRASTO LADOLEMONO
[Spinach with lemon-oil dressing]

Spinach is delightfully versatile and makes a great *spanakopita* or Spanakorizo (page 107), or, for a simpler accompaniment to fish and meat dishes, use one of these methods. Select fresh, tender, deep-green leaf spinach and store covered, in the refrigerator, to keep hydrated. Wash in clear water until no sand remains and avoid soaking. Drain thoroughly or wrap in a towel to absorb excess water. Use the stems of young spinach, but trim those of coarser varieties and save for a soup stock. Spinach leaves will soften quickly during cooking, due to the high water content.

When substituting frozen for fresh spinach, allow to thaw sufficiently to separate the leaves before cooking.

TO SERVE 5 TO 6

2 pounds fresh spinach
Salt and freshly ground pepper
A few chives, chopped
  (optional)

1 sprig fresh mint
¼ cup olive oil
Juice of 1 lemon
Lemon slices for garnish

Wash, drain, and trim the spinach. Put in an enameled pan without water, cover, and cook over medium heat until the leaves wilt (this method is called "panning"), removing the lid several times during the first 5 minutes. Sprinkle with salt and pepper, chives, and mint. Stir with a wooden spoon, then cover and simmer gently 15 to 18 minutes until just tender. Remove from the heat and transfer to a warm serving bowl.

Meanwhile, prepare sauce by mixing the oil with the lemon juice, using a fork or wire whisk. Pour the sauce over the spinach and garnish with lemon slices.

SPANAKI SOTE
[Sautéed spinach]

Here is another delicious style. After heating the spinach until the leaves wilt, sauté in a small amount of olive oil or butter with chopped scallions and dill leaves. Serve with fish or cold meats.

MELITZANES POURE
[*Whipped eggplant*]

Cooking eggplant offers many surprises and delights to those unfamiliar with this "vegetable" (which is really classified as a fruit of the berry family with tomatoes, grapes, and so on). Although not an ancient Greek food, it is one of the most appreciated in Greece, as you will note in the recipes in other chapters. In addition, try *melitzanes tiganites* (fried eggplant), prepared and fried as suggested in Melitzanes Moussaka (page 233), and whipped eggplant, as a mild accompaniment to spicy meat and fish dishes.

TO SERVE 4

> *1 medium eggplant (approximately 1 pound)*
> *¼ cup milk, warmed*
> *2 to 3 tablespoons butter or margarine*
> *Salt and freshly ground pepper*
> *Fresh parsley for garnish*

Bake the eggplant in a moderate oven (350 degrees) for 45 minutes until the skin puckers, then remove from the oven, peel, and discard the skin. Chop the pulp and pound in a mortar, or whip in an electric blender, until smooth and creamy while gradually adding the milk and butter. Season with salt and pepper, garnish with parsley, and serve warm.

ANGINARES A LA POLITA
[*Artichokes, Constantinople style*]

Artichoke season in spring rejuvenates the fundamental feeling Hellenes have for nature and the changing seasons. Though one of the lesser crops and of short duration, artichokes are still plentiful and the marketing excitement is contagious. Yet for some, artichokes represent a luxury, as expressed in the familiar Greek expression, "We don't have bread, and we want artichokes!"

Since the days of Aristophanes, when artichokes were confused with nettles, the delight in cooking them has been firmly established. And so has their gender—feminine—*E anginara*—resolved after Sophocles, who referred to this elegant vegetable in both the feminine ancient form, *E kinara*, and the masculine, *O kinaros*. Coinciding as it does with the prized lamb season and that of several spring vegetables, artichokes are cooked in many delicious combinations. A few are included among the meat dishes (see pages 133 and 141).

Large green-leaved varieties are referred to in Greece as *aspra* (white), and are used for braised and stewed dishes. Smaller, globe varieties with dark green leaves and *kentri* (chokes or "stings") are called *mavra* (black). The latter make excellent salads and appetizers (see page 71).

All artichokes, fresh or frozen, must be rubbed with lemon juice or plunged into acidulated water immediately after cleaning to avoid discoloration. Remove the tough, outer leaves of the fresh artichokes, and cut off the stems. With kitchen shears, snip off the tips of the leaves. When canned or frozen ones are used, cooking time will vary considerably; watch them closely and don't overcook. Usually, fresh baby varieties cook within 15 minutes, while larger sizes may take up to 50.

Hellenes reflect their affinity with the city of Constantinople (now named Istanbul) by clinging to nicknames: *polis* or *polita* are generally understood to mean Constantinople. We immediately adored the dish below when served to us in a resort on the spectacular Vouliagmeni peninsula near Athens. When we complimented him, the energetic chef not only shared his secrets, but also disclosed that he was born in the *polis* where this renowned dish originated. He also introduced *xino* (citric acid which also means "sour") to me, and I have always tried to use citric acid, very successfully, with artichokes, since then.

TO SERVE 5 TO 6

Juice of 1 lemon	*3 small pieces citric acid crystals*
3 tablespoons all-purpose flour	*or juice of 1 lemon*
8 globe artichokes	*3 carrots, scraped and cut into*
3 medium potatoes	*1-inch slices*
1/3 to 1/2 cup olive oil	*4 scallions or 1 onion, peeled and*
	sliced

Combine lemon juice and 2 tablespoons of the flour in an enameled pan with enough water to cover the artichokes. Break off the tough outer leaves of the artichokes, cut off stems, slice off the tips and remove the choke with a spoon. Plunge immediately into the acidulated water. Allow to soak while peeling and quartering lengthwise the potatoes, which should also be soaked in the same pan.

In a small pan combine the oil, citric acid or lemon juice, and remaining flour and cook over low heat until the citric acid melts and the sauce thickens. Strain into a 3-quart enameled pan, add the drained artichokes and potatoes, carrots, scallions, and enough water to cover the vegetables. Cut a small opening in the center of a piece of waxed paper large enough to fit over the vegetables. Place it on the vegetables, or cover them with an inverted plate. Cover the pan and simmer gently 40 minutes, or until tender. Using a slotted spoon, transfer the vegetables to a warm platter and keep warm. Boil the remaining sauce to reduce to 1 cup, if necessary, and spoon over the vegetables. Serve warm or cold as a first course.

Note: Citric acid crystals are available in spice departments.

ANGINARES ME ARAKA
[Artichokes and green peas]

On both islands and mainland, green peas and artichokes are a favorite combination. The flavor is best when using fresh vegetables that will cook simultaneously. If substituting frozen, check the package directions for time and avoid overcooking.

TO SERVE 5 TO 6

3 cups fresh green peas, shelled	1/2 cup canned tomato sauce
6 to 8 artichokes	1 cup water, more if necessary
Juice of 1 lemon	1/4 cup chopped fresh parsley
3 tablespoons all-purpose flour	1 teaspoon dried marjoram
1/2 cup olive oil	leaves, crushed
1 small bunch scallions, washed	Salt and freshly ground pepper
and chopped	1/2 teaspoon granulated sugar

Wash and drain the peas. Pull off the outer leaves of the artichokes, peel around the base, cut off an inch at the top, and cut in half lengthwise. With teaspoon, remove the choke, then plunge the artichokes in acidulated water, made by mixing the lemon juice and the flour with cold water to cover. Allow to soak while preparing the sauce.

Heat the oil in a heatproof casserole and sauté the scallions until translucent. Stir in the tomato sauce and the 1 cup water, then season with the herbs, salt, pepper, and sugar. Drain the artichokes and set into the sauce, then drop the peas around the artichokes. Shake the pan to mix and add enough water to almost cover the vegetables, if necessary. Cover and bake for 35 to 40 minutes in a moderate oven (350 degrees), or simmer on a slow burner; the sauce should be thick. Serve warm or cold.

Note: This is delicious with broiled or roasted meats and poultry.

KOLOKITHIA, KOLOKITHA, KOLOKITHAKIA
[*Zucchini, pumpkin, squash*]

The confused classification of the *kolokithia* family can be traced to the fourth century B.C. Yet the puzzling nomenclature never dulled Greek ardor for these *pepos*, among the most imaginative of vegetable dishes.

Theophrastus had indicated that the composition and nutritional value of these vegetables varied considerably, and could therefore not be classed as one group. More confusion arose from gourds, grown from squash seed imported from India and named *sikya*, which often were called *sikonia*, to differentiate them from Greek kolokynths. But Cnidians called the kolokynth "Indian" while the Hellespontines called the long gourds *sikya*.

A modern Greek, therefore, uses the confusion to advantage when he hears a jumbled story—he dismisses it summarily with *"Kolokithia!"*

A little marketing experience and familiarity with the Greek language diminutive helps, at least for their relative sizes. *Kolokitha* is singular, very large; *kolokithia*, plural and large; and *kolokithakia*, plural and small. In *tavernes*, when faced with *kolokithia* on the menu (which is invariably the case during tourist season), guests are encouraged to visit and select from the kitchen, much more fun than guesswork.

You will find exciting zucchini recipes among casseroles and other baked dishes, cooked with eggs in the egg section, as a cooked salad (particularly the tiny ones) or the larger varieties cooked in a small amount of oil (see Ladera). You will like *kolokithakia tiganita*, good with fish and meat dishes.

KOLOKITHAKIA TIGANITA
[Fried zucchini]

TO SERVE 5 TO 6

> 4 medium zucchini
> Seasoned flour
> Olive or other vegetable oil for frying

Scrub, wash, dry, and cut off the stem ends of the zucchini. Slice into rounds the size of a little finger and dredge with seasoned flour. In a deep pan heat the oil (to a depth of ½ inch) almost to the smoking point and slip in only 3 or 4 zucchini slices without crowding them. Using tongs, turn the zucchini and lift them out when golden chestnut in color. Drain on absorbent paper and continue until all have been fried. Serve warm. Excellent with Skordalia (page 49).

KOLOKITHOKORFADES
[Zucchini blossoms, Cretan style]

A foreigner might say the name of this dish is a Greek tongue-twister, but a Hellene will roll his eyes, sigh, and wait patiently until summer to taste it again. On Crete, a young weaver showed us how she soaked the stems overnight in cold water to allow the blossoms to open. The blossoms must be strictly fresh, and if carefully handled and gently simmered, become a delectable dish.

TO SERVE 5 TO 6

> 30 zucchini blossoms (see note below)
> 3 tablespoons olive oil
> 4 scallions or 1 small onion, minced
> 1 clove garlic, minced
> ⅓ cup raw long-grain white rice

> ½ cup canned tomatoes, drained or canned tomato sauce
> 3 tablespoons chopped fresh parsley
> 3 tablespoons chopped fresh mint or dill leaves
> Salt and freshly ground pepper
> ½ teaspoon granulated sugar

Soak the stems in cold water overnight, without soaking the blossoms. The following day, wash and drain on a towel. Cut off and discard the stems without breaking the blossoms, and set the blossoms aside while you make the filling.

Heat the oil and sauté the scallions until soft. Add the garlic and rice and cook over moderate heat for 2 minutes stirring constantly with a wooden spoon. Stir in the tomatoes, herbs, and enough water to cover the rice, then season with salt and pepper and the sugar. Simmer for 5 minutes, and remove from the heat. Using a teaspoon, stuff each blossom carefully, holding it in the palm of one hand, then close it and lay it on its side in a buttered flameproof casserole large enough to accommodate all the blossoms. Continue until all are filled.

Pour 1 cup of warm water into the casserole. Invert a plate over the flowers, then cover the casserole and simmer over lowest heat about 1½ hours. Check every 30 minutes to see if more water is needed; if so, add warm water (it should all be absorbed when cooked). Serve with poultry, meat, and fish dishes or as a delightful first course.

Note: If zucchini blossoms are unavailable, use Boston-type lettuce, the small leaves especially, blanched 1 minute and drained.

Salads

HORTA VRASTA LADOLEMONO
[*Boiled greens with lemon-oil dressing*]

This is the most traditional year-long salad, changing only with the seasonal crops; it is also the easiest to cook and serve. An excellent accompaniment to fish and meat dishes, it is preferred cold. The most difficult aspect is finding the vegetables. They must be very young and fresh, usually, in large cities, more available in Italian markets. In Greece these greens are delicious, a brighter green, and tender. After boiling, the remaining liquid is not discarded. Someone in the family— usually the one who lives to be ninety-five!—always loves the bitter beverage, with a little lemon juice squeezed in.

You will need at least ½ pound of vegetable per serving, plus more for seconds and for the next day. Since in any case they boil down to a small volume, it is good to cook a large amount. This is only a partial listing: baby squash, dandelions, curly endive, escarole, kale, mustard tops, spinach, chicory. Clean, then wash in several waters and drain. Cook squash (whole) and spinach in small amounts of water, but cook leafy vegetables in large amounts of water, at a very high boil, uncovered, to avoid color change. Season with salt, drain, and serve cold or warm, dressed with Ladolemono (page 54), with fish, egg, and meat dishes.

PANTZARIA SALATA
[Beet salad]

TO SERVE 4 TO 6

> *1 large bunch young beets, leaves included*
> *Ladoxido (page 53)*
> *Grated nutmeg for garnish*

Choose small, tender beets with fresh leaves. Cut off the stems and leaves, wash thoroughly in cold water and set aside, then scrub the beets. Place beet roots in a large saucepan, preferably enameled, and cover with cold water. Cook until tender, rinse in cold water, peel, and slice. Place in center of a serving platter and set aside. Meanwhile, steam or "pan" the stems and leaves until tender (see page 201), cut into fine pieces, and toss with *ladoxido*. Arrange around the sliced beets, which have been sprinkled with the same dressing. Grate nutmeg over the top and serve cold.

Note: This is also a favorite served with Skordalia (page 49) in which case eliminate the nutmeg.

ANGOUROSALATA
[Cucumber salad]

Cucumber salad may be prepared in two ways. The more festive method: choose short, plump cucumbers, peel, cut lengthwise, and using a spoon, scoop out and discard the seeds. Sprinkle with salt. Peel and dice another cucumber, discarding the large seeds. Toss with pepper and Ladoxido (page 53), sprinkle with chopped fresh parsley, and use to stuff the little "boats." Serve on lettuce leaf or plain, half a cucumber per person.

The simpler method is to peel the cucumbers and slice into rings or in large dice, toss with the same seasonings as the first method, and serve in a salad dish. On the islands and in the northern regions, chefs frequently line the cucumber rings in rows, very neatly, with a row of tomatoes next to them.

Or you may fill the cucumber "boats" with a *domatosalata* (see below) with or without the feta, and top with crushed oregano or chopped basil, garnished with a black olive.

DOMATOSALATA ME FETA
[*Tomato salad with feta cheese*]

TO SERVE 1 TO 2

> *3 tablespoons olive oil*
> *Pinch of oregano*
> *Salt and freshly ground black pepper*
> *¼ pound feta cheese, crumbled*
> *2 firm, ripe tomatoes*

Pour the olive oil into a salad bowl, add the oregano and a little salt and pepper and whisk with a fork. Add the crumbled feta and let stand for 10 minutes. When ready to serve, cut the tomatoes into quarters, add to the cheese dressing, toss carefully, and serve. (Or for a Peloponnesos touch, first mash the feta in the oil and use as a dressing on the tomatoes.) You might also pass the vinegar.

Note: In Greece, *domatosalata* is served without the feta unless requested. Tomatoes are usually sliced in neat rings in the north and on Crete, while elsewhere they are more frequently quartered casually.

PATATES SALATA LADOXIDO
[Potato salad with vinegar-oil dressing]

Make a day in advance for a better flavor.

TO SERVE 4

1 pound waxy-type potatoes	Salt and freshly ground pepper
2 scallions, minced	Ladoxido (page 53)
1 stalk celery, chopped fine	3 tablespoons cold water
6 sprigs fresh mint, chopped or	Fresh mint or parsley for garnish
1 teaspoon dried mint,	
crumbled	

Scrub the potatoes, and cover with cold water, and cook until tender. Cool, peel, and slice into thin rounds. Combine in a bowl with all the other ingredients except for the garnish, mixing with a wooden spoon to avoid breaking the potatoes. Taste for seasonings, then cover and refrigerate overnight. Serve warm or cold (to heat, set the bowl over warm water for 30 minutes), garnish with mint or parsley leaves.

SALATA ROSSIKI
[Salad à la Russe, Greek style]

Salata rossiki is a popular choice on menus, amazingly inspiring for the chefs. Their vegetable combinations vary considerably, allowing a delight for the cook and surprises for the guests.

TO SERVE 6

1 cup cooked beans of any kind	1 tablespoon chopped angouraki
1 cup beets, cooked, rinsed, and	tursi (pickle)
sliced	2 tablespoons chopped parsley
1 cup cooked, sliced carrots	1 tablespoon chopped dill
1 cup cooked, cut green beans	1 cup Mayoneza (page 54)
1 cup cooked, drained peas	Vinegar or lemon juice
2 cups cooked, sliced potatoes	3 hard-cooked eggs, cherry or
Salt and freshly ground pepper	sliced tomatoes and 6 black
1 teaspoon chopped capers	olives for garnish
	Lettuce leaves (optional)

In a large bowl combine the vegetables carefully to avoid breaking, and season with salt and pepper. Combine capers, pickle, and fresh herbs, or other favorite condiments, and mix in a small bowl with the mayonnaise. Add vinegar or lemon juice to taste. Mix 3 to 4 tablespoons of dressing into the vegetables and allow to marinate for 1 hour. Arrange in a serving bowl in a mound and cover with the remaining dressing. Garnish decoratively with the eggs, cut in half, around the lower perimeter, then place the tomatoes above the eggs and the olives around upper part of the salad. You may place lettuce around the base, if desired. Keep refrigerated until ready to serve.

LAHANOSALATA
[Cabbage salad]

The status of vegetables is an emotional matter in Greece, as any philhellene knows. Ancient writers had often attributed human qualities to cabbages. They were almost sacred, and Hellenes swore by them. "So help me cabbages" appeared in Greek literature. Eventually (who knows exactly when?), the Greek word for cabbage, *lahano*, developed into the Greek word for vegetables, *lahanika*.

Pomegranate seeds are frequently tossed into cabbage salad: attractive and tasty.

TO SERVE 5 TO 6

1 medium cabbage, washed and shredded	*Juice of 1 lemon*
	Salt and freshly ground pepper
1 large green pepper, sliced into rings	*Pinch of granulated sugar*
	½ cup plain yogurt
1 carrot, scraped and shredded	*½ cup Mayoneza (page 54)*
2 tablespoons chopped fresh parsley	

In a large bowl, combine the cabbage, pepper (saving a few rings for garnish), carrot, and parsley. Sprinkle the lemon juice over, then season with salt and pepper and a pinch of sugar. Combine the yogurt and mayonnaise and taste for seasoning. Toss the salad lightly with the dressing, arrange in a bowl, and garnish with the pepper rings. Chill, and serve cold.

SALATA RIZIOU
[Rice salad]

Leave it to the Hellenes to substitute anything on hand for a new salad! This is a nice salad to serve with shrimp, crab, or other fish dishes.

TO SERVE 4 TO 6

1 cup raw long-grain white rice
Salt
4 scallions, chopped
4 hard-boiled eggs, chopped
1 dill pickle, diced fine
1 green pepper, chopped
2 to 3 canned pimentos, chopped

Freshly ground pepper
Ladoxido (page 53)
Mayonnaise (optional)
Prepared mustard (optional)
Lettuce leaves
Pimentos and black olives for garnish

Cook the rice in salted water, then drain, cool, and combine in a bowl with the scallions, eggs, dill pickle, green pepper, and pimentos. Season with salt, pepper, and the *ladoxido* dressing (mixed with some mayonnaise and prepared mustard, if desired). Chill in a mold, then turn out on lettuce leaves and serve cold, garnished with pimentos and black olives.

HORIATIKI SALATA
[Village salad]

Undoubtedly, the most exciting and colorful Greek salad!

TO SERVE 4

4 to 5 firm, ripe tomatoes
1 clove garlic, cut
1 large cucumber, peeled and sliced
2 firm green peppers, sliced into thin rounds
3 to 4 scallions, green part included, sliced
16 to 20 Greek olives

1/3 pound feta cheese, broken or cut up into pieces the size of a fingertip
1/3 cup Ladoxido (page 53)
Salt and freshly ground black pepper
Chopped fresh parsley and crumbled dried oregano for garnish

Quarter the tomatoes and place in large salad bowl rubbed with the cut garlic clove. Add the cucumber, green peppers, scallions, Greek olives and feta. Shake the *ladoxido* dressing with salt and pepper to taste, then pour over the salad. Toss lightly. Sprinkle with the parsley and oregano and serve immediately.

Note: *Horiatiki salata* may be varied by using onion rings instead of scallions, adding capers, and substituting dill leaves in lieu of oregano.

SAVORY PIES, STUFFED VEGETABLES, AND CASSEROLES

Savory Pies

Sometimes pita *with the flask, sometimes* pita *alone.*

GREEK PROVERB

SAVORY PIES *(pites)* AND CASSEROLES *(tapsiou, tou fournou, pastitsio,* and *moussakades)* are among the most important and most beautifully prepared dishes of the Greek cuisine. They lend themselves perfectly to many of the reasonably priced and highly available foods, and graciously adapt to feeding large groups. Greek women deserve praise for their devotion in the selection of vegetables, particularly for these dishes, and should be emulated. Flavor will be enhanced by choosing sound, fresh vegetables as well as by the choice of cheeses and seasonings.

Another Greek habit to mimic: the substitution of seasonal, available foods. In the provinces the use of tender, wild greens and herbs gleaned from the stony hillsides result in superb dishes. If not from our own gardens, perhaps the specialty markets catering to various cultural groups will offer unusual greens for use in an exciting pie! You may become inventive as the Greeks, who cook with whatever they happen to have. As an example, in addition to using the eggplant in that most famous Melitzanes Moussaka (eggplant *moussaka*, page 233) Greek women have been known to prepare the dish with rice, zucchini, or potatoes or with a combination of two or three vegetables.

Greek cooks pride themselves on homemade pastry for their delicious pies, providing a world of possibilities for the imaginative experimenter. After successfully preparing a large pie, for instance, you may use the fillings to stuff miniature *bourekia* and *pitakia*. In addition to the vegetable, meat, and poultry *pites* presented here, see the chapter on dairy foods (pages 237–258) for classic savory and sweet cheese pies of Greece.

KREATOPITA KEFALLINIAS
[*Kefallinian spicy meat pie*]

On the island of Kefallinia in the Ionian Sea, the Feast Day of Analipseos (Ascension Day) is celebrated with the traditional *kreatopita*. This spicy pie also ushers in the beginning of Lent on the day of Apokreas.

TO SERVE 12

1 small leg of lamb or shank end of large leg, boned and cut in 1-inch cubes, bones reserved
Juice of 1 lemon
¼ cup oil or butter
1 onion, chopped
3 medium potatoes, parboiled in their jackets, peeled, and diced
1 large carrot, parboiled and diced
3 cups parboiled white rice, drained
2 tablespoons tomato purée
1 cup feta cheese, crumbled

½ cup chopped fresh parsley
2 sprigs chopped fresh mint
1 teaspoon dried oregano
1 clove garlic, sliced
1 teaspoon ground cinnamon
Peel of 1 fresh orange or lemon, cut into pieces
Salt and freshly ground pepper
16 sheets commercial filo *pastry, unrolled flat and kept covered to avoid drying, plus 6 to 8 tablespoons melted butter; or 2 homemade pastry sheets (Zymi yia Filo, page 41)*
3 hard-boiled eggs, quartered

215

In a stock pot, cover the lamb bones with cold water. Simmer, covered for 1 hour. Strain, boil down to 1 cup, and set aside. Sprinkle the lemon juice on the lamb cubes. Heat the oil or butter in a heavy pan, add the onions and lamb, and sauté the meat on all sides until the onions are soft without browning. Pour the onions, lamb, and juices into a large bowl. Add the diced potatoes and carrot, rice, tomato purée, cheese, parsley, mint, oregano, garlic, cinnamon, and fruit peel and season with salt and freshly ground pepper. Add enough reserved lamb broth for liquid while the pie bakes, then mix with a wooden spoon.

Butter the bottom and sides of a 9 x 12 x 3-inch baking pan. Spread 8 commercial *filo* sheets, brushing butter in between the sheets, or one homemade pastry sheet in the pan, making sure the pastry fits the sides and bottom of the pan. Pour in the filling, spreading evenly with a spatula. Place the egg quarters here and there across the top and cover with the remaining 8 commercial *filo* sheets, brushing with butter as before, or homemade pastry sheet. Flute the edges with two fingers or a fork and brush the top with butter. Using a sharp knife, score the top 3 commercial *filo* sheets into square or diamond shapes, or prick the homemade pastry with a fork. Bake for 40 to 50 minutes in moderately slow oven (325 degrees), raising the temperature to 350 during the last 10 minutes. Remove from the oven and let stand on a rack for 15 minutes. Cut into diamonds or squares and serve warm.

Διόσμος
Mint

KREATOPITA YIANNIOTIKI
[*Lamb pie, Ioannina style*]

An exciting, substantial, and easy pie from Epirus, prepared with ground lamb and particularly good with homemade *filo*.

TO SERVE 9 TO 12

2 tablespoons butter or margarine
1 medium onion or 4 scallions, chopped
1½ pounds lean lamb (preferably from the leg), ground
1 teaspoon ground cinnamon, or more to taste
Salt and freshly ground pepper
1 cup tomato sauce or purée diluted with water, warmed
½ cup chopped fresh parsley

3 thick or 5 thin slices toast
1½ cups milk
3 eggs, lightly beaten
¾ cup grated mizithra and kefalotyri cheese or substitutes
2 homemade pastry sheets (Zymi yia Filo, page 41); or 12 sheets commercial filo, unrolled flat and kept covered to avoid drying, plus 6 tablespoons melted butter

In a frying pan, heat the butter and cook the onion until translucent. Add the lamb and cook gently, while mashing and stirring with a fork until the raw color disappears. Season the meat with cinnamon, salt, pepper, then stir in the tomato sauce and parsley. Cover the pan and simmer for 20 minutes. (This much can be cooked a day in advance and stored in the refrigerator.) Meanwhile, soak the toast slices in the milk to make a soft mixture, and add to the meat along with the eggs and cheese. Mix the filling with a wooden spoon, taste, and add more cinnamon if you like. Using the *filo* and the melted butter, assemble and bake the pie as described on page 216. Serve warm.

Note: Greek cooks use trimmed-off pieces of dough, shaped into flowers, leaves, and so on, to decorate the crusts of pies. Also, beaten egg may be brushed on the homemade *filo* for a rich glaze.

KREATOPITA THERINI
[*"Summery" meat pie*]

If the ingredients are available in winter, this tasty pie should be called "June in January." Excellent for leftover meats, in which case the vegetables may be simmered and ground leftover meat added toward the end of cooking, just before filling the pie crust.

TO SERVE 9 TO 12

4 scallions or 2 small onions, chopped

3 tablespoons butter or oil

1 pound veal, beef, or lamb, ground

4 small or 2 medium zucchini, scrubbed and cubed

1 eggplant (less than 1 pound), cubed

1 cup canned tomatoes, drained

1/4 cup chopped fresh parsley

Salt and freshly ground pepper

1/2 teaspoon ground coriander or allspice

1 teaspoon dried oregano

1 cup grated cheese

Bread crumbs, if necessary

2 sheets homemade pastry sheets (Zymi yia Filo, page 41); or 9 to 10 sheets commercial filo, unrolled flat and kept covered to avoid drying, plus 6 tablespoons butter

1 egg, beaten (optional)

Sauté the scallions in the butter in a large frying pan and add the meat. Simmer a few minutes, then toss in the zucchini, eggplant, tomatoes, and parsley and season with salt and pepper. Cover the pan and simmer for 30 minutes, adding the coriander and oregano during the last 10 minutes. Remove from the heat and stir in the cheese. (The mixture should be thick; if any liquid remains, dust lightly with bread crumbs to absorb.) If using homemade pastry, line the bottom of a buttered 9 x 12 x 3-inch baking pan, making sure the pastry extends up all sides. Spread the filling in the pan and cover with the remaining pastry, tucking the top over the bottom. Flute all the edges decoratively, and with any remaining dough, cut out and arrange leaves in the corners. Brush the top with the beaten egg for a richer glaze. (If using commercial filo, lay 6 sheets on the bottom and sides, buttering each, and after spreading the filling, cover with the remaining filo sheets, buttering each. Score the top few filo sheets into squares or diamonds.) Bake in a medium oven (350 degrees) for 35 to 40 minutes, until golden in color and the dough is crisp. Remove from the oven, and let stand for 10 minutes, then cut and serve warm.

KOTOPITA

[Chicken pie baked with cheese and herbs]

Chicken pie in January and duck at threshing time!
GREEK PROVERB

TO SERVE 9 TO 12

1 chicken, stewed
¼ cup (4 tablespoons) butter or
margarine
¼ cup all-purpose flour
2½ cups chicken broth or stock,
warmed
¼ cup milk (optional)
3 eggs, lightly beaten
¾ cup mizithra or kefalotyri
grated cheese

Salt and freshly ground pepper
1 teaspoon grated nutmeg
Several thyme or mint leaves,
chopped
12 sheets commercial filo,
unrolled flat and kept covered
to avoid drying, plus 6 table-
spoons melted butter; or 2
sheets homemade filo *pastry*
(Zmi yia Filo, page 41)

Remove the bones and skin from chicken and discard. With your fingers tear the chicken into strips, not too small. Set aside while you prepare the sauce. Melt the butter in a heavy pan, then blend in the flour, without scorching, over medium heat. Remove from the heat for a minute and stir in the warm broth, then return to the heat and cook gently until the sauce boils. Cool. Mix in the milk if the sauce seems too thick, then add the eggs, cheese, a little salt, pepper, nutmeg, and thyme.

Butter a 9 x 12 x 3-inch baking pan and in it spread 6 commercial *filo* sheets, brushing each with butter, or 1 homemade *filo* pastry. Pour in the chicken filling, then cover with the remaining *filo* (buttering each if using commercial *filo*). Tuck the top *filo* over the bottom and flute the edges. If using commercial *filo*, score the top 3 *filo* sheets with a sharp knife, or prick the homemade *filo* with a fork. Bake in a moderate oven (350 degrees) for 40 minutes, or until crisp and a golden chestnut color. Remove from oven and let stand for 15 minutes before cutting into 9 or 12 squares. Serve warm.

Note: In Epirus, *kotopita* is sometimes made with a large amount of onions. If you would like to try it, use the recipe above plus 1 pound of Spanish-type onions. Peel and slice the onions, boil in water for 5 minutes, and drain. Prepare the sauce without the cheese and bake the chicken and onions in the sauce, between homemade *filo*, preferably, or commercial *filo*.

HORTOPITA ME AVGA
[*Pita of greens, herbs, and eggs*]

Traditional and individualistic. Village women learn to gather tender, young greens from their rocky surroundings, which ironically produce the most beautiful wild flowers and delicious greens. When greens are bought in the markets, spinach is the most frequently substituted. Cretans combine dandelions and spinach. This recipe is written as recipes are spoken in Greece, in the warm first-person plural.

TO SERVE 10 TO 12

2 pounds fresh spinach, dandelions, chicory, endive or other greens
Salt (see note below)
½ bunch fresh parsley, chopped
½ bunch fresh dill, chopped
Handful of fresh chervil, chopped
¼ cup butter or margarine
1 bunch scallions, green parts included, chopped
½ teaspoon each ground allspice, cinnamon, and nutmeg

2 teaspoons granulated sugar
Salt and freshly ground pepper
5 eggs, lightly beaten
1 cup crumbled feta cheese
½ to ¾ cup milk
½ cup melted butter or margarine (optional)
12 sheets commercial filo pastry, unrolled flat and kept covered to avoid drying; or Zymi yia Filo (page 41)

First we wash the spinach, trim coarse ends, drain, chop, sprinkle with salt, and squeeze until all the liquid has been drained. Now we combine the spinach in a large bowl with the parsley, dill, and chervil and mix thoroughly. Allowing the greens to stand while heating the ¼ cup butter in a large frying pan, we add the scallions to the butter and sauté them until the white parts are translucent. Continuing to cook over medium heat, we add the greens, the spices, sugar, and enough salt and pepper for seasoning, careful to allow for the additional salt in the feta, which will be added later. We partially cover the pan and simmer for 20 minutes, or until all the liquid has been absorbed, then we remove it from the heat and cool the mixture in a large bowl. Now we add the eggs, feta, and enough milk to saturate the greens, mix, and assemble the *pita* exactly as for Kreatopita Kefallinias (page 215) choosing a *tapsi* large enough to create a finished *pita* about 2 fingers high (15 x 11 x 2 inches, approximately). We bake *hortopita me avga* for 45 minutes in a moderate oven (350 degrees) and allow it to cool slightly before slicing and serving it warm.

Note: You may eliminate the salting of the spinach by panning it, cooking over very low heat until the leaves wilt, and then draining thoroughly.

PITA ME PRASSA THRAKIS
[*Leek pie, Thracian style*]

Leek *pites* are popular in many regions. The Thracians combine the leeks with *trahana* (page 100), which absorbs the leek juices during the baking. Commercial *filo* may be substituted, as it is here, for the dough, which in Thrace is usually rolled at home to a fine thinness. *Pita* is layered in the method used more in the northern region than others. To avoid excess fattiness, spread as little oil as possible between the *filo* sheets. Because of the layers, the *pita* needs more baking time, in a slower oven.

TO MAKE 12 SQUARES

2 pounds leeks
3/4 cup Trahana (page 100)
1 cup grated cheese
Salt and freshly ground pepper
1/2 cup olive or vegetable oil (or half margarine melted)

1 pound commercial filo pastry, unrolled flat and kept covered to avoid drying
1 egg beaten with 1 tablespoon melted butter for glaze (optional)

Clean the leeks thoroughly and mince as fine as possible. Combine in a bowl with the *trahana*, grated cheese, and salt and pepper to taste. In a 9 x 12 x 3-inch baking pan layer 5 sheets of the *filo*, brushing each with oil. (Reserving 5 *filo* sheets for the top, cut the remaining sheets in half to fit the pan without extending up the sides; and keep covered while assembling the *pita*.) Spread a thin layer of leeks over the bottom *filo* sheets. Cover with 3 sheets of *filo*, brushing each with oil, and spread with another layer of leeks. Continue until both leeks and *filo* have been used up. Cover with the reserved 5 *filo* sheets, score with a sharp knife and brush with the glaze, if desired. Bake in a moderately slow oven (325 degrees) for 1¼ hours, or until crisp and golden. Remove from the oven and let stand for 10 minutes before cutting. Serve warm.

Note: If desired, substitute 1½ cups medium Saltsa Aspri (page 50) made with milk or stock for the *trahana*, typical of the other regions.

KOLOKITHOPITA
[*Savory pumpkin pie with wheat, Peloponnesos style*]

A traditional recipe from my grandmother, who learned it in her native Laconia. Served hot or cold, with poultry, game, or meats, this is a substantial dish, especially good when made with homemade pastry.

TO MAKE 12 SQUARES

1 fresh pumpkin (5 pounds)
½ cup pligouri, burghul, or wheat germ
1 small onion, grated
1 tablespoon granulated sugar
5 eggs, lightly beaten

Salt and freshly ground pepper
1½ teaspoons grated nutmeg
½ cup olive oil
2 sheets homemade filo *pastry*
  (Zymi yia Filo, page 41)

Cut the pumpkin in half and discard the seeds (or toast and salt them for a snack). Slice the pumpkin as you would a melon, and peel. Then, using a vegetable scraper, shred the pumpkin meat into long, thin scrapings, to make 8 cups. Place in a large bowl and combine with the *pligouri*, onion, sugar, eggs, salt, pepper, nutmeg, and oil. Mix thoroughly with a wooden spoon.

Spread one pastry sheet on the bottom and sides of a buttered 9 x 12 x 3-inch baking pan. Spread the pumpkin mixture over the pastry and cover with the top pastry sheet. Tuck the top pastry sheet over the bottom and flute decoratively with your fingers, then any remaining pastry into small leaves and decorate the corners. Using a fork, prick your family initials on the top of the pastry to allow steam to escape. Bake in a moderate oven (350 degrees) for 1¼ hours or until the top is a golden chestnut color. Cut into squares and serve warm or cold.

KOLOKITHOPITA THRAKIS

[Sweet pumpkin-walnut "snail" pita, Thracian style]

An exciting flavor and appearance, much fun to roll.

TO MAKE ABOUT 20

> *1 pumpkin (4 to 4½ pounds)*
> *½ cup granulated sugar, more if desired*
> *2 tablespoons ground cinnamon*
> *1 cup chopped walnuts*
> *1 pound commercial* filo *pastry*
> *½ cup olive oil, melted butter or margarine*

Cut the pumpkin in half, remove and discard the seeds, then peel using a sharp knife. Grate the pumpkin on the medium holes of a cheese grater (there should be approximately 4 cups of finely grated pumpkin). Combine in a bowl with the sugar, cinnamon, and walnuts. Taste for flavor, adding more sugar if desired.

Start to roll the "snails." Lay the *filo* flat and deep, covered with a damp towel except when rolling. Brush one *filo* sheet lightly with the oil and fold in half lengthwise. Spread a row of filling (about 3 to 4 tablespoons) across the length of one end of the *filo* to within an inch of each edge. Roll up to seal the filling, forming a long tube. Then, beginning at one end, curl up tightly into a snail-like coil and set on a baking sheet. Continue until all the filling has been used, keeping the *pites* covered with waxed paper or plastic to avoid drying. Brush *pites* with fat and bake in a moderate oven (350 degrees) for 25 minutes or until puffy and crisp. Serve warm or cold with poultry and game dishes.

SPANAKOPITA

[Spinach pie]

Everyone loves *spanakopita*. A delightful reason for the cook: it can be filled and rolled in a dozen ways. The filling below is a delicious one—see the note below for ways to vary the seasonings—and try it in a simple pie or small *pitakia* for appetizers. A delicious cold leftover for the next day.

TO SERVE 9 TO 12

1/3 cup olive oil, butter or margarine
1 small bunch scallions, green parts included, chopped
2 1/2 to 3 pounds spinach, washed and thoroughly drained
1 small bunch fresh parsley, chopped
1 small bunch fresh dill, chopped

Salt and freshly ground pepper
1/2 pound feta cheese, crumbled
3 to 4 eggs, lightly beaten
2 homemade filo pastry sheets (Zymi yia Filo, page 41); or 12 commercial sheets filo, unrolled flat and kept covered to avoid drying, plus 6 tablespoons melted butter
Bread crumbs, if necessary

Heat the oil in a large pan and sauté the scallions until soft. Meanwhile, pan the spinach (cook it without adding water, then drain it thoroughly) or salt and rinse it (the latter method is used extensively in Greece, but is not advisable). Squeeze out excess liquid. Add the spinach to scallions and stir in the parsley, dill, and a very little salt and pepper. Cook gently for 10 minutes, then cool. (This much can be done in advance and stored in the refrigerator.) Using a wooden spoon, stir in the feta and eggs. Now assemble the pie, using either homemade or commercial *filo* according to directions an page 219. (If the filling is too liquid, sprinkle in some bread crumbs before spreading it on the pastry.) Bake in a moderate oven (350 degrees) for 45 minutes, or until the top is golden and flaky. Serve warm or cold.

Note: Some of the favorite variations: Use some nutmeg, or substitute mint for the dill; use grated cheese instead of feta (be discreet with the salt if the cheese is salty); add a small handful of raw long-grain white rice to the filling. You will surely invent your own flavor combination which is why *spanakopita* is so great.

SPANAKOPITES SAMIOTIKES
[Spinach "snail" pita, Samos style]

Samos is famous for its wine, songs, history and beauty, and— among other things—for its spinach pies. These are rolled into graceful "snails" (as they frequently are in Thrace), very simple to make at home.

TO MAKE ABOUT 20

> *1 pound commercial sheets* filo, *unrolled flat and kept covered to avoid drying*
> ½ *cup olive oil and melted butter, mixed*
> *Spinach filling for Spanakopita (page 224)*

Remove one sheet of the *filo* at a time, brush lightly with the fat, then stuff and roll exactly like Kolokithopita Thrakis, page 223, to make snail-like coils. Place them on a baking sheet, brush lightly with fat, then bake in a moderate oven (350 degrees) for 25 minutes, or until puffy and crisp. Serve hot or cold with fish, egg, and meat dishes.

Note: These may be frozen before baking, preferably with waxed paper between them to keep them from sticking.

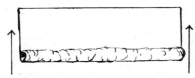

Stuffed Vegetables

KIMA APO MELITZANES
[Eggplant "kima" stuffing]

A superb meat substitute for abstinence (vegetarian) dishes. Use for the meat layer in *moussaka* dishes or to stuff eggplants, tomatoes, or green peppers for a refreshing change. Prepare a day in advance if possible. This is also delicious cold, served with fish and other vegetable dishes.

TO MAKE ABOUT 4 CUPS

3 pounds eggplants (3 medium)
¼ cup olive oil
⅓ cup scallions or shallots, chopped
1 clove garlic, sliced (optional)
¼ cup chopped fresh parsley
2 tablespoons chopped fresh fennel or dill leaves

½ teaspoon allspice, more if necessary
¼ cup dry white wine
2 tablespoons tomato paste diluted with ½ cup water
Salt and freshly ground pepper
½ cup bread crumbs

Cut the eggplants in half lengthwise. With a small knife, cut away the eggplant flesh from the skin without breaking the skin (if planning to stuff the shells, leave ¼ inch of flesh with the skin as a firm base) and set the shells aside. Dice the eggplant flesh and push through the medium blade of a meat grinder as quickly as possible to avoid discoloration. (Or the eggplant may be puréed in a blender, 1 cup at a time.)

Heat the oil in a frying pan and sauté the scallions and garlic. Add the parsley, fennel, allspice, wine, and the diluted tomato paste. Stir in the eggplant pulp, season with salt and pepper, and simmer for 20 minutes. Taste to adjust seasonings. Add the bread crumbs to absorb excess liquid.

Stuff the eggplant shells, if desired, and place in an oiled baking dish. Bake in a moderate oven (350 degrees) for 35 minutes. Serve warm or—particularly good—cold.

DOMATES YEMISTES ME KIMA KAI RIZI
[Tomatoes stuffed with meat and rice]

This is probably the most popular stuffed vegetable dish in Greece, frequently stuffed with herbs and rice without the meat (see note below). We were surprised to find that in Macedonia tomatoes were stuffed upside down, that is, stem side down, rather than with the stem ends for caps, the way we learned. Then we visited the village where my mother was born and found that they too stuffed their tomatoes upside down. Things had changed in the tiny village! It seems more practical for the heavy end to be down, so the recipe is thus presented—but they are delicious with either end up.

TO SERVE 6 TO 8

12 firm, ripe tomatoes
Salt and granulated sugar
3 tablespoons olive oil or butter
1 medium onion, or 3 scallions, chopped fine
2 cloves garlic, chopped
1/4 cup chopped fresh parsley
1/2 pound lean lamb or veal, ground

1/4 cup dry white wine
1/4 cup water
5 to 6 tablespoons raw long-grain white rice
Tomato juice, if necessary
Freshly ground pepper
2 sprigs fresh mint or basil
Pinch of grated nutmeg

Wash the tomatoes, then turn each stem side down, and with a sharp knife carefully cut the end now up to make an opening or "cap" being careful not to detach the cap entirely. With a small spoon, carefully, without breaking the outer skin of the tomatoes, scoop the pulp into a bowl. Place the tomato shells in a baking-serving dish large enough to support them touching. Sprinkle the inside of the shells with salt and sugar.

Meanwhile, prepare the stuffing. Heat the oil in a heavy skillet and add the onions. Cook over moderate heat until soft and transparent, then add the garlic and parsley, and blend. Add the meat, mashing with a fork, then add the wine and water, cover, and simmer for a few minutes. Add the rice and tomato pulp and stir. (Tomato juice may be added if necessary, since the mixture should provide enough liquid for the rice to absorb.) Cover the skillet and simmer about 7 minutes, then add salt, pepper, mint or basil, and nutmeg. Taste for seasoning. Remove

227

from the heat and fill the tomatoes up about two-thirds of the way with the stuffing and liquid. Cover with tomato caps, brush with oil. Bake in a moderate oven (350 degrees) until the rice is tender (approximately 50 minutes to 1 hour), basting inside the tomatoes with liquid released by them. Serve warm.

Note: For Domates Yemistes me Rizi (tomatoes stuffed with rice) use 1¼ cups raw long-grain white rice instead of the meat and rice in the above recipe, eliminate the wine, and include with the other seasonings a few tablespoons each of black raisins and 2 tablespoons pine nuts, if desired. Rice in baked stuffed dishes takes much longer to cook than over a burner. Stuffed green peppers, also popular in Greece, can be made the same way with an entirely different flavor.

LAHANIKA YEMISTA THRAKIS
[*Stuffed vegetables, Thracian style*]

This delightful and colorful dish uses the same stuffing for the varied vegetables. The eggplants and zucchini should be small, so that they match the tomatoes and peppers in size.

TO SERVE 6 TO 8

4 pounds baby eggplants, firm tomatoes, green peppers, and baby zucchini, washed	½ cup raisins
	¼ cup chopped fresh parsley or mint
Salt and granulated sugar	1 stick cinnamon
¼ cup vegetable oil or butter	Freshly ground black pepper
2 to 3 onions, minced	2 cups hot water
1 cup raw long-grained white rice	½ cup tomato juice, if necessary
	3 tablespoons olive oil

Cut the eggplants in half lengthwise and remove the inside portion, being careful not to break the skin. Chop the inside eggplant pieces and reserve for the stuffing. Using sharp knife cut a slice across either end of the tomatoes, not quite all the way, and allow the cut part for "caps." With a spoon carefully remove the pulp, discard seeds, and save pulp for the filling. Season inside tomatoes with a little sugar. Cut off the pepper "caps" at the stem end and save them, remove and discard seeds and sprinkle peppers inside lightly with sugar. Cut the zucchini in half lengthwise, remove pulp and chop it for the filling. Sprinkle zucchini shells with salt. Arrange the vegetables in casserole scooped-out sides up, and set aside while you prepare the filling.

Heat the oil or butter in a frying pan and sauté onions until soft. Stir in the rice and cook for 3 minutes, then add tomato, eggplant and zucchini pulp, raisins, parsley or mint, cinnamon stick, salt and pepper to taste, and enough hot water to cover. You may need to add some tomato juice. Cover and simmer until the rice is partially cooked (approximately 15 minutes). Remove cinnamon. Stuff the vegetables, cover with their "caps," and dribble with oil. Bake about 35 to 40 minutes in a moderate oven (350 degrees). Serve warm or cold.

MELITZANES PAPOUTSAKIA KIMA
[Meat-stuffed eggplant "booties"]

Popular throughout Greece, this dish is made with small eggplants, so the product looks like booties or little shoes. Adapted for our larger eggplants, triple in size, the adaptation could be called *papoutsia* (shoes)! If you find small eggplants, estimate a cup of sauce for every 2 eggplants.

TO SERVE 4 TO 5

3 medium eggplants (less than 1 pound each)	2 tablespoons chopped fresh parsley
Vegetable oil for frying	Salt and freshly ground pepper
2 cups Saltsa Kima (page 52) made with ground lamb	Bread crumbs (optional)
1 clove garlic, crushed	1 cup medium Saltsa Aspri (page 50)
6 tablespoons grated cheese	1 egg, lightly beaten

Wash and dry the eggplants, then cut in half lengthwise. Scoop out enough of the flesh to allow space for stuffing without breaking through the outer skin. Chop the eggplant flesh, then heat a thin layer of oil in a frying pan and sauté over high heat, turning quickly to fry the other side. Lower the heat, cover, and simmer for 5 minutes. Drain the eggplant and combine in a mixing bowl with the *saltsa kima*, garlic, ¼ cup of the cheese, and the parsley. Season lightly. Let stand while preparing the eggplant shells.

Reheat the oil remaining in the frying pan or add a thin layer and when hot, slide the eggplant shells into the pan. Using tongs for turning, fry quickly on both sides. Drain on paper towels and place in a shallow casserole, scooped side up. Fill with the eggplant-meat mixture, sprinkling with bread crumbs if the filling is very liquid. Meanwhile, mix the *saltsa aspri* with the egg and spoon it over the eggplants. Sprinkle with the remaining 2 tablespoons of cheese and some bread crumbs and bake in a moderate oven (350 degrees) for 25 minutes, or until golden and bubbly. Serve warm.

IMAM BAYALDI
[Eggplant stuffed with aromatics]

There should be no merriment about the name of this dish: "The Imam swooned" seems appropriate, since the dish is as colorful to behold and as rich to taste as a vegetable dish can be.

TO SERVE 5

2½ pounds eggplants (about 5 five-inch or 3 long ones)
Salt
3 medium onions, peeled and sliced into thin rings
½ cup water
4 to 5 tablespoons olive oil

5 peeled, sliced fresh tomatoes or 8 canned plum tomatoes, sliced
½ cup chopped fresh parsley
3 to 4 cloves garlic, peeled and sliced lengthwise
Freshly ground pepper
Pinch of granulated sugar
Fresh parsley for garnish

Wash the eggplants, cut off the stem end if using large ones and cut in half lengthwise. With the tip of a sharp knife, make at least 3 lengthwise slashes on the cut sides of the eggplants, being careful not to pierce the skin on the opposite side. Sprinkle with salt and let stand for 30 minutes. Rinse with cold water, dry, and invert to drain.

Meanwhile, put the onions in a small pan with the ½ cup water and simmer a few minutes. Drain and discard the water or save for soup.

In a medium frying pan, heat 2 tablespoons of the oil and sauté the onions until soft, then put approximately a third of them in the bottom of a buttered casserole large enough to accommodate all the eggplants. Set 4 to 5 tomato slices over the onions in the casserole and add the rest of the tomatoes to the onions remaining in the frying pan. Sauté onions and tomatoes for 10 minutes, then stir in all but 2 tablespoons of the parsley and remove from the heat. Set the eggplants into the casserole, tuck a slice of garlic into each eggplant slash, and stuff the slashes with the filling, allowing some to cover the top of the eggplant. Season lightly with salt, pepper, and a pinch of sugar, then dribble the remaining oil and chopped parsley over the eggplants. Cover the casserole with a lid or aluminum foil and bake in a moderate oven (350 degrees) for 30 to 40 minutes, until fork-tender, removing the cover during the last 10 minutes to allow the sauce to thicken. Garnish with parsley and serve warm.

Note: This is excellent as a first course of a subsequently light meal topped with fresh fruit and Turkish coffee.

If you wish you may leave the eggplants whole, slash one side and remove some of the pulp with a small spoon. This pulp is then sautéed with the filling and stuffed into the eggplant, a very attractive method for the smaller eggplants. As you might suspect, both variations may also be prepared on top of the stove.

Casseroles

BRIAMI MYSTRAS
[Multi-vegetable and herb casserole, Mystras style]

Climbing the peaceful hills and exploring the Byzantine churches, we suddenly found ourselves walking into the charming courtyard of Pantanassa. Bright with geraniums and hydrangeas and fragrant with basil in pots, the scrubbed convent seemed like a haven. The nuns described their life and diet, including their version of *briami*, which contains okra, along with other vegetables.

In other regions green peppers are substituted, like the famous French *ratatouille*.

TO SERVE 6 TO 8

1½ pounds potatoes, peeled and sliced into rounds
1½ pounds zucchini, scraped slightly, and sliced into rounds
¾ pound okra, trimmed, soaked in vinegar, and rinsed
1 eggplant (¾ to 1 pound), salted, rinsed, and sliced
1 pound fresh or canned tomatoes, sliced
1 small bunch fresh parsley, chopped
1 small bunch fresh dill, chopped
Salt and freshly ground pepper
½ cup olive oil
4 to 5 scallions or 2 onions, chopped
2 to 3 cloves garlic, minced
Toast or bread crumbs

In a large bowl, place all the vegetables, reserving half the tomatoes. Season with the parsley, dill, salt, and pepper, and mix thoroughly. Layer the vegetables in a large casserole, alternating vegetables as much as possible.

Meanwhile, heat the oil in a small pan and sauté the scallions and garlic, stirring. Chop the remaining tomatoes and add them to the scallions, stirring. Simmer for 10 minutes, then spoon over the vegetables. Dust the top with the crumbs and bake in a moderate oven (350 degrees) for 1 hour. Serve warm or cold.

TOURLOU YUVETSI
[Multi-vegetable and lamb casserole]

A variation: quite a different flavor has *tourlou yuvetsi*: sauté 1 pound lean lamb chunks with a large chopped onion, tuck in among the vegetables, and bake very slowly. Serve warm.

MELITZANES KIMA FOURNOU
[Baked eggplant and ground meat casserole]

TO SERVE 6

2 large eggplants	*1 bay leaf*
Salt	*Fresh parsley*
3 to 4 tablespoons olive oil, more	*2 sprigs fresh thyme*
if necessary	*Salt and freshly ground pepper*
2 cups Saltsa Kima (page 52)	*½ cup toast crumbs*
1 one-pound can peeled plum	
tomatoes	

Wash and dry the eggplants, then cut off the blossom ends, peel, and slice into ¼-inch rounds. Salt both sides. Allow to stand for 30 minutes, then rinse off and dry. In a **heavy frying** pan, heat the oil and quickly fry the eggplant slices on both sides, adding more oil if necessary. Drain on absorbent paper. Butter a 10 x 8 x 2-inch baking-serving casserole and layer half the eggplant slices on the bottom. Spread the *saltsa kima* over the eggplant, and put the remaining eggplant slices over the meat.

Meanwhile, simmer the tomatoes, the bay leaf, 3 sprigs parsley, and thyme for 15 minutes. Season with salt and pepper, then pour over the eggplant and sprinkle with ½ cup chopped parsley and the toast crumbs. Bake in a moderate oven (350 degrees) for 25 minutes, or until crusty and golden. Cut into squares and serve warm.

MELITZANES MOUSSAKA
[Eggplant moussaka]

Moussaka has become synonymous with eggplant moussaka, so much so that many Hellenes and philhellenes never try the splendid variations with other vegetables. *Moussaka* traveled to Greece from the Middle East and became identified as much with Greece as *baklava*, which happens to some dishes!

TO SERVE 8

6 to 8 tablespoons olive oil, more
   if necessary
1 medium or 2 small onions,
   peeled and chopped
1½ pounds lamb, beef, or veal,
   ground
½ cup dry white wine
1½ cups chopped tomatoes or
   tomato sauce
Salt and freshly ground pepper
3 to 4 tablespoons chopped fresh
   parsley

¼ teaspoon dried oregano or
   thyme
½ cup bread crumbs
2 eggs, separated
2½ pounds eggplants (about 3
   medium)
3 cups Saltsa Aspri (page 50)
1 cup grated mizithra and
   kefalotyri cheese or substitutes
Grated nutmeg

Heat 2 tablespoons of the oil in a heavy skillet, then add onions and cook until soft and transparent. Blend in the chopped meat, cover, and simmer a few minutes. Stirring constantly, add the wine, tomatoes, and herbs, then season with salt and pepper, cover, and simmer for 30 minutes. Cool. Add the egg whites and 2 tablespoons of the bread crumbs and blend thoroughly with a spoon.

Partially peel the eggplants by cutting ½-inch strips of skin off lengthwise, cut off the green stem end, then cut in circles or lengthwise into ⅓-inch slices. Salt, rinse, and dry the eggplant slices, then fry lightly on both sides in the remaining hot olive oil, adding more if necessary (or skip the frying of eggplant slices if you wish). Drain.

Prepare the *saltsa aspri* and cool, then add the egg yolks, about half of the grated cheese, and stir well.

Butter a 9 x 12 x 2-inch baking pan and sprinkle lightly with bread crumbs. Line the bottom of the pan with half the eggplant slices, then cover completely with the meat mixture, spreading evenly with a spatula. Layer the remaining eggplant slices over the meat. Cover with the sauce and sprinkle with the remaining cheese, nutmeg, and remaining bread crumbs. Bake in a moderate oven (350 degrees) for about 35 to 40 minutes, or until the top turns golden in color. Remove from the oven to a rack and allow to cool for at least 10 minutes, then cut into squares, transfer to a warm serving platter, and serve warm.

KOLOKITHAKIA MOUSSAKA
[*Zucchini moussaka*]

Adoring *kolokithakia* as they do, the Hellenes had to try it in *moussaka*, in this dish and in other versions layered with tomatoes or potatoes, and still another with equal parts eggplant, potatoes, and zucchini!

TO SERVE 8 TO 9

2½ to 3 pounds zucchini
Vegetable oil for frying
  (optional)
Salt and freshly ground pepper
Bread crumbs
¼ cup chopped fresh parsley
¼ cup chopped fresh basil

4 cups Saltsa Kima (page 52)
2 eggs, separated
2 cups medium Saltsa Aspri
  (page 50)
½ cup grated cheese
½ teaspoon grated nutmeg
½ teaspoon ground cinnamon

Scrub the zucchini, but leave the skin on, unless very tough. Cut off the stem and discard, then slice the zucchini into ⅓-inch circles. If you like, heat a shallow layer of oil in a frying pan and fry the zucchini on both sides. Drain on paper towels, then season lightly with salt and pepper. Oil or butter a 9 x 12 x 3-inch baking pan and dust the bottom with bread crumbs. Layer half of the zucchini in the pan, then sprinkle on half the parsley and basil. Combine the *saltsa kima* with the 2 egg whites and spread evenly over the zucchini in the pan. Cover the meat layer with the remaining zucchini and herbs.

Meanwhile, mix the *saltsa aspri* with the egg yolks, cheese, and spices and spread over the casserole. Sprinkle lightly with bread crumbs, then bake in a moderate oven (350 degrees) for about 35 to 45 minutes, or until golden and steaming. Remove to a rack to cool for 15 minutes, then cut into squares and serve warm.

PILAFI MOUSSAKA
[*Rice moussaka*]

TO SERVE 9

1½ cups raw long-grain white
   rice
Salt
3 cups medium Saltsa Aspri
   (page 50)

¾ cup grated cheese
3 tablespoons melted butter
4 cups Saltsa Kima (page 52)
1 egg, separated
Bread crumbs

Cook the rice in salted water by any method and drain, then drape with a dry towel for 10 minutes. Mix ½ cup of the *saltsa aspri* and ½ cup of the cheese with the rice. Using a brush and the melted butter, butter a 9 x 12 x 3-inch baking pan and spread the rice evenly across the bottom. Combine the *saltsa kima* with ⅓ cup bread crumbs and the egg white and spread evenly over the rice. Combine the remaining sauce with the egg yolk and spread over the meat layer, then sprinkle with the remaining cheese and some bread crumbs on top. Bake in a moderate oven (350 degrees) for 30 to 40 minutes, until golden and bubbly. Remove to a rack to stand for 10 minutes, then cut into squares. Serve warm, with cooked green vegetables, a tomato salad with olives, and chilled wine.

EGGS, DAIRY, AND CHEESE SPECIALTIES

Eggs

AVGA
[Eggs]

If you buy an egg from him, it won't have a yolk inside.
GREEK PROVERB

IN GREECE, EGGS, RAW OR COOKED, must be listed among the most versatile of ancient foods. And it was goose's, peacock's, and fox-goose's eggs that were more highly prized in ancient eras than hen's eggs, although archeologists have found that hen's eggs were used by the early Minoans.

Ancient tradition forbade the eating of domestic birds and their eggs because the cock was consecrated to the goddess Maia. And F. J. Simoons in *Eat Not This Flesh* relates that shepherds on the island of Chios kept cocks, not hens, for fear that hen's eggs would cause sickness among the flocks.* These beliefs have disappeared.

Some very colorful concoctions are among the records of Athenaeus. Imagine an elaborate vegetable appetizer garnished with hard-cooked eggs cut into star shapes. Eggs were also eaten as a dessert with walnuts and almonds, and Antiphanes includes eggs among the im-

* Simoons, F. J., *Eat Not This Flesh: Food Avoidances in the Old World* (Madison, Milwaukee, and London: The University of Wisconsin Press, 1967), p. 72.

237

portant seasonings of his time. Along with crayfish, bulbs, snails, and animal "extremities," eggs were considered potent aphrodisiacs by Alexis, only one of the many writers who discoursed on this subject. In addition, egg cookery must have been highly developed. Among the ancient Greek utensils was one designed with cavities of varying sizes to accommodate different-sized eggs and to keep the egg yolk centered during the cooking!

The ancient Greek word for egg—*oon*—has changed, but not the egg's status, although the Western visitor might argue this point. Restaurants and *tavernes* rarely feature eggs, and most certainly not at breakfast time. The Greek breakfast is quite frugal, more so than the typical continental ones. Because of this, and because eggs are expensive in Greece, mothers are more likely to dole out eggs to their youngsters for *kolatsio*—the brunch between early breakfast and dinner. For these youngsters, the egg will probably be soft-boiled or lightly scrambled with cheese. Delicious soufflés and omelets with sausages or vegetables are prepared on special occasions in the average Greek home. And eggs, whenever available, are used extensively in such things as noodles, breads, *trahana*, cheese and vegetable pies, custards, baked pudding pastries and thickeners.

Certainly, serving eggs as a form of hospitality is an age-old custom. It was probably goose eggs roasted in ashes that Philemon and Baucis served to their visitors in their inimitable example of hospitality, for later in this poignant myth the impoverished couple struggles to catch the goose and prepare it for their guests. Modern Hellenes include eggs—usually stuffed or hard-cooked—among the *orektika* for visitors. And they are also likely to cook an egg especially for a visiting youngster, as a special treat.

In the provinces we often observed that eggs hatched by one of the family's hens were collected to take to market. In homes without hens, eggs are purchased daily, one for each child, for there is a traditional clamor for freshness. A customer often asks, "Is it today's egg?" If it is not, the seller will surely lose a customer.

AVGA KOKKINA PASHALINA
[*Easter or red eggs*]

Easter is the most important religious ceremony of Greece, and its jubilation is ushered in by the traditional cracking of eggs. Probably as much excitement is stirred up in Greek homes over hard-boiled, red, Easter eggs as in Western homes over the Easter bunny. *"Christos anesti —Christ is risen,"* you cry as you hit another's egg with your own. *"Alithos anesti—truly, Christ is risen,"* answers the other. And you turn, with your uncracked, surviving egg in your hand to the next person, to crack shells with him. You repeat, hoping you will be possessor of the strongest shell, which, unbroken, wins—an honor that needs no greater reward. There are a few rules: eggs must be struck directly on top, not on the sides; and the pointed end must attack the pointed end, or the round end, the round end.

Other uses for the Easter eggs are in adding brightness to Tsoureki or Lambropsomo (braided Easter breads; page 270), for which red eggs are baked into the trimmings. Red eggs are also used in baskets for youngsters. As for the eggs earmarked for the family *tsoungrisma* (cracking): no one may have a "crack" at the eggs beforehand. On one unforgettable Easter in our home, my brother woke up early, searched for the strongest red egg, and broke them all in the process!

TO MAKE 2 TO 3 DOZEN EGGS

> *Commercial red egg dye*
> *3/4 to 1 cup vinegar*
> *2 to 3 dozen unbroken eggs, washed and dried*
> *Olive oil for glazing*

Follow the directions of the commercial egg dye, using the vinegar as a mordant. Avoid overcooking. If the egg cracks accidentally, remove it and reserve for another use. After cooking, carefully remove the eggs and set them on dry towels; they will be stained red. Dampen a soft cloth with olive oil and rub each egg, then set on platters or baskets and store in a cool place.

Note: The dye may be used again by adding more vinegar.

KORKADA * AVGO HTIPITO
[*Creamy beaten egg yolk, Peloponnesos style*]

Korkada, or "beaten yolk," is named for the egg yolk, the *korko*. This is a favorite snack for youngsters after their nap, either eaten with a spoon or spread on bread, accompanied by a glass of milk.

For each serving: In a heavy cup, using the curved side of a teaspoon, mix one egg yolk with 2 to 3 teaspoons sugar, depending on how sweet you want the *korkada* to be (we have seen it made with 4 teaspoons of sugar!). After about 10 minutes of beating, the mixture will be almost white, very fluffy, and creamy. A pleasant task for a youngster, who can soon sit down and eat the egg he has beaten. Save the white, covered, in the refrigerator to use in another dish.

KAYIANIA
[Egg and tomato omelet, Peloponnesos style]

A traditional favorite for *kolatsio*—Greek brunch—or a special treat.

TO SERVE 5 TO 6

> *3 to 4 tablespoons olive oil, butter or margarine*
> *4 scallions, green parts included, sliced (optional)*
> *5 ripe tomatoes, peeled and sliced*
> *Salt and freshly ground pepper*
> *1 teaspoon granulated sugar*
> *8 eggs, lightly beaten*
> *Fresh parsley for garnish*

Heat the oil or butter in an omelet pan, add the scallions, and cook until soft. Layer the tomatoes over the scallions and sprinkle with salt, pepper, and the sugar. Cover and simmer for 20 minutes, or until the tomatoes are tender. Pour the eggs over the tomatoes and continue cooking for 4 minutes, then flip the omelet over and cook the bottom until the eggs are a golden chestnut color. Transfer to a warm platter, garnish with parsley, and serve hot.

Note: *Kayiania* is often varied by adding fried *loukanika* (homemade sausage) slices, or slices of kefalotyri cheese.

SFOUGATO
[Savory omelet baked with veal and zucchini, Rhodian style]

Roses and deer are not the only fine things associated with the beautiful island of Rhodes, capital of the Dodecanese. For throughout Greece there is a descriptive rhyme about *Sfougato* asserting how difficult it may be to prepare but certainly easy to eat! The dish is unusual, mild in color and flavor.

TO SERVE 5 TO 6

2 to 3 tablespoons butter or
    margarine
1 onion or 2 to 3 scallions,
    chopped
3/4 pound lean veal, ground
2 medium or 5 small zucchini,
    scrubbed and cubed

Salt and freshly ground pepper
4 sprigs fresh chopped parsley
1/4 cup chopped fresh dill
7 eggs, beaten
Bread crumbs

Heat the butter or margarine in a frying pan, add the onion and cook, without browning, until soft. Using a fork, mash the veal over the onions and cook over medium heat a few minutes, until the color deepens. Add the cubed zucchini, salt and pepper to taste, and enough hot water to cover the bottom of the pan. Stir with a fork, cover the pan, and simmer for 20 minutes. Add the parsley and dill and cook for 5 minutes longer. Remove from the heat and cool, drain of excess liquid, then combine with the beaten eggs.

Sprinkle the bread crumbs lightly on the bottom of a buttered baking-serving casserole (approximately 8 x 11 x 2 inches, or a 2-quart size), then pour in the egg mixture. Bake in a moderate oven (350 degrees) for 25 minutes or until the egg is firm and appears like a yellow pudding. Serve warm.

Note: This is excellent with feta cheese.

Arndor
Dill

SOUFFLE KOLOKITHAKIA
[*Zucchini soufflé*]

An excellent luncheon dish or first course, this will be well worth the effort when you see your guests' eyes gleam at the first taste. Be sure they are seated before presenting the soufflé.

TO SERVE 4 TO 5

4 small zucchini, peel left on, washed and scrubbed with a vegetable brush
Salt
Pinch of chopped fresh basil and parsley
¼ cup (4 tablespoons) butter
¼ cup all-purpose flour
1½ cups milk, warmed

1 cup grated mizithra and kefalotyri cheese, mixed, or hard ricotta and Romano
¼ teaspoon grated nutmeg
Pinch of salt
6 eggs, at room temperature, separated
¼ teaspoon cream of tartar

Parboil the zucchini in a small amount of salt water, along with pinches of basil and parsley. Drain and slice into ½-inch rounds; there should be a heaping cupful. Set aside while you prepare the sauce.

Melt the butter in a saucepan, then remove from the heat and stir in the flour with a whisk. Return to low heat, and cook, stirring, for 30 seconds; do not allow to brown. Remove from the heat, gradually add the milk, stirring constantly, then return to the heat until the sauce boils. When thick, add the cheeses, nutmeg, and a pinch of salt and fold in the zucchini. Beat the yolks in a large bowl until thick and lemon colored. Add a few tablespoons of the sauce-zucchini mixture to the yolks and blend with a wooden spoon, then stir the remaining yolk mixture into the sauce and zucchini.

Preheat the oven to 400 degrees and butter an 8-inch, 1½-quart soufflé dish. Whisk the egg whites until foamy, then sprinkle in the cream of tartar and keep whisking (or beating) to the stiff-peak stage. Add 2 tablespoons of the whites to the sauce mixture, mix, then carefully fold the remaining whites into the sauce, using a rubber spatula in an under-over motion. Gently turn into the buttered soufflé dish, place in the center of the oven, and immediately reduce heat to 375 degrees. Allow to bake for 25 minutes before opening the oven door to check with a toothpick or cake tester. If the tester does not come out clean, leave for 5 to 10 minutes longer, until the soufflé is high and the surface is golden chestnut colored. Serve immediately.

Note: Zucchini or squash pulp may be substituted for slices.

Dairy

GALA
[*Milk*]

Hellenes have been drinking milk since the Bronze Age, but in their own distinctive ways. Fresh goat's milk, boiled and used as quickly as possible, is a traditional favorite. This preference may be based on more than Zeus' predilections, however, since milk from the goat has more calcium, phosphorus, potassium, iron, and fat than cow's milk. In current Greek milk production, goat's milk is slightly less than sheep's milk and both of these types are less than cow's milk production. Buffalo's milk is also produced, but in much smaller quantities.

Increasing refrigeration during the last decade and more milk factories, such as the pasteurizing plant at Gastouni, Elia, have increased commercial production considerably. Yet in many areas we visited, we noted that mothers depend on canned milk or the local shepherds, who sell milk on a daily basis. (And there is a terrible shortage of shepherds, the backbone of the ageless milk "industry.") Indeed, despite the rapid acceleration of commercial milk in Athens and other large cities, such as Patras and Thessaloniki, the villagers living near a shepherd continue to seek sheep's milk, and those who own goats use their supply of milk for drinking and to make cheese. It was a pleasant, indeed to us an unknown, sight to see children walking home bringing milk in a pail.

At the same time, the *galaktopoleion* (milk shop) and many small general stores stock milk from both cows and sheep in some areas, and, the refrigerated milk truck with loudspeaker does a booming business, selling ice cream, milk, yogurt, and other dairy products. Packaged ice cream sandwiches, popsicles, and cones have gained in popularity during the last few years, reflecting the influence of both Italy and the United States.

In the cultural life, milk has many uses, but not in the manner of, say, milk drinking in the United States. Milk is not a typical beverage. Children drink water at the table; adults are likely to drink for breakfast hot milk flavored with coffee and sugar. Milk is used extensively in custards, the famed Galaktoboureko (page 332) and other milk custard pies; breast-feeding has been a frequent theme in poetry, as have been dairy products. Among them, the last verse from Kostas Krystallis's (1868–1894) poem "To the Imperial Eagle" begins:

O eagle, I wish to chew acorns from a gentle oak,
I wish to swallow deer cheese and wild goat's milk. . . .

YAOURTI
[Yogurt]

Yogurt probably originated accidentally among nomadic tribes traveling in the desert. But Hellenes might argue that the gods created it on Mount Olympus. Since its use spread through Bulgaria and the other Balkans into Greece, yogurt has been a perennial mainstay— served with meals, as a separate course, or in cooking other dishes. Greek people particularly like it with rice dishes.

Sheep's milk is prized for making yogurt in spring when sheep are nursing the baby lambs. In summer, when available, cow's or goat's milk is used, particularly the latter, which produces a rich, thick yogurt. Yogurt is readily available throughout Greece for a nominal fee, a perfect snack at any *galaktopoleion* (milk shop) where dairy products are sold. We observed that during their infrequent trips away from their villages, elderly Hellenes (who distrust food not prepared in their own home), *will* order and eat yogurt.

Undoubtedly, there is a vigorous association in Greece between yogurt and good health. In fact, longevity has often been attributed to yogurt and sour-milk products in central Europe, possibly partly because of the favorable conditions produced in the human intestines by the acidity of the yogurt.

In the Greek provinces, yogurt is made at home and the *mayia* (starter, the same word used for yeast) saved for the next fermentation. I have been making it for years, ever since childhood days, when I used to watch the yogurt bag dripping over the sink, producing a yogurt thick enough to slice with a knife. Now we have a Greek *tsantila*, which is actually the cheesecloth used by shepherds to make cheese. A double cheesecloth or linen cloth will serve amiably.

Yogurt is a semisolid cultured or fermented milk containing Bacillus bulgaricus and Streptococcus thermophilus. These organisms present in the "starter," given warmth, will ferment whole or skimmed fresh milk overnight. With a fresh supply of yogurt you can enjoy it in a myriad of delightful ways.

In Greece, yogurt is enjoyed plain as a separate course following the main course or as a snack anytime of the day. As a snack, yogurt is also mixed with honey or sugar and sometimes lemon juice. As a tenderizing agent, yogurt is used with tougher meat cuts, and also to flavor meat and poultry sauces. Try it as the appetizer Tzatziki (page 74), which also makes a good salad; make yogurt-nut cakes; and be sure to serve yogurt with steaming rice and wheat. As exciting to make at home as to see made in the kitchens of a *galaktopoleion* or a *galaktozacharoplasteion* anywhere in Greece! Try serving it thickened by straining through fine linen or a double cheesecloth to remove the whey—utterly delicious.

TO MAKE I QUART

> *1 quart homogenized or skimmed milk*
> *3 tablespoons "starter" yogurt (from previous homemade yogurt or commercial plain yogurt)*

In a heavy pan, bring the milk to a boil over medium heat and simmer 2 minutes, being careful not to scorch the bottom of the pan. Pour the milk into an earthenware or porcelain bowl and allow to cool to approximately 130 degrees on a candy thermometer. The small finger should be able to tolerate the heat to the count of 11, a good test for temperature and most fun. (Unsuccessful attempts to make yogurt are usually a result of the milk cooling too much.) Mix a few tablespoons of the hot milk with the "starter" and then stir it into the milk as quickly as possible. Cover the bowl with a plate and a kitchen towel and set in a draft-free area overnight, or for at least 8 hours. (The bowl may be covered with a blanket or satisfactorily allowed to rest in an unlit oven that has no pilot light.) The yogurt will be semisolid and will appear like commercial yogurt. If desired, it may be drained of excess liquids in one of two ways: either place a clean white napkin on the yogurt, store in the refrigerator, and occasionally squeeze the liquid from the napkin into the sink; or allow the yogurt to drain through double cheesecloth or fine linen which you have tied around the yogurt and hung over the sink. After 2 hours the yogurt will be thick enough to slice, and can be placed in a bowl and then stored in the refrigerator.

Note: Save "starter" for the next yogurt. Also make enough to eat in three days. Yogurt may also be prepared in individual cups allowing a heaping teaspoonful of "starter" per cup.

Cheese Specialties

TYRI
[Cheese]

She [Circe] brought them in and made them sit on chairs and seats, and made for them a potion of cheese and barley meal and yellow honey with Pramnian wine.

HOMER, *The Odyssey*

Cheese became a staple of the Greek diet during the Bronze Age, and there is no indication the trend will ever be reversed. On the contrary, cheese is universally adored. The best cheeses are eaten fresh, in or near the provinces where they are made. They are also salted and treasured during the fall and winter to grate and crumble into the myriad dishes they enhance:

Obviously, from the earliest records on the subject of cheese, they scored in a kaleidoscopic array of specialties. In the *Odyssey* Homer describes cheese dishes served by Circe to Odysseus. In another passage, Nestor grated goat's milk cheese over wine and even added a touch of onion as relish (a Homeric "Gibson"?). During this period, cheese was also served with the meal, as was wine. Considerably earlier, during the Minoan period, archeologists assert that cheeses were made of the milk of goats and sheep of domesticated flocks.

Subsequently, the use of cheese in cooking flourished dramatically.

246

Cheese was baked into bread, served with honey, used as a seasoning or a relish, cooked with vegetables, made into cheesecakes of many kinds, including "breast-shaped" ones by a particularly expressive chef. Especially interesting was the ancient dish *thrion*, often referred to by the comic poets: this was eggs, milk, flour, honey, cheese, and fat, wrapped in fig leaves. How exciting it is, centuries later, to relate these fabulous recipes to modern Greek cooking. The filling for *thrion* is now baked inside *filo* pastry to make Tyropita (pages 254–255). And the fig leaves have been replaced by grapevine leaves, wrapped around Dolmades (page 68).

As a seasoning, the use of cheeses, particularly the salted ones, remains extensive in sauces, gravies, casseroles, soups, forcemeat and stuffing mixtures, savory pies and egg, grain, and vegetable dishes— cheese mellows or sharpens the flavor.

Feta, telemes (another form of feta), kefalotyri, mizithra, and kasseri are by far the outstanding Greek cheeses and are listed in order of quantity of production and consumption. Another cheese seen less frequently on menus is graviera. All are readily available in local shops, and are quite reasonable, with feta leading both in popularity and economy (approximately half the price of the least costly of the other cheeses). In addition, yogurt appears on the cheese list on Greek menus, while Roquefort and Parmesan, found in more expensive restaurants, are increasingly being enjoyed by the more affluent, and are imported into Greece. Cheese is not served as a separate course with fruit, continental style, but as an embellishment to the meal, while fruit constitutes a separate course.

Considering the prominence of cheese in Greek culture and food, the Greek cheese list is quite short. Here it is:

Anthotyro: A Cretan cheese made from goat's milk; full of butterfat, it is soft (slightly firmer than cream cheese) and white (but yellower than feta); substitute soft, unsalted mizithra.

Feta: A distinctive Greek sheep's and goat's milk curd cheese; pure white and flaky, it is salted and stored in brine; it is made throughout Greece and the islands and used extensively in cooking and as table cheese. Feta is packed in wooden barrels in 7-pound pieces (see telemes); there is no substitute.

Graviera: A Greek gruyère-type cheese made of sheep or cow's milk; salted, mild, it is used both for grating into dishes and served with meals.

Kasseri: A mild, creamy cheese that is Cheddar-type in texture, but saltier; made of sheep's or goat's whole milk, it is popular with meals.

Kefalotyri: A very hard, salty, light yellow grating cheese; made of sheep's or goat's milk in some provinces, it is used in many dishes and *pites*; substitute Italian Romano.

Manouri: A soft, unsalted white cheese similar to and sometimes synonymous with mizithra in some regions; made of whey of sheep's and goat's milk; especially used for savory and sweet cheese pies, and desserts, it is also a table cheese; substitute soft, unsalted mizithra.

Mizithra: Two types: (1) soft, unsalted, made of the whey after the curd is removed from goat's or sheep's milk to make feta; a favorite cheese, it is also used in sweet and savory pies; substitute fresh cottage cheese or soft ricotta; and (2) a lightly salted, semihard grating cheese (easier to grate with a fork than grater) and table cheese of delicious, mild flavor; it is also used in various dishes; more difficult to find in the United States than feta, but an excellent substitute is hard Italian ricotta (available in hard and very hard varieties in Italian specialty stores).

Telemes: Another form of feta which differs only in method of packing and shape (see feta). Telemes is packed in square tins and is available in square, 2-pound pieces.

Toulomotyrion: A Cretan sheep's curd cheese; semisoft, flaky and white, it is similar to feta but sweeter and less salty; introduced to Crete by Asia Minor Greeks, it is eaten with meals, salads, fruit, and is especially excellent with grapes; it is prepared in animal hide (hair side in), aged for three months, and sold from the hide; the whey is used to make mizithra or manouri.

FLAOUNES KYPRIOTIKES
[*Cheese-mint tarts, Cyprus style*]

These delicious triangles or squares of cheese and crisp, tasty dough are made for Easter. The recipe has been adapted for available cheese. Cypriots use local haloumi cheese.

TO MAKE 20

½ cup corn oil	2 cups fresh ricotta cheese
3 to 4 eggs	1 cup grated kefalotyri (or
3 pieces mastic	Romano) and kasseri cheese,
4 teaspoons granulated sugar	mixed
¼ cup milk, warmed	2 tablespoons fine semolina
3½ cups all-purpose flour	2 tablespoons finely crushed
1 teaspoon baking powder	mint leaves
¼ teaspoon salt	Sesame seeds

In an electric mixer, beat the corn oil with one of the eggs until thick, then add 3 teaspoons of the sugar. Pound the mastic with the remaining teaspoon sugar and add to the batter, then add the warm milk. In another bowl, sift the flour with the baking powder and salt. Gradually add to the batter, mixing by hand when the dough becomes thick. Knead for 5 to 10 minutes, until elastic and smooth, then cover and let rest a few hours before rolling.

Meanwhile, make the filling. Combine the ricotta, the grated cheese, 1 to 2 eggs, the semolina, and the mint; the filling should be thick and flavorful.

Break off sections of the dough and roll out each as thin as possible. Using a round plate or a pastry cutter, cut 6-inch circles. Fill the center of each with 2 heaping tablespoons of the filling, then fold the sides of the circle over to form squares or triangles or some of each, leaving the cheese filling exposed in the center. Beat the remaining egg and use it to brush the dough edges. Sprinkle the *flaounes* with sesame seeds and bake in a moderate oven (350 degrees) for 20 to 25 minutes, or until the dough is crisp and golden chestnut color and the filling is firm. Serve hot or cold.

Note: Cypriots sometimes substitute cinnamon for mint and add ½ cup raisins along with the cheese. Use cottage or farmer cheese and other favorite grating cheese. The size is a variable as well; the *flaounes* can be prepared bite sized or family sized in an 8- or 9-inch pan.

KALITSOUNIA ME KANELLA
[Sweet cheese-cinnamon "half-moons," Cretan style]

Pastry shops specialize in delectable cheese treats on Crete. We wondered if women baked them at home, and discovered that they certainly do. This is one of the many versions; the following recipe is another. Plan to make, serve, and eat at once. They are best hot and fresh—these are sweet.

TO MAKE ABOUT 20

1½ cups fresh mizithra or fresh ricotta cheese
2 tablespoons grated hard ricotta
2 eggs, separated
½ cup granulated sugar
Ground cinnamon
2 tablespoons melted butter

4 to 5 tablespoons milk
2 cups all-purpose flour
Pinch of salt
3 tablespoons softened butter
1 teaspoon vanilla extract
Water or milk
Confectioners' sugar

For the filling, combine the cheeses, lightly beaten egg yolks, sugar, ½ teaspoon cinnamon, and melted butter in a bowl. The mixture should be thick enough to mound, but not stiff; add 1 tablespoon milk, if necessary. Set aside while you make the dough.

Sift the flour and salt into a bowl, then cut in the butter and mix by rubbing between your fingers. Mix in the vanilla, egg whites, and enough milk to make a soft dough. Knead until smooth and elastic, then break off small pieces and roll as thin as a dime. (The dough will be elastic and can be rolled easily.) Cut into circles 4 inches in diameter (teacup size), then on each circle place a teaspoon of the cheese filling. Wet the circle edge with water or milk and fold over to form a half-moon, then seal with the tines of a fork or a pastry wheel. Arrange the *kalitsounia* on buttered cookie sheets and bake in a moderate oven (350 degrees) for 25 minutes, or until the pastry puffs up and turns a light chestnut color. Remove from the oven, and place on racks, and dust with confectioners' sugar and cinnamon. Serve hot or cold.

Note: See the accompanying sketches for variations on folding *kalitsounia*.

KALITSOUNIA ME SOUSAMI
[*Savory cheese-sesame "half-moons"*]

These are not as sweet as the preceding; they are nice served with pork and veal dishes and a fresh salad.

TO MAKE ABOUT 20

1½ *cups fresh mizithra or ricotta* | 2 *cups all-purpose flour*
cheese | ½ *teaspoon salt*
1 *tablespoon melted butter* | 2 *tablespoons butter or margarine*
2 *eggs* | 8 *to* 10 *tablespoons orange juice*
1 *tablespoon granulated sugar* | *Sesame seeds*

Make the filling by combining the cheese, melted butter, 1 egg, lightly beaten, and sugar in a bowl. Make a soft dough by sifting together the flour and salt, cutting in the butter and mixing well between your fingers. Add only enough orange juice to form a ball. Knead until smooth, then break off and roll as for Kalitsounia me Kanella (page 250). Brush with the second egg, beaten, and sprinkle with the sesame seeds. Bake in a moderate oven (350 degrees) for 25 to 30 minutes, or until puffy and a light chestnut color and serve warm or cold.

Note: Water may be used instead of orange juice for the dough. Also, many Cretans use oil instead of butter, and in some villages *kalitsounia* are fried in hot oil and dusted with cinnamon.

SOUFFLE TYRI
[Savory cheese soufflé]

Soufflés show the rising French influence on Greek cuisine. To taste "Greek," the cheese soufflé must be made with exceptional Greek cheese, which, you will observe, the Hellenes taste before purchasing. Mizithra, kefalotyri, and feta provide fine flavor. Season very carefully with salt, if the cheeses are already very salty.

TO SERVE 5 TO 6

3½ tablespoons butter
3½ tablespoons all-purpose flour
1½ cups hot milk
Salt, if necessary, and white pepper
¼ to ½ teaspoon grated nutmeg

6 eggs, at room temperature, separated
1 cup grated mizithra, kefalotyri, or feta, crumbled (or a combination)
Pinch of cream of tartar

Make a thick white sauce with the butter, flour, and hot milk as directed on page 50. Season with salt (unless the cheeses are salty), white pepper, and nutmeg. Cool slightly, then stir in the egg yolks and all but 2 tablespoons of the cheese. Beat the egg whites with a pinch of salt and the cream of tartar until they form stiff peaks. Stir 2 tablespoons of the whites into the sauce-yolk mixture, carefully, to avoid losing air from the egg whites, then fold remaining whites into the sauce, using an over-under motion with a rubber spatula. Turn into a buttered 8-cup soufflé dish sprinkled with 1 tablespoon of the grated cheese and dust the top with the remaining tablespoon of cheese. Place in the center of a 400-degree oven and immediately turn the heat down to 375 degrees and allow to bake for 30 minutes without opening door. Test for doneness; the soufflé will be done when the tester comes out clean, the soufflé is high, and the top golden. Serve at once.

253

SAVORY CHEESE PIES

TYROPITA NAFPLIOU
[Cheese pie with semolina, Nafplion style]

An unusual treatment of cheese pie, thick and wholesome as made in Nafplion, a town with a cosmopolitan air. In addition to Hellenes, Nafplion has been occupied by Franks, Venetians, and Turks after its legendary creation of Nafplios, son of Poseidon. Either commercial *filo* or homemade *filo* may be used, although the commercial *filo* will bake to a flakier crispness, contrasting nicely with the rich, creamy filling.

TO MAKE 12 SQUARES

3 cups milk
2/3 cup fine semolina
2/3 pound feta cheese, grated with
  a fork
1/3 cup grated kefalotyri or
  Romano cheese
3 eggs, lightly beaten

12 sheets commercial filo, *un-*
  rolled flat and kept covered to
  avoid drying, plus 6 table-
  spoons melted butter; or 2
  sheets homemade filo *pastry*
  (see note below)

In a medium pan, slowly bring the milk to the boiling point without scorching. Gradually add the semolina, stirring constantly with a wooden spoon. Cook until the mixture thickens, then remove from the heat and cool for 10 minutes. Stir in the feta, kefalotyri, and eggs.

Stack 7 sheets of the commercial *filo* pastry on a buttered 9 x 12 x 2- or 8 x 11 x 2-inch pan (the latter will make a thicker pie), brushing each sheet before stacking with warm, melted butter. Turn the filling into the pan and cover with the remaining 5 sheets *filo*, brushing each as well as the top of the *pita*. Score into squares the top sheets, using a sharp knife, then bake in a moderate oven (350 degrees) for 40 minutes, or until crisp and a golden chestnut color. Cool for 10 minutes, then cut into squares and serve warm.

Note: If using homemade *filo,* spread one sheet on the bottom and one over the filling, flute the edges together and prick the top with a fork. Brush the top with butter and bake the same as above.

TYROPITA THRAKIS
[Cheese pie, Thracian style]

Thracians layer their *pites* more like *baklava,* revealing the Asia Minor influence. *Pites* therefore are fascinating to assemble and to see, but require a longer baking time at a lower temperature to bake thoroughly.

TO MAKE 12 SQUARES

1 pound grated feta, mizithra, kefalotyri, or Parmesan cheese
½ cup milk, more if necessary
5 eggs
3 tablespoons chopped fresh mint or 1 tablespoon dried mint

Freshly ground black pepper
1 pound commercial filo sheets, unrolled flat and kept covered to avoid drying
1 cup olive oil and melted butter or margarine, mixed

In a bowl, combine the cheese, milk, eggs, mint, and a few grindings of black pepper. The mixture should not be thick; add more milk if necessary. On the bottom of a 9 x 12 x 3-inch baking pan, stack 5 sheets *filo,* brushing each with oil and butter before stacking. Spread on a thin layer of cheese filling, then cover with 3 additional *filo* sheets, brushing each. Continue until all the *filo,* except for 4 to 5 sheets saved for the top, and filling have been used up. Cover with the reserved 4 to 5 *filo* sheets, brushing each with the fat. Tuck the upper *filo* over the lower neatly, then score the top few sheets into squares with a sharp knife, and brush the surface. Bake in a moderately slow oven (325 degrees) for 1 to 1¼ hours, or until crisp and golden. Remove and let rest for 10 minutes before cutting into squares. Serve warm.

Note: An alternate method of layering in Thrace: After stacking 5 bottom sheets, divide the filling into 2 parts and make only 2 layers, dividing them with 5 *filo* sheets and topping as described above. Bake the same as above. Cover and freeze the remaining *filo* for another recipe.

BOUGATSA
[Sweet fresh cheese in filo with sugar, Cretan style]

A midmorning treat for shoppers in Hania, Crete, is piping hot *bougatsa* from the oven in the little shop. A family owns and runs the business: Father helps roll the filo; Mother cuts, weighs, and sprinkles the pie with sugar; and Grandfather and son help serve. For us, an additional treat was watching the *filo* made in the kitchen. Soft dough is rolled thin, then flipped and "spanked" on the work table—a huge sheet of marble lightly covered with olive oil—then folded around the fresh mizithra cheese and baked in the cavernous brick oven. The result is delectable. Since fresh mizithra is not available in the United States, the following recipe tastes delicious without claiming to be the "real thing." Not terribly sweet, it is lovely for a leisurely brunch.

TO SERVE 6 TO 8 (3 SEVEN-INCH PIES)

> *½ pound cream cheese*
> *1 pound fresh ricotta cheese*
> *1 pound fresh large-curd cottage cheese*
> *Granulated sugar*
> *½ teaspoon grated nutmeg*
> *18 sheets commercial* filo *pastry*
> *½ to ⅔ cup melted butter*

Using an electric mixer, beat the cream cheese at high speed until light and fluffy. Lower the speed and add the ricotta, cottage cheese, 1½ tablespoons sugar, and the nutmeg. Beat for 1 minute at high speed, then set aside while you prepare the *filo*.

Lay the *filo* flat on a table and keep covered with a damp towel over waxed paper or plastic wrap. By stacking 4 sheets, form a base of 15 x 18 inches, brushing the top of each sheet with melted butter as you stack them. Then lay 2 sheets at right angles over the center, using the "base" as a diamond, not as a square, brushing the center of each with butter. Divide the filling into 3 parts and spread one part over the *filo* to form a 7-inch square. Set the rest of the filling aside. Fold the top *filo* sheet over the cheese and brush with butter, and continue folding the *filo* over the cheese to make a square, brushing each time with butter. With a wide spatula, lift the *bougatsa* and invert onto a cookie sheet. Brush the top with butter and set aside.

Repeat with the remaining *filo*, filling until all 3 square pies are folded. Bake in a moderate oven (350 degrees) for 15 to 20 minutes or until the *filo* puffs up and turns a golden chestnut color. Cut into small squares and sprinkle with additional sugar. Serve piping hot.

MELOPITA (SIPHNOPITA)
[*Honey-cheese pie, Siphnos style*]

Melopita is a popular sweet dessert throughout Greece, but the creations on the island of Siphnos have become so famous that the name *siphnopita* is synonymous with *melopita*. Most of the flavor derives from the delicous honey produced on the island. Mizithra in the *hloro* stage—soft and unsalted cheese from fresh ewe's milk—also contributes to the delectable pie. The islanders traditionally prepare and enjoy *melopita* during the climax of their Easter celebration.

TO SERVE 12

> *Flaky pastry (see below)*
> *1 pound fresh mizithra, ricotta, or cottage cheese*
> *½ cup good-quality honey*
> *5 to 6 tablespoons granulated sugar*
> *Ground cinnamon or grated lemon rind*
> *3 to 4 eggs, beaten*

Line a buttered 8 x 11 x 2-inch or 10-inch round baking pan with the pastry, pressing it into the bottom and sides of the pan. Flute the edges with your fingers or with the tines of a fork. Cover with another pan (bottom down) of same size or fill with clean, uncooked dried beans to hold down the pastry, and bake in a moderate oven (350 degrees) for 10 minutes. Remove and let it cool slightly, then remove the extra pie pan or beans. Meanwhile, in a medium bowl, combine the cheese, honey, sugar, and ½ teaspoon ground cinnamon or lemon rind. In another bowl, whisk the eggs, and when well beaten pour into the cheese mixture. Mix thoroughly, using a wooden spoon, and pour into the baked pastry shell. Bake in the center of a moderate oven (350 degrees) for 35 to 40 minutes, or until firm and creamy yellow in color. Sprinkle the entire surface generously with additional ground cinnamon, then cool. To serve, cut into diamond shapes.

FLAKY PASTRY

To make 1 ten-inch pie shell

> *1¾ cups all-purpose flour*
> *1 tablespoon granulated sugar*
> *Pinch of salt*
> *6 tablespoons chilled butter*
> *3 to 4 tablespoons ice water*

Sift the flour, sugar, and salt into a large bowl. Using pastry blender or two knives, cut the chilled butter into the flour until the butter is evenly distributed. Add 3 tablespoons ice water and mix quickly with the fingers, adding 1 more tablespoon water if necessary. Wrap and refrigerate for 1 hour, then roll out on a floured board to a thickness of ⅛ inch.

YEAST BREADS, QUICK BREADS, AND BISCUITS

The kneading trough is greased and sprinkled with poppy-seed, on which dough is spread, and so it does not stick to the trough during the rising. When it is placed in the oven, some coarse meal is sprinkled over the earthenware pan, after which the loaf is laid upon it and takes on a delightful color, like that of smoked cheese. ATHENAEUS

THIS RECIPE IS ONE OF myriad references to bread making recorded by Athenaeus. During the peak period of Greek cookery, the types of breads were even more varied than in modern Greece. Yet in the local *fourno* (oven-bakeshop) of contemporary Greece one can find breads of European, Middle Eastern, and ancient Greek influence. The staple bread is a large, crusty, leavened, either round or long loaf, made with wheat flour (whole wheat in the provinces). Placed in wood- or coke-heated brick ovens, which release high *atmos* (steam) from the pipes, loaves of this bread have the crisp, shiny crust so loved by Hellenes, and are delicious when fresh.

Dilphius of Siphnos was among the early Greeks whose treatises on bread reflected interested research. As early as Dilphius' era (early third century B.C.) wheat was known to be more nourishing and digestible than barley bread, which was also an early favorite. Barley from Lesvos and Thessaly were considered superlative by the great chef

Archestratus, and Thessalian wheats have been famous since his time.

In the various cities of the ancient Greek Empire, the bread bakers and soft loaves of Cappadocia (eastern Asia Minor) were renowned, and so were bakers of Lydia and Phoenicia. Athens bread, too, was mentioned frequently by food writers, including Antiphanes, who wrote:

> How could a man of gentle breeding ever leave this roof,
> when he sees these white-bodied loaves crowding the shelves
> in close ranks, and when he sees, too, how they have changed
> their shape in the oven—deft imitations made by Attic skill,
> which Thearion taught his countrymen?

The great Attic baker Thearion was also mentioned by Plato.

Rolls and buns of unusual shapes, wafer-thin griddle cakes, and both raised and unleavened breads were among the breads of the early Greek cuisine from various regions. Athenaeus also mentions an Attic "sandwich bread," which was eaten with lettuce, and in another reference, "heaping up sandwich bread and muffins." Ancient seasoners included honey, cheese, olives, poppy, sesame, and goat's milk. These seasonings and many more are used in modern breads, reflected in the sampling of bread recipes that follow. Vanilla, cinnamon, cloves, anise, *mastiha,* ouzo, wine, *petimezi* (must syrup), nutmeg, grated orange, and lemon rind, *mahlepi,* and orange juice are dribbled into the fancy breads. Honey, sugar, eggs, milk, and cheese flavor some of the special breads. Raisins, which had been resisted when introduced by nutritionists after World War II in some areas, now spike some of the breads we tasted on Crete and in the northern regions. In the confusing Greek nomenclature, these raisin breads are often called *stafidopita* but are unlike the sweeter raisin cakes having the same name.

Among the special breads woven into Greek cultural life are the Christmas bread, Christopsomo (page 267); New Year's bread, Vasilopita (pages 268 and 269); and Easter bread, Tsoureki (page 270). The glazed, bright breads not only have a luscious flavor, sweetened, enriched with eggs, milk, and sugar, but also have delightful variations in the ways they are rolled, toasted and decorated. For example, Easter sweet breads are baked with red-dyed eggs tucked into their braids and rings, called *tsoureki* or *lambropsomo.* (Easter orange-flavored sweet biscuits introduced by Smyrna Hellenes bearing a diminutive form of the name Tsourekakia [page 284], are not breads.)

Of all the confusing versions, *vasilopita,* which ushers in the New Year (Saint Vasilios Day), takes top prize. Vasilios, sometimes called Basil, was an advocate of Orthodoxy, a writer and a force in leading monks from a merely contemplative to a more active life. He became Bishop of Caesarea in Cappadocia in A.D. 370. *Vasilopita* was named for him, originating during the Byzantine era. In this cookbook, I have divided the sweet breads by method of preparation, including all *vasilopita* yeast breads in this chapter, and all *vasilopita* cakes among the cake recipes (pages 319 and 320). Although I have included only one *christopsomo* and one *tsoureki* recipe, you can rest assured there are individualistic versions. Sweet breads are, after all, for very special days!

For the majority of meals, however, the Hellene is happy with plain, fresh, crusty bread called *artos* or *karveli* (loaf) or *kouloura* (if round), or, as in most homes, *psomi*. Baked at home, it is the bread the mother learned from her mother. Luckily, these wonderful breads have been relatively simple for me to adapt at home using our excellent flours and other ingredients. For I believe that mixing, kneading, punching, and later smelling the aroma of bread baking to be the most completely satisfying culinary experience possible. It is exciting, like stepping into a Greek *fourno* and taking a deep whiff.

The delightful group of "quick breads" in this section, not a bit like "quick breads" of the United States, have always had a special niche in Greek life. Loukoumades (pages 274), Tiganites (pages 275–277), and Svingi (page 275), fried nd topped with honey or syrup, spices and nuts, are delectables made, with slight variations, in provincial homes throughout Greece. Who would deny their origin when reading through the fascinating mementos of ancient writers?

> Sweet, rounded, toasted, honey sesame-biscuits . . .
> Sesame-cheese-and-oil boiled cakes sprinkled with sesame seeds . . .
> A small cake boiled in olive oil and soaked in honey . . .
> Tagenites—flat cakes fried in oil—which steamed when honey was poured on them . . .
> Soft dough is poured upon the frying pan, and on it are spread honey, sesame and cheese . . .

Among the novelty breads, the French influence is evident in Athens, particularly, with its increasing use of croissants, brioches, and choux. The Athenians also favor, though to much less a degree, the United States doughnut. The latter is not as delicious as the Greek "doughnut"—*svingi* (page 275).

Koulourakia fill a unique role as a staple, traditional butter hard biscuit, not terribly sweet, but just perfect. The name comes from *koulouri, kouloura* (round), the original shape of a *koulouraki,* formed by rolling dough into a short rope and joining the edges. There are interesting ways to shape these *koulourakia* and many different ways of mixing them (including some versions on pages 281 to 286).

Paximadia, cut biscuits, must also be counted among the staples. Like *koulourakia,* the *paximadia* belong to the Greek cupboard, symbolic of plenty, a contented soul who has something on hand for dunking into his coffee. *Paximadia* are especially prevalent in the proverbs and, with fish, coffee, and Cognac, are traditionally served in the deceased person's home following a Greek funeral.

However, bread must be singled out as the most significant cultural food, promoted not only by the elevating spirit of Demeter, but also through the Christian influence exemplified by the tradition of Christ's Last Supper. Bread from the *Prosphoron* is the Host during the Divine Liturgy. And bread is distributed after the Orthodox Divine Liturgy to worshipers as *antidoron* ("instead of the Gift" meaning the Host, which is only given in Holy Communion). Children learn early that the last piece, the *boukitsa,* must be eaten, for it contains a symbolic strength. "Whosoever thirsts, dreams of springs, and whoever is hungry, loaves," states the proverb. Yet another varies the beverage and mood—"Without bread and wine, love freezes."

Yeast Breads

PROSFORON
[*Offering bread*]

An important contribution women make to the Orthodox Liturgy is to bake a *prosforon,* which is blessed and cut, at the altar by the priest, during the church service. The custom began among early Christians, who brought bread and wine as an offering, and continues in modern times with the *prosforon,* which means "offering," presented with sweet wine, oil, and incense used for traditional church ceremonies. The bread is stamped before baking with a religious seal or *sfragida* which is often hand-carved in the monasteries. The seal is divided into nine sections and the center one is the most significant, with the symbols IΣ ΧΣ NI KA, Greek initials for "Jesus Christ Conquers." During the Transubstantiation service, this part of the bread is the Host and is mixed with the blessed wine for the Communion cup. Aside from the indispensable seal, the only other unusual treatment of the bread is the total lack of fat or oil during preparation.

TO MAKE 1 LOAF

> *1 package active dry yeast*
> *1½ cups warm water*
> *1 teaspoon salt*
> *4 to 4½ cups flour*
> *1* prosforon sfragida *(seal)*

Combine the yeast and ½ cup of the warm water in a mixing bowl. Cover and allow to double in bulk. Add the remaining warm water, and the salt, and gradually add only enough flour to form a soft ball. Knead for 10 minutes until smooth and elastic, then place in a floured bowl, cover, and set in a warm place to double in bulk.

Punch down the dough and knead for a few minutes on a floured board, then shape into a round loaf and set in a floured 9-inch pan. Flour the *prosforon* seal and press into the center of the loaf. Cover with a clean towel and set in a warm place to rise for 1½ hours or until doubled in bulk. Remove the seal. Bake in a moderately hot oven (375 degrees) for 10 minutes, then, without opening the oven door, lower the heat to 350 and bake for 25 to 30 minutes longer, or until a light chestnut color. Remove from the pan and cool on a rack.

Note: *Sfragida* may be purchased at most Greek specialty stores.

PSOMI
[Bread]

This is the bread my mother learned from her mother and I from mine, so it is called, in our home, "Mother's bread."

TO MAKE 5 LOAVES

3 packages active dry yeast	*6½ teaspoons salt*
2 teaspoons sugar	*3 tablespoons olive oil*
5 to 5¼ cups warm water	*3 tablespoons butter or margarine*
5 pounds unbleached flour	*Melted butter (optional)*

In a small pan or bowl, combine 2 packages of the active dry yeast with 1 teaspoon sugar and 1 cup of the warm water. Cover and let rest until doubled in size (approximately 10 minutes). In a very large bowl or pan, put the flour, salt, remaining teaspoon sugar, the olive oil and butter and rub between your fingers until the mixture resembles a fine cornmeal. Mix in the remaining yeast, undiluted.

Make a well in the center of the flour mixture. Pour into the well the swollen yeast and 4 cups warm water. Using your fingers, mix quickly until a soft dough is formed, adding the additional ¼ cup water, if necessary. Knead, fold, and punch the dough from 15 to 20 minutes, until smooth, satiny, and resilient. Place in a floured bowl, cover with a clean towel, set in a warm draft-free area (oven with *no* pilot light, or covered with wool blanket). Allow to rise until doubled in bulk (approximately 2½ hours). Uncover the dough, punch down, and remove all the dough and place on a floured board. Divide the dough into 5 parts and knead each part separately for a few minutes, then mold with the palms of your hands to form the shape of pans you are going to use.

Oil bottoms and sides of 5 round 8-inch diameter or 9 x 5-inch loaf pans (or any combination you like). Place dough in each pan, cover with clean towels, and set to rise until doubled in bulk again, in the same draft-free area for about 1½ hours. (If using the oven, remove the loaves before preheating.) Bake on the center rack of a 375-degree oven for 10 minutes, then reduce the heat to 350 degrees and continue baking for another 30 to 35 minutes, or until the crust is golden chestnut color. (The loaves may be turned in their pans during the last 10 minutes of baking time for even color.) Remove the loaves from their pans to wire racks, quickly wiping the tops with water-dampened fingers or towel, a Greek baker's trick for glaze. Or you may brush the tops with melted butter. Cool before slicing. Delicious toasted the next day, with butter and honey.

Note: The best test for doneness in baking bread of any kind, I have found, is to remove the loaf from the pan and tap the bottom and sides with your knuckles. When done, the bread will have a hollow sound. This dough may also be used to make rolls and other variations.

LALANGIDES
[*Hot and crisp fried bread curls*]

Announce the time you'll be serving these and the family will arrive promptly. *Lalangides* are ruddy chestnut, crisp, and delicious.

TO MAKE 8 TO 10

After the second rising of one loaf of Psomi (page 264), break off pieces of dough about the size of an orange. Roll the dough pieces into 10-inch ropes and shape any of these ways: Bend the 2 ends toward the center with tips extending in opposite directions and pinch at the juncture; bend into large circles with tips extending in opposite directions; shape into "pretzels." Heat olive or vegetable oil in a deep pan to a depth of 6 inches to 375 degrees. Slip in *lalangides* a few at a time without crowding and fry on both sides. Drain on towels. Serve hot.

PITA LAKONIAS
[*Crisp and salty bread "diamonds," Laconian style*]

For another bread variation that must be eaten hot and fresh: When preparing Psomi (page 264), after the first rising, use one of the loaves and spread the dough into an oiled 9-inch-square or 7 x 11-inch pan and shape into a flat *pita*. Score into generous diamond shapes, cover, and allow to rise with the other loaves until doubled in bulk. Before baking, dribble generously with olive oil and sprinkle with salt, scoring again if shapes are not clearly indented. Bake in 375-degree oven for 40 minutes, reducing heat to 350 during the last 15 minutes. Cut and serve hot.

ELIOPSOMO
[Olive bread with onions and mint, Cyprus style]

Eliopsomo is one of the more unusual non-sweet breads. Use the large, wrinkled Greek olives, and be sure to pit them and discard the pits, since they are indigestible—or worse—if baked in the bread and accidentally swallowed. Otherwise, the bread is a joy to serve with meals or sliced thin with appetizers.

TO MAKE 2 TEN-INCH LOAVES

2 packages active dry yeast
1½ teaspoons granulated sugar
3 cups warm water,
 approximately
10 cups sifted all-purpose flour
5 tablespoons olive oil or other
 vegetable oil
5 teaspoons salt, or less if the
 olives are very salty

1 medium onion, chopped
3 tablespoons chopped fresh mint
 leaves or 4 teaspoons dried
 mint
18 to 20 Amphissa-type Greek
 olives, pitted
Melted butter or oil (optional)

Dissolve the yeast and ½ teaspoon of the sugar in 1½ cups of the water, cover, and let rise until doubled in volume. In a large mixing bowl, combine the flour with the oil, remaining sugar, and the salt, and rub between the fingers. Stir in the onion and mint, make a well in the center, and add the swollen yeast and 1½ cups more warm water. Mix well and work until the dough is soft and elastic, adding more water if necessary. Keeping the olives as large as possible after pitting, add to the dough. Knead for 10 minutes, then place in a large floured bowl, cover, and set in a warm place to double in bulk (2 to 3 hours).

Punch down and divide the dough in half. Knead each piece thoroughly, form 2 large loaves, and set in oiled pans. Cover and allow to rise in a warm place until doubled in bulk. Bake in a moderately hot oven (450 degrees) for 10 minutes, then reduce the heat to 350 degrees for an additional 30 to 35 minutes, or until the loaves are chestnut in color and crisp. Brush with butter, or oil, or wet your fingers with water and run lightly over the tops of the loaves to form glaze. Cool on racks.

SWEET YEAST BREADS

CHRISTOPSOMO
[Fruity, glazed Christmas bread]

A delicious and festive Christmas sweet bread of airy grain, speckled with fruits and with a deep chestnut, soft layered crust— glazed with nuts or fruits. Soak the figs in advance overnight, plan to bake the day before the bread is sliced.

TO MAKE 2 HIGH, ROUND 9-INCH LOAVES

6 dried figs
2 packages active dry yeast
1 cup warm water
¾ cup plus 2 teaspoons
  granulated sugar
7 to 7½ cups flour
1 teaspoon salt
1 to 1½ teaspoons mastic (resin)
1 cup warm milk
3 large eggs, lightly beaten

½ cup melted sweet butter or
  unsalted margarine
¾ cup coarsely chopped walnuts
½ cup light raisins
Glaze (2 tablespoons honey, 2
  tablespoons orange juice, ¼
  cup slivered almonds, mixed;
  or 1 beaten egg white, fine
  granulated sugar and ¼ cup
  glacéed fruit)

Cut off the fig stems, quarter the figs, and place in a small bowl. Barely cover with water, then put a plate over the bowl and let stand overnight. The next day, when ready to mix the bread, dissolve the yeast with the water and 1 teaspoon sugar and let stand, covered, until doubled in volume. Meanwhile, sift 7 cups of the flour with the ¾ cup sugar and the salt into a large mixing bowl. Pound the mastic with the remaining teaspoon sugar (to prevent gumming) until powdered, then add to the flour. Make a well in the flour and add the milk, eggs, butter, figs and their liquid, swollen yeast, walnuts, and raisins and mix with fingers until smooth. Add a little more flour if necessary to form a soft, but not sticky dough and knead for 10 to 15 minutes. Place in a lightly-oiled bowl in a warm place to rise until doubled in bulk (2 hours). Uncover the dough, punch down, and divide into 2 parts. Knead each part for a few minutes, then form into round loaves and place in buttered 9-inch pans. Cover and allow to rise in a warm place until doubled in bulk (1½ hours), then bake in a moderately hot oven (375 degrees) for 20 minutes. Pull out the oven rack to spread on the glaze preferred. The first glaze may be brushed on. If using the second (which will produce a lighter glaze), brush on the egg white, then sprinkle with sugar, then the glacéed fruit. Continue baking at 325 degrees for 35 to 40 minutes, or until bread is a deep shiny chestnut. Cool on racks.

Note: The flavor improves the second day.

VASILOPITA KONSTANTINOUPOLEOS
[*Constantinople New Year's sweet bread*]

Vasilopita was introduced to mainland Greece by Hellenes living on Constantinople (Istanbul) to honor Saint Vasilios (Saint Basil), ironically using the Syrian and Turkish spice *mahlepi!* Despite breaking all rules of bread baking (with such high fat and sugar content), this is one of the most delicious of the Greek sweet breads. A deep chestnut color transforms the soft crust and also the outer layers of this cakelike bread, which has a pale yellow interior, fine grain, and the gentlest aroma. There is no substitute for *mahlepi*; luckily, it is not expensive, and is readily available at Syrian and Greek specialty stores. *Vasilopita* is made differently in some regions (cake versions are included among the cakes, pages 319 to 320), but everywhere the "lucky" coin is inserted for the ceremonial cutting of the bread in the traditional New Year's Day family meal (and in many churches, too). In Greece this coin can be a *lira* (gold coin) or small *drachma* coin, or in the United States a dime or quarter. It is the honor and luck that counts most.

TO MAKE 2 ROUND TEN-INCH LOAVES, OR 2 NINE-INCH AND
1 SEVEN-INCH LOAVES

2 to 3 packages active dry yeast
2 cups plus ½ teaspoon
  granulated sugar
1⅔ cups milk, warmed, more if
  necessary
10¼ cups sifted all-purpose flour
2 teaspoons salt
5 to 6 eggs, lightly beaten

2 cups (1 pound) sweet butter,
  melted and clarified (see page
  40)
1½ teaspoons mahlepi, boiled 2
  minutes in ⅓ cup water and
  strained (see note below)
Sesame seeds

Dissolve the yeast and ½ teaspoon sugar in 1 cup of the warm milk, cover and allow to rise for 15 minutes. Place 10 cups of the flour in a large mixing bowl and stir in the 2 cups sugar and salt. Make a well in the center and add 4 to 5 lightly beaten eggs, the butter, remaining milk, the *mahlepi* water (discard the seeds) and swollen yeast. Mix into a smooth but stiff dough adding additional flour or milk only if necessary. Knead thoroughly for 10 to 20 minutes, then place in a lightly oiled or buttered pan, and allow to rise in a warm, draft-free place until doubled in bulk (2 to 3 hours).

Punch the dough down, then divide into 2 or 3 parts, depending on the size of the loaves desired. Knead each section thoroughly into a round shape and insert the "lucky coin" which has been washed and wrapped in waxed paper through the bottom of the loaf.* Place in a buttered, floured round baking pan, cover, and allow to rise in a warm place until doubled in bulk. With kitchen shears, clip the tops of the loaves decoratively in graceful garlands. Beat the remaining egg and use to brush the tops of the loaves. Dust with sesame seeds, then bake in a hot oven (425 degrees) for 10 minutes, then reduce the heat to 350 for the next 30 minutes. Lower the heat again to 325 and continue baking for 10 minutes or until done. (Check the loaves after 20 minutes and reduce the heat sooner if the crust color is deepening too quickly.) Remove and cool on racks.

* *Note*: If you forgot to insert the "lucky coin" before baking you may slip it in through the bottom after baking. Also, *mahlepi* may be slightly pounded and added to the batter without boiling in water, in which case 1 teaspoon will be sufficient.

VASILOPITA MORAITIKI
[*New Year's Day sweet bread, Peloponnesos style*]

A deep chestnut glaze over a sweet even-grained bread of a light yellow color. (Morea is a nickname for Peloponnesos.)

TO MAKE 2 ROUND 9-INCH LOAVES

2 *packages active dry yeast*	2 *tablespoons butter or margarine*
2 *cups milk, warmed*	1 *teaspoon salt*
¾ *cup plus 1 teaspoon*	5 *eggs, lightly beaten*
granulated sugar	*Grated rind of 1 large orange*
7 *to 7½ cups sifted all-purpose*	*Sesame seeds (optional)*
flour	

In a small bowl, dissolve the yeast in 1 cup of the warm milk with the 1 teaspoon sugar. Cover and let stand for 20 minutes, or until doubled in volume. In a large mixing bowl, place 7 cups of the flour and add the butter, rubbing it between your fingers, then add the ¾ cup sugar and the salt.

Make a well in the center of the flour mixture and pour in the swollen yeast, remaining 1 cup milk, 4 of the lightly beaten eggs, and the grated orange rind. Work with your hands until the dough is smooth, adding ½ cup flour if necessary. Knead for 10 to 15 minutes, then place in a lightly oiled or buttered bowl, cover, and set in a warm, draft-free area until doubled in bulk (2 to 3 hours).

Uncover, punch down, and divide the dough in two. Knead each part for a few minutes and then form round loaves (see note below). Set in buttered round 9-inch pan, cover, and allow to rise in a warm place until doubled in volume, 1½ to 2 hours. Before placing in the oven, snip the surface decoratively with kitchen shears, in rows either circular, curved, or radiating from the center. Beat the remaining egg, and, using a pastry brush, spread it on the surface. Sprinkle lightly with sesame seeds, if desired. Bake for 10 minutes in a moderately hot oven (375 to 400 degrees), then reduce the heat to 350 for an additional 30 to 35 minutes, or until a deep chestnut color. Cool on racks.

Note: Insert the "lucky coin" as described in Vasilopita Konstantinoupoleos (page 268).

TSOUREKI OR LAMBROPSOMO
[Easter sweet bread, Peloponnesos style]

The *tsoureki* is a delightful braided bread, festive and bright with red eggs and shiny glaze during the climax of the Easter day. Though the flavorings and the method of braiding and shaping the dough vary from region to region, it is always sweet. Mothers often shape small portions of the dough into miniature baskets or animals for the children.

FOR 2 BRAIDED LOAVES 13 INCHES LONG OR
2 ROUND 9-INCH LOAVES

1 cup milk	*5 tablespoons orange juice*
½ cup (¼ pound) sweet butter	*1 tablespoon grated orange rind*
1 package active dry yeast	*5½ cups sifted all-purpose flour*
½ cup plus 2 tablespoons	*Melted butter*
granulated sugar	*Red-dyed, hard-boiled eggs*
1 teaspoon salt	*(optional; see page 238)*
2 eggs, beaten	*¼ cup slivered almonds*

In a small saucepan, combine the milk and butter over medium heat and scald. Stir until the butter melts, then pour into a mixing bowl. When lukewarm, sprinkle in the yeast, and with fingers or a heavy spoon gradually stir in the ½ cup sugar until it dissolves. Then add the salt, eggs, 3 tablespoons of the orange juice, and the orange rind, stirring continuously, and gradually add half the flour until the mixture begins to bubble. Continue adding flour gradually by hand; the dough will be sticky, but should not be stiff. Flour your fingers lightly and knead for 15 minutes. Place the dough in a large buttered bowl, brush the dough with melted butter, cover, and place in a warm area to rise until doubled in bulk (approximately 2 to 3 hours).

Punch the dough down and divide into 2 parts. Divide each half into 3 parts and roll each into a long rope about 10 x 2 inches. Braid the three ropes together; pinch to seal the ends if leaving long, or join together to form a round loaf (see note below). Repeat with the other half of the dough to make a second *tsoureki*. Place in large baking pans or on a cookie sheet, cover, and let rise until doubled in bulk (approximately 1½ hours).

Meanwhile, prepare a glaze by mixing the remaining orange juice, remaining sugar, and the almonds in a small bowl. Bake the *tsourekia* in a moderately hot oven (375 degrees) for 20 minutes. Remove from the oven and with a pastry brush glaze the tops and sides of the loaves. Return to the oven and bake for another 15 to 20 minutes until the color is a rich and shiny chestnut.

Note: If using the Easter eggs, tuck them into the center when you shape the loaves, leave until loaves have doubled and bake them with the loaf. After baking, though lovely, the eggs will be inedible. Also, in some provinces, the *tsoureki* is formed with a large braid and a smaller one over it, making a much larger loaf requiring longer baking time.

BREAD RINGS

ARTOKOULOURA KRITIKI
[Bread ring, Cretan style]

Artos is the ancient Greek word for "bread," and *kouloura* means circle or ring. Throughout Greece, *kouloures* are sold by vendors or from the community baker's oven for 2 drachmas. They usually have sesame seeds, as do these exceptionally aromatic ones from Crete.

TO MAKE ABOUT 20

2 packages active dry yeast	2 tablespoons butter or margarine
2 tablespoons plus ½ teaspoon	1 cup milk, warmed
granulated sugar	3 eggs
1 cup warm water	1 teaspoon vanilla extract
7 to 7½ cups all-purpose flour	1 tablespoon orange extract
2 teaspoons salt	Sesame seeds

In a small saucepan or bowl, combine the yeast, ½ teaspoon sugar, and the warm water. Cover and let stand until doubled in volume. Sift 7 cups of the flour, salt, and 2 tablespoons of sugar together into a large bowl. Add the butter, rubbing it into the flour with your fingers. Make a well in the center of the flour mixture and add the swollen yeast, milk, 2 lightly beaten eggs, and vanilla and orange extracts. Mix thoroughly until the dough is soft but not sticky. Work in small amounts of flour or water if necessary, then knead for 10 to 15 minutes, until elastic. Place in a floured bowl, cover, and let rise in a warm place until doubled in bulk.

Punch the dough down, and break off pieces the size of a small orange, and roll them into 16-inch "ropes" as thick as a thumb. Join the ends of each rope into a 6-inch circle, brush with the remaining egg, beaten, and sprinkle with sesame seeds. Set on buttered pans or cookie sheets allowing 3 inches between each. Continue until all are rolled. Cover and let rise for 30 minutes. Bake in a moderately hot oven (375 degrees) for 20 to 25 minutes, lowering the oven to 350 during the last ten minutes. The color will be a light chestnut. Cool on racks.

Note: Both sides may be glazed and covered with sesame seeds.

GYRISTARIA

["Lattice" koulouria, Cyprus style]

Cypriots enjoy many *koulouria* similar to the mainland types and this one with the prefix *gyro* (round and round). Their *haloumotes* are made with their famous haloumi cheese; *tahinopites*, made with *tahini*, and *eliotes*, smaller versions of Eliopsomo (page 266). *Gyristaria* are frequently made by the *prozymi* (predough) method, in which yeast and a small portion of flour and water are allowed to sit until they bubble, then are mixed with the remaining ingredients (also frequently used to make Greek breads).

TO MAKE 12 TO 15

2 packages active dry yeast	*2 teaspoons salt*
1 tablespoon plus ½ teaspoon	*1 teaspoon mastic*
granulated sugar	*1 teaspoon ground cinnamon*
2½ cups warm water	*1 egg, beaten*
6 to 6½ cups all-purpose flour	*Sesame seeds*

In a small bowl or saucepan, combine the yeast, ½ teaspoon sugar, 1½ cups of the warm water, and 2 cups of the flour. Cover and allow to rest in warm place until bubbling. Punch down and combine in a large mixing bowl with the remaining cup warm water, salt, mastic and 1 tablespoon sugar (which have been pounded together), and cinnamon, and gradually add only enough of the remaining 4 to 4½ cups flour until the dough forms a soft ball. Knead for 10 to 15 minutes, until smooth and elastic. Place in a floured bowl, cover, and set in a warm place until doubled in bulk.

Punch down the dough and break off 12 pieces about the size of a small orange. Roll each piece into a rope, then close the ends to form a 6-inch circle. Break off pieces of the remaining dough to roll 6 pencil-thin strips for each dough ring. Attach 3 of the thin strips to each top and 3 to each side of the dough rings, then form a lattice effect by criss-crossing the strips. Attach at the opposite ends. If any dough remains, continue making more. Place on a buttered baking sheet, brush with egg, and sprinkle with sesame seeds. Cover the *gyristaria* and allow to rise for 30 minutes, then bake in a moderately hot oven (375 degrees) for 25 minutes. Cool on racks.

Quick Breads

LOUKOUMADES
[*Fried dough puffs with honey*]

A national, traditional favorite throughout the winter until warm spring. It is fun to see the tiny shops where *loukoumades* are made in the window and where you can stop in for a quick treat. *Loukoumades* are fried in huge pots full of boiling oil. At home use a deep 6-inch pan and oil to a depth of 2½ to 3 inches, saving the oil to use several times before discarding.

You may use any plain yeast dough made with white flour (page 264), or substitute commercial unbaked biscuits (cut into 4 pieces) planning on 4 to 6 puffs per person. Dough made from 1 pound of flour (4 cups) will serve a party of 8. Allow the dough to rise twice.

When ready to fry, heat vegetable or olive oil in a deep fryer almost to the smoking point. Pinch off pieces of dough smaller than a walnut, or use the quartered biscuits, and drop into the oil 4 at a time. Using tongs turn until ruddy chestnut on all sides, lift, and drain on paper towels. Dip in warm honey, sprinkle with ground cinnamon, chopped walnuts, pistachios, or sesame seeds, and serve hot.

SVINGI
[Batter puffs with honey and cinnamon]

Svingi are less filling than *loukoumades* and sometimes referred to as Greek doughnuts. Hot, crisp, and syrupy, *svingi* are fun and quick to make for a cold evening's snack.

TO MAKE 28 TO 30 THREE-INCH PUFFS

1 cup boiling water	*4 eggs*
4 tablespoons butter or margarine	*Olive or other vegetable oil*
¼ teaspoon salt	*Honey, warmed, or a syrup made*
1 tablespoon granulated sugar	*by combining 2 cups*
½ teaspoon grated orange rind	*granulated sugar, 1 cup water,*
1 cup all-purpose flour	*and 2 teaspoons lemon juice*
1 teaspoon baking powder	*Ground cinnamon*

In a medium-sized saucepan, combine the boiling water, butter, salt, sugar, and orange rind. Bring to a boil. Meanwhile, sift together the flour and baking powder. Add the dry ingredients all at once to the hot mixture, beating hard with a wooden spoon over medium heat until the mixture forms a compact mass and leaves the sides of the pan. Remove from the heat and let cool for 1 minute. Add the eggs, one at a time, beating hard after each addition; the mixture should be smooth, glossy, and thick. Heat the oil (which should be 2½ to 3 inches deep) almost to the smoking point, then drop the batter by tablespoons into the oil, without crowding, to form puffs. When the puffs surface, turn them to fry on all sides, using tongs, then lift them out, drain off excess oil on absorbent paper. Place on warm platter and keep warm. If using the syrup, boil the syrup ingredients for 5 minutes; spoon the syrup, or warm honey, over the puffs, sprinkle with cinnamon, and serve hot.

TIGANITES ME FROUTO
[Fruit fritters]

Fritters are probably more distinguishable in how various cultural groups enjoy them than by their ingredients. Greek people will prepare *tiganites* impulsively for a *koliatso*, midmorning or supper snack, with seasonal fruit and fresh honey, for their family group. The word *tiganites* is also tacked onto vegetables fried and served with meals, but the accent is on the fourth syllable—and substance—while the accent for these is on the third—and on fun!

TO SERVE 2 TO 3

1 cup peeled, sliced Greening apples; 1 cup canned pineapple chunks, drained; or 2 ripe, firm bananas
Granulated sugar
2 tablespoons Cointreau or brandy; or 2 to 3 tablespoons kirsch or brandy
2 eggs, separated
⅔ cup cold milk

1 tablespoon olive oil
1 tablespoon brandy or lemon juice
1 cup all-purpose flour
½ teaspoon salt
Vegetable oil for deep frying
Ground cinnamon
Warm honey
Chopped walnuts (optional)

If using the sliced apples, sprinkle lightly with sugar and the Cointreau or brandy, then marinate in the refrigerator for several hours. If using the pineapple chunks, soak them in the kirsch or brandy. If using bananas, have them at hand but do not slice until just ready to fry.

Beat the egg yolks until thick and lemon-colored, then add the cold milk, beating constantly with a wire whisk. Dribble in the olive oil and brandy or lemon juice. Meanwhile sift the flour with the salt and add to the batter gradually. Fold in the egg whites which have been stiffly beaten; the batter will be thick and viscous. Put several pieces of fruit in the batter at a time and make sure they are covered thoroughly.

Add vegetable oil to a deep pan to a depth of at least 4 inches, then heat a temperature of 375 degrees. Drop several of the fritters in at a time, without crowding. When they puff up they should be turned; they should fry to a bright chestnut color on both sides. Drain, then sprinkle with cinnamon and warm honey, or warm honey and chopped walnuts. Serve hot.

Note: In some regions a few tablespoons raisins, chopped dry figs, or nuts may be dropped into the batter. If plain *tiganites* are preferred, beat the egg yolk and white together rather than fold in the egg white separately. Also Petimezi (page 347) is another favored syrup.

TIGANITES KRITIKES
[Pancakes, Cretan style, with honey-sesame-cinnamon syrup]

TO MAKE 15 TO 16

3 eggs
1½ cups milk
1¾ cups flour
¼ teaspoon salt
1 teaspoon baking powder
1 tablespoon granulated sugar

1 to 2 tablespoons butter or
  margarine
1 cup honey
1 tablespoon sesame seeds
½ teaspoon ground cinnamon

In a mixing bowl, whisk the eggs with the milk. In a smaller bowl, combine the flour, salt, baking powder, and sugar. Gradually add the dry ingredients to the liquid, mixing until smooth. Heat a griddle and grease with 1 teaspoon butter or margarine. Pour on ¼ cup batter for each pancake, and when bubbly, turn over and cook on the other side. Keep warm until all have been made, adding butter as needed.

For the accompanying syrup, heat the honey to the boiling point, then remove from the heat and add 1 tablespoon sesame seeds and the cinnamon. Stir and pour into a pitcher. Serve warm, with hot *tiganites.*

FETES
[Egg-bread fried in butter with syrup]

Fetes are believed to have been introduced to mainlanders by Hellenes from Smyrna. Very similar to the American breakfast dish called "French toast."

TO SERVE 5

1 cup sugar
½ cup honey
1 cup water
1 stick cinnamon
2 cloves
1 tablespoon lemon juice
3 eggs

½ cup milk
Pinch of salt
5 slices white bread, cut in half
4 to 5 tablespoons butter or
  margarine
Ground cinnamon

Combine the sugar, honey, water, spices, and lemon juice in a saucepan, bring to a boil and boil for 10 minutes. Remove the spices and set aside.

Beat the eggs in a shallow bowl, add the milk and salt, and whisk until mixed. Dip the bread slices in the mixture and soak on both sides until all the egg has been absorbed. Heat 1 tablespoon of the butter for each slice in frying pan and toast the egg-soaked bread on both sides over low heat until crisp and golden chestnut and continue frying other slices. Dust with cinnamon and serve with the warm syrup.

BOBOTA
[Corn bread]

Corn bread is not yet a favorite in Greece because it is identified with periods of occupation and the hunger that was a concomitant. Yet the corn breads I found there are flavorful. I tested this recipe, made with commercial cornmeal.

TO SERVE 9

1½ cups white or yellow
  cornmeal
½ cup all-purpose flour
3 teaspoons baking powder
½ teaspoon baking soda
½ teaspoon salt
¼ cup granulated sugar
½ cup orange juice

2 tablespoons vegetable oil
2 tablespoons butter or
  margarine, melted
½ to ¾ cup water
1 teaspoon grated orange rind
½ cup raisins
¼ cup honey

In a large bowl, sift together the dry ingredients. In a measuring cup, combine the orange juice, oil, and melted butter; add enough water to make 1 cup. Make a well in the center of the dry ingredients, pour in the cupful of wet ingredients and stir with a wooden spoon. The batter should be thick but not too stiff; add ¼ cup water if necessary. Blend in the orange rind and raisins and pour into a buttered 7 x 7 x 2-inch baking pan. Bake on the center rack of a moderately hot oven (375 degrees) for 30 minutes, or until a rich, golden color. Remove from the oven but leave in the pan. Make a syrup by boiling the honey with ¼ cup water for 1 minute. Pour the syrup over the *bobota*, cool in the pan, and cut into squares. Serve on individual plates.

Biscuits

PAXIMADIA ME GLYKANISON
[Anise double-baked biscuits]

Paximadia are found in every Greek cupboard and variations are as plentiful as cooks. They are not shaped by hand, therefore quicker to make than *koulourakia* and not as sweet. This version is of dry texture, thirsty to be dunked.

TO MAKE 35, 3 X 1¼-INCH BISCUITS

2 eggs	2½ to 2¾ cups all-purpose flour
¾ cup granulated sugar	2 teaspoons baking powder
Juice of 1 lemon, strained	¼ teaspoon salt
1 to 1½ tablespoons aniseed	¼ cup vegetable oil

Using an electric mixer, beat the eggs until light, then add the sugar gradually and the lemon juice. Beat at high speed for 2 minutes. Lower the speed and add the aniseed. Meanwhile sift together the 2½ cups of flour, baking powder, and salt and gradually add half of this mixture to the batter. Then add the oil alternately with the remaining flour mixture. When the batter thickens, remove the beaters and continue mixing by hand, adding only enough flour to form a soft ball. Knead for 5 minutes, then divide into 3 equal parts.

Shape each dough section into a long rectangle about 3 inches wide and less than an inch high. The sides along the length of the dough should slope gently down (like the bottom of a sliding board). Place dough sections on a greased cookie sheet and bake in a moderate oven (350 degrees) for 15 minutes. Remove from oven and raise the oven temperature to 425. (At this point the dough will not have a rich color.) Using a very sharp knife, slice the dough sections diagonally into ⅝-inch slices (for maximum length). Turn each slice on the same cookie sheet with a cut side up. Bake for 6 minutes in the 425-degree oven, turning once to toast the other side. The *paximadia* will have a rich chestnut color. Remove from the oven and cool on racks.

Note: This is a quick method and successful if you watch the second bake carefully. If you are willing to take the time for a drier product, allow the dough to cool thoroughly after the first bake. Then slice diagonally and toast in hot oven. You may use 1 teaspoon vanilla, orange, or lemon extract instead of aniseed for flavoring.

SAVAYAR
[*Savoyard "ladyfingers"*]

Crisp and delicately flavored, these are used as the popular accompaniment to many desserts and compotes, and have excellent lasting qualities.

TO MAKE 4 DOZEN

> *3 eggs, separated*
> *1 cup plus 2 tablespoons sugar*
> *½ teaspoon vanilla extract*
> *1 cup plus 2 tablespoons sifted cake flour*
> *Confectioners' sugar*

Using an electric mixer, beat the egg yolks until lemon colored, then gradually beat in the sugar and vanilla. Continue beating until thick. Using a whisk, beat the egg whites until stiff but not dry. Gently fold the egg whites and flour alternately into the yolk mixture.

Meanwhile butter and lightly flour cookie sheets. Fill a pastry bag, using a wide, flat opening, with the batter. Squeeze 3-inch straight cookies out onto the cookie sheets, allowing 2 inches between each. Dust very lightly with confectioners' sugar, then bake for 15 minutes in a moderate oven (350 degrees) until delicately gold colored around the edges, without browning. Remove from the oven and lift from the cookie sheets with a flat spatula. Cool on racks and store in airtight containers.

BISCUITS FORMED BY HAND

KOULOURAKIA
[Hand-rolled biscuits]

In provinces and islands where homes are not equipped with ovens, it is a common sight to see women or children carrying their trays lined with *koulourakia* to the *fourno* to be baked. Though there are individualistic methods of mixing and seasoning, it is amazing that the shapes and the controlled amount of sweetness are quite similar. Vanilla, orange, *petimezi* (must syrup), ouzo, and *mastiha* are the most typical flavors, egg and sesame for glaze. The color is golden, the texture crisp, the flavor wholesome and not too sweet.

TO MAKE 11 TO 12 DOZEN

1 cup (½ pound) butter or margarine	*1 teaspoon vanilla extract*
2 cups granulated sugar	*4 teaspoons baking powder*
2 eggs plus 4 egg yolks	*6½ to 6¾ cups all-purpose flour*
2 tablespoons Cognac	*½ cup heavy cream*
	Sesame seeds (optional)

Using an electric mixer, cream the butter in a large bowl until fluffy. Gradually add the sugar, one of the eggs and the yolks, beaten, Cognac, and vanilla, mixing on medium speed.

Meanwhile, sift the baking powder with flour. Gradually add to the batter, alternately with the cream, beating well after each addition. Beat in the last few cups of flour by hand, until the dough is soft. Knead for a few minutes, then refrigerate for a few hours. Remove from the refrigerator approximately 30 minutes before rolling and baking.

To roll any type *koulourakia, moustokouloura*, Cretan *tsourekakia*, etc., dough should be soft and shiny from kneading. Break off pieces larger than a walnut and roll on a board to form a dough rope about 6 inches long and a finger (⅓-inch) in diameter. (The finger size distinguishes cooks and most Greek women make them thick. The important thing is to be consistent so that they all bake at the same rate.) After rolling this rope you can create many shapes: to make the traditional ring just join the edges; make a snail-shape by winding the rope from one end to form concentric rings; another is to begin rolling from either end toward the center to form concentric rings either meeting in the center, or, begin rolling from either end, one side under and one side over, to meet at a diagonal. Another interesting group of shapes is made with a slightly longer rope, about 8 to 9 inches. Fold the rope in half, then twist four or five times; another, after twisting join the ends to form a twisted ring; another, after twisting bend in half and curl each end outward. Variations on the octopus shape is another group made by an untwisted dough rope: bend the rope in half and curl the ends outward 2 or 3 times keeping them close to the center; another, bend the rope in half and curl the ends into tight circles in the same direction. As you roll them, place *koulourakia* on buttered or oiled cookie sheets allowing 1½ inches between each. Brush with the remaining beaten egg for glaze, sprinkle with sesame, if desired, and bake in a moderate oven (350 to 360 degrees) for 15 to 18 minutes until the glaze is golden orange. Remove from the sheet and cool on racks. Store in covered containers.

KOULOURAKIA ME PORTOKALI
[*Orange-flavored koulourakia*]

Youngsters like the flavor of this version, not as rich as the one above, crisper when made with margarine.

TO MAKE 11 TO 12 DOZEN

> *4 eggs, separated, plus 1 egg yolk*
> *2 cups granulated sugar*
> *Juice of one orange (⅓ cup)*
> *2 teaspoons vanilla extract*
> *½ cup (¼ pound) plus 4 tablespoons butter or margarine, melted*
> *3 teaspoons baking powder*
> *6 to 7 cups all-purpose flour*

Using an electric mixer beat the egg whites until stiff in a large bowl. Beating constantly on medium speed, gradually add the 4 yolks one at a time, the sugar, the orange juice, the vanilla, and the melted butter or margarine.

Meanwhile, sift the baking powder with the first cup of flour and gradually add to the batter. Continue adding only enough of the flour to form a soft ball, mixing by hand when the mixture becomes too stiff for the electric mixer. Knead until elastic. Follow directions for rolling and baking Koulourakia (page 281), using the remaining egg yolk for glazing before baking.

MOUSTOKOULOURA
[*Must-syrup koulourakia*]

An ancient method uses must in baked products. Particularly festive for holidays after the grape harvest, these are crisp, of fine texture and aromatic.

TO MAKE 10 DOZEN

1 cup light vegetable oil or olive oil
1¼ cups granulated sugar
1 cup Petimezi (page 347) (see note below)
½ teaspoon ground cinnamon
¼ teaspoon ground cloves

½ teaspoon grated nutmeg
2 tablespoons lemon juice
1 tablespoon brandy or ouzo
1 teaspoon baking soda
6 to 6½ cups all-purpose flour
1 to 2 egg whites

Beat the oil with the sugar on medium speed of an electric mixer for 5 minutes. Gradually add the *petimezi* and spices. In a cup, combine the lemon juice, brandy and baking soda (it will fizz) and enough water to fill the cup; add to the batter, then gradually beat in the flour; when the batter thickens, remove the beaters and continue to mix by hand until the dough is soft enough to roll and elastic. Knead for a few minutes, then roll into desired shapes as described for Koulourakia (page 281) and place on cookie sheets. Beat the egg white with a fork and brush on the surface. Bake in a moderately hot oven (370 degrees) for 15 minutes, or until a light chestnut color. Cool on racks.

Note: You may substitute Saltsa Mavrodaphni (page 347) if *petimezi* is not available.

KOULOURAKIA METHISMENA
[*"Tipsy" koulourakia*]

You won't get tipsy eating these, but you might while sniffing them baking. *Mastiha* adds the aromatic scent.

TO MAKE ABOUT 60

½ cup plus 2 tablespoons butter
  or vegetable oil
¾ cup plus 1 teaspoon granulated sugar
3 eggs
½ cup mastiha (90-proof
  cordial)

1 teaspoon mastic (resin)
1 teaspoon sugar
4½ cups all-purpose flour
1 teaspoon baking soda
1 teaspoon salt
Slivered almonds for garnish
  (optional)

Cream the butter or oil and ¾ cup of the sugar using an electric mixer. Add 2 of the eggs, one at a time, beating well after each addition. Gradually add the *mastiha*, beating on low speed. Pound the mastic with 1 teaspoon sugar in a mortar and add to the batter. Sift 4 cups of flour with the soda and salt and gradually add to the batter, then remove the beaters and finish by hand, kneading thoroughly and adding only enough flour to make a soft dough. Allow to rest for 10 to 15 minutes, then roll by hand into desired shapes and set on cookie sheets. Brush with the remaining egg, beaten, and garnish each *koulouraki* with an almond sliver, if desired. Bake for 15 to 18 minutes in a moderate oven (350 degrees) until a light chestnut color. Cool on racks and store in covered containers.

Note: Ouzo may be substituted for the *mastiha*. Use grated lemon or orange rind rather than the *mastic* as flavoring.

TSOUREKAKIA
[*Koulourakia, Cretan style*]

These flavorsome Cretan *koulourakia* are similar to the mainland variations, rolled into many snail shapes. Although more costly than other leavening agents, and available at pharmacies, the bicarbonate of ammonia is very effective and produces a light product, worth the additional effort, because it volatilizes during baking and leaves no residue. It is used extensively in many regions.

TO MAKE 5 DOZEN

½ cup (¼ pound) butter or margarine
¾ cup granulated sugar
3 eggs, lightly beaten
½ cup milk, warmed
3 teaspoons bicarbonate of ammonia or 2 teaspoons baking powder

2 teaspoons orange flower water
1 teaspoon vanilla extract (optional)
3 to 3½ cups sifted all-purpose flour
Sesame seeds (optional)

Using an electric mixer, cream the butter or margarine until fluffy. Gradually add the sugar and 2 of the eggs, beating thoroughly on medium speed. Meanwhile, mix the warm milk with the bicarbonate of ammonia and flavorings. Add to the batter, alternately with the sifted flour, until the dough is soft. Knead for a few minutes, then roll into desired shapes indicated for Koulourakia (page 281), glaze with the remaining egg, beaten, and sesame seeds, and bake.

ALMYRA
[Salty koulourakia, Macedonia style]

A totally different flavor, a newer adaptation of the traditional shape and color, and excellent with aperitifs and appetizers. We first tasted these in Macedonia. They were easy to adapt at home with Greek cheese. (Do not offer any to Greek "old-timers" without a warning, because the taste surprise may be too great!)

TO MAKE 4 DOZEN

3 cups all-purpose flour
1½ teaspoons salt (reduce to ½ teaspoon if the cheese is very salty)
1 teaspoon dried mustard
Dash of cayenne
1 teaspoon baking powder

½ cup butter or margarine, softened
¾ cup kefalotyri or Romano cheese, grated
2 egg yolks and 1 whole egg
2 tablespoons ouzo
2 to 3 tablespoons water

In a large mixing bowl, sift together the flour, salt, mustard, cayenne, and baking powder. Work the butter in with your fingers, then add the cheese and 2 egg yolks and mix thoroughly. Combine the ouzo and 2 tablespoons of the water in a cup and add to the dough, mixing to gather the dough into a ball. Use more water in droplets, if needed. Knead until smooth, for 5 to 10 minutes, then break off walnut-sized pieces and roll each into a pencil-thin rope 6 inches long, rolling the two ends to points. Twist to form a circle, with the two points extending about ½ inch beyond the juncture, in opposite directions, and set on a buttered cookie sheet. Continue until all are shaped. Brush the surface with the remaining egg, beaten, and bake in a 360-degree oven for 18 minutes or until the glaze is a deep gold. Remove to a rack to cool, and store in covered containers.

FRUITS, NUTS, AND DESSERTS

Fruits

FRESH SEASONAL FRUIT CLIMAXES most major meals in Greece. Although served as a separate course, it is not considered a "dessert," simply *frouta*. (The ancient word for fruit and fruit trees—*opora*—is used less in everyday speech but remains in related words, such as fruit bowls, fruit shops.) Whether in a family setting or *taverna*, there is an obvious relaxation with the fruit course, in contrast to the light-hearted animation of the *orektika* course and the concentration and intensity of the entrée or main course. Naturally, this pleasure mounts with the deeply established anticipation of fruit—because Hellenes pride themselves on their excellent varieties. But also, an additional warmth develops during the unhurried peeling, coring, and passing of fruit around the table.

This is traditionally done by the father, who spears on a fork and passes a good portion of apple, pear, orange, peach, or other fruit. All eyes watch the guest, who has the privilege of being the first taster. The fruit is accepted, the guest begins, and then the family members begin tasting. Each person chooses and peels his own, but the passing continues. Sharing not only allows personal interaction, but also permits everyone to sample more than one fruit served during the meal. And when the fruit meets expectations, the meal ends on a sweet note! But if not, oh, what a calamity!

While emphasis at table is on flavor rather than elaborate service, the selection and washing of fruit are critical. Scrutiny is obvious in the markets. An argument can flare up if the retailer tries to include a bad fruit. In Greek homes we have seen fruits scrubbed with soap and rinsed many times in water to remove all traces of poisonous insecticides. Perhaps as a habit derived from years without refrigeration, fruit is purchased as close to serving time as possible, then cleaned and eaten at room temperature, except for melons, which are chilled.

Frequently, in Greece, grape clusters are served in small bowls in ice water. Each grape is picked off individually and individually enjoyed. (When one of our youngsters popped a grape cluster into his mouth, pulling out the stems with one yank to relish a mouthful of grapes, he was given an on-the-spot lesson in grape-eating etiquette by a Greek relative.)

Figs are so adored, as they ripen on family trees, that their progress is a daily report: "Ah, next week we will eat figs." "Be sure to come back when the figs are ripe." "We will eat figs together," is the same as promising sure ecstasy. When finally they are ready and a family member picks a handful and brings them into the home, everything stops. Breathlessly the fig is peeled and luxuriatingly savored.

Homer was among the earliest poets stimulated by nature, as exemplified in the fifth book of the *Odyssey*. Describing a Greek garden, he says: "In it flourish tall trees, pears and pomegranates and apples full of fruit, also sweet figs and bounteous olives. Here too a fertile vineyard has been planted. . . ." Homer's list includes the fruits enjoyed by Minoans during the early Bronze Age, to which acorns might be added.

Historians recorded Plato's love for figs. Philip of Macedon and Alexander the Great were apple lovers. According to Athenaeus, Alexander, when in Babylonia, filled his ships with apples.

In Greek parlance fruit plays a dominant role. "Soft as a melon" describes a weak man, and "Thousand vineyards, ten grapes" means poor earnings or profits. Greek Aesop's fables, which for centuries were spoken before they were recorded, are full of fruit. When the fox could not reach the prize, "sour grapes" became a universal consolation for sore losers. Figs and filberts were the symbols in the fable about the greedy boy who tried to grab more than he could handle.

Fruits, significant throughout Greek mythology, often decided the fates of the gods. The "golden apple" award of Paris to Aphrodite, as fairest above Hera and Athena, sharpened the rivalry that contributed to the Trojan War. Pomegranate seeds eaten by Persephone doomed her to Hades for part of each year. Tantalus had the worst fate of all, seeing, but unable to grasp, as Homer wrote in the *Odyssey*: "Then leafy-crested trees dropped down their fruit—pears, pomegranates, apples with shining fruit, sweet figs and thrifty olives. But when the old man stretched his hand to take, a breeze would toss them toward the dusky clouds." It is not surprising that the English word "tantalize" is derived from his name.

Fresh fruits remain a special part of the Greek diet. However, compotes, preserves and marmalades, *granites* (page 296) and sherbets, are also part of the picture. Of these, the most significant role in Greek cultural life is played by the varieties of *glyka tou koutaliou* ("spoon sweets"). Serving them to visitors is a ritualistic custom maintained in the provinces and by city hostesses who were raised in the provinces.

GLYKA TOU KOUTALIOU
[*Spoon sweet preserves*]

Glyka tou Koutaliou (sweets of the spoon) are the most Greek expressions of traditional hospitality to visitors. Fragrant and spicy fruits and vegetables cooked to a smooth perfection in syrup by Greek women exemplify one of their proudest skills. "My sister makes the best *fraoula glyko*," a Macedonian woman told me; she took me to visit her sister, who promptly served the delicious strawberry preserve. "My mother had tricks in making *vyssino glyko*. Mine never tastes the same," an Athenian friend apologized, although hers tasted superb to me.

Certainly cooking fruits in syrup is an ancient method in Greece. Diocles of Carystus, physician and author of health treatises in the fourth century B.C., wrote, "The melon is more laxative if cooked in syrup." So strong has the tradition remained through the centuries that immigrants to America (including my mother, who arrived at the age of seven in 1909 and learned from her mother) continued the practice. I can remember the exciting cooking sessions at home with Mother's sisters and sisters-in-law, and also the eagerness with which I passed the tray (knowing some of the visitors' praise would be beamed on me).

Mother used garden roses for *triandafilo glyko* (rose-petal jam) before Japanese beetles took over. But it was pounds and pounds of fresh sour cherries that particularly entranced me, and I loved the freedom of joining my aunts in pitting them, and hearing the endless joviality.

Skill and great care marks the cooking of syrup (made, in Greece, without adding pectin) and avoiding the overcooking of fruit. So complex is this process, that it must be learned through years of observation, helping, and a few disasters. Several ladies could not give me their recipe, nor describe it—as though it were an indefinable mystery. "*Einai diskolo*—it is difficult," they say.

I have watched women stand endlessly as the fruit cooks, pouring a spoonful to test the various thread stages of the syrup. "*Na min desi* —do not bind," orders for a light syrup for cakes and pastries, or "*Na desi kala*—bind it well (or let it reach the large thread stage)," for spoon sweets. Another device is adding glucose or lemon juice to syrup to avoid crystallization of the sugar (a trick used in making fruit ices and *granites*, as well).

A word about the cultural use of spoon sweets is needed at this juncture, since I am aware of the puzzling reaction of uninitiated visitors. It is customary in all Greek regions, as well as traditional Greek-American homes, that a teaspoon or so of the preserve and its syrup is scooped onto a dessert plate with the teaspoon. Plate and spoon are set on a tray with a glass of ice water, one of each for each guest (family members customarily are not served). Each guest lifts a plate and slowly relishes the spoon sweet, then sets the plate down when finished, and lifts the ice water, toasts and compliments the hostess, the host if it happens to be his nameday, or offers good wishes for a coming wedding, etc., then drinks the water. As you might expect in a traditional setting, there is specific protocol in serving older guests first, and unfortunately, offended feelings if the guest does not accept the spoon sweet.

As for the idea of eating anything so sweet, so horrifying to some visitors, it is not surprising considering the Greek dietary pattern. There is a long break between the main dinner and late evening supper, and after a nap, how refreshing it is to enjoy a sweet (usually with Turkish coffee as well) and the ice water. Aside from learning more about jelly making, you can use spoon sweets as you would any other preserved fruit. The varieties in Greece are endless, using fruits or vegetables and nuts, and I wish they could all be included.

NUTS, CANDIES, AND DESSERTS

Hellenes enjoy their nuts. They munch on them, combine them with dried fruits and munch on them, make interesting candies and desserts with them. Try Amygdalota (page 303) and Pasteli (page 304), both excellent for flavor and lasting qualities, descendants, no doubt, of the ancient nut and honey treats. Almonds, pine nuts, chestnuts, filberts (hazelnuts), acorns (called Zeus-acorns), walnuts (identified with Persia), and pistachios, which apparently traveled to Greece from Arabia and Syria—all were mentioned by ancient Greek writers. Except for acorns, which are not eaten, all the nuts are among today's Greek favorites. Peanuts originating in South America, unknown to ancient Hellenes, are known and used in Greece but less than the other nuts. Chocolate may also be counted among the newer ingredients, and with nuts, turn into Troufes Sokolatas (page 306), which you will enjoy making.

Halva, rizogalo, and *moustalevria,* included in this chapter's recipes, are among traditional desserts made at home for family, not necessarily for a holiday. Krema Savayar Santigi (page 307) is among the continental desserts increasingly made at home. For festive cakes and pastries turn to page 311.

[*Fresh Fruit*]

Wash, dry and arrange ripe, fresh fruit in an attractive bowl. Serve as a separate course following the main course with a dessert plate, fruit knives, and forks for each guest. Serve the fruit whole, and unpeeled, and allow each guest to peel his or her selection. Pineapple and melons should be served cleaned and cut on individual plates.

ANANAS
[*Pineapple*]

On a cutting board, using a heavy, sharp knife, cut off the spiked leaf end of a ripe pineapple. Hold the pineapple, cut side up, and slice down the entire rind, exposing the fruit. Continue cutting and turning until all rind is cut away. Then cut off the stem end. Slice the pineapple in long strips and discard the tough center core. Slice again, across the pineapple, into serving pieces. Arrange in fruit bowl. Sprinkle with brandy or Cointreau and chill.

Or pineapple may also be cut lengthwise into sixths, melon style, leaving the spiked leaves intact. Run the tip of the knife between the rind and fruit, to separate them. Leaving the fruit in place, cut down into serving pieces. Serve chilled, in the rind.

PEPONI
[Melon]

Greek melons have a sweet, unforgettable flavor. They are more expensive than Greek watermelons, ripening in greatest quantity at summer's peak. Although grown in all regions, the outstanding melons come from Argos in Peloponnesos.

Using a sharp knife, cut off the stem end of melon or cantaloupe. Cut in half and discard the seeds. Depending on size, cut each half into 2 to 3 sections lengthwise. Serve on individual plates, garnished with fresh mint.

PEPONI ME LIKER
[Melon compote with liqueur]

After cutting the melon from rind and discarding seeds, cut into bite-sized pieces. Pour droplets of fine liqueur over the melon and chill.

PEPONI ME FOUNTOUKIA
[Melon compote with filberts]

Prepare Peponi me Liker (see above), keeping the rind in as large pieces as possible if you wish to use as cups, allowing a generous portion per person. Just before serving, mix in 1 full tablespoon roasted chopped filberts for each portion. Serve in dessert cups or in the melon or cantaloupe rind, which has been fluted with a sharp knife. Serve chilled, on green fruit tree leaves.

FROUTA FRESKA MAZENTOUAN
[Fresh fruit Macedoine]

Macedoine is the French for Macedonia, and has become syn-onymous with a bowl of mixed fruit or vegetables.

TO SERVE 6 TO 8

1 watermelon
Peaches, pears, plums, apricots, grapes, and other fresh fruits in season
Granulated sugar
2 to 3 tablespoons brandy, kirsch, or other liqueur
5 to 6 fresh mint leaves, washed
½ cup blanched, chopped almonds
Sprigs of fresh mint for garnish

Using a sharp knife, cut the watermelon in half lengthwise, then care-fully scoop out fruit, reserving the rind. Remove and discard the seeds. Cut the fruit into spoon-sized pieces, or using a melon-ball cutter, make balls. Place in a large bowl. Wash, peel, and dice as many varied seasonal fresh fruits as possible and add to the bowl. If using seed grapes, cut in half and pit. Sprinkle lightly with sugar and a few tablespoons of the brandy, kirsch, or liqueur. Tuck the fresh mint leaves among the fruit, then chill in the refrigerator.

Meanwhile, using a small sharp knife, cut the rim of one of the reserved watermelon rind halves at a sharp angle to form sawteeth, discarding the small pieces. Remove the fruit from the refrigerator, mix in the blanched, chopped almonds, and fill the watermelon "bowl." Garnish with sprigs of mint and chill until ready to serve.

Note: Use the remaining watermelon rind to make preserves (page 299).

FRANGOSYKA
[Prickly pear cactus fruit]

After hearing so much about this wild fruit for many years, and finally tasting it, I feel it deserves a place among the Greek wild foods (although it is also harvested and sold in fruit shops). After peeling the spiky yellow and red skin, the fruit, whose seeds are also edible, is soft as a peach, and it tastes a little like a pear and a peach. But a few Hellenes we know refuse to let it pass through their lips. Why should they, when peaches and melons ripen at the same time?

SIKA ME KARYDIA
[Figs with walnuts]

Walnuts have the distinction of having the same name as the generic term for nut in Greece. (They are also a favorite source of dye in the vegetable family.) Munching this wonderful combination makes the winter months pleasanter for provincial Hellenes. Prepare from one to dozens, either one minute or weeks before eating. Or better, gather family and friends with a bowl of walnuts and bowl of figs and make them as you nibble. But do try it.

TO MAKE 4 DOZEN

> 40 dried figs
> 24 walnuts, shelled and halved

With a sharp knife, cut the stem off the fig, and using your fingers, pry open without breaking the other side. Stuff the fig with a walnut half, then close the fig over the nut. Serve plain, or with stuffed dates, almond balls, and fresh fruit. Store in covered containers.

Note: For another exciting variation: Stuff dates with the walnuts and roll in fine granulated sugar.

KOMPOSTA
[Compote]

Fruit compotes are more likely to be served in the late afternoon for a sweet snack rather than after meals, when fresh fruits are preferred. The following method may be used for any fresh seasonal fruit, to be used within a few days or preserved in sterile jars and sealed.

Compote syrup: Boil 2 cups sugar and 1 cup water and 1 tablespoon lemon juice for 7 minutes. Add any of the following fruit and cook only until a needle can penetrate easily. Cool in syrup, then chill. Serve cold with Savayar (page 280).

6 to 8 hard, tart cooking apples, peeled, cored, and quartered. Add 1 stick cinnamon and 3 cloves to the syrup.

20 to 24 dried figs, soaked in semi-sweet red wine or water until hydrated, or 20 to 24 fresh figs, washed and peeled. Substitute 1 two-inch piece vanilla bean for the lemon juice in the syrup.

1 pound prunes. Wash and soak prunes in 1 cup cold water until hydrated (stirring frequently). Use the soaking water to make the syrup, adding 1 lemon peel and 1 orange peel. Or instead of peels, use 1 teaspoon rosewater or orange flower water for flavoring.

1 pint strawberries. Wash and hull, then put in a bowl and pour the boiling syrup over. Substitute 2 tablespoons brandy, kirsch, or other liqueur for the lemon juice in the syrup.

For an exciting variation with wine . . .

KOMPOSTA AHLADIA KRASATA
[Pear compote in wine]

TO SERVE 5

> *5 pears, peeled, cored, and halved*
> *Juice of 1 lemon*
> *1½ cups semi-sweet red wine*
> *1¼ cups granulated sugar*
> *½ teaspoon grated orange, lemon, or tangerine rind*

Place the pear halves in a bowl and sprinkle with the lemon juice. In a small saucepan, bring the semi-sweet red wine to a boil with the sugar. Simmer for 7 minutes. Add the pears and lemon juice and cook until a needle penetrates the fruit easily. Add the grated rind. Cool, then chill. Serve cold.

MYLA ME MOSHATO
[Apples with muscatel]

This excellent apple dessert, which originated in Athens, uses a Greek muscatel and tart apples.

TO SERVE 6

> 6 tart cooking apples, peeled and cored
> 1/4 cup (4 tablespoons) sweet butter or unsalted margarine
> 1/4 cup granulated sugar
> 1/2 cup muscatel wine
> Pinch each of cinnamon and nutmeg
> Whipped cream or vanilla ice cream (optional)

Slice the apples into thin, uniform slices. Melt the butter in a saucepan and add the apples. Cook over moderate heat, turning the apples on both sides, and sprinkle with the sugar. Cover and simmer for 5 minutes, then pour the wine over the apples, shaking the pan to mix. Continue cooking, uncovered, over low heat until the apples are tender but not too soft and the sauce is thick. Sprinkle with cinnamon and nutmeg toward the end of cooking. Serve warm, with whipped cream, or a scoop of ice cream, if desired.

ICED FRUIT DESSERTS

GRANITA LEMONATA
[Lemon ice]

This is delicious and refreshing as any available commercially. For another Greek version, granita vyssino (sour-cherry ice), substitute sour-cherry juice.

TO SERVE 8 TO 9

> 1 1/2 cups granulated sugar
> 1/2 cup light corn syrup
> 7 3/4 cups water
> 1 1/2 cups fresh lemon juice (8 to 10 lemons), strained

1 tablespoon grated lemon rind
Fresh mint leaves for garnish

Boil the sugar, corn syrup, and water for 7 minutes, then remove from the heat, cool for 10 minutes and stir in the lemon juice and rind. Pour into ice cube trays and freeze (about 3 hours for 1 inch of liquid), then remove from the trays and break into smaller pieces using an ice pick. Beat small portions in a glass with a spoon, or beat at low speed on the electric mixer and gradually increase the speed. Transfer to an electric blender and whip at highest speed until soft, smooth, and milky white. Serve immediately, garnished with mint. Delicious with Savayar (page 280) or another crisp cookie.

Note: You can also freeze in parfait glasses after whipping, until 1 hour or so before serving, then place in the refrigerator to thaw. You may use 2 cups sugar and 8 cups of water if you eliminate the corn syrup.

PEPONI PAGOTO

[*Melon ice*]

In Epirus, on a hot summer day, we were refreshed by the *peponi pagoto*. When we complimented the chef, he told us that "all you need are melons of excellent aroma, sugar and water." His *pagoto* was made by churning in a hand freezer. The recipe has been adapted to make in the refrigerator, but aromatic melons are still a prerequisite.

TO SERVE 8

2½ cups granulated sugar
1½ cups water
2 honeydew melons
Juice of 1 orange, strained
Juice of 1 lemon, strained
Fresh mint leaves for garnish

Combine the sugar and water in a heavy pan and stir over moderate heat until dissolved. Cook until the syrup reaches 230 degrees on a candy thermometer (approximately 10 minutes). Meanwhile, cut the melons in half, discard the seeds, and scoop the melon pulp into a funnel sieve or food mill. Push through the sieve, discarding any fibers left in it. Measure 5 cups of puréed melon. Pour it into the syrup, stir, and allow to cool, then stir in the orange and lemon juice. Pour into a freezer tray and freeze (approximately 3 hours), then remove and push through an ice crusher. The mixture will be soft. Pour back into the freezer tray. Repeat the freezing and breaking of ice particles by pushing through the ice crusher. Fill 8 parfait or sherbet glasses and freeze again, removing to the refrigerator 30 minutes before serving. Garnish with mint leaves.

PRESERVES

PORTOKALOFLOUDO GLYKO
[Orange-rind preserves, Peloponnesos style]

When we were youngsters, helping mother prepare orange and grapefruit rinds, rolled and strung, was a delightful chore. Although this method takes a good deal of time, the result is absolutely lovely. Many hands working together make this fun.

MAKES ABOUT 2 QUARTS PER DOZEN NAVEL ORANGES

Very thick-skinned navel oranges are indispensable for this recipe. Before peeling the fruit (for a milder-flavored preserve) lightly grate the orange rind and reserve the grating for another use. When peeling the oranges, use a small, sharp knife and begin at the stem end in a circular motion, turning the orange and cutting about ⅓ inch wide in a continuous strip.

Place rinds of at least one dozen oranges in a large enameled pot, cover with cold water and bring to a boil. Immediately pour off the water. Cover again with cold water, bring to a boil and pour off the water. Repeat twice more, then drain. Measure the rinds in a 4-cup container and reserve an equal volume of sugar to use later in the recipe (8 cups rinds, 8 cups sugar). Take each strip of rind and roll tightly into a small roll that will fit easily into a teaspoon. With a clean sewing needle and double white thread, sew through the center of the roll. Continue until all the rind is rolled and strung, and be sure the string ends are knotted.

Place the measured sugar and half the volume of water (8 cups sugar, 4 cups water) in a large saucepan and bring to a boil, stirring constantly. Cook 15 minutes, then add the rinds on their strings and continue cooking. Remove the rinds when a needle will pierce them easily, but continue cooking the syrup until it reaches the large-thread stage. Remove from heat, add the orange rinds (still on strings) and the juice of 1 lemon strained. Cool the rinds in the syrup. Cut and remove the strings (the rind is now permanently rolled) and store in sealed containers.

Note: Frapa glyko (grapefruit rind preserves) may be prepared the same way, substituting grapefruit for orange rinds.

KYDONI GLYKO

[Quince preserves with rose geranium and almonds]

One of the real delicacies of the spoon-sweet family, aromatic with rose geranium.

TO MAKE 1 QUART

> *3 pounds quinces*
> *1 quart water*
> *6 cups (3 pounds) sugar*
> *Juice of 1 lemon*
> *4 to 5 rose geranium leaves*
> *½ cup almonds, blanched and quartered lengthwise*

Wash, peel, and coarsely grate the quinces, discarding the cores. Combine the grated quince with the water and the sugar in a large saucepan, and gradually bring to a boil, stirring constantly until the sugar is dissolved. Lower the heat and cook until the syrup thickens and reaches the large-thread stage. Add the lemon juice and rose geranium and stir in the almonds. Cool, then remove the geranium leaves. Seal in an airtight glass container.

Note: You may prefer to slice the quinces in thin strips with a very sharp knife: more work, but prettier. The cooking time varies according to the size of the cuttings, usually about one hour.

KARPOUZI FLOUDA GLYKO

[Watermelon rind preserves]

Preserve any quantity of watermelon rind with this recipe. The finished preserve will be about one-third the size of the uncooked rind. Choose the early thick rinds to preserve.

With a sharp knife, cut off and discard the green skin from the thick rind of a watermelon, leaving on a thin layer of the red fruit if it remains after the fruit has been served. Cut the rind in pieces approximately 1 by 1½ inches. Place in a large pot, cover with cold water, bring to boil, and drain. Repeat three times, then wrap the rind in a towel for 1 to 2 hours to absorb excess moisture from the rind. (If you wish you may leave wrapped overnight in the refrigerator at this stage.)

In a bowl large enough to hold rind, place 1 quart water and stir in 1 teaspoon of powdered lime. Drop the rind into the lime solution to harden and soak from 15 to 30 minutes. (If preparing more than 4 cups rind increase the lime solution proportionately.) Drain and rinse in cold water, then allow to drain thoroughly. Wrap again in a dry towel and allow to stand at least 3 hours to remove excessive moisture.

Unwrap the towel and measure the rind and an equal volume of granulated sugar. (If preserving 4 cups rind, use 4 cups sugar.) In a heavy pot, layer the rind and sugar. Add ½ cup water and an additional ½ cup sugar for each 4 cups rind. Set over medium heat, stir with a wooden spoon until dissolved, and bring to a boil. Add 3 to 4 whole cloves and a small cinnamon stick for each 4 cups rind. Boil until the rind is translucent and the syrup thick, approximately 1¼ hours. Remove the spices. Stir in 2 tablespoons of Cointreau or other liqueur for each 4 cups rind, then cool. Spoon into clean jars and seal.

DOMATOULES GLYKO
[Spicy cherry tomato spoon sweet]

From start to finish the tomatoes need a delicate touch and will furnish a reward—a succulent, translucent tomato preserve of rosy-orange color cloaking a crunchy almond. This is an excellent recipe when cherry tomatoes are plentiful on the vines.

TO MAKE ABOUT 1 QUART

3 pounds cherry tomatoes (3 pints)	2 cups water
	1 cinnamon stick
Boiling water to cover tomatoes	8–10 cloves
2 teaspoons slaked lime (calcium hydroxide) from pharmacy	6–8 allspice seeds
	Grated rind of 1 lemon
2 quarts water	1 cup blanched almonds
5 cups sugar	

Wash the firm, ripe cherry tomatoes and blanch in boiling water. Drain and slip off the skins, and place in a large bowl. Meanwhile combine the lime with 2 quarts water and shake thoroughly, allowing residue to settle to the bottom of jar. Pour the lime water over tomatoes and soak 10 minutes. Lift tomatoes out of water with a slotted spoon and save the lime water. Using tip of sharp knife incise bottom of each tomato with a small cross. Slightly squeeze and simultaneously shake each tomato to discard seeds and put back into the lime water to soak another 30 minutes until firm. Drain, thoroughly inverted, on linen towels. To make the syrup, combine the sugar and 2 cups water in jelly pan, stir and bring to boil. Skim, add the spices and boil for 10 minutes. Carefully slip in the tomatoes and continue boiling 5 minutes. Remove from heat. Cool tomatoes overnight in syrup. Next day, remove the tomatoes. Add the grated lemon rind to syrup and continue cooking to soft ball stage. Remove from heat, add tomatoes. Cool. Slip an almond inside each tomato. Store cherry tomatoes in sealed containers.

FRAOULA GLYKO
[Strawberry preserves]

Strawberries soaked in lime water will be firmer than if unsoaked, a trick Greek women use in all regions, although this recipe is from western Macedonia.

Use any quantity of fresh, firm strawberries and an equal weight of granulated sugar. Hull the strawberries and wash them thoroughly several times, then drain on dry towels. Place the strawberries in an enamel pan or bowl and soak for 2 hours in lime water solution (1 teaspoon of powdered lime for each quart of water). Drain, then rinse the strawberries in cold water, and spread on dry towels to drain thoroughly. Place the strawberries in a heavy saucepan with the juice of 1 lemon for each pound of strawberries, then cover with an equal weight of sugar and allow to rest overnight.

The next day, place the pan with strawberries over medium heat and bring to a boil, stirring occasionally. Cook until the syrup reaches the large-thread stage, cool and store in glass containers.

Note: If strawberries are not soaked in lime water, remove them from the syrup with a slotted spoon when a needle will pierce them easily. Continue cooking the syrup until it reaches the large-thread stage, then add the strawberries and cool.

VYSSINO GLYKO
[*Sour-cherry preserve*]

When fresh sour cherries are unavailable, canned sour cherries may be substituted for this irresistible delight. This is particularly distinctive and refreshing when made into the beverage *vyssinada*, a generous helping of preserves in ice water.

TO MAKE ABOUT 1¾ QUARTS

4 one-pound cans sour cherries (approximately 6 cups cherries), drained
1 cup sour-cherry liquid from can (see note below)
9 cups (4½ pounds) granulated sugar
Juice of 1 lemon, strained

In a large, heavy saucepan, combine the cherries, 1 cup of sour-cherry liquid, and sugar, layering the cherries and sugar. Place the pan over low heat until the sugar dissolves, stirring constantly. After the mixture boils, remove the foamy scum from the surface with a spoon. Boil for 10 minutes, then, using a slotted spoon, remove the cherries and place in a bowl. Continue boiling the syrup until the large-thread stage (approximately 35 minutes). Add the cherries to the syrup, along with the lemon juice and allow to cool overnight in the syrup. The next day, spoon into clean, airtight jars.

Nuts

AMYGDALOTA
[Almond candy]

"Candy" might be misleading for this ancient sweet, since it is baked like a cookie. Easy to prepare, *amygdalota* are also called *rozethes* or *troufes* in various regions, and shaped into balls, bells, or pears, or the more popular almond shapes. Delicious and rich, *amygdalota* should, preferably, be one-bite size.

TO MAKE 75 ALMOND-SHAPED CANDIES (1½ INCHES)

3 cups blanched, peeled, and finely ground almonds	2 tablespoons honey
⅔ cup granulated sugar	2 tablespoons warm water
2 tablespoons cracker crumbs or toast crumbs	Whole cloves (optional)
	Rose water
	Confectioners' sugar

Mix together the almonds, sugar, crumbs, honey, and warm water; the mixture will be stiff. Knead and mix thoroughly for a few minutes, then flour your fingers, pinch off pieces the size of almonds and form into almond shapes in the palms of your hands. Stud the end of each with a whole clove, if desired, to serve as a stem and a "handle." Place all the "almonds" on a well-greased cookie sheet. Bake in a slow oven (250 degrees) to dry, allowing 15 minutes for a soft candy or up to 25 minutes for drier candy. (A higher oven will not spoil the *amygdalota* but will toast the almonds to produce an altogether different flavor.) Remove from the oven and cool 1 minute, then either dip into or sprinkle with rose water and roll in confectioners' sugar. Cool thoroughly and store in covered tins; *amygdalota* keep for several weeks. Serve as a candy or as a garnish for various cakes and pastries for a large buffet.

AMYGDALOTA KRITIKA
[*Amygdalota, Cretan style*]

Combine and knead 2 cups blanched, finely ground almonds with 1 cup granulated sugar and 6 egg whites. Wet your fingers with rose water and shape into balls. Proceed to bake as above.

Note: After unsealing rose water or orange flower water, store in the refrigerator.

PASTELI
[*Sesame seed and honey candy*]

Pasteli is probably a very ancient candy in Greece, with honey always the oldest sweetener and sesame among the earliest seeds for spicing. Various regions specialize in distinctive variations, including Kalamata (also famous for the delicious olives), where pistachios lend their flavor, and on Andros in the Cyclades, where walnuts contribute their texture (page 305). Among its charms, *pasteli* has excellent storing qualities.

To make any desired amount, use equal weights of honey and sesame seeds. In a heavy pan bring honey to very firm ball stage (250 to 256 degrees). Stir in the sesame seeds and continue cooking until the mixture comes to a bubbling boil. Spread on a marble slab or tray moistened with orange flower water and spread to a ½-inch thickness. Cool; then cut into small diamonds or squares.

PASTELI ME FISTIKIA
[*Pistachio and honey candy, Peloponnesos style*]

TO MAKE 50 ONE-INCH SQUARES

> *1 pound fresh, unsalted pistachio nuts*
> *1¼ cups sugar*
> *1 cup honey*
> *1½ cups water*
> *Butter or oil*

Peel and place pistachios on a baking sheet, then put in a slow oven (250 degrees) to roast for 20 minutes. Remove from the oven and cut into quarters.

Meanwhile combine the sugar, honey, and water in a heavy pan, and stir over medium heat until dissolved. Lower the heat and boil to the very firm ball stage (250 to 256 degrees), toss in the pistachios and stir, then remove from the heat. Butter or oil a marble slab, jelly roll, or any aluminum pan and quickly spread the candy using a spatula or knife. Allow to cool, then cut into squares and store in covered containers.

Note: A Greek pastry chef told me that glucose and honey are usually used for this excellent treat.

PASTELI ME KARYDIA

[Sesame seed and honey candy with walnuts, Andros style]

TO MAKE 70 ONE-BY-TWO-INCH CANDIES

> *4 cups coarsely chopped walnuts*
> *⅓ cups zwieback or toast crumbs*
> *1½ cups honey*
> *1 cup granulated sugar*
> *Orange flower water*
> *1½ cups sesame seeds*

In a large bowl, combine the walnuts and crumbs and set aside. In a heavy saucepan, combine the honey and sugar and set over medium heat. Stirring constantly, bring to a boil. Continue to boil, uncovered, until the syrup reaches the very firm ball stage (250 to 256 degrees), then remove from the heat. Add the syrup to the walnut-crumb mixture, stirring with a heavy wooden spoon.

Meanwhile, have ready a marble slab or tray moistened slightly with orange flower water and sprinkled generously with sesame seeds (a 12 x 18-inch surface will be sufficient). Spread the walnut-syrup mixture onto the sesame-covered surface, spreading to a ½-inch thickness with a spatula and fingers moistened with orange flower water. Sprinkle liberally with sesame seeds. Cool, then cut into diamond shapes. Store indefinitely in covered tins.

Note: The flavor improves after a few days. Also, in Greece, *pasteli* is frequently served on bright orange tree leaves.

TROUFES SOKOLATAS
[Chocolate-nut candy balls]

A popular Athenian candy. Of the various treats bearing this name, all rich, this version is the quickest to make. Success depends on using a chocolate of good quality.

TO MAKE 40 BALLS, ONE INCH IN DIAMETER

1 cup (8 ounces) sweet chocolate of good flavor
½ cup blanched, finely ground almonds
1 cup finely ground walnuts
2 teaspoons brandy or rum
½ cup confectioners' sugar
Confectioners' sugar or finely ground almonds for rolling candy

In the top of a double boiler melt the chocolate over warm water, then remove from the heat. Stirring with a wooden spoon add the ½ cup almonds, walnuts, brandy or rum, and enough of the confectioners' sugar to form a workable mass. While the chocolate is still warm, break off small pieces and roll in your palms to form small balls. Roll the candy in either the confectioners' sugar or almonds. Cool. Store in covered containers.

Desserts

HALVA
[Spicy syrup semolina pudding]

A traditional and classic sweet. Though known by its Turkish name, *halva* desserts probably descended from *amorai*—pudding baked with honey sauce. A wholesome "family" dessert rather than a party type, this is my favorite method, although there are many baked versions.

TO SERVE 12 TO 15

3 cups water
2 cups granulated sugar
1 cinnamon stick
3 whole cloves
Peel of 1 lemon or 1 tablespoon
    lemon juice
½ cup (¼ pound) butter

1 cup coarse semolina or farina
4 to 5 tablespoons pine nuts
2 tablespoons blanched,
    chopped almonds
2 to 3 tablespoons whole
    blanched almonds for garnish

Combine the water, sugar, cinnamon stick, cloves, and lemon peel or juice in a heavy saucepan and bring to a boil. Boil for 10 minutes, then cool.

Meanwhile, slowly melt the butter in a heavy saucepan, and cook for several minutes, without browning. Stirring constantly with a wooden spoon, slowly add the semolina or farina. Cook over low heat until the mixture turns a golden chestnut color; do not brown. Add 2 tablespoons of the pine nuts and the chopped almonds and continue cooking 1 more minute.

Remove cinnamon stick, cloves, and peel from the cooled syrup. Gradually add the syrup to the semolina mixture, stirring with a long-handled wooden spoon; the mixture will bubble furiously. Cook over the lowest possible heat until the syrup has been absorbed and the mixture thickens. Remove from the heat and drape with a clean towel for 10 minutes. Turn into a mold, spreading with a knife or spatula. Cool, then reverse onto a serving platter, sprinkle with cinnamon, and garnish decoratively with the remaining pine nuts and the whole almonds. Cut into small, diamond-shaped pieces.

KREMA SAVAYAR SANTIGI
[Molded berry cream dessert with ladyfingers]

Dribbled with brandy and unmolded on a pretty plate, this is an admired dessert (with variations) in Athens. Use a charlotte or other deep mold of 1-quart capacity, and sweet, fresh berries or other fruit. Frequently, the mold is filled with cooked pudding, which jells in the refrigerator. The mold must be same height or slightly taller than the *savayar* (ladyfingers).

TO SERVE 6 TO 8

10 to 12 Savayar (page 280)
2 to 3 tablespoons brandy
1 pint heavy cream
4 teaspoons sugar
½ teaspoon vanilla extract
4 to 5 egg whites, at room
temperature

¼ teaspoon cream of tartar
1 cup fresh berries, soaked in
brandy and drained
Fresh berries and fruit tree leaves
for garnish (optional)

Stand the *savayar*, flat side toward the center of a 1-quart mold, against the sides, to test the number needed to line the mold. Dribble them with brandy and let stand in the mold while preparing the filling.

Beat the cream with 1 teaspoon of the sugar and the vanilla until just stiff, then refrigerate. Beat the egg whites with the cream of tartar until soft peaks form and gradually add the remaining sugar. Continue beating to the firm peak stage. Remove the whipped cream from the refrigerator and fold the egg whites carefully into the cream, then fold in the fruit. Fill the mold, keeping the ladyfingers erect, then freeze.

To unmold, stand for a few seconds in warm water, slip the tip of the knife around the edges and invert with a quick shake over a chilled platter. Garnish with fresh berries and fruit tree leaves, if desired, and serve with additional *savayar*.

RIZOGALO
[Rice pudding]

Delicious and traditional. Hellenes may not admit they did not invent this creamy dessert because they invented a name for it! You will find *rizogalo* (which means "rice-milk") in the Greek milk shops (where you will also find yogurt) for a snack, with vanilla or cinnamon, not with the rose-water flavoring of the Persian rice pudding.

TO SERVE 6 TO 8

8 cups milk
1 cup raw long-grain white rice
¾ cup sugar
4 tablespoons butter

1 stick cinnamon and 3 whole
cloves (optional)
1 teaspoon vanilla
2 eggs, slightly beaten
Ground cinnamon

In a heavy saucepan, pour the cold milk, add the rice, sugar, and butter. Cook over low heat, stirring frequently until thickened, approximately 1 hour, adding cinnamon stick and cloves for flavor, if desired, during the last 15 minutes. Remove from the heat, stir in the vanilla, then remove the cinnamon stick and cloves.

Beat the eggs lightly in a small bowl, then add one tablespoon of the hot pudding mixture into the eggs, stir and repeat twice. Add the egg mixture into the pudding, stirring until mixed thoroughly. Pour into individual serving dishes or large serving bowl. Sprinkle with ground cinnamon, cool, then chill. Serve cold.

Note: You may use a vanilla bean, added with the rice, instead of stick cinnamon and cloves, or substitute grated lemon rind for all the other flavorings.

MOUSTALEVRIA
[*Must dessert*]

Moustalevria is named for its basic ingredients—*moustos* (must) and *alevri* (flour). Thus a quantity of sweet grapes and a little flour and seasonings can make this unusual treat—which is too firm to be a "pudding," and not as sweet as "candy." The method and ingredients, however, would put it in the class of soft candy in the starch-jelly family.

Hellenes get excited about *moustalevria*, and always maneuver to eat some. My father tells a sad-funny story about *moustalevria*. When crossing the first time from Greece to the United States (as a teenager), he had about ten pounds as a gift for relatives. But when the sailors heard about the delicious cargo, they ate it all before the ship docked.

Because grapes vary in sugar and water content, at least 10 pounds of sweet grapes are recommended for an end product of 24 to 30 pieces of *moustalevria*. After straining and clearing the must, the cook measures the syrup (Petimezi, page 347) to estimate the amount of flour needed. Sesame seeds and ground cinnamon, or nuts and cinnamon are the usual flavorings of this modern candy, which sounds like a direct descendant of the ancient *mustacea*.

Actually, two operations are involved, first making the *petimezi* and from it making the *moustalevria*.

7 cups strained unfermented must (juice of fresh grapes)
1 cup all-purpose flour
¼ cup blanched, chopped almonds
¼ cup chopped walnuts
Ground cinnamon

Using the must, follow the directions for making Petimezi (page 347). After straining the cleared must syrup (discarding the ash at the bottom), bring to a boil and cook for 20 minutes. Cool.

Combine the flour with 2 cups of the cooled *petimezi* in a small bowl. Bring the remaining syrup in the pan to a boil, and gradually add the syrup-flour mixture, stirring constantly. Lower the heat to minimum and cook until the soft ball stage (a drop of the mixture on a plate will remain round), stirring all the time. Pour the *moustalevria* on a large platter or several small plates and allow to cool and set. Sprinkle with nuts or sesame seeds and cinnamon and cut into squares. Store in covered tins indefinitely.

CAKES, SYRUP CAKES, AND PASTRIES

UNLIKE THE CUSTOM IN MOST Western and Middle Eastern cultures, the Greek meal does not include sweets. The huge family of *zacharoplastika*, including *glykismata* (sweets), *glyka tou koutaliou* (spoon sweets), *epidorpia* (desserts), *tourtes* (cakes), *glykes pites* (sweet syrup cakes), *glykismata me filo* (*filo* pastries), *koulourakia* (biscuits, and so on), form an integral part of Greek cultural life, however.

To avoid overwhelming the reader with a deluge of sweets recipes, I have scrupulously selected from many more Greek favorites, grouped them by type, and described their role in Greek life whenever possible. Holidays and special occasions herald the preparation of a special treat— Baklava (page 337), Galaktoboureko (page 332), Amygdalopita (page 324), Melomakarona (page 315), Kourambiedes (page 314), Karydopita (page 322), or perhaps a sweet yeast bread. Casual visits demand more casual refreshment: possibly *tourta*, small cakes, and almond-paste candies, which stay fresh a long time if stored in tins. Another sweet may be chosen when meeting a friend in the evening for the walk in the *plateia*, a beverage or favorite syrup in ice water: *Vysinnada* or *glyko vanilias* as *anapsistika* (refreshment). Yet a *paximadi* or *koulouraki* with coffee may be all that is necessary to ease the long wait between meals, or to offer to a business acquaintance who visits your office or place of business.

We know that the traditional climax of a Greek dinner is the enjoyment of fresh seasonal fruits. This habit does not preclude the occasional preparation of special *epidorpia* as a treat for guests or an expression of love for the family. Puddings, sherbets, custards, compotes, tartlets, and gelatin and nut desserts may be counted among these. In addition to the homemade ones, some elaborate frosted, layered, decorated, filled concoctions make their richness felt in Greek homes. In fact, stepping into a fancy *zacharoplasteion* (pastry and confectionery shop) in Athens recently, I wondered if I was in Vienna. Here one may sit and eat the dessert or buy some to carry home. Or both.

The usual Greek hostess is never, but *never*, caught by a visitor without something sweet to serve, preferably homemade, especially spoon sweets. *Paximadia*, *koulourakia*, stuffed dried fruits, chocolate treats, or small cakes are never too far from the serving tray. Holidays inspire, in addition to special dishes or breads, one special sweet, possibly two, but not a huge assortment. There is a marked difference between the traditional home of any class, whether urban or provincial, and the small percentage of "international" Hellenes. The food habits and ambience of the former are the more typical of Greece.

Outside Greece, particularly in the United States, visitors to a typical Greek-American family for a "little buffet" or party will probably be overwhelmed by the display of homemade pastries and cakes on the dessert board. Church suppers and functions where many women contribute their specialties can be staggering to the eyes and taste buds. Nothing could create a more false impression of sweets as used in Greece. This lavish display is a Greek-American phenomenon. Since I grew up in the midst of this gradual adaptation of Greek foods in America, I had to visit the various regions of Greece many times to be sure of the "old way." Naturally, certain changes occur in food habits, and confectionery methods, as people move into new settings and sense outside influences. Yet how amazingly the Greek people manage to preserve those customs, dishes, and cooking methods which they consider important.

In my reading of Athenaeus I found an account of a "sumptuous wedding banquet" held in Macedonia about 300 B.C. as related by Hippolochus, one of the twenty men who were guests (no bride is mentioned). I was especially delighted to find this passage because of the familiarity of foods, and because the desserts sound very much like the sweets of modern Greece, but carried home in "happy baskets" (the original doggie bags?). The elaborate courses began with chickens, ducks, ring doves, geese, hares, goats, molded cakes, pigeons, doves, and partridges, continually washed down with Thasian, Mendaean and Lesbian wines, amidst flowers and dancing girls who "looked quite naked." Gold and silver jars filled with perfume were gifts for guests. Courses continued with crystal platters full of all kinds of baked fish accompanied by Cappadocian loaves (which the guests offered to slaves). The guests received gold tiaras with that course, and another double jar of perfume. Drinking steadily, they enjoyed more dancing girls, merrymaking, and entertainment. More food—"Erymanthian" boars, on square platters trimmed with gold, the meat skewered with silver spears. The pièce de résistance, however, was a whole roast pig on a huge silver platter that was gilded all over. Roasted inside the pig was "thrushes, ducks, warblers in unlimited number, pease purée poured over eggs, oysters and scallops," all towering high. "After this we drank," said Hippolochus. When the banquet was drawing to a close, slaves began stuffing guests' baskets (a Macedonian practice at large dinners). The concluding courses were desserts in ivory baskets and flat cakes of every variety—Cretan, Attic, Samian. "We arose and took our leave, quite sober, because we were apprehensive for the safety of the wealth we took with us." In fact, he admitted the gifts of gold were enough to buy houses, land, or slaves. Indicative of the impatience of Hellenes with the habits of other regions, he quips, "But you, staying in Athens, think it happiness rather to listen to the precepts of Theophrastus, eating wild thyme and rocket-seed and your esteemed roll . . ."

Philoxenus of Cythera, a century earlier, had written of "flower-leaved cakes, fresh confections spiced, puff-cakes of wheat with frosting large as the pot." Other writers reported "oil and honey cakes," other sweet cakes. Along with these, the following excerpt, attributed to Archestratus, established *zacharoplastiki* and the Greek sweet-tooth, obviously forerunners of today's variety and habits: "Yet accept a cheese cake made in Athens, or failing that, if you get one from somewhere else, go out and demand some Attic honey, since that will make your cheese cake superb."

Cakes

KOURAMBIEDES
[Powdered small butter holiday cakes]

Traditionally prepared for Christmas and New Year's Day, *kou-rambiedes* require tremendous skill. A superlative *kourambie* leaves a lasting memory—it melts in the mouth and the taster's eyes glow as he rolls the flavor over his tongue, swallows, and sighs ecstatically. Experts take pride in whipping the butter for an hour or so by hand and adding each ingredient very slowly. Through experience, the cook learns exactly how much flour is needed before rolling and baking, as well as how to remove the *kourambiedes* from the baking sheets and roll in powdered sugar on all sides.

TO MAKE APPROXIMATELY 50

1 cup (½ pound) sweet butter
1 pound plus ½ cup sifted
  confectioners' sugar
1 egg yolk
2 tablespoons brandy, Cognac, or
  mastiha

1 teaspoon vanilla extract
1 teaspoon baking powder
2½ to 2¾ cups sifted cake flour,
  more if necessary
50 whole cloves, approximately
Rose water

In a large bowl, whip the sweet butter by hand or using an electric mixer for approximately 45 minutes, until it is fluffy, white, and sounds like the sea lapping against rocks. Continuing to beat on medium speed if using an electric mixer, gradually add the ½ cup confectioners' sugar, egg yolk, and flavorings.

Meanwhile, sift the baking powder with the flour and gradually add to the batter, mixing by hand and working the flour thoroughly into the mixture before adding more. Knead until a soft, buttery dough is formed that will stay together when a little is rolled in the palms of your hands. Break off pieces slightly larger in size than a walnut, then roll in your palms and shape with your fingers into half-moons, pear shapes, S-curves, mounded circles pinched gently on top with three fingers, and mounded triangles—all traditional shapes. Insert the tip of a whole clove in center of each or in the narrow ends of the pear-shaped *kourambiedes*. Place on cookie sheets allowing an inch between each. Bake on the center rack of a moderate oven (350 degrees) for 12 to 15 minutes or until golden colored, not chestnut. Remove from the oven and sprinkle rose water lightly on the *kourambiedes* with your fingers. Using a flat spatula, carefully lift each *kourambie* and place on a generous layer of sifted confectioners' sugar. (Sift the sugar over the bottom of a cardboard box or onto waxed paper, so that excess sugar may be reused.) Immediately sift more confectioners' sugar on top to cover the *kourambiedes*. Allow to cool for 10 to 15 minutes before lifting and rolling to be sure they are evenly coated. When thoroughly cool, store in tins. Serve *kourambiedes* on dessert plates with freshly sifted confectioners' sugar on each.

MELOMAKARONA * PHOENIKIA
["*Phoenicians*"]

Ancient and traditional small, spicy baked and syruped cakes, these are perfect for a large buffet. The nickname asserts their introduction into Greece by the Phoenicians, but not with these ingredients! Within my lifetime I have seen the oil give way to butter and semolina succumb to flour.

Prepare the syrup and filling first. You may prefer to try once without the filling, which is an equally festive way.

TO MAKE 40 TO 50

1½ cups honey
1½ cups granulated sugar
1 cup water
1 tablespoon lemon juice
1 pound plus 2 ounces finely chopped walnuts
1¼ cups (½ pound plus 4 tablespoons) softened sweet butter
4 teaspoons ground cinnamon, additional for sprinkling

1½ cups light vegetable oil
½ cup confectioners' sugar
Juice of 2 large oranges, strained
2 tablespoons Cognac or brandy
¼ teaspoon ground cloves
½ teaspoon grated nutmeg
1 teaspoon baking powder
½ teaspoon baking soda
6 to 7 cups all-purpose flour

Combine the honey, granulated sugar, water, and lemon juice in a saucepan and boil for 5 minutes. Remove from the heat. Combine the

1 pound finely chopped walnuts with ¼ cup of the softened sweet butter, 2 teaspoons of the cinnamon, and 5 tablespoons of the syrup. Reserve the remaining syrup and set the filling aside while you prepare the dough.

Using an electric mixer, cream the remaining butter (1 cup) with the oil until light and fluffy. Gradually add the confectioners' sugar, beating on medium speed. Add the orange juice slowly to the batter, along with the Cognac or brandy, 1 teaspoon of the cinnamon, and the other spices. In a small bowl, sift the baking powder, soda, and 2 cups of the flour together. Slowly add the flour mixture to the batter and beat for a few minutes. Continuing to mix by hand, add only enough remaining flour to make a soft dough. Knead.

Break off small pieces of the dough and shape with your fingers into oblongs about 2½ inches long and 1 inch high. Flatten between your palms and place 1 teaspoon of the filling mixture in the center. Work the dough around the filling to enclose it completely and press firmly to seal. This procedure sounds difficult, but with many hands it is quite simple. Place on a cookie sheet and continue until all the cakes are shaped. Bake in a moderate oven (350 degrees) for 25 minutes, then cool on a rack. Bring the syrup back to a boil. Dip each cake into the syrup and arrange on a platter. Sprinkle with the remaining chopped walnuts and teaspoon cinnamon, or more if desired. Cool before storing.

Note: You may bake and cool *melomakarona*, store a few days in advance and dip in syrup as described above a day or so before serving. The flavor improves after a few days.

YAOURTINI
[Brandied yogurt cake]

A heady cake to attract attention on the buffet table. Double the recipe if serving 10 to 15 persons.

TO SERVE 6

½ cup sweet butter	1 cup plain yogurt
1 cup granulated sugar	1 teaspoon baking soda
2 large eggs	1 tablespoon good quality brandy
1⅔ cups all-purpose flour	Confectioners' sugar
2 teaspoons baking powder	Slivered blanched almonds
¼ teaspoon salt	Candied cherries, sliced

With an electric mixer, beat butter until light, then cream with the sugar for 5 minutes. Lower the speed. Add the eggs, beating well after each addition. Meanwhile, sift the flour together with the baking powder and salt. Mix yogurt with the baking soda. Add the dry ingredients and yogurt alternately to the batter, beating on low speed. Pour in the brandy, turn the mixer up to high speed, and beat for 1 to 2 minutes. Turn into a buttered 9-inch tube pan or square pan, place in a preheated 375-degree oven, and lower the heat immediately to moderate (350 degrees). Bake for 35 to 40 minutes or until the cake is an even, light chestnut color and springs back to the touch. Remove the pan to a rack, then turn out of the pan on to a rack after a few minutes. Dust with confectioners' sugar while warm. When cool, dust again lightly and garnish with the almonds and cherries, arranging them in circles on top.

Note: If doubling the recipe use a larger pan.

TOURTA ATHINEIKI
[*Orange-walnut cake, Athens style*]

Excellent and dependable cake very much like the cakes served in Greece with the continental breakfast. Of dry texture, the cake has a fragrant aroma and the walnuts seem to absorb the orange flavor.

TO SERVE 8 TO 10

1 cup (½ pound) sweet butter	3 cups all-purpose flour
2 cups granulated sugar	1 teaspoon baking powder
4 eggs	¼ teaspoon salt
Juice of 1 orange	1 cup coarsely chopped walnuts
Grated rind of 1 orange	Confectioners' sugar (optional)

Cream the butter until light and fluffy, then gradually add the sugar. Continuing to beat, add the eggs one at a time, beating well, on medium speed, after each addition. Gradually add the orange juice and rind.

Meanwhile, sift the flour with the baking powder and salt and gradually add to the batter. Add the walnuts last, blend another minute on medium high speed, and pour into a greased and lightly floured 8-inch tube pan. Bake in a moderate oven (350 degrees) for 25 to 30 minutes until the color is a light chestnut and the cake springs back to the touch. (Watch carefully because this cake bakes quickly.) Turn onto a wire rack, round side up. Dust with confectioners' sugar and cool thoroughly before slicing.

TOURTA ME YAOURTI KAI STAFIDES
[*Spicy yogurt cake layered with raisins*]

One of many delightful cakes and *pites* made with yogurt.

TO SERVE 9

½ cup (¼ pound) sweet butter or margarine	*1 teaspoon baking soda*
	1 teaspoon vanilla extract
1 cup granulated sugar	*¾ cup raisins*
3 eggs	*1 teaspoon ground cinnamon*
2 cups sifted all-purpose flour	*½ teaspoon grated nutmeg*
2 teaspoons baking powder	*¼ teaspoon ground cloves*
1 teaspoon salt	*½ cup chopped walnuts*
1 cup plain yogurt	*(optional)*

Cream the butter and sugar together, then add the eggs, one at a time, beating well after each addition. Meanwhile, sift the flour with the baking powder and salt and add gradually to the batter, beating on medium speed. Combine the yogurt with the baking soda and add to the batter, a few tablespoons at a time, along with the vanilla.

Mix together the raisins, spices, and if desired, the walnuts. Pour half the batter into a buttered 9-inch-square pan and sprinkle half the raisin mixture evenly over it. Pour in the rest of the batter and top with the raisin mixture. Bake in a moderate oven (350 degrees) for 40 to 45 minutes, or until the cake springs back to the touch of your finger. Remove to a cake rack and cool in the pan. Cut into square or diamond shapes when cool.

Note: Cupcakes are more popular than cake squares in the larger Greek cities. This recipe would make a dozen cupcakes.

TAHINOPITA NISTISIMI
[*Tahini Lenten cake*]

People, especially cooks, show their ingenuity in the way they brighten fasting days. *Tahinopita* is an example. Chewy and packed with nuts, fruits, and raisins, this makes an excellent party treat for children. Greek people make versions of this cake during Lenten days, substituting *tahini* for fat.

TO MAKE 36 BARS, 1¼ x 3 INCHES

1 cup tahini
1 cup granulated sugar
2 tablespoons Cognac
1 teaspoon baking soda
1½ to 2 cups sifted all-purpose
  flour
2 teaspoons ground cinnamon

2 cups chopped walnuts, light
  raisins, and glacéed fruit peel,
  mixed
1 cup orange juice
½ cup water, if necessary
Confectioners' sugar

Mix the *tahini*, if the oil has separated to the top, measure, and beat in a large bowl, using an electric mixer or wooden spoon. Continuing to beat, gradually add the sugar. Combine the Cognac and baking soda and add them to the mixture. Sift 1½ cups of the flour with the cinnamon and mix in the walnuts, raisins, and glacéed fruit peel. Add the flour mixture and orange juice alternately to the batter, mixing thoroughly after each. (If using an electric mixer, start beating by hand.) Add only enough water or flour to make the batter pour; it will be thicker than an average cake batter. Butter the bottom and sides of a 9 x 12 x 2-inch baking pan and line the bottom with buttered waxed paper. Pour the batter into the pan and spread evenly, then bake in a moderate oven (350 degrees) for 45 minutes, or until a deep chestnut color. Remove and cool in the pan, dusting with confectioners' sugar when warm. Cool, then cut into bars or diamond shapes and store in covered tins.

Note: 1 cup each of walnuts and light raisins may be used if glacéed fruits are unavailable. *Tahini* is sold in Greek and Middle Eastern specialty stores.

VASILOPITA PORTOKALION THRAKIS
[*Orange vasilopita cake, Thracian style*]

Vasilopita as made in Alexandroupolis (the last stop before Turkey) is a luscious cake, yellow-orange, heavy grained, and with a sweet flavor. The coin (a drachma—honor and good luck for the winner) is inserted in the batter, and the cake is cut at the climax of the traditional New Year's Day meal. In Thrace there is no glaze—just a fine, orangey-chestnut crust.

TO MAKE 1 ROUND 10-INCH CAKE

1 cup (½ pound) plus 1 table-
spoon sweet butter
4 cups (2 pounds) sifted
confectioners' sugar
6 eggs, at room temperature

4⅓ cups all-purpose flour
2 teaspoons baking powder
1 teaspoon baking soda
Grated rind of 2 oranges
Juice of 5 oranges

Using an electric mixer or beating by hand, beat the butter until soft and fluffy. Gradually add the sugar, beating on medium speed. Add the eggs one at a time, beating thoroughly after each addition. Meanwhile, sift the flour, baking powder, and soda together. Combine the orange rind with the orange juice, then, beginning and ending with the flour mixture, add the dry and liquid ingredients to the batter, a few tablespoons at a time, beating on medium speed.

Butter and flour a round 10-inch pan. Turn the batter into the pan and bake in a moderate oven (350 degrees) for 1 hour, then lower the heat to 325 and continue baking for an additional 20 minutes, or slightly longer, until a cake tester comes out clean. (The center of the cake will require the longest.) Set on a cake rack for 15 minutes before removing from the pan. Cool.

Note: The coin may be slipped into the cake before or after baking. Either way, wash the coin, rub with lemon and salt, wash again, and dry.

VASILOPITA SMYRNIS
[New Year's "cake," Smyrna style]

Greek people originally from Smyrna bake an unusual *vasilopita*. The top is glazed and stamped with a Byzantine two-headed eagle (with eyes of clove), of a heavy, crumbly texture. It is also unusual because it is a kneaded cake.

TO MAKE 1 ROUND 10-INCH CAKE

*1 cup (½ pound) softened sweet
   butter
1 cup plus 2 tablespoons granulated sugar
3 eggs at room temperature
Grated rind of 1 navel orange
⅓ cup orange juice or milk*

*4 cups cake flour
2 teaspoons baking powder
½ teaspoon salt
Byzantine eagle stamp (available
   at Greek specialty stores)
Whole cloves*

Using an electric mixer, cream the butter until light and fluffy, then gradually add the sugar and continue to beat for 5 minutes. Lower the speed and add 2 of the eggs, one at a time, then the orange rind and very gradually the orange juice. Sift the flour with the baking powder and salt and gradually add to the batter, mixing in the last cupful by hand and kneading thoroughly for several minutes.

Butter the pan as well as a piece of waxed paper that has been cut to fit the bottom. Shape the dough into a round cake to fit the pan and set on the waxed paper. Stamp with the Byzantine eagle and decorate the edges using 2 forks. Stud the eyes with whole cloves. Bake in moderate oven (350 degrees) for 45 minutes until light chestnut in color, brushing with the remaining egg, lightly beaten, after the first 20 minutes. (The glaze may be brushed on before baking, but it will deepen the color of the crust to a dark chestnut.) Cool on a rack for 15 minutes before removing from the pan.

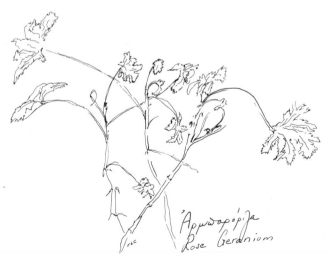

Αρμωαρόρἰα
Rose Geranium

Syrup Cakes

KARYDOPITA
[*Walnut syrup sponge cake*]

Traditional and famous syrup cake throughout Greece, this is one of the richer versions which you would enjoy making in advance and serving dainty portions for a tea or buffet.

TO MAKE A SHEET CAKE 15½ X 11 X 2 INCHES BEFORE CUTTING
(SERVES 20 TO 24)

3 cups water
4 cups (2 pounds) granulated sugar
Peel of 1 orange or lemon
2 cloves
18 eggs, separated, at room temperature
5 tablespoons Cognac

1 teaspoon vanilla extract
½ teaspoon baking soda
1 six-ounce package zwieback, crushed fine
1 pound shelled walnuts (approximately 4 cups), coarsely chopped
1 teaspoon ground cinnamon

Combine the water, 2½ cups of the sugar, orange or lemon peel, and cloves in a saucepan and boil for 10 minutes. Remove the peel and cloves and cool.

Meanwhile, using an electric mixer, beat the egg yolks until light and lemon colored, and gradually add the remaining 1½ cups sugar. In a separate bowl, mix the Cognac, vanilla extract, and baking soda and slowly add to the yolks and sugar. Combine the zwieback, walnuts, and cinnamon, and gradually add to the batter, mixing on low speed.

Meanwhile, beat the egg whites until soft peaks form. Slowly fold into the cake batter, then pour into a greased 15½ x 11 x 2-inch *tapsi* or baking pan. Bake in a moderate oven (350 degrees) for 30 minutes, or until a deep chestnut color. Remove from the oven and set on a wire rack. Spoon the cooled syrup over the cake and allow it to cool in the pan. Cut into traditional diamond shapes (see sketch page 45), according to the desired size.

322

REVANI

[Semolina-almond sponge cake with syrup]

An amiable Metsovon chef shared his delicious recipe for *revani*, freshly made the day we stopped in the unique town nestled in the Pindus Mountains. His ingredients and proportions exactly match those of *revani* recipes of the tip of Peloponnesos and Athens, with slight variations in flavorings and sugar concentration in the syrup. Some chefs add the brandy to the syrup and the orange flavor to the cake batter, using extract, juice, or grated orange peel, but both flavorings permeate *revani*, sooner or later. *Revani* may be made by separating eggs and folding the beaten whites into the batter. Having tried both methods, I find the following one simpler, producing a light, fine-grained cake of yellow-orange color.

TO MAKE 18 TO 20 "DIAMONDS"

2½ *cups granulated sugar*
3 *cups cold water*
1 *small stick cinnamon*
3 *to 4 whole cloves*
Peel of 1 orange or 1 teaspoon
   orange extract
1 *cup (½ pound) sweet butter*
6 *eggs at room temperature*

1 *cup all-purpose flour*
1 *cup fine semolina*
3 *teaspoons baking powder*
1 *cup blanched, peeled and finely*
   chopped almonds
1 *teaspoon vanilla extract*
2 *tablespoons brandy*

Combine 1½ cups of the sugar with the cold water in a saucepan and cook until dissolved, then add the cinnamon stick, cloves, and orange peel and simmer for 15 minutes. Remove the flavorings. Cool.

Using an electric mixer, beat the butter in a large bowl until fluffy. Gradually add the remaining sugar, beating on medium speed, then add the eggs, one at a time, beating thoroughly after each addition, without rushing. Meanwhile, sift the flour, semolina, baking powder, and almonds together. Very gradually add to the batter, beating on medium speed, then pour in the vanilla and brandy and give the batter a last whirl on high speed for a few seconds. Pour immediately into a buttered 9 x 12 x 3-inch cake pan and bake on the center rack of a moderate oven (350 degrees) for 30 to 35 minutes, or until the cake springs back when touched by a finger. Remove from the oven and set the pan on a cake rack. Using a sharp knife, score the cake into diamond shapes (see sketch page 45). Spoon the cooled syrup over the entire cake and cool.

Note: Each piece may be attractively garnished with a candied or maraschino cherry slice in the center and almond slivers angled on each side.

AMYGDALOPITA
[*Brandied almond honey cake*]

Of the infinite versions, there is always one better *amygdalopita*, and that applies to this one, which I have reduced for a smaller group. Very sweet syrup.

TO SERVE 10 TO 12

1 cup honey	*Pinch of salt*
1 cup sugar	*¾ teaspoon ground cinnamon*
1 cup water	*½ teaspoon grated nutmeg*
1 teaspoon lemon juice	*¼ teaspoon ground cloves*
1 tablespoon brandy	*4 tablespoons milk*
½ cup (¼ pound) sweet butter	*1 tablespoon grated orange rind*
3 eggs, separated	*1 cup blanched, coarsely chopped*
1 cup all-purpose flour	*almonds*
1½ teaspoons baking powder	

Combine the honey, ⅓ cup of sugar, and water in a saucepan, stir, and bring to a boil. Skim off the foam and simmer for 5 minutes, then remove from the heat. Stir in the lemon juice and cool, then mix in the brandy. Set aside while you prepare the cake. Using an electric mixer, beat the butter until fluffy and gradually add the remaining sugar and the egg yolks, beating thoroughly. Sift the flour with the baking powder, salt, and spices. Lower the speed and add the dry ingredients to the batter alternately with the milk, then stir in the orange rind and almonds.

Meanwhile, beat the egg whites until firm peaks form and fold carefully into the batter. Pour into a buttered 8 x 8 x 3-inch baking pan and bake in a moderate oven (350 degrees) for 30 to 35 minutes until the cake springs back when touched by a finger. Put the pan on a rack and cut into diamond shapes. Spoon the cooled syrup over the cake, cool, and store in the refrigerator until ready to serve.

DIPLES

*[Crisp bubble bows, knots, and rolls
honeyed with nuts and cinnamon]*

A popular, traditional village sweet for festive occasions—requiring great skill. *Diples* crumble in the mouth, a magnificent balance between crisp and syrup, when expertly made. Usually every family has one "expert," and in ours it was Stavroula Lagakos, our grandmother, who died at ninety-five while I was writing this book. Many of her proverbs and memories of village life, including this recipe, remain as her legacy. I wrote the recipe, watching her mix and roll the *diples*, when she was in her late eighties. Using a long *plasti* intent on creating a perfect *filo* as we watched, she rolled and stroked the *filo* until soft as, but thinner than, a chamois, gathering strength from our admiration—and the Cognac she sipped after adding one jigger to the mixture!

Prepare and fry in advance, store in tins, and pour honey over them just before serving the *diples*, sprinkled with nuts and cinnamon, of course. Similar pastries are called *lyhnarakia* (little lamps) in Athens and *xerotigana* in Crete.

TO MAKE 4 TO 5 DOZEN

5 egg yolks
1 egg white
2 tablespoons butter
1/4 cup confectioners' sugar
1 jigger brandy or Cognac
Grated rind of 1 small orange
1/2 teaspoon vanilla extract
1 teaspoon baking powder

1/4 teaspoon baking soda
2 1/2 to 2 3/4 cups all-purpose flour
*Olive or other vegetable oil for
  deep frying*
Honey, warmed
Chopped walnuts
Ground cinnamon

Beat the egg yolks and egg white until light and fluffy, using an electric mixer. Gradually add the butter, sugar, brandy, orange rind, and vanilla, continuing to beat. Sift the baking powder and soda with 1 cup of the flour and gradually add to the batter, mixing on low speed. Continuing to mix by hand, add enough flour to make a soft dough. Knead until the dough is elastic and smooth, then divide into 3 balls. Lightly flour a large board, and using a *plasti* (clean broom handle), roll each ball until noodle thin.

The trick to creating an even *filo* for *diples* or noodles is to rotate the dough each time. Roll the dough around the *plasti*, give it 3 or 4 quick slaps on the table by pushing at each end with the palms of your hands and then bringing it back toward you. Turn the *plasti* a quarter circle, unroll slowly with your left hand, and with your right hand on the dough, gently stretch it evenly. Flour the dough lightly. Repeat this slapping motion, which stretches the dough, and turning a quarter circle each time, and the dough will be smooth and thin.

Using a sharp knife, cut into any of the following sizes and cover until ready to fry (usually one person fries and another cuts, alternating on whim).

> 4 x 1½ inches—for rolls, bows, and knots
> 16 x ¾ inches—for roses, rosettes
> 4 x 2 inches—for folds

To fry rolls and folds: In deep but not too wide pan, heat oil to a depth of 4 inches. When the oil reaches a temperature of 350 degrees regulate to maintain the temperature and drop in one piece of the dough; it will bubble immediately. Using 2 forks, fold in half and turn over to fry to an even golden color; or if making rolls, turn in one end and roll up quickly to the other. Remove with forks carefully, so as not to crumble the pastry, and set on paper toweling to drain. Cool on racks.

To fry: Pinch the dough in center before frying as above.

To fry knots: Make a lengthwise slash in the center of the dough; slip one end of the dough into slash to form the "knot." Fry as above.

To fry roses: Shape "roses" by winding long dough strips around the fingers of one hand, first using 2 fingers to make a circle, then 3 fingers, and another circle around 4 fingers to make concentric rings or "roses" about the size of a demitasse saucer. Place on a slotted spoon and lower into the hot fat, one at a time.

To serve, pour warm honey over the *diples* and dust with cinnamon and chopped walnuts.

Note: Cretans also sprinkle sesame seeds over *diples* before serving.

DAKTILA KYRION KYPRIOTIKA
[*Ladyfinger nut rolls, Cyprus style*]

Stuffed, fried, and dipped in honey-sugar syrup, these are delicious made a day in advance.

TO MAKE ABOUT 30 NUT ROLLS

2 cups plus 3 tablespoons granu-
    lated sugar
1 1/4 cups water, approximately
1/4 cup honey
1 stick cinnamon
2 cloves
2 tablespoons plus 2 teaspoons
    lemon juice
2 to 2 1/4 cups all-purpose flour
1 teaspoon salt

1/4 cup (4 tablespoons) sweet
    butter
2 tablespoons lemon juice
4 to 6 tablespoons water
3/4 cup blanched, coarsely
    chopped almonds
2 teaspoons ground cinnamon
Peanut or corn oil for deep frying
Finely chopped almonds

Combine the 2 cups sugar, 1 cup of the water, honey, the cinnamon stick, cloves, and the 2 teaspoons lemon juice in a saucepan and boil for 5 minutes. Remove the spices and cool thoroughly.

Meanwhile, sift 2 cups of the flour with the salt in a large mixing bowl and work in the butter with your fingers or a pastry blender. Add the 2 tablespoons lemon juice and enough water, a quarter cup or more, to form the dough into a large ball. Use flour sparingly on the board, and knead for 5 to 10 minutes. Cover and let rest an hour, then roll out as thin as possible on a lightly floured board. Using a sharp knife, cut into rectangles about 2 x 3 inches. In a small bowl, thoroughly combine the almonds, 3 tablespoons sugar, and the ground cinnamon. Spread a teaspoon of the nut mixture across the 2-inch width of one of the rectangles, roll up, moisten the end of the dough with cold water, and seal. Set on a buttered cookie sheet and continue until all the "fingers" are rolled.

In a deep pan, heat oil to 375 degrees and fry 3 or 4 rolls at a time, turning with tongs until a rich chestnut color on all sides. Drain a moment on absorbent towels, then dip in the cooled syrup, drain, and place on a platter. Continue until all are fried, being careful to keep the oil hot without smoking. When all have been dipped, sprinkle with finely chopped almonds.

Small Pastries

RAFIOLA KOKOKARION
[Coconut pastries stuffed with glacéed fruit, Cretan style]

In a Cretan *zacharoplasteion*, we were so intrigued by these coconut pastries (among the newer breed) that I tried them at home. You can expect the potato pastry to be a bit difficult to manipulate, and you can also anticipate compliments on the results. Attractive and tasty, not excessively sweet.

TO MAKE 20 HALF-CIRCLES

3 potatoes
3 tablespoons granulated sugar
Pinch of salt
2 egg yolks
4 cups finely shredded coconut

1½ cups glacéed fruit (cherries, apricots, lemon, orange, pear, and so on)
Confectioners' sugar

Boil the potatoes in their jackets until fork-tender, then drain and remove the skins and all spots. Return the potatoes to the pan and dry over medium heat, shaking the pan constantly. Push the potatoes through a mill or ricer, then combine in a large bowl with the sugar and salt. When somewhat cool, add the egg yolks and coconut and knead until smooth. Refrigerate for 2 hours.

Remove the dough from the refrigerator and knead until smooth enough to roll. If sticky, dust lightly with flour. Roll out on a floured board to ¼ inch thickness, then, using a glass with a 3½-inch diameter, cut the pastry into rounds.

Meanwhile, mince the glacéed fruit. Place 1 tablespoon on the center of each of the pastry rounds. Lift one side with a spatula and fold over the other half, forming a half-circle. Press the edges together and place on a baking sheet. Continue until all have been stuffed, then bake in a moderate oven (350 degrees) for 15 minutes, or until firm; the pastries will be white. Remove and cool for 10 minutes, then roll in confectioners' sugar and cool completely. Store in a covered container.

Note: In Crete this pastry is cut with a serrated pastry cutter producing an attractive edging.

LOUKOUMIA KYPRIOTIKA
[*Nut-stuffed semolina pastries, Cyprus style*]

Delicious. The first step begins the evening before.

TO MAKE ABOUT 30 TWO-INCH OVALS

½ cup (¼ pound) sweet butter
1¼ cups fine semolina
Orange flower water
¼ teaspoon salt
5 to 6 tablespoons warm water

1 cup chopped unsalted pistachios
4½ tablespoons granulated sugar
1 tablespoon ground cinnamon
Confectioners' sugar

In a small, heavy saucepan, bring the butter to bubbling over medium heat and stir in the fine semolina. Transfer to a small bowl, cover, and let stand overnight at room temperature. The next day, uncover and add 2 teaspoons orange flower water, the salt, and gradually the warm water, working with your fingers to make a firm dough. Knead for 5 minutes, then cover and let rest for 1 hour. Meanwhile, combine the pistachios, sugar, and ground cinnamon in a small bowl.

Break off pieces of dough slightly larger in size than a walnut. Work in your fingers to form a ball. Press the center with your thumb to make a large well and fill with 1 teaspoon of the nut mixture, then cover over with dough and shape into an oval. Set on a cookie sheet and continue until all the pastries are shaped. Bake in a moderate oven (350 degrees) for 30 to 35 minutes or until the yellow color has become a light, not a deep, chestnut. Remove to racks and cool for 10 minutes, then dip quickly into orange flower water and roll in confectioners' sugar. Cool before storing.

Note: You may substitute blanched almonds for the pistachios and peanut oil for the butter.

PATOUDIA

[Aromatic stuffed pastries, Cretan style]

A fragrant and chewy delight (make a few days in advance).

TO MAKE ABOUT 45 TWO-INCH SQUARES

¾ cup light vegetable and olive oils, mixed
¼ cup orange juice
¼ cup lemon juice
¼ cup water
¼ cup granulated sugar
4 cups plus 2 tablespoons all-purpose flour

1 teaspoon salt
½ teaspoon baking soda
¾ cup ground walnuts
¾ cup blanched ground almonds
¾ cup honey
⅓ cup sesame seeds
⅓ cup rose water, approximately
Confectioners' sugar

In a large bowl, combine the oils, orange and lemon juices, water, and sugar. Mix thoroughly, using your hand or a spoon. Sift the flour with the salt and soda and stir into the liquid ingredients. Knead until smooth, then cover and refrigerate for several hours, removing to room temperature 1 hour before rolling.

Meanwhile, in a medium-sized bowl, combine the ground walnuts, ground almonds, honey, and sesame seeds to make a stiff filling. Set aside.

On a floured board, roll out the dough to a thin sheet, then cut the pastry into 3½-inch squares with a sharp knife. Place 1 teaspoon filling in center of each square, then dampen the edges of the square with water. Lift the corners of each square toward the center and press gently to seal. Set on a cookie sheet until all are stuffed, then bake in a moderate oven (350 degrees) for 25 minutes, or until golden in color. Cool for 10 minutes, then dip each pastry into rose water and roll in confectioners' sugar.

PASTA FLORA
[Latticed fruit-filled sheet pastry, Athens style]

Attractive, tasty, and rich, this should be cut into dainty squares. You will need both dough and filling ingredients before beginning.

TO MAKE 3 DOZEN 1½-INCH SQUARES

1 cup (½ pound) sweet butter
½ cup granulated sugar
2 eggs
6 tablespoons Cognac
2 to 2½ cups all-purpose flour
¼ teaspoon salt
½ teaspoon baking powder
2 cups canned or fresh stewed apricots

3 to 4 dried figs
⅓ cup raisins
Grated rind of 1 orange
1 cup apricot jam
1 tablespoon lemon juice (optional)
2 teaspoons cornstarch
⅓ cup orange juice

Using an electric mixer, beat the butter until light and fluffy and gradually add the sugar, 1 egg and an egg yolk, and 3 tablespoons of the Cognac, beating thoroughly after each addition. Sift 2 cups of the flour with the salt and baking powder and add slowly to the batter, while beating on medium speed. Remove the beaters and finish by hand, adding only enough flour to make a soft dough. Knead. Cover and refrigerate for at least 30 minutes.

Meanwhile, slice the apricots into uniform pieces and place in an enameled pan. Soak the figs and raisins in the remaining Cognac until swollen, then mince and add to the apricots along with the orange rind, jam, and lemon juice, if desired. Combine the cornstarch with the orange juice and stir into the apricot mixture, then cook over medium heat until thick, stirring constantly with a wooden spoon. Cool.

Remove the dough from the refrigerator and set aside about one-third for the latticed top. Using your fingers (the dough will be too soft to roll), press the larger portion of dough into a buttered 9 x 12 x 2-inch baking pan, pressing evenly about ¼ inch up the sides. Pour the filling into the dough-lined pan.

Divide the remaining dough into walnut-sized balls and roll each ball into ½-inch strips. Using the strips, make a lattice over the top of the pastry. If using a glaze, beat the remaining egg white slightly with a fork and brush on the dough strips. Bake in a moderate oven (350 degrees) for 45 minutes, or until golden in color. Remove and cool in the pan on a rack. To serve, cut into 1½-inch (or smaller) squares with a sharp knife.

Note: You may use peaches and peach jam, strawberries and strawberry jam, and so on, instead of apricots; also diced candied peel adds a colorful note when substituting for figs; and slivered almonds may be added to the filling.

FILO PASTRIES

GALAKTOBOUREKO
[*Syrupy milk custard dessert baked in filo*]

This is a traditional dessert that is made in all regions; this recipe comes from Macedonia. *Galakto* is a derivative of *gala*, or "milk" in Greek, and *boureko* belongs in the family of *bourekia*, or "stuffed." A Greek pastry baker assured us the *galaktoboureko* is a distinctly Greek pastry baked only in Greece. "Difficult to make" is a misconception: This is simple as any custard. It is delicious fresh, but may be stored in the refrigerator a day or two.

TO MAKE 20 TO 24 SQUARES

6 cups milk
1 cup fine semolina
3½ tablespoons cornstarch
3 cups granulated sugar
¼ teaspoon salt
6 eggs
1 teaspoon vanilla extract (optional)

1 tablespoon butter
12 sheets commercial filo, unrolled flat and kept covered to avoid drying
¾ cup hot melted butter
1 cup water
Peel of 1 lemon or orange
2 tablespoons fine brandy or Cognac (optional)

In a heavy-bottomed, 3-quart saucepan, bring the milk gradually to a boil; do not allow it to scorch. Meanwhile, sift the semolina, cornstarch, 1 cup of the sugar, and salt together and gradually add to the boiling milk, stirring constantly with a wooden spoon. Cook slowly over medium heat until the mixture thickens and comes to a full boil, then remove from the heat.

Beat the eggs on high speed of an electric mixer. Gradually add ½ cup sugar and continue beating until very thick and fluffy, about 10 minutes, then add the vanilla. Stirring constantly, add the eggs to the hot pudding. Partially cover the pan and allow to cool. Butter a 9 x 12 x 3-inch baking pan and cover the bottom with 7 sheets of the *filo*, brushing butter generously between each and making sure that a few sheets come up the pan sides. Pour the custard into the pan over the *filo*. Cover with the 5 remaining sheets, brushing butter between each and on the surface. With the tip of a very sharp knife, score the top *filo* sheets into square or diamond shapes, being careful not to score as deeply as the custard. Bake on the center rack of a moderate (350-degree) oven for 40 to 45 minutes, until crisp and golden chestnut in color and the custard is firm.

Meanwhile, boil the remaining 1½ cups sugar with the water and lemon or orange peel for 5 minutes. Add the brandy or Cognac, if desired, and set aside.

Remove the *galaktoboureko* from the oven and set on a cake rack. Spoon the hot syrup over the entire *galaktoboureko*, particularly the edges. Cool thoroughly before cutting and serving. Store in the refrigerator.

FLOYERES

[Pastry "flutes" stuffed with brandied nuts]

Also called *poura* (cigars) and *daktila kyrion* (ladies' fingers). The same mixture may be rolled into *trigona* (three-cornered) pastries by rolling like *tyropites* (page 65).

TO MAKE 40 SIX-INCH OR 60 FOUR-INCH PASTRIES

3 cups plus 2 to 3 tablespoons granulated sugar
2 cups water
1 stick cinnamon
2 whole cloves
1 tablespoon lemon juice
Rind of ½ lemon, left whole
1 pound mixed walnuts and almonds, medium, coarsely ground

5 tablespoons fine brandy
½ teaspoon grated lemon rind
1 teaspoon ground cinnamon
¼ teaspoon ground cloves
1 egg, slightly beaten
¼ cup toast or zwieback crumbs, approximately
1 pound commercial filo pastry
1½ cups melted butter

333

Boil the 3 cups sugar, water, cinnamon stick, cloves, lemon juice and lemon rind for 10 minutes, then remove the rind and cool.

Meanwhile, in a mixing bowl, combine the nuts, 4 tablespoons of the brandy, the grated lemon rind, spices, 2 to 3 tablespoons sugar, the egg, and enough of the crumbs to absorb excess liquid; the mixture should not be too stiff.

Unroll the pastry sheets and cut in half or thirds lengthwise, depending on the size pastry you prefer. Keep covered with damp towel until rolling. Brush each *filo* sheet with warm melted butter, fold in half, and brush with butter again. Spread 1 tablespoon of the filling along one narrow end, fold the *filo* ½ inch toward the center on each side and roll up tightly, keeping opposite edges parallel. Arrange on a baking sheet. Continue until all pastries have been rolled, then pour remaining butter over them. Bake in a moderate oven (350 degrees) until golden and crisp, about 25 minutes. Remove from the oven, pour over the cooled syrup, to which the remaining tablespoon brandy has been added, and cool thoroughly. Serve on individual plates or arrange on a serving platter.

KADAIFI

[*Baked kadaifi pastry, sheet style*]

Simple and quick! The large, impressive *kadaifi* rolls are the more famous method. Walnuts may be mixed with the almonds.

TO SERVE 12 TO 16

1 pound commercial raw kadaifi *pastry*	*Ground cinnamon*
½ cup melted sweet butter	*½ cup orange juice (optional)*
1½ cups blanched finely chopped almonds	*2 cups water*
	½ cup honey
3½ cups granulated sugar	*2 tablespoons lemon juice*

Open the raw *kadaifi* pastry to the air for 10 to 15 minutes. Spread half the pastry evenly over the bottom of a 9 x 12 x 3-inch baking pan and brush with half the butter. Meanwhile, combine the almonds, ½ cup sugar, 1 tablespoon cinnamon, and orange juice in a small bowl. (The orange juice will make the mixture like a paste that can be spread with a knife.) Spread the almond mixture over the *kadaifi* and cover with the remaining pastry. Brush with the remaining butter and bake in a moderate oven (350 degrees) for 40 minutes or slightly longer, until golden on top.

Meanwhile, boil the remaining 3 cups sugar with water for 5 minutes. Stir in the honey and lemon juice, bring to a boil and keep hot. When done, remove the pastry to a rack to cool in the pan, then spoon the hot syrup over the pastry. Cover with a dry towel and allow to cool thoroughly. When cool, cut into square or diamond shapes of any desired size. Dust with additional ground cinnamon just before serving on dessert plates.

[*Kadaifi rolls*]

This is the more familiar version in Greece.

TO MAKE 18 TO 20 ROLLS

Unwrap 1 pound commercial raw *kadaifi* pastry and divide into lengthwise sections approximately 4 to 5 inches wide. There should be enough to make 18 to 20 rolls of traditional size; these can be individualized in size at the outset.

Prepare the recipe above, but using double the amount of sweet butter. On one end of each pastry section, place 2 teaspoonfuls of almond mixture. Roll up to other end, tightly or loosely as desired, and place on a buttered baking sheet. Repeat until all the pastry is rolled and lined up, not too tightly on the pan. Brush or spoon hot butter on the *kadaifi* and bake for approximately 35 to 40 minutes, or until golden. Remove from the oven, leave in the pan, and spoon the hot syrup over the pastry. Complete as described above.

KOPENHAI
[*Almond spongecake with filo and syrup, Athens style*]

Created to honor King George I of Greece when the Danish prince began his reign in 1862, and named for his native Copenhagen, this confection is a combination (very rich) pastry–almond spongecake topped with *filo* and syrup.

TO SERVE 16 TO 20

1 cup granulated sugar
1 cup plus 1 tablespoon water
1 tablespoon lemon juice
½ cup (¼ pound) sweet butter
2 egg yolks, at room temperature
2 cups sifted confectioners' sugar
1¾ cups sifted all-purpose flour
Pinch of salt
1 teaspoon baking powder
Ground cinnamon
4 to 5 tablespoons apricot jam

4 egg yolks, at room temperature
2 tablespoons brandy
1½ cups blanched finely ground
    almonds
3 pieces zwieback, crushed fine
¼ teaspoon grated nutmeg
6 egg whites, at room temperature
4 sheets commercial filo pastry,
    unrolled flat and kept covered
    to avoid drying
6 tablespoons melted butter

Combine the granulated sugar, 1 cup water, and the lemon juice in a saucepan and boil for 5 minutes. Cool.

Meanwhile cream the butter until light, using an electric mixer. Gradually add the 2 yolks and 1 cup of the confectioners' sugar. Sift 1 cup of the flour with the salt, baking powder, and a pinch of ground cinnamon and gradually add to the butter mixture, then add the remaining flour and knead the dough by hand for several minutes. Press into the bottom of a buttered 8 x 11 x 3-inch baking pan, allowing the sides to rise only slightly above the level at pan bottom. Bake in a moderate oven (350 degrees) for 6 minutes, then remove and spread with the apricot jam. Set aside while you prepare the filling.

Beat the 4 egg yolks using an electric mixer, and gradually add ½ cup of the confectioners' sugar, the brandy and the 1 tablespoon water. Combine the almonds, zwieback crumbs, ½ teaspoon cinnamon, and the nutmeg in a small bowl and add them gradually to the egg yolk mixture on low speed or with a large wooden spoon by hand. (The mixture will be thick, but if too stiff add 1 to 2 tablespoons water.) In a medium bowl, beat the egg whites, using a balloon whisk, and when thick gradually add the remaining ½ cup confectioners' sugar. Continue beating until stiff peaks form. Drop several tablespoons into the yolk-almond mixture and stir, then fold in the remaining egg whites with an over-under motion, avoiding losing the air incorporated into the whites.

Turn the filling into the jam-covered dough and cover with the 4 filo sheets, brushing butter generously on each and on the surface. With a sharp knife score the top 2 sheets, carefully estimating the number of "diamonds" (see page 45). Bake in a moderate oven (350 degrees) for 20 minutes then reduce heat to 325 degrees and continue baking for 20 to 25 minutes longer or until the top is golden and crisp. Remove to a rack, in the pan, and spoon cooled syrup over. Cool. Cut into diamonds and serve each piece individually.

BAKLAVA

Baklava is a gala pastry prepared for very special occasions: name day celebrations, christenings, holidays. Women frequently carry their *tapsi*, prepared and assembled at home, to the local baker to be baked to crisp perfection. Greek villagers pound their cloves and cinnamon in a *goudi* with *goudoheri* (mortar and pestle). Most frequently they use a mixture of walnuts and almonds, although all-almond *baklava* has a certain snob appeal and an excellent flavor when baked with freshly shelled almonds.

Syrup flavorings vary. Honey, Cognac, lemon peel and juice, cinnamon, and cloves are most characteristic of the Greek *baklava.* Consequently, the aroma is spicier and the syrup tarter than in the Middle Eastern *baklava*, where cardamom and rose-water syrup are especially preferred. Aside from individual variations, the rule for syrup generally dictates that it be cool to pour over hot *baklava* from the oven, or hot to add to cool *baklava*, for maximum flakiness.

TO MAKE 60 TO 70 "DIAMONDS"

3½ cups granulated sugar
2½ cups water
2 tablespoons honey (optional)
Rind of 1 lemon
1 stick cinnamon
3 to 4 whole cloves
1¼ pounds English walnuts and blanched almonds, medium finely chopped

2 teaspoons ground cinnamon
1 scant teaspoon ground cloves
1½ pounds commercial filo *pastry*
1 pound sweet butter, melted and clarified (see page 40)

Combine 3 cups of the sugar, the water, honey, lemon rind, and whole spices in a saucepan and bring to a boil. Lower the heat and simmer for 15 minutes, then remove the lemon peel and spices and cool.

Meanwhile, in a large bowl, combine the nuts, remaining ½ cup sugar, and ground spices and set aside. Read commercial *filo* directions for handling and for scoring *baklava* (page 44). Lay the *filo* sheets flat, cover with a damp towel, and keep covered except when removing to assemble the *baklava*. Count 8 *filo* sheets, fold, cover, and refrigerate to reserve for the top. Using a large pastry brush, butter an 11½ x 15½ x 3-inch *tapsi* or baking pan. Lay a *filo* sheet on the bottom of the pan, brush with warm butter, and repeat using 8 sheets. Scoop up a handful of the nut-spice mixture and sprinkle over the top *filo* sheet inside the pan. Lay on 3 more *filo* sheets, brushing each with butter, and sprinkle again with the nut mixture. Continue until all the nuts and *filo* are used. (The important things here are to butter each *filo* and to spread the nuts evenly. The way to do the latter is to rotate the pan several times during the procedure.) Now you can remove the reserved sheets from refrigerator and spread over the top, brushing on each sheet.

Using a long, very sharp knife, score the *baklava* from top to bottom into diamond shapes planning in advance the size desired. Be sure the knife touches the bottom of the pan as you cut. (Small sizes that will fit into fluted cupcake baking cups are ideal for buffets.) Heat the remaining butter to sizzling and pour over the top. Bake in a slow oven (300 degrees) for 1¼ hours or until golden chestnut in color and flaky. (A perfect *baklava* is evenly colored, requiring both skill and a well-regulated oven that will not brown the bottom faster than the top.) Remove from the oven (in the pan) to a rack, and spoon the cooled syrup over the entire pastry. Cool in the pan, then serve each piece individually.

Note: A tip from a Greek *zacharoplasti* (pastry maker): If the oven does have a tendency to darken the bottom of the *baklava* faster than the top, set the *baklava* pan in another, slightly larger one with a non-conductive substance between.

For variations on this delicious theme: some chefs sprinkle nuts between each *filo* sheet (with very chewy results), others between every other one. I have also noticed some who concentrate the nuts in a few spots and leave large quantities of *filo* between. In Epirus a tiny slash is made in the center of each *baklava* "diamond" (before baking) and a slivered almond inserted in each slash. You may use all walnuts, almonds, or pistachios, or, as in Sparta, add some sesame seeds. Enjoy your own personal combination.

BEVERAGES, SYRUPS, AND WINES

——————

RARITIES IN GREECE WOULD BE (1) a table set without a pitcher of ice water and (2) Hellenes sitting around the table not drinking and nibbling.

A rendezvous anywhere, anytime, signals a drink. If you visit a home, the host or hostess will offer refreshments almost immediately upon your arrival. Meeting in a *plateia,* popularly referred to as the *nymphoagora* (bridal market), you will finish your walk by sitting around a table. To accompany an aperitif, something is brought to nibble on—*meze, orektika, stragalia, fistikia, passa tempo;* with Kafe (Turkish coffee; page 342), a sweet, or perhaps *paximadi* or *koulouraki.* Drinking and eating in Greece are inseparable.

The noteworthy exception to this custom, however, is a good drink of cold water. And next to this obvious appreciation of fresh water, Greek people favor ouzo, retsina wine and *mastiha,* which can have startling effects on the tongue and olfactory nerves. But Hellenes also enjoy beverages made from fruits, nuts, vegetables, and herbs, as well as teas, milk with chocolate, and especially coffee. They have a delightful habit of preparing nut and fruit syrups and mixing a few tablespoons in ice water to create the excellent Soumada (page 349) or Vyssinada (page 348) and others. Mineral waters are also popular, as are beers. And of course, the Greek love of wines with or without resin is legendary.

Many families prepare liqueurs with mulberries (favorite berries since ancient times), coffee, almonds, oranges, cherries, sour cherries, or prunes, adding *katharo oinopnevma* (pure alcohol), which is readily available and legal. No wonder that the variety of beverages produced in Greek homes always amazes me; each situation seems to suggest a different drink. Culturally, lines dividing alcoholic beverages are sharp ones: Cognac is for men and served anytime (not necessarily after dinner, continental style) and liqueur is for ladies (served on formal visits). Cognac is served at the family home following a funeral; liqueur is for baptisms, weddings, happy occasions. Commercial products are excellent. Among the delicious liqueurs there are apricot, cherry and other fruit flavors, and an aromatic one made from roses.

Many contemporary beverages are reminders of Hippocrates. In his *Regimen,* the noted physician recommended herbal drinks: beverages of raisins, grapes, and pomegranate; diuretic juices of celery, garlic, clover, fennel, leek, mint and parsley, as well as of others; hydromel (honey and water); oxymel (honey and vinegar), which as honey and lemon juice is a famous Greek therapy for sore throats, colds, and hoarseness!

Beverages

IDOR * NERO
[*Water*]

Water is almost sacred in Greece, and the traveler learns its value quickly. Hellenes flock around the gushing mountain springs in summer as youngsters in the United States would rush to a refreshment stand. There is usually a communal cup chained to the spring, but most Greek people carry cups, jugs, and all kinds of *hydriai,* including the new plastic ones, evoking images of fountain scenes on old vases. If there is a spigot, the last to drink turns it off. A drink from these springs is safe and cold and has a most wonderful, natural taste. And in moving away from the spring after having sipped from a cupped hand, you raise your fingers to cool your brow.

During a viciously hot summer day on the Athens Acropolis, as the sun rose overhead, everyone crowded about the only fountain for a drink. Instead of drinking, one tourist put her head under the spray. It does not take long to learn in Greece.

Large Greek cities are well equipped with fresh, drinkable water, as are the smaller towns. But villagers, in many instances, continue to depend on wells. The water is analyzed, and where a neighbor owns land with a superior well, the water is shared. For as a Greek land owner phrased it when we walked with a friend to fill her container from the superior well, "It is God's water."

This appreciation for water has been reinforced by poets, philosophers, and politicians since ancient times. Homer in the *Iliad* suggested that water was so blessed that the gods were born of Ocean, Titan lord of the river Ocean. During the Golden Age, the statesman Pericles restored a springhouse. By the time of Aristotle, much planning had resulted in the development of water supplies and drainage. Excavations of the Agora at Athens disclosed more than four hundred wells and cisterns. Aristotle had suggested in his *Politics* that there be "large and capacious cisterns of rainwater" to supplement the inadequate natural water supply in case of wars.

Cisterns are still needed, and the flat-roofed homes on the islands have homemade eaves and troughs to channel rainwater into the deep cisterns. In small villages usually youngsters have the chore of dropping a bucket on a rope and hoisting it up. We pulled a few buckets and soon realized the weight of water! Cistern water is usually used for bathing and watering plants and animals, and the well water for drinking and cooking.

The tradition of sharing this sacrosanct element might be traced to Solon's laws in the sixth century B.C. The great statesman specified that the public well could be used if within half a mile of a person's property. Farther away, individuals were encouraged to dig their own wells, but if unsuccessful they could fill a five-gallon jar twice daily from a neighbor's well.

Greek life for men in those days centered around the agora, where public fountains and a fountain house were indispensable items. Aristophanes wrote in his *Lysistrata*:

Just now I filled my pitcher at the fountain;
It's a difficult task, with the crowd and the din and the clatter of pots.

Vase painters used this daily task as one of their most delightful subjects. Sometimes the pitchers must have fallen into the well: Literary references indicate that meat hooks were used to grasp and retrieve containers.

And of course, in addition to fountains, there were *perirrhanteria*, basins for sprinkling water for purification on entering the agora. The sacred water in these *perirrhanteria* was carefully guarded to deny it to unworthy cowards and deserters in order to maintain the sanctity of the agora. As Hippocrates wrote: "We ourselves set boundaries for the gods of their sacred places, so that no one may enter if he is not pure, and going in we sprinkle ourselves." Except for the obvious pleasure of springs and public water fountains, the ancient agora sprinkling died away. But it continues in the Church, where blessed water plays a part in the important rituals, beginning with the Baptism.

KAFE
[*Turkish coffee*]

Kafe in Greece means Turkish coffee. Its preparation, time, place, and method of serving are highly ritualistic, and the accompanying pleasure of drinking it may be the only one Greeks begrudgingly attribute to centuries of Turkish domination. The words *kafe* and "coffee" come from the Arabic *kahveh*. As a beverage, coffee was introduced into Europe during the reign of Suleiman the Magnificent (ca. 1496–1566). When prepared with expertise, *kafe* topped with *kaimaki* (froth) is a favorite refreshment after the nap, when visiting, or in the late evening.

At home, a spoon sweet is served on a dessert plate with ice water, and the *kafe* either accompanies or follows the sweet. In Athens, Plateia Syntagmatos, the large Constitution Square facing Parliament, livens with chatter as people sit for hours at the tables and chairs covering the square. Waiters serve *kafe* and other refreshments for the *kafeneia* (coffee houses) lining the square. On smaller Omonia or on the grounds of the National Archeological Museum, tables are fewer and groups smaller, but patrons may sit for hours drinking from a cup no deeper than your little finger.

The real *kafeneia* are sacrosanct meeting places—for men only. These *kafeneia*, in the provinces, islands, and quieter districts of large cities, are havens for most of their day. The men play *hartakia* (cards), *tavli* (backgammon), or *billiardo* (billiards). And in older establishments, we have been told, the men still smoke a *narghi le!* This is a Middle Eastern pipe which is designed with a long hose. The smoke passes through water and is cooled. The name derived from the Persian

342

word for coconut tree, *nargil*, probably because the pipe is made from a coconut shell.

Coffee machines turning out poor imitations of Turkish coffee taste worse because of the disappointment. This is a personal reaction, because I enjoy making Turkish coffee in a *briki*—or having someone else make it in a *briki*—and drinking it. Generally, the real thing should be ordered in a coffee shop rather than a *zacharoplasteion*. If in doubt, walk into the kitchen and look for the small, long-handled *briki*.

To simplify this ritualistic beverage, I list the known versions in Greece as you might order them in a coffee shop:

> *Metrios vrastos*—medium strong, minimum sugar, boiled
> *Varys glykos*—strong and sweet
> *Glykos vrastos*—sweet and boiled
> *Sketos*—no sugar

To make at home: you will need a *briki* (coffee maker usually enough for 2 or 3 cups); demitasse cups with straight sides; Turkish coffee (no substitute), sugar, and a teaspoon.

For the average drinker, *metrios vrastos* will be made like this:

In the *briki*, pour 1 Turkish cupful cold water for each cup prepared (the fewer the better because the *kaimaki* [froth] won't have to be divided). Measure 1 level teaspoon sugar per cup and add to the water in the *briki*, then 1 level teaspoon coffee per cup and stir into the *briki*. Place over medium heat and stir until dissolved. Hold on to the *briki* and remove it from heat as soon as it boils up. The *kaimaki* will settle down, and you can put it over the heat to boil up once or twice more for maximum *kaimaki*. If preparing more than one cupful, divide the *kaimaki* and fill the cups to the very brim (they won't spill over), then serve with ice water.

In Greece, coffee drinkers can tell how the coffee was poured into the cup (from a height in a steady stream or from low level). But I guarantee that if you serve them *kafe* with *kaimaki*, no one will be disappointed, no matter how you may pour it.

343

KAFE ME GALA
[Turkish coffee with milk]

Greek adults enjoy this delicious milk beverage for breakfast, and drinking it is not unusual for Greek youngsters, either. I myself have loved it since childhood, when an old-fashioned aunt made it for me when I visited her. Also, at the local *zacharoplasteion* (sweets shop) or *galaktopoleion* (milk and dairy shop) this is a popular midmorning snack. Only early birds get the fresh milk, however, in provinces and islands where the local supply is limited. This is served in a glass in Greece.

To make at home, combine 1 cup or glass of milk with ½ to 1 teaspoon Turkish coffee and 1 to 1½ teaspoons sugar. Stir over medium heat until the mixture is dissolved and it reaches a boil. Pour into a glass or cup and serve hot.

TEÏON (TSAI)
[Herb teas and "ptisanes"]

Herbs have been a brewers' delight in Greece for centuries and remain an aromatic national habit, even though the sorcerers and witch doctors with which they have often been identified have disappeared. All joking aside, Hippocrates might have started it, or recorded it, for his identification with herbs is more than legendary. And his famous barley water, the *ptisane*, evolved into the French word *tisane*, which we use to describe any of these delightful, special brews, not necessarily from barley.

When our children caught severe colds in Athens during the mid-1950s, the family physician prescribed *tilion* for head colds, *faskomilo* for chest colds. *Chamomili* cures a mild upset stomach and also is relaxing at bedtime. Hippocrates also used warm *chamomili* to treat wounds. He probably contributed as much to develop confidence in herbs as he did to the family budget. What could be more economical and at the same time bring one closer to nature than to grow herbs for cooking and *tisanes*?

Unlike Western tea—ritualistic in preparation for social purposes, and ceremonial in service—the Greek herb teas are simply boiled briefly, strained, and sweetened with sugar. The only ritual is the individual one of brewing a cup as an endearing expression for a loved one, a personal home "remedy," a comfort. Preparing these teas is also relaxing for the one brewing, for there is an aroma, an indescribable fragrance in these herbs, as well as rich color. Drink them hot and sweet.

Teas are referred to as *teïon* and *tsai*, from the Chinese words, but herb teas are described simply by the name of the herb. The favorites are: *diosmon* (mint); *faskomilon* (sage); *glykanison* (aniseed); *chamomili* (chamomile); *sampoukos* (elder blossom); *tilion* (lime flower). These are available in Greece and in specialty Greek and Middle Eastern stores in the United States.

To brew 1 cup:
Combine a scant teaspoon of herb or spice with one cup cold water. Bring to a boil, then remove from the heat and allow to steep for a few minutes. Strain into cup, sweeten to taste, and serve hot.

Accustomed to fragrances, Greek ladies invariably serve black tea spiced.
For 4 cups:
Boil 4½ cups water with a 1-inch cinnamon stick and 2 cloves for 2 minutes. Remove and discard the spices, then use the water to steep black tea for 5 minutes with a ½-inch piece of lemon rind. Pour into cups and serve hot, plain or sweetened.

Or for a stronger version:
To each cup add 1 teaspoon fine brandy or Cognac.

OUZO

This favorite is sipped straight or mixed with water, usually as an aperitif. However, "ouzo on the rocks" has become a popular favorite. And with a magical trick of its own, the clear liquor will turn milky white on the ice!

ZESTI NICHTA
[Hot night]

TO SERVE 2

Juice of 1 large lemon
2 to 3 tablespoons fine brandy or cherry liqueur
2 tablespoons granulated sugar
Club soda, chilled

Combine the lemon juice, brandy or liqueur, and sugar, then divide into 2 highball glasses. Pour enough club soda into each glass to fill it about two-thirds full, add an ice cube in each, if you like, stir and serve.

SAMPANIA ME FROUTA KAI KRASI
[Greek champagne punch]

You will not find this punch at the average Greek *glendi*. A sophisticated, delightful beverage in which you may use your favorite, seasonal fruits.

TO MAKE APPROXIMATELY 5½ QUARTS

2 bananas, sliced
1 sixteen-ounce can sliced pineapple
1 cup Cognac or brandy
2 oranges, rinds included, sliced
1 bottle Greek champagne, chilled

2 bottles Greek muscatel, chilled
2 quarts club soda (or less for stronger punch)
Granulated sugar or honey
Fresh sliced strawberries and mint leaves for garnish

Marinate the bananas and pineapple slices in the Cognac or brandy for 1 to 2 hours, then place in a punch bowl. Add the sliced oranges, champagne, wine, and as much club soda as you like. Sweeten with the sugar or honey and garnish with the strawberries or mint leaves. Or, better, make a frozen mold using the strawberries and mint leaves with water in an attractive ring- or fruit-shape. Unmold after mixing punch and allow it to float on top but be sure to reduce the amount of soda in the punch.

346

Syrups

SALTSA MAVRODAPHNI
[*Sweet mavrodaphne wine sauce*]

A wonderful use of the superb mavrodaphne wine, very new, very Athenian. I have used this as a substitute for *koulourakia* which require *petimezi* (not in *moustalevria*, however). Also tasty poured over ice cream and other desserts.

TO MAKE APPROXIMATELY 1½ CUPS

> *1¼ cups mavrodaphne wine*
> *1¼ cups orange juice*
> *½ cup granulated sugar*
> *Grated rind from 1 orange*

Combine all the ingredients in a small saucepan and stir over medium heat until dissolved. Boil 10 minutes and cool. Store in a jar in the refrigerator.

PETIMEZI
[*Unfermented must syrup*]

Petimezi is syrup made from must, *moustos* in Greek. If prepared when sweet grapes are ripe and plentiful, *petimezi* may be stored indefinitely with other bottled syrups. It is an outstanding Greek ingredient for flavoring cakes, cookies, quick breads (as a syrup instead of honey), and for the favorite, which makes Greek eyes sparkle at the mere mention of its name—Moustalevria (page 309).

Use fresh sweet grapes, such as red Emperor or sweet light seedless grapes. To estimate the amount: whole grapes will yield about half their volume in juice. You will also need *stahti* (wood ash), to clear the grape juice, and if unavailable in specialty stores, use any clean ash, sifted, about 1 tablespoon for each 4 cups of grape must.

Wash grapes, remove the stems, then push through a food mill. Strain the juice and discard the pulp. Tie wood ashes in a linen or muslin cloth, set into a saucepan with the grape juice and boil for 10 minutes. Remove the bag with the ashes and allow the juice to stand overnight. Next day, carefully pour off the juice. Discard any remaining ash residue which has settled on the bottom. Return juice to the pan, bring to boil, and boil to the large-thread stage (234 degrees). Cool, then store in jars until ready to use.

VYSSINADA
[Sour-cherry syrup in ice water]

The Greek penchant for refreshment results in infinite syrups made through the ages from juices of fruit. Syrups are stirred into ice water for a quick energy booster, and might have begun with the custom of serving spoon sweets with ice water. I have often seen Hellenes put their chosen *glyko tou koutaliou* right into their ice water and sip it.

From this magical custom an array of drinks evolved, and are called by the name of their major ingredient whether a fruit or nut or flavoring such as vanilla or *mastiha*. *Vyssinada* is the most famous and most popular, and for my taste, the most delicious. Follow the same procedure for juice or pulp of apricots, peaches, plums, berries, or raisins and enjoy a few tablespoons in a tall glass of ice water and a long spoon on a hot summer day.

TO MAKE ABOUT 2 CUPS OF SYRUP

>2¼ cups sour-cherry liquid (from canned sour cherries)
>2¼ cups sugar

In a heavy pan dissolve the liquid and sugar over medium heat, stirring until dissolved. When the mixture boils, remove the scum from the surface and continue cooking to the large-thread stage (234 degrees on a candy thermometer). Cool. Pour into jars and refrigerate until ready to use. Serve in ice water on ice cream, and ices.

SOUMADA

[Almond syrup in ice water]

Gentle almond flavors this syrup, which is traditionally served at wedding receptions in Greece, and also for a refreshing cold drink anytime, especially in summer.

TO MAKE 1 QUART OF THE SYRUP

> *1 cup blanched, chopped almonds*
> *3 cups granulated sugar*
> *4¼ cups water*
> *½ teaspoon almond extract or rose water*

Pound a few tablespoons of the almonds at a time in a wooden mortar, using a few teaspoons of the sugar and water each time. The mixture will become paste. Transfer to a bowl and continue until all are pounded. Combine the remaining sugar and water in a large heavy saucepan and let boil for 15 minutes, removing the scum from the surface. Stir in the almond paste and continue cooking for 15 minutes, making sure that the syrup does not boil over. Stir frequently; the syrup will be milky and foamy.

Remove the syrup from the heat and cool thoroughly, then strain through a double cheesecloth, squeezing out all the almond syrup. Save the almonds remaining in the cloth for another purpose (see note below). Flavor the syrup with the almond extract or rose water; store in covered jars in the refrigerator. Serve 2 to 3 tablespoons of the syrup in ice water to make *soumada*.

Note: The remaining almonds should be toasted in a slow oven to dry before storing and may be used as a garnish for cakes and other desserts.

YPOVRIHIA

["Submarines"—syrup drinks in ice water]

Syrup beverages now have a very descriptive nickname—submarine—the syrup is submerged in water. Two favorites on the mainland and on the islands are made with *mastiha* and vanilla. The following recipe is for *mastiha* syrup, flavorful, and as prepared in Greece could be classified a fondant.

TO MAKE APPROXIMATELY 1¾ CUPS OF "MASTIHA" SYRUP

> *4 cups (2 pounds) plus ½ teaspoon granulated sugar*
> *2 cups water*
> *1 egg white*
> *Juice of ½ lemon*
> *2½ teaspoons mastic (resin)*

Combine the 4 cups of sugar, water, and egg white in a heavy saucepan and stir over medium heat until dissolved. When the mixture boils, skim off the foam and coagulated egg white from the surface and the sides of the pan with a dampened cloth. Cook to the soft ball stage (238 degrees), or until a drop forms a soft ball in a glass of cold water. Do not overcook. Stir the lemon juice into the syrup and pour into medium bowl without scraping the crystals from the sides of the pan. (Or before pouring, wipe off the crystals from the sides with a dampened cloth.) Allow the syrup to cool to 100 degrees without stirring as it cools.

Meanwhile, pound the ½ teaspoon sugar and *mastiha* in a mortar until finely pulverized. Pour into the syrup gradually, beating with a paddle or wooden spoon until white and creamy. Store in tightly covered jars.

Wines

OINOS * KRASI
[*Wine*]

While the origin of the ancient Greek word for wine—*oinos*—may be controversial, the attitudes, use, and association of wine with Greece since mythological times remains clear and indisputable. Since the vine spread from Egypt to Palestine and then to Thrace, and was carried on his boat's mast by Dionysos into Attica, according to a delightful myth, grapes and wine have flourished in Greece. In addition,

Hellenes transplanted vines to their early colonies in Sicily, Malaga, Jerez, and the Rhone Valley, where they subsequently matured. This was especially rewarding during the later eras, when Greek production declined and the vines might have been lost to posterity. Viticulture in Europe, Asia, and the Americas by now has expanded to over twenty-five milllion acres. Of this, the Greek people produce one million tons a year from all their vines.

Both love of wines and virtue in moderate drinking are part of Hellenic culture. Homer believed that the ancient word for wine was derived from *onesis* (to benefit). "There is no moment more pleasurable than when the guests, sitting around a well-laden table, lend their ear to the voice of a singer, while the cup-bearer, having drawn wine from the amphoras, moves round the table to pour into each and every cup in turn."

Centuries later Plato, who praised wine as a relaxer and enervator of body vigor, nevertheless cautioned against the duplicity of wine. His explanation of the etymology of the word asserted his position. The word *oinos*, Plato believed, was from *oinous*, which means "fill the brain with false impressions."

This good warning apparently fell on many deaf ears, for throughout Greek history, revelry has been promoted by drinking songs such as the one from Hedylus (280 B.C.): "Let us drink. For, indeed, over wine we may find some new, some elegant, some honey-sweet turn of speech. Soak me with jars of Chian wine and say: 'Enjoy yourself, Hedylus.' I hate living emptily, not drunk with wine."

Though refuted by some historians, evidence remains that Alexander the Great was known to succumb enough to the overpowering effects of wine to sleep two days and nights. In fact, he lost sexual potency, another ill effect of alcohol.

The ambivalent nature of wine typified the nature of Dionysos, god of the vine, the ancient god with the most lasting influence in Greece, born of Zeus and Semele. Dionysian inspiration in the arts was dual—kind and pleasurable, very often compared also to a bull and a leopard.

Though we personally have never seen a drunken person in Greece, there has to be some reason for the many nicknames for overdrinkers:

Bekros: one who hits the bottle.
Krasopateras: Wine-bibber, literally "wine father."
Krasopotis: Wine-bibber, literally "wine drinker."
Krasokanata: Wine-bibber, literally "wine pitcher."

Methismenos: Drunk; *oligon methismenos*: a little drunk, tipsy.

Geropotiri: Heavy drinker, literally "strong-glass."

Ta kopanai: "He hits them" (traditionally, before drinking all in the company clink their glasses together and toast each other's health).

Oinofligos: Tipsy, drunkard.

Oinolippos: Drunk with wine.

Oinomanis: Wine-bibber, literally "wine maniac."

Oinopnevmatodis: Alcoholic.

Stoupi: Stone drunk.

Incidentally, the ancient *oinos* is still used (in addition to the above list), although in common usage *krasi* describes the wines. A Greek wine shop is called *oinopoleion*, and a wine expert is *oinologos*.

On the one hand, "wine is truth and reveals the heart of man," Philochorus said. But "too much wine makes you babble too much," another Hellene, Ephippus, stated. So who can doubt the two-sided spirit of wine?

Hippocrates' classification of wines in his *Regimen* is still influential in Greece. His analysis includes effects on body moisture and processes:

Soft dark wines make the body moister.

Sweet dark wines make the body moister and weaker.

Harsh white wines produce heat without drying the body.

Thin wines pass better through the urine.

Boiled-down wine warms the body, moistens, and is nutritious.

Two ancient customs have survived for most Hellenes when drinking wine that may have prevented serious alcoholism (the lowest in Europe statistically). First, wine is frequently mixed with water, an early practice, since the gods were said to have diluted their nectar with water. Secondly, Greek people eat before and during drinking rather than indulging on an empty stomach.

Wine remains a staple, always appearing on the table with major meals, next to the water pitcher and bread. In fact, the per capita consumption is fifty to seventy pints annually. Greeks love their local wines (with excellent reason). We have pleasant memories of buying these delicious wines from huge barrels in Athens during the mid-1950s for five drachmas a bottle, but this custom has unfortunately disappeared from even the neighborhood lanes of Athens. However, on Crete and in some provinces, buying wine from the barrel is still possible.

On islands and in villages, the small producers are gradually buckling to the rapid expansion of the wine industry within the last two decades. Plant capacity, which in 1952 was 135,000, rose to 311,000 tons in the early 1970s.

Outstanding Greek vineyards flourish primarily in Peloponnesos, where forty-four of the one hundred eighty bottling plants are located near the vineyards. In the central regions, the Mantineia grapes produce the balanced white wines. In the Patras region, the famous Mavrodaphne wine of the Mavroudi grape thrives. And along the banks of the azure Gulf of Corinth, the Nemea wines develop. Famous dry white Demesticha, Santa Helena, Santa Laoura, and Antika wines all flourish in the Peloponnesos.

Attica remains a rich contributor of the Saviatiano grapes, famous since antiquity for excellent wines. Attica's production remains higher than other areas of central Grece, which currently maintains thirty-seven plants.

Macedonia grows the Popolka grape of Niaousta, one of the numerous distinctive wines of the other Greek regions. From Thessaly comes the red Rapsani and Ambelakia wines. Zitsa, a semisweet white wine, originates in Epirus.

And among the renowned island wines are those of Samos, particularly the Muscat de Samos dessert wines. The volcanic soils of Santorini produce the Nychteri and Vino Santo wines. Dry white wines are nurtured in Rhodes and Zante, while Levkadia produces red wines. A fine rosé comes from Kefallinia, where the Mavroudi grape for Mavrodaphne also flourishes excellently.

Wines are produced in the various regions of Crete, which, with twenty-six plants, has the third largest production of Greece. In the western region are the red, full-bodied Kastelli-Kissamou wines, and the Latiko grape, which gives deep red wines, or the *mavro* (black) wines, as Cretans and northerners usually call them. Ketsifali (red) and Mandilare (red) are produced in the Heraklion region and in Xania, the Romeidon (red) wines.

As for the retsina, beloved by Hellenes and disdained by many tourists, it is made by flavoring wine with resin during fermentation, not by any particular grape or vine. Resin comes from the pine tree *Calitris quadrivalvis*. Retsina wines are usually aged less than a year for a lighter taste, and are added to the dry white and rosé (*kokkinelli*) wines of major companies. The same wines are usually also available *aretsinata* (not resinated).

Comparatively, dry white wines compose the most important category: 274,000 tons, as compared to the 155,000 tons of dry red wines, the latest available statistics. Sweet Greek wines, though popular, constitute a smaller group, about 24,000 tons.

During the same period, brandy production expanded to 482 tons, while other liqueurs almost doubled to 602 tons. Of these, ouzo is perhaps the most famous, with a distinctive licorice flavor, originating in Thessaly during the mid-eighteenth century.

Certainly, in cookery, the ancient practices have not died away. Old sources remind us that chefs used to mix wines with dough, sweeten them with honey for flavor, or use them in fish dishes and casseroles. Today, wines are used as tenderizing agents in marinades and for zest and aroma in numerous meat and fish dishes and sauces. In addition, brandies and liqueurs are dribbled into cakes, cookies, breads, syrups, desserts, and fruit compotes for a delicate aroma and taste—which cannot intoxicate.

In cooking, the best-flavored available wines should be used. Among the Greek wines, in recipes requiring "dry white," select strong and dry ones without resin. Do not use sour or fruity wines. Also, dry white Pinot Chardonnay and good light domestic vermouth wines may be substituted.

When dry red ones are needed, full-bodied Greek, Burgundy, and Bordeaux should be used. Greek brandies, Cognacs and liqueurs, ouzo, and *mastiha* are excellent in desserts, as are Cointreau and Grand Marnier. Greek muscatels are delicious with fruit compotes and pastries.

In addition to uses in cookery, wines with meals and with appetizers or other informal moments can be selected from local wines on hand:

With appetizers, snacks: Vermouth types; light, dry aromatic wines; ouzo
With fish, poultry, white meats, egg dishes, oysters, specialty meats: Light, dry wines (retsina or *aretsinato*)
With red meats, game, cheese, rich dishes and specialty meats: Red full-bodied and dry rosé wines
With fruit, desserts, cheese, dried fruits, pastries: Sweet and semisweet red wines; muscatel
For festive occasions, desserts, special meals: Champagne, champagne punch.

Index

Vilma Liacouras Chantiles

Vilma Liacouras Chantiles, a first-generation American of Greek parentage, has been working on this book all of her life so far, and will continue to do so as she enjoys frequent voyages to the land of her forebears. Her formal education is in the fields of home economics, music, and languages. Married and the mother of three children, Mrs. Chantiles teaches at New York University and makes her home in Scarsdale, New York.